McDougal Littell

WORLD HISTORY
PATTERNS OF INTERACTION

Reading Study Guide

McDougal Littell
A HOUGHTON MIFFLIN COMPANY
Evanston, Illinois • Boston • Dallas

Copyright © 1999 by McDougal Littell Inc. All rights reserved.

Permission is hereby granted to teachers to reprint or photocopy in classroom quantities the pages or sheets in this work that carry a McDougal Littell copyright notice. These pages are designed to be reproduced by teachers for use in their classes with accompanying McDougal Littell material, provided each copy made shows the copyright notice. Such copies may not be sold, and further distribution is expressly prohibited. Except as authorized above, prior written permission must be obtained from McDougal Littell Inc. to reproduce or transmit this work or portions thereof in any other form or by any other electronic or mechanical means, including any information storage or retrieval system, unless expressly permitted by federal copyright law. Address inquiries to Manager, Rights and Permissions, McDougal Littell Inc., P.O. Box 1667, Evanston, Illinois 60204.

Printed in the United States of America.

ISBN 0-395-95204-2

2 3 4 5 6 7 8 9 - RRW - 03 02 01 00 99

Contents

UNIT 1 Beginnings of Civilization, 4 Million B.C.–200 B.C.

Chapter 1 The Peopling of the World, Prehistory–2500 B.C.

Section 1 Study Guide: Human Origins in Africa 5
Section 2 Study Guide: Humans Try to Control Nature 7
Section 3 Study Guide: Patterns of Change: Civilization 9
Glossary and AFTER YOU READ 11

Chapter 2 Early River Valley Civilizations, 3500 B.C.–450 B.C.

Section 1 Study Guide: City–States in Mesopotamia 13
Section 2 Study Guide: Pyramids on the Nile 15
Section 3 Study Guide: Planned Cities on the Indus 17
Section 4 Study Guide: River Dynasties in China 19
Glossary and AFTER YOU READ 21

Chapter 3 People and Ideas on the Move, 3500 B.C.–259 B.C.

Section 1 Study Guide: Indo-European Migrations 23
Section 2 Study Guide: Roots of Hinduism and Buddhism 25
Section 3 Study Guide: Seafaring Traders Extend Boundaries 27
Section 4 Study Guide: The Origins of Judaism 29
Glossary and AFTER YOU READ 31

Chapter 4 First Age of Empires, 1570 B.C.–200 B.C.

Section 1 Study Guide: The Empires of Egypt and Nubia Collide 33
Section 2 Study Guide: Assyria Dominates the Fertile Crescent 35
Section 3 Study Guide: Persia Unites Many Lands 37
Section 4 Study Guide: An Empire Unifies China 39
Glossary and AFTER YOU READ 41

UNIT 2 New Directions in Government and Society 2000, B.C.–A.D. 700

Chapter 5 Classical Greece, 2000 B.C.–300 B.C.

Section 1 Study Guide: Cultures of the Mountains and the Sea 43
Section 2 Study Guide: Warring City–States 45
Section 3 Study Guide: Democracy and Greece's Golden Age 47
Section 4 Study Guide: Alexander—Empire Builder 49
Section 5 Study Guide: The Spread of Hellenistic Culture 51
Glossary and AFTER YOU READ 53

Chapter 6 Ancient Rome and Early Christianity, 500 B.C.–A.D. 500

Section 1 Study Guide: The Romans Create a Republic 55
Section 2 Study Guide: The Roman Empire Brings Change......................... 57
Section 3 Study Guide: The Rise of Christianity 59
Section 4 Study Guide: The Decline of the Roman Empire 61
Section 5 Study Guide: Rome and the Roots of Western Civilization............ 63
Glossary and AFTER YOU READ 65

Chapter 7 India and China Establish Empires, 300 B.C.–A.D. 550

Section 1 Study Guide: First Empires of India.. 67
Section 2 Study Guide: Trade Spreads Indian Religions and Cultur............. 69
Section 3 Study Guide: Han Emperors in China 71
Glossary and AFTER YOU READ 73

Chapter 8 African Civilizations, 1500 B.C.–A.D. 500

Section 1 Study Guide: Diverse Societies in Africa 75
Section 2 Study Guide: The Kingdom of Aksum and East African Trade 77
Section 3 Study Guide: Patterns of Change: Migration 79
Glossary and AFTER YOU READ 81

Chapter 9 The Americas: A Separate World, 40,000 B.C.–A.D. 700

Section 1 Study Guide: Hunters and Farmers in the Americas..................... 83
Section 2 Study Guide: Early Mesoamerican Civilizations 85
Section 3 Study Guide: Early Civilizations of the Andes 87
Glossary and AFTER YOU READ 89

UNIT 3 An Age of Exchange and Encounter, 500–1500

Chapter 10 The Muslim World, 600–1250

Section 1 Study Guide: The Rise of Islam 91
Section 2 Study Guide: The Spread of Islam 93
Section 3 Study Guide: Muslim Achievement 95
Glossary and AFTER YOU READ 97

Chapter 11 Byzantines, Russians, and Turks Interact, 500–1500

Section 1 Study Guide: Byzantium Becomes the New Rome 99
Section 2 Study Guide: Russians Adapt Byzantine Culture......................... 101
Section 3 Study Guide: Turkish Empires Rise in Anatolia........................... 103
Glossary and AFTER YOU READ 105

Chapter 12   Empires in East Asia, 600–1350

    Section 1 Study Guide: Two Great Dynasties in China 107
    Section 2 Study Guide: The Mongol Conquests... 109
    Section 3 Study Guide: Empire of the Great Khan 111
    Section 4 Study Guide: Feudal Powers in Japan 113
    Section 5 Study Guide: Kingdoms of Southeast Asia and Korea 115
    Glossary and AFTER YOU READ 117

Chapter 13   European Middle Ages, 500–1200

    Section 1 Study Guide: Germanic Kingdoms Unite Under Charlemagne .. 119
    Section 2 Study Guide: Feudalism in Europe 121
    Section 3 Study Guide: The Age of Chivalry 123
    Section 4 Study Guide: The Church Wields Power 125
    Glossary and AFTER YOU READ 127

Chapter 14   The Formation of Western Europe, 800–1500

    Section 1 Study Guide: Church Reform and the Crusades 129
    Section 2 Study Guide: Trade, Towns, and Financial Revolution 131
    Section 3 Study Guide: England and France Develop................................ 133
    Section 4 Study Guide: A Century of Turmoil 135
    Glossary and AFTER YOU READ 137

Chapter 15   Societies and Empires of Africa, 800–1500

    Section 1 Study Guide: North and Central African Societies 139
    Section 2 Study Guide: West African Empires and Civilization 141
    Section 3 Study Guide: Eastern City–States and Southern Empire 143
    Glossary and AFTER YOU READ 145

UNIT 4   Connecting Hemispheres, 900–1800

Chapter 16   People and Empires in the Americas, 900–1500

    Section 1 Study Guide: Diverse Societies of North America...................... 147
    Section 2 Study Guide: Mayan Kings and Cities 149
    Section 3 Study Guide: The Aztecs Control Central Mexico...................... 151
    Section 4 Study Guide: The Inca Create a Mountain Empire..................... 153
    Glossary and AFTER YOU READ 155

Chapter 17   European Renaissance and Reformation, 1300–1600

    Section 1 Study Guide: Italy: Birthplace of the Renaissance...................... 157
    Section 2 Study Guide: The Northern Renaissance 159
    Section 3 Study Guide: Luther Starts the Reformation 161
    Section 4 Study Guide: The Reformation Continues 163
    Glossary and AFTER YOU READ 165

Chapter 18 The Muslim World Expands, 1300–1700

Section 1 Study Guide: The Ottomans Build a Vast Empire 167
Section 2 Study Guide: Patterns of Change: Cultural Blending 169
Section 3 Study Guide: The Mughals Establish an Empire in India 171
Glossary and AFTER YOU READ 173

Chapter 19 An Age of Exploration and Isolation, 1400–1800

Section 1 Study Guide: Europeans Explore the East 175
Section 2 Study Guide: China Rejects European Outreach 177
Section 3 Study Guide: Japan Limits Western Contacts 179
Glossary and AFTER YOU READ 181

Chapter 20 The Atlantic World, 1492–1800

Section 1 Study Guide: Spanish Conquests in the Americas 183
Section 2 Study Guide: Competing Claims in North America 185
Section 3 Study Guide: The Atlantic Slave Trade 187
Section 4 Study Guide: The Columbian Exchange and Global Trade 189
Glossary and AFTER YOU READ 191

UNIT 5 Absolutism to Revolution, 1500–1900

Chapter 21 Absolute Monarchs in Europe, 1500–1800

Section 1 Study Guide: Spain's Empire and European Absolutism 193
Section 2 Study Guide: France's Ultimate Monarch 195
Section 3 Study Guide: Central European Monarchs Clash 197
Section 4 Study Guide: Russian Czars Increase Power 199
Section 5 Study Guide: Parliament Limits the English Monarchy 201
Glossary and AFTER YOU READ 203

Chapter 22 Enlightenment and Revolution, 1550–1789

Section 1 Study Guide: The Scientific Revolution 205
Section 2 Study Guide: The Enlightenment in Europe 207
Section 3 Study Guide: The Spread of Enlightenment Ideas 209
Section 4 Study Guide: American Revolution: The Birth of a Republic 211
Glossary and AFTER YOU READ 213

Chapter 23 The French Revolution and Napoleon, 1789–1815

Section 1 Study Guide: Revolution Threatens the French King 215
Section 2 Study Guide: Revolution Brings Reform and Terror 217
Section 3 Study Guide: Napoleon Forges an Empire 219
Section 4 Study Guide: Napoleon's Empire Collapses 221
Section 5 Study Guide: The Congress of Vienna Convenes 223
Glossary and AFTER YOU READ 225

Chapter 24 Nationalist Revolutions Sweep the West, 1789–1900

Section 1 Study Guide: Latin American Peoples Win Independence 227
Section 2 Study Guide: Revolutions Disrupt Europe 229
Section 3 Study Guide: Patterns of Change: Nationalism 231
Section 4 Study Guide: Revolutions in the Arts 233
Glossary and AFTER YOU READ 235

UNIT 6 Industrialism and the Race for Empire, 1700–1914

Chapter 25 The Industrial Revolution, 1700–1900

Section 1 Study Guide: The Beginnings of Industrialization 237
Section 2 Study Guide: Patterns of Change: Industrialization 239
Section 3 Study Guide: Industrialization Spreads 241
Section 4 Study Guide: An Age of Reforms 243
Glossary and AFTER YOU READ 245

Chapter 26 An Age of Democracy and Progress, 1815–1914

Section 1 Study Guide: Democratic Reform and Activism 247
Section 2 Study Guide: Self-Rule for British Colonies 249
Section 3 Study Guide: Expansion and Crisis in the United States 251
Section 4 Study Guide: Nineteenth-Century Progress 253
Glossary and AFTER YOU READ 255

Chapter 27 The Age of Imperialism, 1850–1914

Section 1 Study Guide: Imperialists Divide Africa 257
Section 2 Study Guide: Patterns of Change: Imperialism 259
Section 3 Study Guide: Muslim Lands Fall to Imperialist Demands 261
Section 4 Study Guide: British Imperialism in India 263
Section 5 Study Guide: Western Powers Rule Southeast Asia 265
Glossary and AFTER YOU READ 267

Chapter 28 Transformations Around the Globe, 1800–1914

Section 1 Study Guide: China Responds to Pressure from the West 269
Section 2 Study Guide: Japan Modernizes 271
Section 3 Study Guide: U.S. Economic Imperialism in Latin America 273
Section 4 Study Guide: The Mexican Revolution 275
Glossary and AFTER YOU READ 277

UNIT 7 The World at War, 1900–1945

Chapter 29 The Great War, 1914–1918
- Section 1 Study Guide: The Stage Is Set for War 279
- Section 2 Study Guide: War Consumes Europe 281
- Section 3 Study Guide: War Affects the World 283
- Section 4 Study Guide: A Flawed Peace 285
- Glossary and AFTER YOU READ 287

Chapter 30 Revolution and Nationalism, 1900–1939
- Section 1 Study Guide: Revolutions in Russia 289
- Section 2 Study Guide: Patterns of Change: Totalitarianism 291
- Section 3 Study Guide: Collapse of Chinese Imperial Rule 293
- Section 4 Study Guide: Nationalism in India and Southwest Asia 295
- Glossary and AFTER YOU READ 297

Chapter 31 Years of Crisis, 1919–1939
- Section 1 Study Guide: An Age of Uncertainty 299
- Section 2 Study Guide: A Global Depression 301
- Section 3 Study Guide: Fascism Rises in Europe 303
- Section 4 Study Guide: Aggressors on the March 305
- Glossary and AFTER YOU READ 307

Chapter 32 World War II, 1939–1945
- Section 1 Study Guide: Hitler's Lightning War 309
- Section 2 Study Guide: Japan Strikes in the Pacific 311
- Section 3 Study Guide: The Holocaust 313
- Section 4 Study Guide: The Allies Are Victorious 315
- Section 5 Study Guide: The Devastation of Europe and Japan 317
- Glossary and AFTER YOU READ 319

UNIT 8 Perspectives on the Present, 1945–Present

Chapter 33 Restructuring the Postwar World, 1945–Present
- Section 1 Study Guide: Two Superpowers Face Off 321
- Section 2 Study Guide: Communists Triumph in China 323
- Section 3 Study Guide: War in Korea and Vietnam 325
- Section 4 Study Guide: Cold War Around the World 327
- Section 5 Study Guide: The Cold War Thaws 329
- Glossary and AFTER YOU READ 331

Chapter 34 The Colonies Become New Nations, 1945–Present

Section 1 Study Guide: The Indian Subcontinent Gains Independence 333
Section 2 Study Guide: Southeast Asian Nations Gain Independence 335
Section 3 Study Guide: New Nations in Africa 337
Section 4 Study Guide: Conflicts in the Middle East 339
Glossary and AFTER YOU READ 341

Chapter 35 Struggles for Democracy, 1945–Present

Section 1 Study Guide: Patterns of Change: Democracy 343
Section 2 Study Guide: Democratic Challenges in African Nations 345
Section 3 Study Guide: Gorbachev Moves Toward Democracy 347
Section 4 Study Guide: Collapse of the Soviet Union 349
Section 5 Study Guide: China Follows Its Own Path 351
Glossary and AFTER YOU READ 353

Chapter 36 Global Interdependence, 1960–Present

Section 1 Study Guide: Science and Technology Shape Human Outlook .. 355
Section 2 Study Guide: Global Economic Development 357
Section 3 Study Guide: Global Security Issues 359
Section 4 Study Guide: Cultures Blend in a Global Age 361
Glossary and AFTER YOU READ 363

Being a Strategic Reader
Strategies for Reading Your History Book

UNDERSTANDING THE BIG PICTURE

History is filled with people, events, facts, and details. Sometimes you can get lost in all the details. This is why the most important strategy to remember as you read a history textbook is to form the "big picture" of history. As you read, keep asking yourself, "What is the main idea?" When you do this, the details will make more sense.

Use the strategies shown here to help you read *World History: Patterns of Interaction*.

Strategy: Read "Main Idea" and "Why It Matters Now" to begin forming the "big picture" of the section.
Try This: What do you think will be the subject of this section?

Strategy: Look at the heads and subheads in each section to get a general understanding of the subject.
Try This: Preview the head and subheads on pages 724 and 725. What do you expect to learn in this section?

Strategy: Look closely at the photographs, art, and other illustrations in the text. Be sure to read the captions.
Try This: Look at the photograph. What does it show about peasant farming in Latin America?

Strategy: Look for key terms and names, which are in dark type in the section. The text gives clues to the important terms and names in the section.
Try This: Read the terms. Then look at pages 724 and 725. Which of the terms appears on these pages? How did you recognize it?

---

3 U.S. Economic Imperialism in Latin America

TERMS & NAMES
- caudillo
- Monroe Doctrine
- Jose Marti
- Spanish-American War
- Panama Canal
- Roosevelt Corollary

MAIN IDEA
The United States put increasing economic and political pressure on Latin America during the 19th century.

WHY IT MATTERS NOW
This policy set the stage for 20th-century relations between Latin America and the United States.

SETTING THE STAGE Latin America's long struggle to gain independence from colonial domination between the late 18th and the mid-19th centuries left the new nations in shambles. Weeds choked off farm fields. Cities and towns collapsed. The new nations faced a struggle for recovery as difficult as their struggle for independence had been.

Latin America After Independence
Political independence meant little for most citizens of the new Latin American nations. The majority remained poor, illiterate laborers caught up in a cycle of poverty.

Colonial Legacy During colonial times, most Latin Americans worked for large landowners. The employers paid their workers with vouchers that could be used only at their own supply stores. Since wages were low and prices were high, workers went into debt. Their debt accumulated and passed from one generation to the next. These "free" workers were almost like slaves in a system known as peonage.

The landowners, on the other hand, only got wealthier after independence. Many new Latin American governments took over the lands owned by native peoples and by the Catholic Church. They then put those lands up for sale. Wealthy landowners were the only people able to afford to buy them, and they snapped them up. But as one Argentinean newspaper reported, "Their greed for land does not equal their ability to use it intelligently." The unequal distribution of land and its poor use combined to prevent social and economic development in Latin America.

The land—and its rich resources—was and is Latin America's major asset. The peasants worked all of their lives in the fields and remained poor and propertyless, as many still are today.

Political Instability Political instability also was a widespread problem in 19th-century Latin America. Many Latin American army leaders had gained fame and power during their long struggle for independence. They often continued to assert their power. They controlled the new nations as dictators, or **caudillos**. By 1830, nearly all the countries of Latin America were ruled by caudillos. One typical caudillo was Juan Vicente Gómez. He was a ruthless man who ruled Venezuela for nearly 30 years after seizing power in 1908. "All Venezuela is my cattle ranch," he once boasted.

There were some exceptions, however. Reform-minded presidents, such as Argentina's Domingo Sarmiento, made strong commitments to improving education. During Sarmiento's presidency, between 1868 and 1874, the number of students in Argentina doubled. But such reformers usually didn't stay in office long. Eventually a caudillo would return to power, forcing the reformer out at the point of a bayonet or gun.

The caudillos found little opposition. The upper classes usually supported them because they opposed giving power to the lower classes. In addition, Latin Americans had gained little experience with democracy under European colonial rule. So the dictatorship of a caudillo did not seem unusual to them. But even when caudillos

724 Chapter 28

X BEING A STRATEGIC READER

Strategy: Preview the maps in each section. Think about how geography affected historical events.
Try This: Look closely at the map. What is the map about?

Latin America, 1830

Cacao—was used as a medium of exchange as well as a beverage by the Maya and Aztec.

Bananas—have been a staple food in the New World since the 1500s.

Coffee—plant is a source of cattle feed, alcohol, and fuel oil, as well as a beverage.

Cotton—is used throughout the world as a source of clothing in temperate climates.

Nitrates—disputes over ownership of these deposits led to war between Chile, Bolivia, and Peru in the late 1800s.

Sugar cane—plant is a source of cattle feed, rum, paper, and wallboard, as well as a sweetener.

Wool—the Latin American highlands offer ideal conditions for breeding sheep for their wool.

Natural Resources: Bananas, Cacao, Cattle, Coffee, Corn, Cotton, Gold, Nitrates, Silver, Sugar cane, Wheat, Wool

1825 Year of independence

GEOGRAPHY SKILLBUILDER: Interpreting Maps
1. **Region** Which Latin American countries remained under colonial rule in 1830?
2. **Human-Environment Interaction** Which country had the most different types of natural resources?

THINK THROUGH HISTORY
A. Identifying Problems What difficulties did lower-class Latin Americans continue to face after independence?

weren't in power, most Latin Americans still lacked a voice in the government. Voting rights—and so, political power—were restricted to the relatively few members of the upper and middle classes who owned property or could read.

Economies Grow Under Foreign Influence

When colonial rule ended in Latin America in the early 1800s, the new nations were no longer restricted to trading with colonial powers. Britain and, later, the United States, became Latin America's main trading partners.

Old Products and New Markets No matter with whom the new Latin American nations were trading, their economies continued to depend on exports. As during the colonial era, each country concentrated on one or two products. With advances in technology, however, Latin America's exports grew. The development of the steamship and the building of railroads in the 19th century, for example, greatly increased Latin American trade. Toward the end of the century, the invention of refrigeration helped increase Latin America's exports. The sale of beef, fruits and vegetables, and other perishable goods soared.

But foreign nations benefited far more from the increased trade than Latin America did. In exchange for their exports, Latin Americans imported European and North American manufactured goods. They therefore had little reason to develop their own manufacturing industries. And as long as Latin America remained unindustrialized, it could not play a leading role on the world stage.

Outside Investment and Interference Furthermore, Latin American countries used little of their export income to build roads, schools, or hospitals. Nor did they

Transformations Around the Globe 725

Strategy: Use the Think Through History questions to check your understanding as you read.
Try This: Read Question A. How would the details in the text help you answer the question?

Strategy: Look at charts and graphs that present ideas in visual ways.
Try This: Study the chart below. What does the chart show?

The Marshall Plan

Country	Millions of Dollars
Great Britain	2,826
France	2,445
Italy	1,316
West Germany	1,297
Holland	877
Austria	561
Belgium/Lux.	547
Greece	515
Denmark	257
Norway	237
Turkey	153
Ireland	146
Sweden	119
Portugal	51
Yugoslavia	33
Iceland	29
Other	350

Source: *Problemes Économiques No. 306*

SKILLBUILDER: Interpreting Charts
1. Which country received the most aid from the United States?
2. Why do you think Great Britain and France received so much aid?

BEING A STRATEGIC READER 1

Being a Strategic Reader
How to Use This Reading Study Guide

The purpose of this *Reading Study Guide* is to help you read and understand your history textbook, *World History: Patterns of Interaction.* You can use this *Reading Study Guide* in two ways.

1. **Use the *Reading Study Guide* side-by-side with your history book.**
   - Turn to the section that you are going to read in the textbook. Then, next to the book, put the pages from the *Reading Study Guide* that accompany that section. All of the heads in the *Reading Study Guide* match the heads in the textbook.
   - Use the *Reading Study Guide* to help you read and organize the information in the textbook.

2. **Use the *Reading Study Guide* to study for tests on the textbook.**
   - Reread the summary of every chapter.
   - Review the definitions of the Terms and Names in the *Reading Study Guide*.
   - Review the diagram of information that you filled out as you read the summaries.
   - Review your answers to questions.

Strategy: Fill in the diagram as you read. The diagram will help you organize information in the section.
Try This: What is the purpose of this diagram?

Strategy: Read the Terms and Names and the definition of each. The Terms and Names are in dark type in the section.
Try This: What are the definitions of "indulgence" and "annul"?

Strategy: Read the summary. It contains the main ideas and the key information under the head.
Try This: What do you think this section will be about?

Name _____ Date _____

CHAPTER 17 Section 3 (pages 428–432)

Luther Starts the Reformation

BEFORE YOU READ
In the last section, you saw how the Renaissance spread to Northern Europe.
In this section, you will see how Renaissance ideas helped bring about the Reformation.

AS YOU READ
Use the chart below to take notes on the responses to Luther's challenge.

TERMS AND NAMES
indulgence Release from punishments due for a sin
Reformation 16th-century movement for religious reform, leading to the founding of new Christian churches
Lutheran Member of a Protestant church founded on the teachings of Martin Luther
Protestant Member of a Christian church founded on the principles of the Reformation
Peace of Augsburg Agreement in 1555 declaring that the religion of each German state would be decided by its ruler
annul Cancel or put an end to
Anglican Relating to the Church of England

BATTLE/POLITICAL ISSUE	EFFECT
Responses to Luther's Challenge	The Pope threatens Luther with excommunication.

Causes of the Reformation (page 428)
Why was the Church criticized?

By 1500, the influence of the Church on the lives of people had weakened. Some people resented paying taxes to support the Church in Rome. Others sharply criticized the Church for some of its practices. Popes seemed more concerned with luxury and political power than with spiritual matters. The lower *clergy* had faults too. Many local priests lacked education and were not able to teach people. Some lived immoral lives.

Reformers urged the Church to change its ways to become more spiritual and humble. Christian humanists such as Erasmus and Thomas More added their voices to calls for change. In the early 1500s, the calls grew louder.

1. What kinds of changes did Church critics want to make?
_____
_____
_____

CHAPTER 17 EUROPEAN RENAISSANCE AND REFORMATION **161**

---

2 BEING A STRATEGIC READER

Luther Challenges the Church
(page 429)

How *did the Reformation begin?*

In 1517, a German monk named Martin Luther protested the actions of a Church official. That person was selling **indulgences**. An indulgence was a kind of forgiveness. By paying money to the Church, people thought they could win *salvation*.

Luther challenged this practice and others. He posted a written protest on the door of a castle church. His words were printed and spread throughout Germany. This was the beginning of the **Reformation**, a movement for reform that led to the founding of new Christian churches.

2. What role did Martin Luther play in the Reformation?

_____

_____

The Response to Luther (pages 429–430)

What *effects did Luther's protest have?*

Pope Leo X punished Luther for his views, but he refused to change them. Holy Roman Emperor Charles V, a strong Catholic, called Luther an outlaw. Luther's books were burned. But it was too late. Many of his ideas were already being practiced. The **Lutheran** Church started around 1522.

<u>In 1524, peasants in Germany hoped to use Luther's ideas about Christian freedom to change society.</u> They demanded an end to serfdom—a condition like slavery. When it was not granted, they revolted. Luther disagreed with this *revolt*. German princes killed thousands in putting the revolt down.

Some *nobles* supported Luther's ideas. They saw a chance to weaken the emperor's power over them. Other German princes joined forces against Luther's supporters. They signed an agreement to remain loyal to the pope and the emperor. Supporters of Luther's ideas *protested* this agreement. They were called the Protestants. Eventually, the term **Protestant** meant Christians who belonged to non-Catholic churches.

War broke out between Catholic and Protestant forces in Germany. It finally ended in 1555 with the **Peace of Augsburg**. This treaty granted each prince the right to decide whether his subjects would be Catholic or Protestant.

3. Why did Luther's ideas lead to war?

_____

_____

England Becomes Protestant
(pages 431–432)

How *did England become Protestant?*

The Catholic Church faced another challenge to its power in England. Henry VIII, the king, was married to a Spanish princess. She gave birth to a daughter. England had never had a female ruler. Henry feared a civil war would start if he had no son. He believed his wife was too old to have another child. He tried to get the pope to **annul**, or put an end to the marriage, so he could remarry. The pope refused.

To remarry, Henry had to get out of the Catholic church. In 1534, Henry had *Parliament* pass laws that created the Church of England. These laws made the king or queen, not the pope, head of the Church of England. Henry no longer had to obey the pope. Henry remarried five times. His only son was from his third wife.

One of Henry's daughters, Elizabeth, became queen in 1558. She finished creating a separate English church. The new church was called **Anglican**. It had some practices that would appeal to both Protestants and Catholics. In this way, Elizabeth hoped to end religious conflict.

Elizabeth's England had to face a threat from Catholic Spain, too. In 1588, King Philip II launched a huge fleet of ships—known as the Spanish Armada—to invade England. This fleet was defeated by a combination of English fighting skill and a terrible storm.

4. What role did Henry VIII play in creating the Church of England?

_____

_____

Strategy: When you see a word in italic type, read the definition in the Glossary at the end of the chapter.
Try This: What does *Parliament* mean? Look at the Glossary on the next page to find the definition.

Strategy: Answer the question at the end of each part.
Try This: Write an answer to Question 4.

Strategy: Underline main ideas and key information as you read.
Try This: Read the summary under the head "The Response to Luther." Underline information that you think is important. One important idea is already underlined.

Being a Strategic Reader
How to Use This Reading Study Guide

At the end of every chapter in the *Reading Study Guide*, you will find a Glossary and a section called After You Read. The Glossary gives definitions of all the words in italic type in the chapter summaries.

After You Read is a two-page chapter review. Use After You Read to identify those parts of the chapter that you need to study more for the test on the chapter.

Name _____ Date _____

Glossary   **CHAPTER 17** European Renaissance and Reformation

bubonic plague Deadly disease that spread across Europe and Asia in the mid-14th century, killing millions of people
classical related to ancient Greece and Rome and emphasizing ideas of order, balance, and harmony
clergy Religious officials
doctrines Principles; statements of policy
landscapes Pictures showing scenery or land forms

merchants storekeepers and traders
movable type Printing blocks that did not have to be made one by one but could be moved into new positions and reused
nobles People of high rank
oil-based paints Paints that are made with oil; the oil dries slowly and allows for details, blending, and changes
Parliament Law-making body in England

peasant related to poor or lower class people who worked the land
protested Actively disagreed
realistic Lifelike
revolt Uprising, rebellion
salvation Freedom from the effects of sin
sculptors People who create works of art by carving
spiritual sacred; related to religion
three-dimensional Having length, width, and height; giving a sense of depth

AFTER YOU READ
Terms and Names

A. Fill in the blank with the name or term that best completes the paragraph.

Presbyterian
Anabaptists
Anglican
Lutheran
Reformation
Protestant

In Germany, Martin Luther began a movement for religious change called the **1** _____ . He and his followers began a separate religious group called the **2** _____ Church. In England, Elizabeth finished and headed the **3** _____ church. In Scotland, John Knox established yet another branch of the **4** _____ faith. His church was the **5** _____ Church. Other Protestant reformers included the **6** _____, who believed in separation of church and state

B. Write the letter of the name or term next to the description that be...

a. Jesuits
b. secular
c. Calvinism
d. Peace of Augsburg
e. patrons
f. indulgence
g. Utopia

____ **1.** Focus on human
____ **2.** An agreement in German state w...
____ **3.** Concerned with...
____ **4.** Doctrine that G... including which
____ **5.** Use of native la...
____ **6.** Body of religious reformer John C...
____ **7.** Members of the gious order fou...

AFTER YOU READ (continued)   **CHAPTER 17** European Renaissance and Reformation

Main Ideas

1. What changes in the arts occurred during the Italian Renaissance?
   _____
   _____

2. What changes in learning and the arts occurred during the Northern Renaissance?
   _____
   _____

3. What changes in the Christian Church did Martin Luther bring about?
   _____
   _____

4. How did the Reformation in Germany change German political life?
   _____
   _____

5. Why and how did the Church change in England?
   _____
   _____

Thinking Critically
Answer the following questions on a separate sheet of paper.

1. How did the Northern Renaissance differ from the Italian Renaissance?
2. Which leader—Henry VIII or Luther—do you think had a greater impact? Explain why.

Strategy: Review all of the Terms and Names before completing Parts A and B of After You Read.
Try This: Use the *Reading Study Guide* for Chapter 1 to answer Questions A 1-5.

Strategy: Review the chapter summaries before completing the Main Ideas questions. Write a complete sentence for every answer.
Try This: In your own words, what is Question 1 asking for?

Strategy: Write one or two paragraphs for every Thinking Critically question.
Try This: In your own words, what is Question 1 asking for?

4 BEING A STRATEGIC READER

Name _____ Date _____

CHAPTER 1 Section 1 (pages 7–11)

Human Origins in Africa

BEFORE YOU READ

In this section, you will read about the earliest humans.

AS YOU READ

Use the time line below to take notes on the earliest humans.

> **TERMS AND NAMES**
> **artifact** Remains, such as tools, jewelry, and other human-made objects
> **culture** People's way of life
> **hominid** Human or other creatures that walks upright
> **Paleolithic Age** Old Stone Age
> **Neolithic Age** New Stone Age
> **technology** Ways of applying knowledge, tools, and inventions to meet needs
> ***Homo sapiens*** Species name for modern humans

- 3.6 million years ago — Hominids appear.
- 1.6 million years ago
- 25 million years ago
- 200,000 years ago

Scientists Search for Human Origins (pages 7–8)

How do scientists learn about early humans?

People can learn about the past by using written records. But these records cover only the last 5,000 years or so of human life. To learn about the time before written records, scientists called *archaeologists* use special skills and tools.

Archaeologists work at places called *digs*. They uncover **artifacts**: tools, jewelry, or other things made by people. Archaeologists also dig up bones—the bones of ancient humans and of the animals that lived with them. Some of these bones have become *fossils*, meaning they have survived over time because they were preserved in stone. By studying bones and artifacts, scientists learn about the **culture,** or way of life, of early humans.

In the early 1970s, archaeologists in East Africa found the footprints of humanlike beings, called *australopithencines*. Humans and other creatures that walk upright, such as australopithecines, are called **hominids**. They lived about 3.6 million years ago.

Because these early beings walked upright, they could travel long distances more easily than four-footed ones. They could also use their free arms to carry food, tools, and children. They also had an *opposable thumb* that could move across the palms of their hands and touch their other fingers. The opposable thumb allowed them to pick up and hold objects.

1. What were the first humanlike beings, and where were they found?

_____

_____

CHAPTER 1 THE PEOPLING OF THE WORLD **5**

Progress During the Old Stone Age (pages 8–9)

What advances did hominids make during the Stone Age?

Humans made important advances during a period called the Stone Age, when people used tools made of stone. At this time, they also began to use fire and learned to speak.

Scientists divide the Stone Age into two parts. The **Paleolithic Age,** or Old Stone Age, began about 2.5 million years ago and lasted until about 8000 B.C. The **Neolithic Age,** or New Stone Age, went from about 8000 B.C. to around 3000 B.C.

Much of the Old Stone Age overlapped the Ice Age, when the earth was colder than it is now. Huge sheets of ice—*glaciers*—covered much of the land. About 10,000 years ago, the earth's temperature increased. The ice sheets grew smaller. People began to roam wider stretches of land.

In East Africa, archaeologists found a hominid fossil that they named *Homo habilis*. The name means "man of skill." The fossil was given this name because the site also held tools made of lava rock. *Homo habilis* lived about 2.5 million years ago.

About 1.6 million years ago, another kind of hominid lived. This one was *Homo erectus*. *Homo erectus* began to use tools for special purposes. That is when **technology** began. *Homo erectus* dug for food in the ground, cut meat from animal bones, and scraped animal skins. *Homo erectus* also used fire and may have had the first spoken language.

2. Who were *Homo habilis* and *Homo erectus*?

_____

_____

_____

_____

The Dawn of Modern Humans (pages 9–11)

Who were the Neanderthals and Cro-Magnons?

Many scientists believe that by about 200,000 years ago *Homo erectus* developed into humans, or **Homo sapiens.** One group of early humans, the *Neanderthals,* lived in caves or built shelters of wood or animal skins. They were once thought to be rough and wild people. Now scientists think that they may have held religious beliefs. One site suggests that they buried their dead. These people found ways to survive the freezing cold of the Ice Age. About 30,000 years ago, though, the Neanderthals strangely disappeared.

About 10,000 years before these people vanished, the *Cro-Magnons* appeared. Their bodies were just like those of modern people. Scientists think that these people worked with one another in planning large-scale hunts of animals. They may have also had more skill at speaking than did the Neanderthals. Because they had these skills, the Cro-Magnons were better at finding food. That may explain why Cro-Magnons survived and Neanderthals did not.

3. How is the species *Homo sapiens* different from earlier hominids?

_____

_____

_____

_____

_____

Name _____ Date _____

CHAPTER 1 Section 2 (pages 12–16)

Humans Try to Control Nature

BEFORE YOU READ

In the last section, you read about the earliest humans.

In this section, you will read about the development of agriculture and a settled way of life.

AS YOU READ

Use the web below to take notes on changes in human culture.

TERMS AND NAMES
nomad Person who wanders from place to place
hunter-gatherer Person whose food supply depends on hunting animals and collecting plant foods
Neolithic Revolution Agricultural revolution that occurred during the Neolithic period
slash-and-burn farming Early farming method that some groups used to clear fields
domestication Taming of animals

- Tools and Art (Fish Hooks)
- Farming Methods
- Changes in Human Culture
- Farming Villages

Achievements in Technology and Art (page 12)

What advances occurred in technology and art?

The first humans had faced a struggle for survival. For thousands and thousands of years, they had two concerns: finding food and protecting themselves. They used fire, built shelters, made clothes, and developed spoken language. These areas of life are all part of culture. Human culture changed over time as new tools replaced old and people tested new ideas. Later some modern humans increased the pace of change.

The people who had lived in the early part of the Old Stone Age were **nomads.** They moved from place to place. They were **hunter-gatherers.** They found food by hunting and gathering nuts, berries, and roots. The Cro-Magnon people, who came later, made tools to help them in their search.

These early modern humans used many tools—more than 100 different ones. They used stone, bone, and wood. They made knives, hooks, and bone needles.

Cro-Magnon people also created works of art, including painting. Thousands of years ago, artists mixed charcoal, mud, and animal blood to make paint. They used this paint to draw pictures of animals on cave walls and rocks.

1. In what ways did Cro-Magnon people change human culture?

_____

_____

CHAPTER 1 THE PEOPLING OF THE WORLD **7**

The Neolithic Revolution (pages 14–15)

What was the Neolithic Revolution?

For centuries, humans lived by hunting and gathering. Humans lived in small groups of only 20 or 30 people. They often returned to a certain area in the same season each year because they knew it would be rich in food at that time.

Over the years, some humans realized that they could leave plant seeds in an area one year and find plants growing there the next year. This was the beginning of a new part of human life: farming.

Scientists think that the climate became warmer all around the world at about the same time. Humans' new knowledge about planting seeds combined with this warmer climate to create the **Neolithic Revolution**—the agricultural revolution that occurred during the Neolithic period.

Instead of relying on gathering food, people began to produce food. One early farming method was **slash-and-burn farming.** That meant cutting trees and burning them to clear a field. The ashes were used to fertilize the soil.

Along with growing food, they also began to raise animals. They tamed horses, dogs, goats, and pigs. **Domestication** is the taming of animals.

Archaeologists have studied a site in the northeastern part of the modern nation of Iraq. It is called *Jarmo*. The people who lived in this region began farming and raising animals about 7000 B.C.

2. How did life change during the Neolithic Revolution?

_____
_____

Villages Grow and Prosper (pages 15–16)

How did the growth of farming villages change life?

People began to farm in many spots all over the world. The study of one village in modern-day Turkey shows what early farming communities were like.

The village grew on the good land near a river. Some workers grew wheat, barley, and peas. Others raised sheep and cattle. Because these workers produced enough food for all the people, others could begin developing other kinds of skills. Some made pots out of clay that they baked—the first *pottery*. Others worked as weavers. Some artists decorated the village. Archaeologists have found wall paintings that show animals and hunting scenes. They have found evidence that the people had a religion, too.

Early farming villagers had problems, too. If the farm crop failed or the lack of rain caused a drought, people starved. Floods and fires caused damage and death. With more people living near each other than before, diseases spread easily. Still, some of these early villages grew into great cities.

3. What problems did early farming villages face?

_____
_____

Agricultural Revolution
Population

(Graph showing World Population in millions vs. Years Ago in thousands, with lines for Post-Agricultural Revolution, Agricultural Revolution, and Hunting-Gathering Stage)

Skillbuilder

1. When did the Agricultural Revolution begin?

_____
_____

2. When was population growth the greatest?

_____
_____

Name _____ Date _____

CHAPTER 1 Section 3 (pages 17–21)

Patterns of Change: Civilization

BEFORE YOU READ

In the last section, you read about the development of agriculture and a settled way of life.

In this section, you will read about factors leading to the rise of civilizations.

AS YOU READ

Use the chart below to take notes on how civilizations develop.

TERMS AND NAMES
civilization Culture with advanced cities, specialized workers, complex institutions, record keeping, and technology
specialization Development of skills in a specific kind of work
artisan Skilled worker that makes goods by hand
institution Long-lasting pattern of organization in a community
scribe Professional record keeper
cuneiform Wedge-shaped writing developed in Sumer
Bronze Age Time when people began using bronze
barter Trading goods and services without money
ziggurat Pyramid-shaped monument; part of a temple in Sumer

FEATURES OF CIVILZATION	EXAMPLES FROM UR
1. Advanced Cities	
2.	
3.	
4.	
5.	

Villages Grow into Cities (pages 17–18)

What changed as villages grew into cities?

Over time, farmers developed new tools—hoes and plow sticks. These helped them grow even more food. They decided to plant larger areas of land. The people in some villages began to irrigate the land, bringing water to new areas. People invented the wheel for carts and the sail for boats. These new inventions made it easier to travel between distant villages and to trade.

Life became more complex as the villages began to grow. People were divided into social

CHAPTER 1 THE PEOPLING OF THE WORLD **9**

classes. Some people had more wealth and power than others. People began to worship gods and goddesses that they felt would protect their crops and make their harvests large.

1. How did life become more complex?

_____

_____

_____

_____

What Is Civilization? (pages 18–19)
What makes a civilization?

The first civilization arose in a region of Southwest Asia known as Sumer. It was between the Tigris and Euphrates rivers of modern Iraq. A **civilization** has five features.

First, a civilization has advanced cities that contain many people and serve as centers for trade.

Second, civilizations have specialized workers. **Specialization** is the development of skills needed for one specific kind of work. Skilled workers who make goods by hand are called **artisans.**

Third, civilizations have complex institutions. Government, organized religion, and an economy are examples of complex **institutions.**

A fourth feature of civilizations is record-keeping, which is needed to keep track of laws, debts, and payments. It also creates the need for writing. **Scribes** were people who used writing to keep records. **Cuneiform,** which means "wedge shaped," was a form of writing invented in Sumer.

Fifth, civilizations have advanced technology that can provide new tools and methods to solve problems.

Sumer had all the features of a civilization. One of the new technologies in Sumer was making a metal called bronze. The term **Bronze Age** refers to the time when people began using bronze to make tools and weapons.

2. Name the five features of a civilization.

_____

_____

_____

_____

_____

_____

Civilization Emerges in Ur
(pages 20–21)
What was civilization like in Ur?

One of the early cities of Sumer was named Ur. The city was surrounded by walls built of mud dried into bricks. Ur held about 30,000 people. Social classes included rulers and priests, traders, craft workers, and artists.

Farmers outside the city walls raised the food for them all. Some workers dug ditches to carry water to the fields. Officials of the city government planned all this activity.

Inside the city, metalworkers made bronze points for spears. Potters made clay pots. Traders met people from other areas. They traded the spear points and pots for goods that Ur could not produce. This way of trading goods and services without money is called **barter.** Sometimes their deals were written down by scribes.

Ur's most important building was the temple. Part of the temple was a **ziggurat,** a pyramid-shaped structure. Priests there led the city's religious life.

3. What social classes existed in Ur?

_____

_____

_____

_____

_____

Name _____ Date _____

Glossary — CHAPTER 1 The Peopling of the World

archaeologists Scientists who learn about past human life and activities

australopithecines A type of prehistoric hominid

Cro-Magnons Early humans who walked erect and appeared about 40,000 years ago

digs Explorations usually done by digging dirt or sand in search of evidence from the past

fossils Remains of life preserved in stone

glaciers Huge sheets of ice

Homo erectus Early human who used tools for special purposes

Homo habilis Hominid called "man of skill"

Jarmo Site in Iraq where people were farming and raising animals by 7000 B.C.

Neanderthals Early humans who walked erect and vanished mysteriously

opposable thumb Physical feature that sets humans apart from animals by enabling them to pick up and hold objects

pottery Pots and other objects made from baked clay

AFTER YOU READ

Terms and Names

A. Write the name or term in each blank that best completes the meaning of the paragraph.

Neolithic Age

Paleolithic Age

hominids

technology

Homo sapiens

Homo habilis, Homo erectus, Neanderthals, and Cro-Magnons are all examples of **1** _____. Evidence of these early humans was discovered by archaeologists. This evidence dates back to both the **2** _____, which lasted until about 8,000 B.C. and the later **3** _____ . One important change between *Homo habilis* and *Homo erectus* was probably in developing **4** _____ . *Homo erectus* is believed to have used intelligence to create tools. After *Homo habilis* and *Homo erectus,* **5** _____ appeared.

B. Write the letter of the name or term next to the description that explains it best.

a. institution

b. domestication

c. ziggurat

d. specialization

e. cuneiform

____ **1.** Development of skills for a specific type of work

____ **2.** Pyramid-shaped structure that was part of a Sumerian temple

____ **3.** Taming of animals

____ **4.** Wedge-shaped writing developed in Sumer

____ **5.** Long-lasting pattern of organization in a community

Name _____ Date _____

AFTER YOU READ (continued) CHAPTER 1 The Peopling of the World

Main Ideas

1. How and where do scientists find evidence of early human life?

2. What hominids developed during the Old Stone Age?

3. How were the Neanderthals and the Cro-Magnons alike and different?

4. People who lived in the early part of the Old Stone Age were nomads. What was their life like?

5. Name five features of Ur that show it was a civilization.

Thinking Critically

Answer the following questions on a separate sheet of paper.

1. How did the Cro-Magnons differ from early hunter-gatherers?
2. Why was the development of farming so important?

Name _____ Date _____

CHAPTER 2 Section 1 (pages 27–32)

City-States in Mesopotamia

BEFORE YOU READ

In the last chapter, you read about the earliest humans and the first civilization.

In this section, you will learn more about early civilization in a part of Mesopotamia called Sumer.

AS YOU READ

Use the chart below to take notes on Sumer.

TERMS AND NAMES

Fertile Crescent Arc of rich farmland in southwest Asia between the Persian Gulf and the Mediterranean Sea

silt Thick bed of rich mud deposited on the plain as a result of a river's flooding

irrigation System of bringing water to fields

city-state Political unit much like an independent country

dynasty Series of rulers from a single family

cultural diffusion New ideas spreading from one culture to another

polytheism Belief in many gods

empire Peoples, nations, or independent states under control of one ruler

Hammurabi Babylonian ruler famous for his code of laws

SUMER	NOTES
Geography	• part of Fertile Crescent • rich soil from flooding of rivers • problems: needed to irrigate, defend, find materials they did not have

Geography of the Fertile Crescent (pages 27–28)

What problems did the Sumerians face?

There is an *arc* of rich land in Southwest Asia that is called the **Fertile Crescent.** Two of its rivers, the Tigris and the Euphrates, flood in the spring. This flooding leaves rich mud, called **silt,** in the plain between the rivers. Because of this, many thousands of years ago humans began to settle in that plain, known as Mesopotamia. They grew wheat and barley. It was here that the first civilization began.

About 3500 B.C., the Sumerians moved into this region and settled. They faced three problems. First, the floods were not regular, and once they passed, the hot sun quickly baked the land into clay. Second, the small farming villages had no protection against enemies. Third, the area lacked stone, wood, and metal to use for tools.

The Sumerians solved these problems. They dug **irrigation** ditches from the river to their fields

CHAPTER 2 EARLY RIVER VALLEY CIVILIZATIONS **13**

so they could bring water to their crops. They built walls of baked mud around their villages for *defense*. Because they could grow more food than they needed, they traded the extra for stone, wood, and metal from other lands.

1. How did the Sumerians solve the problems they faced?

_____

_____

Sumerians Create City-States
(page 29)

How did the Sumerians govern?

Several large city-states were at the center of the Sumerian world. These **city-states** had control over a surrounding area. They could act independently, much like a country does today. Slowly, some people rose to power in a number of the city-states. They became rulers, as did their children after them. Rule of an area by the same family is called a **dynasty**.

As population and trade grew, Sumerians came into contact with other peoples. Their own ideas affected others. The Sumerians also got ideas from other cultures. This process of spreading ideas or products is called **cultural diffusion**.

2. Who governed the city-states?

_____

_____

Sumerian Culture (pages 29–31)

What did the Sumerians believe and accomplish?

The Sumerians believed in **polytheism**, or many gods. Each god had power over different forces of nature or parts of their lives. Sumerians believed that people were just the servants of the gods. Souls of the dead went to a joyless place under the earth's crust. These views spread to other areas and shaped the ideas of other peoples.

Society was divided into social classes. At the top were the priests and kings, after whom came wealthy merchants. Next were workers in fields and workshops. Slaves made up the lowest level. Women could enter most careers and could own property. But there were some limits on them.

The people of Sumer invented the sail, the wheel, and the plow. They were the first to use bronze. They also developed the first writing system—on clay tablets. They invented arithmetic and geometry, which they used to help build large structures.

3. How was Sumerian society organized?

_____

_____

The First Empire Builders (pages 31–32)

Who built the world's first empire?

Centuries of fighting between the city-states made the Sumerians weak. In 2350 B.C., the conqueror Sargon defeated Sumer and captured other cities to the north. He built the world's first **empire**. An empire brings together several peoples, nations, or previously independent states. It puts them under the control of one ruler.

A few hundred years later, a different group of people conquered the Sumerians. These people built a capital at Babylon, establishing the Babylonian Empire. They were led by a king named **Hammurabi**. He is famous for his code of laws. It was a harsh code that punished people for wrongdoing. However, it also made it clear that the government had some responsibility for taking care of its people.

4. Why was Hammurabi's Code important?

_____

_____

Name _____ Date _____

CHAPTER 2 Section 2 (pages 33–39)

Pyramids on the Nile

BEFORE YOU READ

In the last section, you read about the city-states that arose in Mesopotamia.

In this section, you will learn about early civilization along the Nile.

AS YOU READ

Use the web below to show how Egypt was unified, what its culture was like, and how it fell.

TERMS AND NAMES
cataract Rapids or waterfall in a river
delta Marshy area at the mouth of a river
Menes King of Upper Egypt who united Upper and Lower Egypt
pharaoh Egyptian ruler thought of as a god
theocracy Government in which the ruler is considered to be a divine figure
pyramid Resting place for Egyptian kings after death
mummification Process by which a body is preserved after death
hieroglyphics Egyptian writing system
papyrus Plant used to make a paper like material

Unification: Menes brings Lower Egypt and Upper Egypt together

Culture:

Egypt

Fall:

The Geography of Egypt (pages 33–35)

What was the key feature of early Egypt's geography?

Another civilization arose along the banks of the Nile River of East Africa. The Nile flows to the North, toward the Mediterranean Sea. It, too, floods each year. The waters leave rich soil on the river banks. There the people of ancient Egypt grew food and began to build their own culture. They worshipped the Nile as a life-giving god.

For many centuries, the people of Egypt lived in two kingdoms, Upper Egypt and Lower Egypt. Upper Egypt extended north from the Nile's first area of rapids, or **cataracts,** to the Nile **delta.** The delta is a broad, marshy, triangular area of rich land. Lower Egypt began here and continued north to the Mediterranean, just 100 miles away.

CHAPTER 2 EARLY RIVER VALLEY CIVILIZATIONS **15**

1. How did the Nile create boundaries?

_____
_____
_____

Egypt Unites into a Kingdom
(pages 35–36)

Who ruled the kingdom?

About 3100 B.C., the king of Upper Egypt, **Menes,** united the two kingdoms. In the years between 2660 and 2180 B.C., the basic marks of the culture of Egypt arose. Ruling over the land was the **pharaoh.** He was not only a king but was also seen as a god. A government in which a ruler is seen as a divine figure is a **theocracy.**

Pharaohs believed they would rule the land after their death. So these kings built themselves magnificent tombs. The tombs were huge **pyramids** made out of *massive* limestone blocks.

2. Why did pharaohs build pyramids?

_____
_____

Egyptian Culture; Chariot Riders Invade Egypt (pages 36–39)

What were the features of Egyptian culture?

Egyptians believed in many gods and in an afterlife. One god, they thought, weighed the hearts of each dead person. Hearts judged heavy with sin were eaten by a beast. Good people, with *featherweight* hearts, would live forever in a beautiful Other World. To prepare for this, Egyptians preserved a dead person's body by **mummification.** This kept the body from decaying.

The pharaoh and his family were at the top of Egyptian society. Below them were people of wealth who owned large amounts of land, the priests, and members of the government and army. Then came the middle class—*merchants* and people who worked in crafts. At the bottom were the peasants. In later times, the Egyptians had slaves. People could move from one rank of society to another. Those who could read and write held important positions.

The Egyptians, like the Sumerians, developed a way of writing. In their **hieroglyphics,** pictures stood for sounds. The pictures could be put together to make words and sentences. At first they wrote on stone. Later they began to make a kind of paper from the **papyrus** plant. The Egyptians invented a system of written numbers and a calendar. Their calendar had 12 months, each of which had 30 days. They were famous in the ancient world for their ideas in medicine.

After 2180 B.C., the pharaohs lost power. Egypt went through a time of troubles. Then strong rulers once again took control. They ruled for four centuries until a group of Asians called the Hyksos arrived in horse-drawn chariots. The land fell to these invaders in 1640 B.C.

3. How was Egyptian society organized?

_____
_____
_____
_____

Name _____ Date _____

CHAPTER 2 Section 3 (pages 42–45)

Planned Cities on the Indus

TERMS AND NAMES
subcontinent Land mass that is a distinct part of a continent
monsoon Seasonal wind

BEFORE YOU READ

In the last section, you read about the development of culture along the Nile.

In this section, you will learn about the first civilization in India.

AS YOU READ

Use the chart below to take notes on the civilization of the Indus.

INDUS CIVILIZATION	NOTES
geography	• subcontinent separate from other areas • rich soil from flooding of rivers • problems: unpredictable river, winds

The Geography of South Asia
(pages 42–43)

What is a subcontinent?

South Asia—modern India, Pakistan, and Bangladesh—is a subcontinent. It is separated from the rest of Asia by tall mountains. Just below the mountains are two large plains that hold the Ganges and Indus rivers. The high mountains gave the people safety from invaders. Because they lived close to the sea, the people could travel over the water to trade with other peoples.

The people along the Indus River faced many of the same challenges that the people in Mesopotamia did. Their river flooded each year and left soil good for farming. But the floods did not occur at the same time each year. Also, the river sometimes changed course. The region's weather caused problems, too. Each winter, strong winds blew dry air across the area. Each spring, the winds brought heavy rains. These seasonal winds are called monsoons.

1. What challenges did the people along the Indus River face?

_____

_____

CHAPTER 2 EARLY RIVER VALLEY CIVILIZATIONS 17

Civilization Emerges on the Indus (pages 43–45)

What were cities like on the Indus?

Historians cannot understand the writings of the people who settled in the Indus Valley. So, they have not learned much about these people. They do know that they were farming along the river by about 3200 B.C. They also know that the culture of these people covered an area larger than either Mesopotamia or Egypt.

About 2500 B.C., these people began building their first cities. In Mesopotamia, cities were a jumble of winding streets. In the Indus Valley, however, the builders carefully planned their cities. They made a *grid* of streets. They built an area called a *citadel* that was easy to defend. All the important buildings were here. They also had systems for carrying water and sewage.

The civilization of the Indus was peaceful. Because the houses were mostly alike, scholars think that the Indus culture did not have big differences between social classes. Few weapons have been found at the sites of these ancient cities. This indicates that warfare was not common.

These early people left an important mark on the region. Some religious objects include symbols that became part of later Indian culture. Historians also think that the people of the area traded with the people of Mesopotamia.

2. Name two conclusions that have been drawn about Indus River culture.

_____

_____

Mysterious End to Indus Valley Culture (page 45)

How did Indus Valley culture end?

Around 1750 B.C., the cities began to show signs of decline. The Indus Valley civilization collapsed around 1500 B.C. No one knows the reason, but there are three possibilities. The Indus River may have changed its course. This would stop the good effects of the yearly floods. The people may have overworked the land. This would have left the soil too poor to produce crops. Lastly, perhaps a group of invaders defeated the Indus civilization.

3. Name three reasons why Indus Valley civilization may have ended.

_____

_____

In their private baths, people took showers by pouring pitchers of water over their head.

Wastes drained though clay pipes into brick sewers running below the streets.

Skillbuilder
Use the illustration to answer the questions.

1. What advance in technology is shown in this illustration?

_____

_____

2. What happened to the wastewater?

_____

_____

Name _____ Date _____

CHAPTER 2 Section 4 (pages 46–51)

River Dynasties in China

BEFORE YOU READ

In the last section, you read about Indus Valley culture.

In this section, you will learn about the earliest cultures in China.

AS YOU READ

Use the chart below to take notes on how geography and early cultures influenced the development of Chinese culture.

TERMS AND NAMES
loess Fertile soil
oracle bone Animals bone used by ancient Chinese priests to communicate with the gods
Mandate of Heaven Divine approval of the ruler
dynastic cycle Pattern of rise, fall, and replacement of dynasties
feudalism Political system in which nobles or lords are granted the use of lands that belong to the king

Geography	Shang Culture	Zhou Culture
developed apart from other cultures		

→ Chinese Culture ←

The Geography of China (page 46)

How did geography affect China's past?

The last of the great early civilizations arose in China and continues to this day. China's geography caused it to develop apart from other cultures.

A great ocean, huge deserts, and high mountains isolate China from other areas. The mountains did not protect China totally, however. People living to the north and west invaded the land many times during Chinese history.

There are two rich rivers within China—the Huang He and the Yangtze. Almost all the good farmland in China lies between these rivers. The Huang He deposited huge amounts of silt when it overflowed. This silt is fertile soil called **loess**. The Chinese people also made use of the flood waters of these rivers.

1. Why did China develop apart from other cultures?

_____

_____

Civilization Emerges in Shang Times (pages 47–48)

What was the Shang Dynasty?

A few thousand years ago, some people began to farm along China's rivers. About 2000 B.C., the first dynasty of rulers brought government to China.

CHAPTER 2 EARLY RIVER VALLEY CIVILIZATIONS 19

Around 1500 B.C., a new dynasty, the Shang, began to rule. This dynasty left the first written records in China. Objects found in their palaces and tombs also tell us much about their society. Chinese people built their buildings of wood, not mud-dried brick as the other early cultures did. Huge walls made of earth surrounded these buildings to protect them. The walls were needed because it was a time of constant war.

The king and the *nobles* who helped him fight these wars were at the top of Shang society. At the bottom was the mass of peasants who lived in simple huts outside the city walls. They worked hard on the farms, using wooden tools because the Shang believed that bronze was too good to be used for farming.

2. What were three features of Shang culture?

_____

_____

The Origins of Chinese Culture
(pages 48–49)

What beliefs shaped Shang society?

Shang society was held together by a strong belief in the importance of the group—all the people—and not any single person. The most important part of society was the family. Children grew up learning to respect their parents.

The family played a central role in Chinese religion, too. The Chinese thought that family members who had died could still influence the lives of family members who were alive. They gave respect to dead members of the family, hoping to keep them happy. Through the spirits of their *ancestors*, the Shang also asked for advice from the gods. They used **oracle bones** to do this. These were animal bones and shells. Priests wrote questions on them. Then they touched them with something hot. The priest interpreted the cracks that resulted to find their answers.

The Chinese system of writing differed from those of other groups. Symbols stood for ideas, not sounds. This allowed the many different groups in China to understand the same writing even though each had a special spoken language. The written language had thousands of symbols, however. This made it very hard to learn. Only specially trained people learned to read and write.

3. Name three important values of Shang culture.

_____

_____

_____

Zhou Bring New Ideas (pages 50–51)

Who were the Zhou?

About 1027 B.C., a new group, the Zhou, took control of China. They adopted Shang culture. They also started an idea of royalty that was new to China. Good rulers, they said, got authority to rule from heaven. This was known as the **Mandate of Heaven.** They claimed the Shang rulers were not just and had lost the favor of the gods. That is why they had to be replaced. From then on, the Chinese believed in *divine* rule. However, it also meant that disasters such as floods or war pointed to a ruler that had lost the support of the gods and needed to be replaced. Until the early 1900s, the Chinese had one dynasty after another. This pattern of rise, fall, and replacement of dynasties is known as the **dynastic cycle.**

The Zhou gave members of the royal family and other nobles the rights to large areas of land. They established **feudalism.** Feudalism is a political system in which the nobles owe loyalty to the king. The nobles promise to fight for the rulers and to protect the peasants who live on the land.

Eventually the Zhou rulers lost all power. The nobles fought each other for control of China in a period called the *"time of the warring states."* It lasted many hundred years. The Chinese people suffered during this time.

4. Name two important changes brought about by the Zhou.

_____

_____

_____

Name _____ Date _____

Glossary — CHAPTER 2 Early River Valley Civilizations

ancestors Long-ago relatives
arc Curved shape
citadel Fort or other stronghold
defense Protection against enemies
divine Godlike
featherweight Extremely light; as light as a feather
grid Large square or rectangle evenly divided into squares or rectangles
massive Huge
merchants People who sell goods; shopkeepers
nobles People just below rulers or kings in wealth and power
"time of the warring states" Time after the Zhou lost power when nobles fought each other for control of China

AFTER YOU READ

TERMS AND NAMES

A. Write the name or term in each blank that best completes the meaning of the paragraph.

mummification
theocracy
pharaoh
Menes
pyramids

A king named **1** _____ brought together Upper Egypt and Lower Egypt to create one kingdom. The ruler of the kingdom was the **2** _____. This ruler was seen as a divine figure. This meant the government was a **3** _____. It also helps explain why the rulers built **4** _____ for themselves. They were preparing for rule after their death. To preserve their bodies for this future life, a process called **5** _____ was used.

B. Write the letter of the term next to the description that explains it best.

a. monsoon   ____ **1.** Several peoples or nations brought together under one rule

b. loess   ____ **2.** System of bringing water to fields

c. irrigation ____ **3.** Fertile soil deposited by flooding

d. dynasty   ____ **4.** Seasonal wind

e. empire   ____ **5.** Series of rulers from a single family

Name _____ Date _____

AFTER YOU READ (continued)   CHAP 2   Early River Valley Civilizations

Main Ideas

1. In Sumer, what was a city-state?

_____
_____
_____

2. What did Sargon and Hammurabi have in common?

_____
_____
_____

3. Name three effects of the Nile on the life and culture of ancient Egypt.

_____
_____
_____
_____

4. How did Indus Valley civilization end?

_____
_____
_____

5. What is a dynastic cycle, and where did it occur?

_____
_____
_____

Thinking Critically

Answer the following questions on a separate sheet of paper.

1. Describe the earliest civilization that grew up along the Indus River.

2. Explain the importance of family in early Chinese culture.

Name _____ Date _____

CHAPTER 3 Section 1 (pages 57–61)

Indo-European Migrations

TERMS AND NAMES
Indo-Europeans Group of Asian peoples who migrated to many different places
steppes Dry grasslands
migration Movement of people from one place to another
Hittites Group of Indo-European peoples who occupied Anatolia
Anatolia Large peninsula in modern-day Turkey
Aryans Group of Indo-Europeans
Vedas Sacred literature of the Aryans
Brahmin Priest
caste Class
Mahabharata Poem that tells the story of a great war

BEFORE YOU READ

In the last chapter, you read about peoples who built civilizations in the great river valleys.

In this section, you will learn about the movements of two groups of people who lived on the grasslands of Asia.

AS YOU READ

Use the chart below to take notes on where each group migrated and on the features of its culture.

```
           Indo-Europeans
           /            \
     Hittites          Aryans
   • occupied Anatolia
```

Indo-Europeans Migrate (page 57)

Who were the Indo-Europeans?

The **Indo-Europeans** were a group of peoples who came from the **steppes**—the dry grasslands of western Asia. The Indo-Europeans rode horses and tended cattle, sheep, and goats. They spoke many different languages, but all of them came from the same original language.

For some reason, starting about 1700 B.C., the Indo-Europeans began to leave their homeland. They moved into some of the settled areas and began to conquer them. These **migrations,** movements of people from one region to another, took place over a long period of time.

1. What happened to the Indo-Europeans?

_____
_____
_____
_____

Hittites Blend Empire and Technology (pages 58–59)

Who were the Hittites?

The **Hittites** were one of these Indo-European peoples. They rode two-wheeled chariots and used

CHAPTER 3 PEOPLE AND IDEAS ON THE MOVE **23**

iron weapons to conquer **Anatolia.** Anatolia is also called Asia Minor. It is a huge *peninsula* in modern-day Turkey. The Hittites moved farther and took the ancient lands of Mesopotamia. When they moved to the south, they ran into the Egyptians. Neither side was able to defeat the other. So, they decided to make peace.

The Hittites adopted many features of the culture that had grown in Mesopotamia before they arrived. They changed others to suit their own ideas. Their laws, for instance, were less harsh than the code of Hammurabi. The Hittites ruled their Southwest Asian empire from about 2000 to 1190 B.C. Then they fell to a new wave of invaders.

2. How did the Hittites react to the culture they found in Mesopotamia?

_____
_____
_____
_____

Aryan Invaders Transform India
(pages 59–61)

Who were the Aryans?

The **Aryans** were another group of Indo-European people. They moved into what is now India and *transformed* it. They first captured the land of the people of the Indus Valley. *Archaeology* tells almost nothing about the Aryans. But their sacred literature, the **Vedas,** tells a lot about them.

The Aryans were divided into three classes of people. There were priests (**Brahmins**), warriors, and peasants or traders. They viewed the non-Aryans living in the area as a fourth class. Over time, they made many rules for how people in these classes, or **castes,** could interact with one another. People were born into their caste for life. Some "impure" people lived in a group outside this class system. They were butchers, grave diggers, and trash collectors. Because they did work that was thought unclean, they were called *"untouchables."*

Over many centuries, the Aryans took more and more of what is now India. Eventually many powerful people tried to create their own kingdoms. They fought each other until one kingdom, Magadha, won control over almost all of India. Around this time, an *epic* poem, the **Mahabharata,** was written. It tells of the blending of cultures at the time. It also sets down ideals that were to become important in Hindu life.

3. What is the caste system?

_____
_____
_____
_____
_____

Name _____ Date _____

CHAPTER 3 Section 2 (pages 62–66)

Roots of Hinduism and Buddhism

TERMS AND NAMES
reincarnation Belief that the soul is reborn
karma Good or bad deeds
Jainism Religion that teaches every living creature has a soul and no living creature can be harmed
Siddhartha Gautama Founder of Buddhism
enlightenment Wisdom
nirvana Buddha's word for release from selfishness and pain

BEFORE YOU READ

In the last section, you read about the Hittites and the Aryans.

In this section, you will learn about the roots of Hinduism and Buddhism.

AS YOU READ

Use the chart below to show features of Hinduism, Buddhism, and also Jainism.

```
                    World Religions
                    /      |      \
            Hinduism    Buddhism   Jainism
         • collection
           of beliefs
```

Hinduism Develops Over Centuries (pages 62–64)

What is Hinduism?

Hinduism is a collection of religious beliefs that forms no one system. Unlike many religions, it was not founded by only one person. It is a religion that allows great variety for its followers. Certain ideas became common to the beliefs of all Hindus.

Hindus believe that each person has a soul. However, there is also a larger soul, called *Brahman*, that brings together all the individual souls. A person's goal is to become free of desire and not bothered by suffering. When that takes place, the person's soul wins escape from life on Earth. Hindus believe in **reincarnation.** They believe the soul is born again into another body after death. In the next life, the soul has another chance to learn its lessons. According to Hindus, how a person behaves in one life has an effect on the person's next life. This is the soul's **karma**—good or bad deeds.

Another religion that arose in India was **Jainism.** It was started by Mahavira, a man who lived from about 599 to 527 B.C. He believed that every creature in the world—even an animal—has

CHAPTER 3 PEOPLE AND IDEAS ON THE MOVE **25**

a soul. Because of that, people must be sure not to harm any creature. Today, Jains take jobs that are certain not to hurt living things.

1. Name three Hindu beliefs.

_____

_____

_____

The Buddha Seeks Enlightenment (pages 64–66)

What is Buddhism?

Another new religion, Buddhism, arose about the same time as Hinduism and Jainism. Buddhism has millions of followers all around the world. It was started around 528 B.C. by **Siddhartha Gautama.**

Siddhartha searched for a way that would allow him to escape the suffering of human life. He spent many years searching for this answer. He was looking for **enlightenment,** or wisdom. Finally, he sat down and *meditated* under a tree. After 49 days, he had his answer. He was now called the Buddha, which means the "enlightened one."

The Buddha began to teach others how to attain enlightenment. They were to follow a plan of behavior called the Eightfold Path—right views, right resolve, right speech, right conduct, right livelihood, right effort, right mindfulness, and right concentration. This would lead to **nirvana,** or a release from selfishness and pain.

As with Hinduism, the Buddha taught that the soul would be reborn into a new life. This chain of new lives would continue until the soul, like Buddha, reached understanding.

These ideas attracted many followers. Many people who lived in the lower classes of Indian society saw these ideas as a chance to escape from the limits placed on them. This teaching also spread in southern India. There the Aryans did not have much influence. Some followers took the ideas to other lands.

In the centuries after Buddha's death in 483 B.C., Buddhism appeared in Southeast Asia. Later it was carried to China and then to Korea and Japan. Merchants and traders played an important role in spreading the religion. Strangely, in India where Buddhism was founded, the religion faded. Many places that are important to Buddhism remain in India, however. Buddhists from around the world come there to visit locations connected to the life of Buddha.

2. Name four basic beliefs of Buddhism.

_____

_____

_____

Four Noble Truths of Buddhism	
First Noble Truth	Everything in life is suffering and sorrow.
Second Noble Truth	The cause of all suffering is people's selfish desire for the temporary pleasures of this world.
Third Noble Truth	The way to end all suffering is to end all desires.
Fourth Noble Truth	The way to overcome such desires and attain enlightenment is to follow the Eightfold Path, which is called the Middle Way between desires and self-denial.

Skillbuilder

Use the chart to answer the questions.

1. What is the subject of the first three noble truths?

_____

_____

2. What is the Eightfold Path?

_____

_____

Name _____ Date _____

CHAPTER 3 Section 3 (pages 67–71)

Seafaring Traders Extend Boundaries

TERMS AND NAMES
Minoans Group of powerful seafaring people
Aegean Sea Sea between modern-day Greece and Turkey
Knossos Minoan capital city
King Minos King of Knossos
Phoenicians Most powerful traders along the Mediterranean

BEFORE YOU READ
In the last section, you read about major religions that developed in India.

In this section, you will learn about traders whose influence spread throughout the Mediterranean.

AS YOU READ
Use the web below to take notes on how trade spread both products and culture.

- **Minoans** — sent products as well as art and culture
- **Phoenicians**
- **Trading Networks**

(center: **Ancient Mediterranean Trade**)

Minoans Trade Far and Wide
(pages 67–68)

Who were the Minoans?

In the Mediterranean area, a new culture arose on the island of Crete. The **Minoans** were peaceful people who lived in rich cities that were safe from invaders. They controlled trade in their area, Crete. Crete is a large island on the southern edge of the **Aegean Sea.** The Minoans sent their fine pottery, swords, and metal drinking cups to other lands. They also sent other countries their style of art and architecture. This style later had influence on the art of Greece.

Archaeologists have explored the ruins of **Knossos,** the capital city of the Minoans. It was the archeologists that first called the culture Minoan, after its famous ruler, **King Minos.** They found beautiful wall paintings that offer views of Minoan culture. One interesting feature of Minoan life was the high position that women appear to have held. An earth goddess seems to have headed all the gods of Crete, and women ruled over some important religious places. Women did not play such

CHAPTER 3 PEOPLE AND IDEAS ON THE MOVE **27**

important roles among other peoples who lived nearby.

Minoan cities were damaged in 1470 B.C. by a series of disasters. First, a number of earthquakes rocked the island, destroying buildings. Then a volcano exploded on a nearby island. That was followed by huge waves and clouds of white ash from the volcano's fire. These shocks seem to have been too much for the Minoans. The Minoan civilization ended about 1200 B.C.

1. What were three important features of Minoan culture?

_____

_____

_____

Phoenicians Spread Trade and Civilization (pages 68–69)

Who were the Phoenicians?

Another group of people arose in the Mediterranean. They lived in several city-states in what is today Lebanon. They traded far and wide. Some may have even sailed as far as Britain—and perhaps around Africa. They were the **Phoenicians.**

The Phoenicians put *colonies* all along the Mediterranean coast. Colonies were 30 miles apart. This was the distance that one of their ships could travel in a day. One of those colonies, Carthage, in North Africa, later became a major power in the Mediterranean world. Phoenicians traded such goods as wine, weapons, metals, ivory, slaves, and objects made of wood and glass. They also made a purple dye that was highly valued.

The important achievement of the Phoenicians was their alphabet. They used symbols to stand for the sounds of consonants. They brought their system of writing to other lands such as Greece, where Greeks changed the form of some letters. The alphabet that we use today, however, had its beginnings in Phoenician writing.

2. How did the Phoenicians spread their culture?

_____

_____

_____

_____

The Long Reach of Ancient Trade (page 71)

What were the major trading networks?

Trading networks also connected the Mediterranean Sea with other centers of world commerce in South and East Asia. Some routes went across Central Asia by land. Some sea routes went across the Arabian Sea. These networks helped people exchange products and information. Traders carried ideas, religious beliefs, art, and ways of living. They did not just trade goods. They also helped "trade" culture.

3. Why were trade networks so important?

_____

_____

_____

_____

Name _____ Date _____

CHAPTER 3 Section 4 (pages 72–76)

The Origins of Judaism

TERMS AND NAMES
Palestine Region on the eastern end of the Mediterranean Sea
Canaan Ancient home of the Hebrews
Torah First five books of the Hebrew Bible
Abraham "Father" or the first of the Hebrew people
monotheism Belief in a single god
covenant Mutual promise between god and the Hebrews
Moses According to the Torah, the man that led the Jews out of slavery
Israel Region on the eastern end of the Mediterranean Sea
Judah Hebrew kingdom in Palestine
tribute Payment made by a weaker power to a stronger power

BEFORE YOU READ

In the last section, you read about the spread of culture through trade.

In this section, you will learn about the *origins* of Judaism.

AS YOU READ

Uses the chart below to take notes on the beginnings of Judaism.

Promised Land	Kingdom of Israel	Babylonian Captivity
• Canaan in Palestine		

The Search for a Promised Land
(pages 72–75)

Where did the Hebrews claim land?

The Hebrews made a claim to an important piece of land, the area now called **Palestine.** They believed the land had been promised to them by God. Their ancient home was the area of Palestine called **Canaan.** This region sat on the eastern edge of the Mediterranean Sea and on the Red Sea, which led to the Indian Ocean. It opened to the trade of many lands. Most of what we know about the early history of the Hebrews comes from the **Torah,** the sacred book of the Hebrews.

The story of the Hebrews began in Mesopotamia. There, according to the Torah, God chose a man named **Abraham** to be the "father," or the first of the Hebrews. God told Abraham to move his family to Palestine. Abraham promised that he and his people would always obey God. (The Hebrews were among the world's earliest peoples to believe in one god, or **monotheism.**) God, in turn, promised to always protect them from their enemies. This was the first of many **covenants**—promises between God and the Hebrews.

CHAPTER 3 PEOPLE AND IDEAS ON THE MOVE **29**

When their crops failed, the Hebrews moved to Egypt around 1650 B.C. Over time, they were forced to become slaves. After many years, they fled. The Hebrews called this mass departure *"the Exodus."*

According to the Torah, a man named Moses led them out of Egypt between 1300 and 1200 B.C. They wandered 40 years in a wilderness. During that time, the Torah says, God gave **Moses** the Ten Commandments. These were the laws that the Hebrews were to follow. For the second time, God promised to protect them in return for their obedience to his laws.

After Moses died, the Hebrews finally reached Palestine and settled. There they began to adopt new ways of life. They often fought with other peoples living in the area, as each group tried to control the best land and other resources.

The Hebrews were organized into twelve groups, called *tribes.* Each tribe was separate from the others. But in times of danger they would unite under leaders called *judges.* One of those judges was a woman named Deborah. It was unusual for women in Hebrew society to hold such a position. Women usually were expected to stay home and raise children.

The Hebrews had other leaders called *prophets.* They said that they were messengers sent by God to tell the people how he wanted them to act. These prophets told the people that they had two duties: to worship God and to deal in just and fair ways with one another. With this message, religion was changing. Instead of being a part of life run by priests, it was now a matter of each person living a *moral* life.

1. What role did Abraham play in early Hebrew history?

_____

_____

_____

The Kingdom of Israel (pages 75–76)
How was Israel formed?

After the exile, the only large tribe left was the tribe of Judah. As a result, the Hebrews came to be known as the Jews. Their religion was called Judaism.

From about 1020 to 922 B.C., the Jews were united into one kingdom, **Israel.** Three kings helped unite them. The first, Saul, drove off their enemies. The second, David, made Jerusalem the capital. The third, Solomon, built a magnificent temple to be used to worship God.

After Solomon's death, though, the kingdom split into two parts. Israel was in the north, and **Judah** was in the south. For the next two centuries, each of the kingdoms had times of prosperity, followed by low periods.

2. How was Israel split?

_____

_____

_____

The Babylonian Captivity (page 76)
Who conquered Israel and Judah?

Disaster came when both kingdoms lost their independence. Israel and Judah began to pay tribute to Assyria. **Tribute** is money paid by a weaker power to a stronger power to make sure it does not attack.

Eventually, the northern kingdom fell to the Assyrians. Later, the southern kingdom fell to the Babylonians. Many Jews were forced into exile in Babylon. They lived there for many years during what was known as the Babylonian *Captivity.* Then the Babylonians themselves were conquered by the Persian king Cyrus the Great. The new ruler let 40,000 Jews return home.

3. What was the Babylonian Captivity?

_____

_____

_____

Name _____ Date _____

Glossary **CHAPTER 3** People and Ideas on the Move

archaeology Study of past human life and activities
Brahman Larger soul that brings together individual souls, in Hinduism.
captivity State of being kept against one's will
colonies Lands under the control of another power
epic Long poem that tells a story; long story written in poetry
Exodus Mass departure of Jews from Egypt
judge Leader of a Hebrew tribe
meditated Cleared the mind of everyday thought
moral Based on principles of right and wrong
origins Beginnings
peninsula Body of land surrounded on three sides by water
prophet Leader whom the Hebrews believed to be a messenger of god
transform Change
tribe One of twelve original groups of Hebrews
untouchables People thought of as unclean and therefore outside the caste system

AFTER YOU READ

Terms and Names

A. Write the name or term in each blank that best completes the meaning of the paragraph.

Anatolia
Aryans
Indo-Europeans
steppes
migrations

Thousands of years ago, there were peoples in Asia called **1** _____. They herded animals on dry grasslands known as **2** _____. Over several centuries, a number of **3** _____ of these peoples took place. They settled in many different areas. One group occupied Asia Minor, or **4** _____. They were the Hittites. Another group settled in the Indus River Valley of what is now India. They were the **5** _____.

B. Write the letter of the name or term next to the description that explains it best.

a. monotheism
b. reincarnation
c. karma
d. nirvana
e. covenant

____ **1.** Release from selfishness and pain
____ **2.** Agreement between God and the Hebrew people
____ **3.** Good or bad deeds
____ **4.** Belief that an individual soul is reborn again and again
____ **5.** Belief in one god

CHAPTER 3 PEOPLE AND IDEAS ON THE MOVE **31**

Name _____ Date _____

AFTER YOU READ (continued) CHAPTER 3 People and Ideas on the Move

Main Ideas

1. How did Aryan invaders change India?
_____
_____
_____

2. What makes Hinduism different from other religions?
_____
_____
_____

3. What was Siddhartha Gautama looking for, and how did he find it?
_____
_____
_____
_____

4. What may have caused the end of Minoan civilization?
_____
_____
_____

5. What role did Moses play in early Jewish history?
_____
_____
_____
_____

Thinking Critically

Answer the following questions on a separate sheet of paper.

1. What effect did the Minoans and Phoenicians have on neighboring cultures?

2. What was unique about the religious beliefs of the Hebrews?

Name _____ Date _____

CHAPTER 4 Section 1 (pages 83–87)

The Empires of Egypt and Nubia Collide

TERMS AND NAMES
Hyksos Invaders that ruled Egypt from 1640 to 1570 B.C.
New Kingdom Period after the Hyksos rulers
Hatshepsut New Kingdom ruler who encouraged trade
Thutmose III Warlike ruler; stepson of Hatshepsut
Nubia Region of Africa bordering Egypt
Ramses II Pharaoh and great builder of Egypt
Kush Nubian kingdom
Piankhi Kushite king who forced the Libyans out of Egypt
Meroë Home and trading center of the Kush kingdom

BEFORE YOU READ

In the last section, you read about the religion of the ancient Hebrews.

In this section, you will read about the interaction of Egypt and Nubia.

AS YOU READ

Use the time line below to take notes on changes in Egypt and Nubia.

1570 B.C. Beginning of the New Kingdom	1075 B.C.	350 A.D.

1200 B.C.	250 B.C.

The New Kingdom of Egypt
(pages 83–84)

What happened during the New Kingdom?

At the end of its second period of glory, power struggles weakened Egypt. New invaders, the **Hyksos,** arrived. They had the chariot. Egyptians had never seen this war machine before. The Hyksos ruled Egypt for many years until the pharaohs took back their land. Then they began some *conquests* of their own. The time from 1570 to 1075 B.C. is called the **New Kingdom.** In this third period, Egypt was richer and more powerful than ever.

Hatshepsut was one of the rulers of the New Kingdom. She encouraged trade. Her stepson, **Thutmose III,** was a much more warlike ruler. He and other pharaohs of this New Kingdom brought Egyptian rule to Syria and Palestine in the east. They also moved south into **Nubia.** This was a part of Africa near where the Nile began. From Nubia, they took valuable goods, such as ivory, gold, and cattle. They also brought back slaves. The Egyptians and Nubians would maintain close contact for hundreds of years.

The pharaohs of the New Kingdom did not

CHAPTER 4 FIRST AGE OF EMPIRES 33

build pyramids, like those who had come before. Instead, they built great tombs in a secret place called the *Valley of the Kings*. Some pharaohs also built huge palaces for themselves or temples to the Egyptian gods.

Ramses II stood out among the great builders of the New Kingdom. He reigned from about 1290 to 1244 B.C.

1. What was the relationship between Nubia and Egypt during the New Kingdom?

_____
_____
_____

The Empire Declines (pages 84–85)
How did Egypt lose power?

Around 1200 B.C., invaders attacked the eastern Mediterranean. They brought trouble with them. Some of these invaders were called the "People of the Sea." They attacked the Egyptian empire. They attacked the Hittite kingdom, too.

As the power of Egypt fell, the land broke into many small kingdoms. People from Libya began to invade Egypt. They took control of the land. They followed the Egyptian way of life.

2. Who invaded Egypt?

_____
_____

The Kushites Conquer the Nile Region (pages 85–87)
How did the Kushites rule?

As Egypt grew weaker, the Nubian kingdom of **Kush** became more powerful. Under Egyptian rule, the people of Kush accepted many Egyptian traditions and customs. They felt that they had to protect Egyptian values.

A Kushite king named **Piankhi** moved into Egypt to force out the Libyans. He united the Nile Valley. He wanted to bring back Egypt's glory. The Kushites ruled Egypt for a few decades. Then the Assyrians invaded. They forced the Kushites back to their home.

3. How did the Kushites view Egyptian culture?

_____
_____
_____

The Golden Age of Meroë (page 87)
What was Meroë?

The Kushite kings settled in the city of **Meroë**, south of Egypt. Their kingdom entered a golden age. The city played an important role in trade. Meroë also became an important center for making iron and iron weapons.

Traders in the city brought their iron to the ports of the Red Sea. These goods were taken on ships to Arabia and India. The traders from Meroë, in the meantime, brought back jewelry, cloth, silver lamps, and glass bottles. The city thrived from about 250 B.C. to about A.D. 150. By A.D. 350 Meroë had fallen to rival Aksum, a seaport farther south.

4. Why was Meroë important?

_____
_____
_____

Name _____ Date _____

CHAPTER 4 Section 2 (pages 88–91)

Assyria Dominates the Fertile Crescent

BEFORE YOU READ

In the last section, you read about Egypt and Nubia.

In this section, you will read about the Assyrians, the people who took over Egypt.

AS YOU READ

Use the chart below to take notes on Assyria.

TERMS AND NAMES
Assyria Powerful empire in northern Mesopotamia
Sennacherib Assyrian king and empire builder
Nineveh Assyria's capital on the Tigris River
Ashurbanipal Assyrian king who gathered writing tablets from many lands
Medes People who helped to destroy the Assyrian empire
Chaldeans People who helped to destroy the Assyrian empire
Nebuchadnezzar Chaldean king who rebuilt Babylon

ASSYRIA	
Military might	defended themselves first; then conquered others

A Mighty Military Machine
(pages 88–89)

Who were the Assyrians?

For a time, **Assyria** was the greatest power in Southwest Asia. The Assyrians began as a farming people in the northern part of Mesopotamia. Because their homes were open to attack, they formed a strong fighting force. Soon they turned to conquest. Assyrian kings, including the fierce **Sennacherib,** built an empire that stretched from east and north of the Tigris River all the way to central Egypt.

The Assyrians used many different methods to win their battles. Their soldiers carried strong iron-tipped spears and iron swords. They used *cavalry*—troops on horses. They used large numbers of men with bows. They dug tunnels under city walls to weaken them. They used heavy battering rams to knock down the wooden gates of the city.

The Assyrians conquered almost everything in their path. They usually killed or enslaved those they defeated. Some Assyrian kings bragged about their cruelty toward people they captured.

Sometimes conquered peoples would revolt. Assyrians wanted to stop these rebellions. They forced groups of captives to leave their homelands. Then the captives were too far away to cause trouble.

1. What made the Assyrians such a strong fighting force?

_____

_____

CHAPTER 4 FIRST AGE OF EMPIRES **35**

An Expanding Empire (pages 89–90)

Whom did the Assyrians conquer?

Between 850 and 650 B.C., the Assyrians conquered all of Mesopotamia along with Syria and Palestine. Then they took modern Turkey and Egypt. They ruled by putting in power kings who would support them. They also collected taxes and tribute—yearly payments from peoples who were weaker. If a city did not pay, the Assyrian army moved in and destroyed it.

The Assyrian kings were builders, too. One built the city of **Nineveh** on the north branch of the Tigris River. It was the largest city of its day. The city was surrounded with walls.

Another king, **Ashurbanipal,** gathered thousands of writing tablets from the lands that had been taken. Some of these tablets were dictionaries. The dictionary tablets were very important. When these were found in modern times, they provided the key to reading many languages of the ancient world.

2. Besides conquering other people, what did the Assyrians accomplish?

_____
_____
_____
_____

The Empire Crumbles (pages 90–91)

Why did the Assyrians fall?

The Assyrians had also made many enemies over the years. After a while, those enemies banded together. An army made up of **Medes, Chaldeans,** and others struck back. In 612 B.C., they destroyed the city of Ninevah. Many people in the area were glad that the city was in ruins.

The Chaldeans, who had ruled the area earlier, took control of Mesopotamia again. A Chaldean king named **Nebuchadnezzar** rebuilt the city of Babylon. Once more it was one of the greatest cities of the world. The city included famous hanging gardens with many different plants from the cool mountain regions. Slaves watered the plants with hidden pumps.

Babylon also featured a *ziggurat*. This step-shaped pyramid soared 300 feet into the air. It was the tallest building in Babylon. At night, priests would study the stars and the planets. They recorded what they saw. This was the beginning of the science of *astronomy*.

3. Who were the Chaldeans?

_____
_____
_____
_____

Name _____ Date _____

CHAPTER 4 Section 3 (pages 92–96)

Persia Unites Many Lands

TERMS AND NAMES
Cyrus Persian king who created a huge empire
Cambyses Cyrus's son
Darius Persian king who put satraps in place and built the Royal Road
satrap Governor who ruled locally
Royal Road Road that helped unify the Persian Empire
Zoroaster Persian prophet and religious reformer

BEFORE YOU READ

In the last section, you read about the military might of the Assyrians.

In this section, you will read about the wise rule of the Persians.

AS YOU READ

Use the chart below to take notes on key people in the rise of Persia, its rule, and its religion.

Cyrus	general and king who conquered a huge empire
Cambyses	
Darius	
Zoroaster	

The Rise of Persia (pages 92–93)

How did Persia come to power?

Persia, a new power, arose east of Mesopotamia, in modern Iran. The area had good farmland. It was also rich in minerals. There were mines of copper, lead, gold, and silver.

The Persians joined with other forces to help defeat the Assyrians. About 550 B.C., the Persians began their own conquests.

Their king was **Cyrus,** an excellent general. His troops rode swift ponies and used short bows that could be fired quickly. Cyrus led his army to conquer a huge empire. It stretched from the Indus Valley in India all the way through Mesopotamia to Turkey. The empire covered about 2,500 miles. Cyrus took all this land in just over 10 years.

Cyrus won this vast land in part because of the wise way he treated the people there. Cyrus did not follow the the examples of the Assyrians. They destroyed towns and cities. Cyrus, however, made sure that his army did not harm the people he conquered. He allowed the people to practice their old religions, too. Cyrus let the Hebrews return to

CHAPTER 4 FIRST AGE OF EMPIRES **37**

Jerusalem and rebuild their temple there. Cyrus was also a great warrior. He was killed in battle.

1. What made Cyrus a great leader?

_____

_____

_____

Persian Rule and Religion
(pages 93–96)

Who was Darius?

Cyrus died in 530 B.C. The kings who followed him had to decide how to run the vast new empire. His son, **Cambyses,** conquered Egypt. Cambyses was not like his father. He was not wise or understanding. He did not respect the Egyptians and their way of life.

The next king, **Darius,** proved as able as Cyrus. Darius put down several revolts. He won more land for the empire and created a government for the empire. Only Greece escaped Persian control.

Darius divided the land into 20 *provinces,* each holding a certain group of people. He allowed each group to practice its own religion, speak its own language, and obey many of its own laws. He also put royal governors—**satraps**—in place to make sure that the people obeyed his laws.

Darius built the **Royal Road** to unite his large empire. This excellent road system ran 1,677 miles. Royal messengers on horses could travel this distance in about seven days. The Royal Road made communication better within the empire. Transportation became easier too.

Darius also had metal coins made that could be used for business anywhere in the empire. The coins had a standard value. This money system, along with the Royal Road, helped increase trade.

During the Persian Empire, a new religion arose in Southwest Asia. A prophet named **Zoroaster** said there were two powerful gods. One stood for truth and light. The other represented evil and darkness. The two gods were in a constant struggle. People needed to choose truth and light to enter paradise. These ideas influenced later religions.

The Persians left their mark in history. They were fair and understanding. The Persians showed respect for other cultures. Their government brought order to Southwest Asia.

2. How did Darius change Persia?

_____

_____

_____

_____

Name _____ Date _____

CHAPTER 4 Section 4 (pages 97–101)

An Empire Unifies China

BEFORE YOU READ

In the last section, you read about the Persian empire.

In this section, you will learn how China was restored to order.

AS YOU READ

Use a chart like the one below to take notes on new ideas and changes in China that restored order.

TERMS AND NAMES
Confucius China's most influential scholar
filial piety Children's respect for their parents and elders
bureaucracy Organization of government into agencies and departments
Daoism Philosophy of Laozi that puts people in touch with the forces of nature
Legalism Chinese idea that a highly efficient and powerful government is the key to social order
I Ching Chinese book that gave advice on practical and everyday problems
yin and yang Powers that govern the natural rhythms of life and must be balanced
Qin dynasty Dynasty that unified China
Shi Huangdi First emperor of China; leader of the Qin Dynasty
autocracy Government in which the ruler has unlimited power

Ideas about social order	Ideas about government	Ideas about nature	New political rule
Confucius stresses five basic relationships			

→ Order in China ←

Philosophy and the Social Order
(pages 97–99)

How did new ideas change China?

After the fall of the Zhou dynasty, China became a land of troubles. Ancient Chinese values were forgotten. Civilization seemed doomed. Yet some thinkers tried to find ways to restore these values.

One of the most important thinkers was Confucius. He was born in 551 B.C. Confucius believed that order could return. But first, the people would have to work at five basic relationships. These were ruler and subject, father and son, husband and wife, older and younger brothers, and friend and friend. The family relationships, he thought, were the most important. Confucius stressed that children should practice **filial piety.** This is respect for parents and elders.

Confucius also tried to make government better.

CHAPTER 4 FIRST AGE OF EMPIRES 39

He helped create the basis of a **bureaucracy.** This is a system of departments and agencies for running the government. Education was important for the people who held jobs in this kind of government. Over time, the ideas of Confucius spread to other countries of East Asia.

Another thinker of this period was Laozi. He said nature follows a universal force called the Dao, or "the Way." His beliefs are called **Daoism.**

Other thinkers formed a set of beliefs called **Legalism.** They said the government should use the law to restore order in China.

Some Chinese people looked for practical advice in solving problems. They might refer to a book called *I Ching.* It was based on the idea of **yin and yang.** These two powers represented the harmony between opposite forces in the universe.

1. What were three thinkers or new ideas that changed China?

_____

_____

The Qin Dynasty (pages 99–101)

What happened during the Qin Dynasty?

A 13-year-old ruler became ruler of the **Qin Dynasty.** He ended the troubles of the warring states. This young ruler used the ideas of Legalism to unite China. After ruling for 20 years, he took a new name—**Shi Huangdi.** This means "First Emperor."

Shi Huangdi doubled the size of China. He established an **autocracy.** In this kind of government, a ruler has unlimited power. Shi Huangdi forced wealthy *nobles* to give up their land in the country and move to his capital city. He destroyed his enemies. The emperor wanted to control ideas, too. He ordered his government to burn books.

Shi Huangdi also had peasants build a network of roads that linked one corner of the empire to another. He set standards for writing, law, money, and weights and measures to be followed throughout the empire.

In the past, some Chinese rulers had built sections of wall to try to block attacks from northern nomads. Shi Huangdi had hundreds of thousands of poor people connect these sections of wall and make a huge barrier. When finished, the Great Wall of China stretched 1,400 miles.

These steps won the emperor little support. When he died, his son took the throne. Just three years into his *reign*, peasants revolted and managed to overthrow the emperor. By 202 B.C., the Qin dynasty had given way to the Han dynasty.

2. Name two changes that Shi Huangdi made.

_____

_____

Daoism	Legalism
• The natural order is more important than the social order.	• A highly efficient and powerful government is the key to social order.
• A universal force guides all things.	• Punishments are useful to maintain social order.
• Human beings should live simply and in harmony with nature.	• Thinkers and their ideas should be strictly controlled by the government.

Skillbuilder

Use the chart to answer the questions.

1. Which set of ideas places more importance on social order?

_____

_____

2. In what ways are these ideas opposite?

_____

_____

Name _____ Date _____

Glossary   CHAPTER 4   First Age of Empires 1570 B.C.–200 B.C.

astronomy Study of heavenly bodies
cavalry Troops riding horses
conquests Acts of conquering or taking over
dominates Has control over
nobles Wealthy landowners just below the level of emperor or king
province Outside territory controlled or ruled by another area or country
reign Rule by a king or other power
unifies Brings together as one
Valley of the Kings Place where New Kingdom pharaohs built tombs
ziggurat Step-shaped pyramid

AFTER YOU READ

Names and Terms

A. Write the name or term in each blank that best completes the meaning of the paragraph.

bureaucracy
Legalism
autocracy
Confucius
Shi Huangdi

After the time of the warring states in China, new ideas were formed. Many of these came from an important thinker named **1** _____. He wanted to organize society around five basic relationships. He also favored creating a **2** _____ in the government. More ideas about changing government came from **3** _____. This way of thinking urged rich rewards for those who carried out their duties and strong punishments for those who did not. The leader of the Qin Dynasty and the new emperor of China, **4** _____, also had strong ideas about government. He established an **5** _____, a government in which the ruler has unlimited power.

B. Write the letter of the name next to the description that explains it best.

a. Cyrus
b. Sennacherib
c. Nineveh
d. Darius
e. Nebuchadnezzar

____ **1.** Persian ruler and builder of the Royal Road
____ **2.** Founder of the Persian empire
____ **3.** Capital of Assyria
____ **4.** Chaldean king who restored Babylon
____ **5.** Assyrian king and warrior

CHAPTER 4   FIRST AGE OF EMPIRES   41

Name _____ Date _____

AFTER YOU READ (continued)   CHAPTER 4   First Age of Empires
1570 B.C.–200 B.C.

Main Ideas

1. What was Meroë?

_____
_____
_____

2. What did Nebuchadnezzar accomplish?

_____
_____
_____

3. Name three things for which Cyrus might be remembered.

_____
_____
_____
_____

4. Explain the ideas of Zoroaster.

_____
_____
_____

5. Name the five relationships that Confucius said people should work at.

_____
_____
_____
_____

Thinking Critically

Answer the following questions on a separate sheet of paper.

1. Explain the relationship of Kush to Egypt.

2. How did Shi Huangdi unite his empire?

42   CHAPTER 4   REVIEW

Name _____ Date _____

CHAPTER 5 Section 1 (pages 111–114)

Cultures of the Mountains and the Sea

BEFORE YOU READ
In the last section, you read about belief systems in ancient China and the Qin dynasty.

In this section, you will read about the development of culture in ancient Greece.

AS YOU READ
Use the chart below to take notes on ancient Greek life.

TERMS AND NAMES
Mycenaeans Group who settled on the Greek mainland around 2000 B.C.
Trojan War War in which the Mycenaeans attacked the city of Troy
Dorians Group of people who migrated into the Greek mainland
Homer Greek poet who composed *The Iliad* and *The Odyssey*
epics Heroic stories told in the form of long poems
myths Traditional stories that explain why the world is the way it is

Geography	Mycenaens	Dorians
mountains and valleys separated areas		

Geography Shapes Greek Life
(pages 111–112)

How did geography influence the Greeks?

The lives of the ancient Greeks were shaped by the geography of their land. Greece is a rocky land with high mountains and deep valleys. These land forms were like barriers. Moving over the land was difficult. For these reasons, Greeks living in different areas could not be easily *united*.

Good farmland covered only about one-fourth of Greece and could not support many people. Only certain crops could be grown. Therefore, the Greeks' choice of foods was somewhat limited. Their diet included grains, grapes, and olives. The need for more living space and the lack of good farmland may have influenced the Greeks to find new colonies.

The Greeks had easy access to the sea, however. They became excellent sailors. Trade became important because Greece had few natural resources.

The climate is mild. As a result, Greek people

CHAPTER 5 CLASSICAL GREECE **43**

spent much time outdoors. They attended public events and even *conducted* government outside.

1. Why was sea trade important for the Greeks?

_____

_____

_____

Mycenaean Civilization Develops (pages 112–113)

Who were the Mycenaeans?

A large wave of people moved from Europe, India, and Southwest Asia. Some of these people settled on the Greek mainland around 2000 B.C. They were later called **Mycenaeans.** They were ruled by powerful warrior-kings.

The Mycenaeans developed a strong culture. They borrowed from the Minoan culture of Crete. They adapted the Minoan form of writing and some religious beliefs. The Mycenaeans also became interested in trade.

According to legend, Mycenaeans fought a long war with the people of Troy, a city in Turkey. This conflict was called the **Trojan War.**

The war was said to have started because a Trojan youth kidnapped a Greek woman. Her name was Helen. She was the beautiful wife of a Greek king. The Greek army later destroyed Troy.

2. How were the Mycenaeans influenced by the Minoans?

_____

_____

_____

Greek Culture Declines Under the Dorians (pages 113–114)

What was Greece like under the Dorians?

The culture of the Mycenaeans fell about 1200 B.C. Sea raiders destroyed their palaces. A less advanced people called the **Dorians** occupied the land. For the next 400 years, Greece went into decline. No written records exist from this period. Little is known about this era.

The spoken word lived on, however. A great storyteller named **Homer** made up **epics,** long poems, based on tales he heard. Epics are about heroes and their deeds.

Homer's two great epics were *The Iliad* and *The Odyssey*. Both center on the heroes of the Trojan War. The heroes of *The Iliad* are warriors. Homer tells about their courage and noble actions in battle. The main hero of *The Odyssey* is a Greek warrior named Odysseus. Most of this epic takes place after the Trojan War. Odysseus has many adventures during his long journey home.

The Greeks also created a rich set of **myths.** These stories explain the actions of gods and events in nature. In Greek myths, gods often act like humans. For example, they show feelings, such as love, hate, and jealousy. Unlike humans, though, the Greek gods lived forever.

3. How did Homer keep Greek culture alive under the Dorians?

_____

_____

_____

_____

Name _____ Date _____

CHAPTER 5 Section 2 (pages 115–119)

Warring City-States

BEFORE YOU READ

In the last section, you read about the rise of early cultures in Greece.

In this section, you will read about city-states and their governments.

AS YOU READ

Use the chart below to take notes on the city-states.

TERMS AND NAMES
polis City-state of ancient Greece
acropolis Hilltop in an ancient Greek city
monarchy Government ruled by a king or queen
aristocracy Government ruled by a small group of noble families
oligarchy Government ruled by a few powerful people
phalanx Side-by-side fighting formation of Greek foot soldiers
tyrant Powerful rulers who controlled a city-state's government
helot Peasant forced to stay on the land
democracy Rule by the people
Persian Wars Wars between the Greek and the Persian empire

Government	city-state—main political unit ways to rule city-states—monarchy, aristocracy, oligarchy
Sparta	
Athens	
Persian War	

Rule and Order in Greek City-States (pages 115–116)

How were city-states governed?

The center of Greek life was the **polis,** or city-state. This name was given to Greek cities and the countryside villages surrounding them. MEN would gather in the marketplace or on a hilltop in the polis called an **acropolis** to conduct business.

Each city-state was independent. These city-states had different kinds of government. Some had a **monarchy,** a government ruled by a king or queen. Some had an **aristocracy,** a government ruled by a small group of noble families. Later, some formed an **oligarchy,** a government ruled by a few powerful people.

Over the years, the Greeks developed the ability to make iron weapons. Because these cost less than weapons made of bronze, more people could afford them. Soon each city-state had its own army. In this army, soldiers stood side by side. They had a spear in one hand and a shield in the other. Together they formed a **phalanx.**

Sometimes, the poor—who knew how to

CHAPTER 5 CLASSICAL GREECE **45**

fight—rose up against the nobles. Powerful individuals called **tyrants** sometimes won support from these groups. Tyrants would then rule the city-state. Sometimes, the rule of the city-state passed from one tyrant to another.

1. What types of government existed in the city-states?

_____

_____

Sparta Builds a Military State
(page 116)

How was Sparta governed?

One very strong city-state was Sparta, in the south of Greece. It conquered its neighbor Messenia. The people of Messenia became **helots.** They were peasants forced to stay on the land they worked. They had to give the Spartans half their crops.

An *assembly*, the Council of Elders, and elected officials governed Sparta. Two kings ruled over Sparta's military. Sparta prized military skills. Boys joined the army at the age of seven and went through a long period of training as soldiers. Spartan women ran the family estates, freeing their husbands to serve in the army.

2. What was Sparta's focus as a city-state?

_____

_____

Athens Builds a Limited Democracy (pages 117–118)

How was Athens governed?

Athens, another city-state, developed in a very different way. In Athens, wealthy nobles and poor people *clashed*. They struggled for power. In 594 B.C., the nobles gave Solon the power to change the government of Athens. Solon was a trusted statesman. He gave citizens a greater voice. He made it possible for any citizen of Athens to join discussions in the assembly, which approved laws. The conflict between the rich and the poor did not end, however. More changes were needed.

Reformers in Athens tried to build a **democracy,** or government by the people. Not everyone was involved in making political decisions, though. Only free adult men were citizens. Women and slaves had few rights. They had no roles in political life.

3. Why was Athens not a full democracy?

_____

_____

_____

The Persian Wars (pages 118–119)

Who fought the Persian Wars?

The **Persian Wars** were fought between Greece and the Persian Empire. In 490 B.C., Persian ships landed 25,000 soldiers on the coast of Greece. At the Battle of Marathon, the Greeks won a tremendous victory that saved Athens.

Ten years later, the Persians returned. The Greeks lost a battle on land, despite the heroic efforts of a small band of Spartans. The Persians also burned Athens. However, the ships of Athens won a great sea battle. The Spartans followed it with another victory on land. The threat from Persia was over.

4. What was the outcome of the Persian Wars?

_____

_____

_____

Name _____   Date _____

CHAPTER 5 Section 3 (pages 120–125)

Democracy and Greece's Golden Age

TERMS AND NAMES
direct democracy Form of government in which citizens rule directly
classical art Art in which harmony, order, and balance were emphasized
tragedy Serious drama dealing with the downfall of a hero or noble character
comedy Light and amusing play that may poke fun at serious subjects
Peloponnesian War War in which Athens and its allies were defeated by Sparta and its allies
philosophers Thinkers who use logic and reason to explore life's big questions
Socrates Greek thinker who explored truth and justice and developed a method of questioning and answering
Plato Socrates' student who wrote *The Republic,* a view of the ideal society
Aristotle Plato's student who developed a method for testing and organizing ideas.

BEFORE YOU READ

In the last section, you read about the government of the city-states.

In this section, you will read about democracy and the Golden Age of Greece.

AS YOU READ

Use the web below to show characteristics and events of Greece's Golden Age.

```
      Democracy                          Art
   direct democracy
                  \        /
                Golden Age
                 of Greece
                  /        \
      Drama                          Philosophy
```

Pericles' Three Goals for Athens
(pages 120–121)

How did Pericles change Athens?

Pericles led Athens during its golden age. He served in this role from 461 to 429 B.C. Greek culture reached new heights under his leadership. Pericles was had a great influence over Athens. Pericles took many steps to make Athens better.

He set three goals. One goal was to make Athens more democratic. More people served in the government. Pericles helped bring about **direct democracy.** This meant that citizens ruled directly and not through representatives. An assembly of male citizens had a voice in making laws for Athens.

Another goal was to make Athens stronger. Pericles tried to increase its wealth and power. He

CHAPTER 5 CLASSICAL GREECE **47**

helped build up Athens navy. It became the strongest in the Mediterranean.

Another goal was to make Athens beautiful. Pericles used money from the empire to buy gold, ivory, and marble. He helped fund great works of art.

1. What were Pericles' three main goals for Athens?

_____

_____

Greek Styles in Art (page 121)
How was Greek art unique?

One of the glories of Athens was the *Parthenon*. This temple was built to honor the goddess Athena. It is a masterpiece of art. Like other buildings and sculptures in Greece, it is an example of **classical art.** It reflects order, balance, and *proportion*.

2. Why was the Parthenon built?

_____

_____

Greek Drama (pages 121–123)
What kinds of drama did Greeks produce?

Athens also became home to a group of very skilled playwrights. Some wrote **tragedies.** These plays were about the pain and suffering of human life. Love, hate, and war were common themes. The main characters were called tragic heroes. They had flaws that caused their downfall.

Other playwrights wrote **comedies.** These plays made audiences laugh about important ideas. Some plays were critical of customs, politics, and people. Such performances showed that Athens was a free and open society.

3. What was the purpose of Greek comedies?

_____

_____

Spartans and Athenians Go to War (pages 123–124)
What was the Peloponnesian War?

After being *rivals* for many years, Sparta and Athens finally went to war. The **Peloponnesian War** began in 431 B.C. The conflict ended badly for Athens. In 430 B.C. a horrible *plague* killed a great many people in Athens. After several battles, the war dragged on. Finally, Athens gave up in 404 B.C. Athens had lost its empire.

4. What was the result of the Peloponnesian War?

_____

_____

Philosophers Search for the Truth (pages 124–125)
What did philosophers contribute to Greek culture?

After Athens' defeat, this city-state became home to several **philosophers.** They were thinkers who tried to understand human life. One of these great thinkers was **Socrates.** He believed deeply in truth and justice. Yet many people did not trust him. They thought his teachings were a danger to young people. Socrates was brought to trial and condemned to death.

His pupil, **Plato,** recorded many of Socrates' ideas. Plato became an important thinker in his own right. Plato's student, **Aristotle,** wrote books that summarized the knowledge of the Greeks. He also developed a way of reasoning. His system of logic became the foundation of scientific thought used today.

5. Who were three important Greek philosophers?

_____

_____

Name _____ Date _____

CHAPTER 5 Section 4 (pages 128–131)

Alexander—Empire Builder

TERMS AND NAMES
Macedonia Region north of Greece
Philip II King of Macedonia who conquered Greece
Demosthenes Greek orator
Alexander the Great Philip's II son who established a huge empire
Darius III Persian King

BEFORE YOU READ

In the last section, you read about the Golden Age of Greece and the fall of Athens.

In this section, you will learn about Alexander the Great and his empire.

AS YOU READ

Use the diagram below to take notes on Alexander's invasions.

Persia
In 334 B.C. soldiers invade Anatolia.

Egypt

India

→ **Alexander's Invasions**

Philip Builds Macedonia's Power
(pages 128–129)

Who were the Macedonians?

In 359 B.C., **Philip II** became king of **Macedonia,** located north of Greece. He was a strong leader and trained his troops to be tough fighters. Philip prepared his army to invade Greece.

The Athenian *orator* **Demosthenes** tried to warn the Greeks. He told them about Philip's plans. But they united too late to save themselves. The Macedonians won. Greek independence was now over.

Philip planned to invade Persia next. He never got the chance. He was killed. His son Alexander became king at age 20. He became known as **Alexander the Great.**

1. How did Greek independence end?

_____
_____
_____

Alexander Defeats Persia
(pages 129–130)

How did Alexander defeat Persia?

Alexander was a brilliant general, just like his father. He was prepared to carry out his father's dream of world *conquest*. In 334 B.C., Alexander invaded Persia. After Alexander's first victory, the king of Persia, **Darius III,** raised a huge army to face him. Alexander then used a surprise attack. Darius III had to retreat.

CHAPTER 5 CLASSICAL GREECE 49

Alexander then moved south to enter Egypt. He was crowned pharaoh and founded a city that he named for himself—Alexandria. He then turned back to Persia and won another great battle. It ended all Persian resistance. The empire was his.

2. What two kingdoms did Alexander defeat?

_____

_____

Alexander's Other Conquests
(pages 130–131)

How far east did Alexander push?

Alexander pushed east, taking his army as far as India. He moved deep into that country. After many years of marching and fighting, however, his soldiers wanted to return home. Alexander agreed and turned back. On the way home, he began to make plans for how to govern his new empire. Then he suddenly fell ill and died. He was not yet 33 years old.

Three of Alexander's generals divided his empire. One ruled Macedonia and Greece. Another took control of Egypt. The third became ruler of the lands that used to be in the Persian Empire. Alexander's empire was not long-lasting. Yet it had important effects. After Alexander, the people of Greece and Persia and all the lands between mixed together and shared ideas and culture.

3. How did Alexander's power come to an end?

_____

_____

Alexander's Empire and Its Legacy 336-306 B.C.

ALEXANDER'S EMPIRE

- **336 B.C.** Philip II was assassinated. Alexander became king of Macedonia at age 20.
- **334 B.C.** Alexander led 35,000 soldiers across the Hellespont or Dardanelles into Anatolia.
- **332 B.C.** Alexander entered Egypt and founded the city of Alexandria.
- **327 B.C.** Alexander's army reached the Indus Valley.
- **323 B.C.** Alexander caught fever and died at age 32. His generals began a power struggle.
- **323 B.C.** Ptolemy seized Egypt and became a pharaoh. (EGYPT)
- **312 B.C.** Seleucus took Persian Empire and then died. (PERSIA)
- **306 B.C.** Antigonus I became king of Macedonia. (MACEDONIA)

Skillbuilder
Use the timeline to answer the questions.

1. How many years did Alexander serve as king?

_____

2. How was Alexander's empire divided after his death?

_____

Name _____ Date _____

CHAPTER 5 Section 5 (pages 132–135)

The Spread of Hellenistic Culture

BEFORE YOU READ

In the last section, you read about the military conquests of Alexander the Great.

In this section, you will learn about the spread of Hellenistic culture.

AS YOU READ

Use the web below to take notes on developments in Hellenistic culture.

TERMS AND NAMES
Hellenistic Relating to the culture that blended Greek with Egyptian, Persian, and Indian influences
Alexandria Egyptian city that was the center of Hellenistic culture
Euclid Greek mathematician and pioneer in geometry
Archimedes Greek scientist, inventor, and mathematician
Colossus of Rhodes Huge bronze statue created on the island of Rhodes

- Science: *observation that sun is larger than Earth*
- Museums/Libraries
- Mathematics
- Philosophy
- Art
- (center) Hellenistic Culture

Hellenistic Culture in Alexandria
(pages 132–133)

What was Hellenistic culture?

A new culture arose—the **Hellenistic** culture. It blended Greek with Egyptian, Persian, and Indian influences. The center of this culture was **Alexandria,** Egypt. This city was located near the mouth of the Nile River on the Mediterranean Sea. Alexandria had a ship harbor. Trade was lively. Alexandria had a large population. These people were from many different countries.

Alexandria was also a beautiful city. Its huge lighthouse towered over the harbor. Its famous museum had works of art, a zoo, and a garden. Alexandria had the first true research library. It held half-million scrolls of papyrus. These contained everything known in the Hellenistic world.

1. Give two reasons why Alexandria became a center of Hellenistic culture.

_____

_____

CHAPTER 5 CLASSICAL GREECE **51**

Science and Technology (pages 133–134)

What *new ideas arose in science, technology, and mathematics?*

While scholars kept what was known about science alive, others learned new ideas. Some used an *observatory* to look at the stars and planets. One of these *astronomers* developed the idea that the sun was actually larger than Earth. No one had believed this before.

The thinkers in Alexandria also made advances in mathematics. **Euclid** wrote a book with the basic ideas of geometry. His approach is still used today. **Archimedes** invented many clever machines. One was the pulley. Another is called Archimedes screw. Its purpose was to bring water from a lower level to a higher one. It was used to bring water to fields being farmed.

2. What two inventions did Archimedes make?

_____

_____

Philosophy and Art (pages 134–135)

What *new developments occurred in philosophy and the arts?*

Two new schools of philosophy arose in these times. The *Stoics* argued that people should live a good life to keep themselves in harmony with natural laws. Desire, power, and wealth led people down the wrong path. The *Epicureans* said that people could rely only on what they learned from their five senses. They urged everyone to live moral lives.

The arts were also important in Hellenistic times. Great achievements occurred in sculpture. Sculpture in the earlier Greek style aimed at showing perfect forms. In the Hellenistic age, sculpted figures were more realistic and emotional. The largest known Hellenistic statue is the **Colossus of Rhodes.** It was over 100 feet high.

3. How were Hellenistic sculptures different from earlier Greek sculptures?

_____

_____

Greek Astronomy

The Earth	The Sun	The Solar System
Erastosthenes' estimate of the circumference—24,662 miles; actual circumference—24,860 miles	Aristarches' estimate—300 times the size of earth; The sun is actually 1.3 million times the size of the earth	Ptolemy's view of the universe: Saturn, Jupiter, Mars, Sun, Venus, Moon, Mercury, Earth

Skillbuilder

1. Which of the Greek ideas shown above was least accurate?

_____

2. Which of the two estimates shown above is more accurate?

_____

Name _____ Date _____

Glossary
CHAPTER 5 Classical Greece 2000 B.C. –300 B.C.

assembly Law-making body in ancient Greece
astronomers Scientists who study the stars and planets
clashed Disagreed strongly
conducted Did the work of
conquest Act of conquering or taking over
enactment Officially becoming law

Epicureans Philosophers who said people could rely only on what they learned through their five senses
noble Of very high rank
observatory Place for observing the movement of heavenly bodies
orator Public speaker; speech maker
Parthenon Temple in ancient Greece that is a masterpiece of classical art

plague Deadly disease that often spreads quickly killing many
proportion A pleasing arrangement
rivals Competitor; people or groups determined to outdo each other
Stoics Philosophers who said people should live a moral life to keep them in harmony with natural laws
united Brought together as one

AFTER YOU READ

Names and Terms

A. Write the name or term in each blank that best completes the meaning of the paragraph.

Aristotle

classical art

Socrates

direct democracy

Plato

Three of the greatest gifts to western culture from ancient Greece were developments in democracy, philosophy, and art. The Athenians had a form of democracy in which all citizens and not just their representatives participated. This was **1** _____. In art, the Greeks valued balance, order, and proportion. They gave the world **2** _____. In philosophy, three Greek thinkers have influenced western thought. The philosopher **3** _____ encouraged his thinkers to examine their beliefs and developed a method of questioning and answering still used today. His student, **4** _____, was also an important thinker. The philosopher **5** _____ invented a way of thinking logically.

B. Write the letter of the name next to the description that explains it best.

a. Archimedes
b. Philip II
c. Darius III
d. Demosthenes
e. Homer

____ **1.** Leader of Macedonia who conquered Greece
____ **2.** Persian king who fought Alexander the Great
____ **3.** Greek poet
____ **4.** Inventor of the pulley
____ **5.** Greek orator

Name _____ Date _____

AFTER YOU READ (continued)

CHAPTER 5 Classical Greece
2000 B.C. –300 B.C.

Main Ideas

1. Give three examples of how the geography of Greece affected its civilization.

_____
_____
_____

2. What war did Athens and Sparta fight, and how did it end?

_____
_____
_____

3. How was Athens governed under Pericles?

_____
_____
_____

4. Where did Alexander the Great turn back and why?

_____
_____
_____

5. Name an advance made in science, technology, and mathematics during Hellenistic times.

_____
_____
_____

Thinking Critically

Answer the following questions on a separate sheet of paper.

1. Compare and contrast Athens and Sparta.

2. Discuss the features of Alexandria that show it was a center of Hellenistic culture.

Name _____ Date _____

CHAPTER 6 Section 1 (pages 141–145)

The Romans Create a Republic

BEFORE YOU READ
In the last section, you read about Hellenistic culture. In this section, you will read about the Roman republic.

AS YOU READ
Use the chart below to take notes on early Rome.

TERMS AND NAMES
republic Government in which citizens have the right to select their own leader
patrician Aristocratic landowner
plebeian Farmer, artisan, or merchant; commoner
tribune Official who helped the plebeians protect their rights
consul Official who was like a king
senate Aristocratic branch of Rome's government
dictator Roman leader who had absolute power to make laws and command the army for a brief period
legion Military unit of the ancient Roman army
Hannibal Carthaginian general who invaded northern Italy
Scipio Roman general who defeated Hannibal

EARLY ROME	
Geography	On river Midpoint of the Mediterranean
Government	
Growth	

The Beginnings of Rome (page 141)
Where was Rome founded?
The city of Rome was founded by the Latin people on a river in the center of Italy. It was a good location, which gave them a chance to control all of Italy. It put them near to the midpoint of the Mediterranean Sea. Two other groups lived in what is now Italy: the Greeks in the south, and the *Etruscans* in the north. The Romans borrowed some ideas from both peoples.

1. What were the advantages of Rome's location?

_____

_____

The Early Republic (pages 142–144)
How was Rome governed?
In 509 B.C., Romans overthrew the Etruscan king who had ruled over his people and over Rome. The Romans said Rome was now a **republic.** The peo-

CHAPTER 6 ANCIENT ROME AND EARLY CHRISTIANITY **55**

ple had the power to vote and choose leaders.

Two groups struggled for power in the new republic. One was the **patricians.** They were the *aristocratic* landowners who held most of the power. The other group was the **plebeians.** They were the common farmers, *artisans,* and merchants who made up most of the population. At first, the patricians had the most power. Over time, the plebeians got the right to form their own *assembly*. They could elect representatives called **tribunes.**

The basis for Roman law was the *Twelve Tables*. This set of rules said that all free citizens were protected by law.

The government had three parts. Two **consuls,** or officials, were elected each year. They led the government and the army.

The second part of the government was the **senate.** It usually had 300 members chosen from the upper classes. The senate passed laws.

The third, and most democratic, part of government was the assemblies. The assemblies included members from different parts of society, such as citizen-soldiers or plebeians. The assemblies could also make laws.

If there were a crisis, the republic could appoint a **dictator.** This was a leader with absolute power. The dictator made laws and commanded the army. But his power lasted for only six months.

Any citizen who owned property had to serve in the army. Roman soldiers were organized into military units called legions. The Roman **legion** was made up of some 5,000 heavily armed foot soldiers.

2. What were the three main parts of Roman government?

_____
_____
_____
_____

Rome Spreads Its Power
(pages 144–145)

How did Rome spread its power?

In the fourth century B.C., Rome began to get larger. Within 150 years, it had captured almost all of Italy. Rome allowed some of the conquered peoples to enjoy the benefits of citizenship. With its good location, Rome saw a growth in trade. This brought it into conflict with Carthage, a trading city in North Africa.

From 264 to 146 B.C., Rome and Carthage fought three bitter wars called the *Punic Wars*. In the first, Rome won control of the island of Sicily. In the second, **Hannibal,** a brilliant Carthaginian general invaded northern Italy. He and his soldiers did much damage. But he was unable to take Rome. It took an equally brilliant Roman general, **Scipio,** to defeat him. By the time of the third war, Carthage was no longer a threat to Rome. Even so, Rome destroyed the city and made its people slaves. Carthage became a new Roman province.

3. What happened as a result of the wars with Carthage?

_____
_____
_____
_____
_____
_____

Name _____ Date _____

CHAPTER 6 Section 2 (pages 146–152)

The Roman Empire Brings Change

BEFORE YOU READ

In the last section, you read about the creation of the Roman republic.

In this section, you will read about the problems of the republic and its collapse.

AS YOU READ

Use the chart below to take notes on the end of the Roman republic and the Roman Empire.

TERMS AND NAMES
civil war Conflict between two groups in the same country
Julius Caesar Ambitious leader who brought order to Rome
triumvirate Group of three rulers
absolute ruler Ruler who has total power
Augustus First ruler of imperial Rome
Pax Romana Period of Roman peace and prosperity
gladiator Professional fighter

Collapse of the Republic	conflict between rich and poor
A Powerful Empire	power struggles
Life in Imperial Rome	civil wars

Expansion Creates Problems in the Republic; The Republic Collapses (pages 146–148)

What conflicts existed in Rome?

Rome's victory in Carthage brought conflict between the rich and poor in Rome. **Civil war**—fighting between groups in the same country—broke out. Leading generals fought for power.

Julius Caesar tried to take control. First he joined with two others—Crassus, a wealthy man, and Pompey, a successful general. They formed a **triumvirate**—a group of three leaders. For the next ten years, the triumvirate ruled Rome.

Caesar gained fame with several victories in battle. Pompey feared Caesar as a result. The two fought another civil war that lasted several years. Caesar won the civil war and then governed as an **absolute ruler.**

Caesar made some reforms that increased his popularity. But some members of the senate mistrusted him. They killed him because they feared he wanted to become king.

Once again, Rome suffered civil war. Caesar's nephew was the winner. He took the title **Augustus,** meaning "*exalted* one." The Roman empire was now ruled by one man.

1. How did Caesar's rule lead to the end of the republic?

_____

_____

CHAPTER 6 ANCIENT ROME AND EARLY CHRISTIANITY 57

A Vast and Powerful Empire
(pages 148–150)

What was the Pax Romana?

For about 200 years, the Roman empire was a great power. Its population of between 60 and 80 million enjoyed peace and prosperity. This period is known as the **Pax Romana**—Roman peace.

The empire stretched around the Mediterranean, from modern Syria and Turkey west and north to England and Germany. It relied on farming, which employed 90 percent of all workers.

Trade was also important. Traders used common coins to buy and sell goods. Coins made trading easier.

Rome had a vast trading network. Goods traveled throughout the empire by ship and along the Roman roads. Trading ships were protected by the Roman navy.

The army defended all these the people and Roman territories from attack. Many of the army's troops came from the conquered peoples. Once they finished their time in the army, they became Roman citizens.

Augustus was Rome's ablest emperor. He brought peace to the frontier, built many public buildings, and created a lasting government. He also set up a civil service. That is, he paid workers to manage the affairs of government.

Between A.D. 96 and A.D. 180, the Five Good Emperors ruled Rome. The death of Marcus Aurelius in A.D. 180 marked the beginning of the decline of the Roman Empire and the end of *Pax Romana*.

2. How were the people of the empire employed?

_____
_____
_____
_____

Life in Imperial Rome (pages 150–152)

How did the quality of Roman life vary?

Throughout its history, Romans valued discipline, strength, and loyalty. The family was the center of Roman society. The oldest man in the family had complete authority in the household. He controlled all the property, too.

Women enjoyed more rights in Rome than in other ancient cultures. They could own property and *testify* in court. But women could not vote. Parents hoped to have boys and not girls because boys could become citizens. A few wealthy children went to school. Poor children did not go to school. They had to work.

The Romans made more use of slaves than any civilization before. About one third of the people were slaves. Most slaves came from conquered lands. Slaves worked in the city and on farms. Some slaves were forced to become **gladiators**. Gladiators were professional fighters who fought to the death in public contests. Slaves did revolt from time to time. None of these revolts succeeded.

Quality of life in *imperial* Rome depended on social position. The wealthy ate well and enjoyed luxuries. The poor—including many people in Rome itself—had no jobs and received food from the government. Housing was poor. People lived in constant danger of fire. To distract people from their problems, the government gave many celebrations and *spectacles*.

3. Who were the slaves, and what work did they do?

_____
_____
_____
_____

Name _____ Date _____

CHAPTER 6 Section 3 (pages 153–157)

The Rise of Christianity

BEFORE YOU READ

In the last section, you read about the *Pax Romana*.

In this section, you will read about the development of Christianity.

AS YOU READ

Use the chart below to take notes on the beginnings and the spread of Christianity.

TERMS AND NAMES
Jesus Leader who came to be known as Christ and was believed to be a savior
apostle Close follower of Jesus
Peter First apostle who helped spread Christianity through Syria and Palestine
Paul Apostle who played a key role in the spread of Christianity throughout the Roman Empire
Diaspora Moving away of the Jews from their homeland in Palestine
bishop Head of all churches in one area
pope Head of the Christian Church
Constantine Roman emperor who ended persecution of Christians
heresy Any belief that questioned the basic teachings of the church

LEADER	RELIGIOUS INFLUENCE
Jesus	spread message of love believed by some to be Messiah
Peter	
Paul	
Constantine	

Jews Come Under Roman Rule; The Life and Teachings of Jesus
(pages 153–154)

Why did people believe Jesus was the savior?

One group of people that lost its land to the Romans was the Jews. Many Jews wanted the Romans to leave their land.

Others hoped for the coming of the *Messiah*—the savior. According to Jewish tradition, God promised that the Messiah would restore the kingdom of the Jews.

Jesus was born in Judea. At about age 30, Jesus began to preach. His message included many ideas from Jewish traditions, such as the principles of the Ten Commandments and the belief in one God. According to close followers, who were later called **apostles,** Jesus performed many miracles. His fame grew. Some believed him to be the long-awaited Messiah.

Jewish leaders did not believe that his teachings

CHAPTER 6 ANCIENT ROME AND EARLY CHRISTIANITY **59**

were those of God. Roman leaders feared he would *incite* the people. The Romans arrested Jesus and put him to death.

After his death, Jesus's followers said that he appeared to them again and then went to heaven. They said this proved he was the Messiah. They called him Christ. This is the Greek word for savior. His followers came to be called Christians. Led by **Peter,** the first apostle, they spread his teachings throughout Palestine and Syria.

1. Why was Jesus put to death?

_____

_____

_____

_____

Christianity Spreads Through the Empire (page 155)

How did Christianity spread through the empire?

At first Jesus's followers were all Jewish. Later, under one apostle, **Paul,** Christians began to look to all people, even non-Jews, to join the church. The leaders of the early church traveled throughout the empire spreading the teachings of Jesus.

During this time, Jews made attempts to break free of the Romans. These movements did not succeed. Most Jews were driven from their homeland into *exile*. This scattering of the Jews is called the **Diaspora.**

At the same time, Roman leaders tried to punish the Christians. Some were put to death or killed by wild animals in the arena. But Christianity continued to spread. After almost 200 years, millions of people across the empire became Christians.

2. What did the Romans do to the Jews?

_____

_____

_____

_____

_____

_____

A World Religion (pages 156–157)

Why did Christianity spread?

Christianity spread for several reasons. First, it accepted all believers: rich or poor, male or female. Second, it gave hope to the powerless. Third, it appealed to those who were bothered by the lack of *morality* in Rome. Fourth, it offered a personal relationship with god. Fifth, it offered the promise of life after death.

As the church grew, it became more organized. Priests were in charge of small churches. **Bishops** were in charge of all the churches in one area. The **pope** was in charge of all. The pope was the head of the Christian Church.

In A.D. 313, Christianity entered a new era. The Roman emperor **Constantine** said that Christians would no longer be *persecuted*. He gave his official approval to Christianity. A few decades later, Christianity became the empire's official religion.

While Christianity grew in power, it went through changes. Church leaders sometimes disagreed over basic beliefs and argued about them. Church leaders called any belief that appeared to contradict the basic teachings a **heresy.** From time to time, councils met to end disagreements and define beliefs.

3. How was the church organized?

_____

_____

_____

_____

_____

60 CHAPTER 6 SECTION 3

Name _____   Date _____

CHAPTER 6 Section 4 (pages 158–162)

The Decline of the Roman Empire

TERMS AND NAMES
inflation Large drop in the value of money and rise in the prices of goods
mercenary Foreign soldiers who fought for money
Diocletian Strong-willed army leader and Roman emperor
Constantinople New name for Byzantium under Constantine
Alaric Visigoth king
Attila Powerful chieftain of Huns

BEFORE YOU READ
In the last section, you read about the spread of Christianity.
In this section, you will learn how the Roman empire collapsed.

AS YOU READ
Use the time line below to take notes on the fall of the empire.

A.D. 260	A.D. 324	A.D. 476
Persians capture Valerian		

A.D. 284	A.D. 444

A Century of Crisis (pages 158–159)
What problems did Rome face?

Rome entered a period of decline after the reign of Marcus Aurelius ended in 180 A.D. Rome suffered economic problems. Trade slowed as raiders threatened ships and *caravans* on sea and land. The economy suffered from **inflation**—a drastic drop in the value of money and a rise in prices. Food supplies also dropped as tired soil, warfare, and high taxes cut the amount of grain and other foods produced on farms.

The empire also had military problems. German tribes caused trouble on the frontiers. Persians defeated the Romans in A.D. 260 and captured the emperor. Roman soldiers could no longer be counted on. Instead, **mercenaries**—soldiers who fight for money—had to be hired. At the same time, Roman generals fought one another for control of the empire.

1. What economic problems did Rome face?

_____
_____

Emperors Attempt Reform
(pages 159–160)
What changes did the emperors make?

Diocletian took the throne as emperor in 284. He passed many new laws to try to fix the economy. He tried to restore the status of the emperor by naming

CHAPTER 6 ANCIENT ROME AND EARLY CHRISTIANITY **61**

himself a son of the chief Roman god. He even divided the empire into eastern and western halves to make it easier to govern.

Many of these changes were continued by Constantine. He became emperor of both halves of the empire in 324. A few years later, Constantine moved the capital of the empire to a new city in northwestern Turkey where Europe and Asia meet. The city was *Byzantium*. Now it was given a new name—**Constantinople,** the city of Constantine.

2. Who was Constantine?

___

Invaders Overrun the Western Empire (pages 160–162)

Who overran Rome?

Reforms delayed the end of the Roman empire but could not prevent its fall. The eastern part of the empire remained strong and unified. But troubles continued in the west. Germanic tribes moved into the empire. They were trying to escape from the *Huns*—fierce nomadic people from central Asia—who were moving into their land.

The Roman armies in the west collapsed. German armies twice entered Rome itself. In 408 Visigoths led by their king, **Alaric,** put the city under siege. In 444, the Huns united under a powerful chieftain named **Attila**. Attila and his armies terrorized both halves of the empire.

The invasions continued after Attila's death. The Germans had arrived for good. By 476 German peoples controlled many areas of Europe. That year a German general removed the last western Roman emperor from the throne.

3. What role did Attila play in the collapse of Rome?

___

Multiple Causes: Fall of the Western Roman Empire

Contributing Factors

Political	Social	Economic	Military
• Political office seen as burden, not reward • Military interference in politics • Civil war and unrest • Division of empire • Moving of capital to Byzantium	• Decline in interest in public affairs • Low confidence in empire • Disloyalty, lack of patriotism, corruption • Contrast between rich and poor	• Poor harvests • Disruption of trade • No more war plunder • Gold and silver drain • Inflation • Crushing tax burden • Widening gap between rich and poor and increasingly impoverished Western empire	• Threat from northern European tribes • Low funds for defense • Problems recruiting Roman citizens; recruiting of non-Romans • Decline of patriotism and loyalty among soldiers

Immediate Causes

• Pressure from Huns   • Invasion by Germanic tribes and by Huns   • Sack of Rome   • Conquest by invaders

FALL OF ROMAN EMPIRE

Skillbuilder

1. What were the four immediate causes of the fall of Rome?

2. Which of the social factors do you think was most important? Why?

Name _____ Date _____

CHAPTER 6 Section 5 (pages 164–167)

Rome and the Roots of Western Civilization

TERMS AND NAMES
Greco-Roman culture Culture developed from the blending of Greek, Hellenistic, and Roman cultures
Pompeii Roman town covered by the eruption of Mount Vesuvius
Virgil Roman poet who wrote the Aeneid
Tacitus Roman historian who recorded the good and bad of imperial Rome
aqueduct Pipeline or channel built to carry water

BEFORE YOU READ

In the last section, you read about the decline of Rome.

In this section, you will learn about the contributions of Rome to Western civilization.

AS YOU READ

Use the web below to take notes on Rome's influence on the western world.

- **Art** — classical sculpture, mosaics, painting
- **Literature**
- **History**
- **Engineering**
- **Rome's Influence**
- **Law**
- **Language**

The Legacy of Greco-Roman Civilization (pages 164–165)

What is Greco-Roman culture?

Rome took aspects of Greek and Hellenistic culture and added ideas of its own. The mixing of Greek, Hellenistic, and Roman culture produced a new culture, called **Greco-Roman culture.** This is also often called classical civilization.

Roman artists, philosophers, and writers did not just copy Greek works. They created a style of their own for their own purposes. Much of Roman art had practical purposes. It was aimed at educating the public.

One example of the mixing of cultures occurred in sculpture. Romans borrowed Greek ideas but made their sculptures more realistic. The Romans also developed a kind of sculpture in which images stood out from a flat background.

Romans were skilled at creating pictures made from tiny tiles, a process called *mosaic*. But Romans were perhaps most skilled at painting. The best examples of Roman painting are found in the Roman town of **Pompeii.** Pompeii was covered with ash after a Volcanic eruption. The ash preserved many works of art and culture.

In both literature and philosophy, Romans were inspired by the Greeks. The poet **Virgil** wrote the most famous work of Latin literature, the *Aeneid*. It was modeled on the Greek epics of Homer.

The Romans also produced some important histories. **Tacitus** is an important Roman historian. Among ancient historians, he is known for presenting accurate facts. He described the good and bad parts of imperial Rome in his *Annals* and *Histories*.

1. Name three Roman cultural achievements.

_____
_____
_____
_____

Roman Achievements (pages 165–167)

What were Rome's most major contributions to Western culture?

The Roman language, Latin, was important in European history. It was the official language of the Roman Catholic Church into the 20th century. Many European languages developed from Latin, including French, Spanish, Portuguese, Italian, and Romanian. And many Latin words are used in other languages, including English.

Romans also became famous for their skill at engineering. They used arches and domes to build large, impressive buildings. Many of these forms are still used today. They also built an excellent system of roads and several **aqueducts.** Aqueducts carried water from distant lakes or rivers to large cities.

But Rome's most lasting influence was in the field of law. Roman government set standards of law that still influence people today. Some of the most important principles of Roman law were:

- All persons had the right to equal treatment under the law.
- A person was considered innocent until proven guilty.
- The burden of proof rested with the accuser rather than the accused.
- A person should be punished only for actions, not for thoughts.
- Any law that seemed unreasonable or unfair could be set aside.

2. What important standards of law were set by the Romans?

_____
_____
_____
_____
_____

Name _____ Date _____

Glossary
CHAPTER 6 Ancient Rome and Early Christianity

aristocratic Belonging to the highest class
artisans Skilled workers
assembly Gathering; group of people organized to make laws for a community
Byzantium City in northwestern Turkey that was renamed Constantinople after Constantine made it the capital of the Roman empire
caravans Traders traveling together
Etruscans People who lived in the north of what is now Italy before the Romans
exalted Honored, praised, glorified
exile State of being sent away from or removed from one's own country
Huns Fierce nomadic tribes from central Asia
imperial Related to an empire
incite To provoke or urge on
Messiah Savior; name given by some to Jesus
morality Code of right and wrong, good and evil
mosaic Type of art in which designs are made using tiny tiles
persecuted Oppressed or harassed unfairly, especially for beliefs or heritage
Punic Wars Three wars fought between Rome and Carthage from 264 to 146 B.C.
spectacle Something to be seen or viewed
testify Make a statement in court
Twelve Tables Set of rules protecting all Roman citizens

AFTER YOU READ

Terms and Names

A. Write the name or term in each blank that best completes the meaning of the paragraph.

triumvirate

Augustus

absolute ruler

civil war

Julius Caesar

After Rome's victory in Carthage, **1** _____ broke out in Rome. When it ended, **2** _____ tried to take control. First, he joined with two others to form a **3** _____. When this government collapsed, he became an **4** _____. Because he then had so much power, some feared he wanted to be king and killed him. Eventually, his rule was followed by that of **5** _____, the new emperor.

B. Write the letter of the term next to the description that explains it best.

a. patricians

b. plebeians

c. apostles

d. mercenaries

e. gladiators

____ **1.** Healthy males forced to become professional fighters

____ **2.** Aristocratic landowners in ancient Rome

____ **3.** Foreign soldiers who fought for money

____ **4.** First close followers of Jesus

____ **5.** Common artisans, farmers, and merchants in ancient Rome

Name _____ Date _____

AFTER YOU READ (continued)   CHAPTER 6   Ancient Rome and Early Christianity

Main Ideas

1. What was the Roman legion, and who served in it?
_____
_____
_____

2. What was the Pax Romana?
_____
_____
_____

3. Name three reactions to the teachings of Jesus.
_____
_____
_____

4. What changes did Diocletian make?
_____
_____
_____

5. Explain what is meant by the term Greco-Roman culture.
_____
_____
_____

Thinking Critically

Answer the following questions on a separate sheet of paper.

1. Why was Paul so important in the history of Christianity?

2. Explain this statement: Rome's most lasting influence was in the field of law.

Name _____ Date _____

CHAPTER 7 Section 1 (pages 173–176)

First Empires of India

BEFORE YOU READ

In the last section, you read about the influence ancient Rome.

In this section, you will read about the Mauryan and Gupta Empires in India.

AS YOU READ

Use the time line below to take notes on the first empires of India.

TERMS AND NAMES

Mauryan Empire First empire in India, founded by Chandragupta Maurya

Asoka Grandson of Chandragupta; leader who brought the Mauryan Empire to its greatest height

religious toleration Acceptance of the right of people to have differing religious beliefs

Tamil Language of southern India; also the people who speak that language

Gupta Empire Second empire in India, founded by Chandra Gupta I

patriarchal Relating to a social system in which the father is the head of the family

matriarchal Relating to a social system in which the mother is the head of the family

```
┌─────────────────────────┐     ┌─────────────────────────┐
│       321 B.C.          │     │        A.D. 320         │
│ Chandragupta Maurya     │     │                         │
│ starts the Mauryan      │     │                         │
│ Empire                  │     │                         │
└─────────────────────────┘     └─────────────────────────┘
                    │                   │
                    └─────────┬─────────┘
                    ┌─────────────────────────┐
                    │        269 B.C.         │
                    │                         │
                    └─────────────────────────┘
```

Chandragupta Maurya Builds an Empire (pages 173–174)

How did the Mauryan Empire begin?

In 321 B.C., Chandragupta Maurya used his army to defeat the king of eastern India. He became king and started the **Mauryan Empire.**

Chandragupta then moved west. In 305 B.C., he began to challenge Seleucus, one of Alexander the Great's generals. The two armies fought for several years. Eventually Chandragupta won. For the first time, northern India was joined under the rule of one person.

Chandragupta was a harsh ruler. He charged a heavy tax on farmers—one-half of the crop they grew each year. He used this wealth to build a huge army. He controlled his government by carefully choosing officials and watching them closely. He split his empire into four *provinces,* each ruled by a prince. These areas, in turn, were divided into smaller pieces that were run by members of the government. Life in Chandragupta's court was rich. The palace and capital city were beautiful.

Chandragupta's grandson, **Asoka,** took the throne in 269 B.C. He brought the Mauryan Empire to its greatest height. At first he was a warlike king and fought many fierce battles with an

CHAPTER 7 INDIA AND CHINA ESTABLISH EMPIRES 67

enemy to the south. Then he decided to accept the teachings of the Buddha.

Asoka promised to rule in a fair and just way. He issued laws that urged his subjects to avoid violence. He urged **religious toleration.** This is acceptance of people's rights to differing religious beliefs. He made great roads so that people could travel easily. Soon after Asoka died, however, his empire collapsed.

1. What changes did Asoka make in the Mauryan Empire?

_____

_____

A Period of Turmoil (pages 174–175)
What troubles did India face?

For 500 years after Asoka, India was a land of troubles. In the center of India, a new kingdom—the Andhra Dynasty—*dominated* the region. In the northwest, many Greeks, Persians, and Central Asians entered the land. They were fleeing the invasions of others. These peoples added new ideas and languages to India's rich mix of culture. In the south, three different kingdoms fought each other off and on. The people who lived in this region spoke the **Tamil** language. They are called the Tamil people.

2. Who are the Tamils?

_____

_____

_____

The Gupta Empire (pages 175–176)
What was life like in the Gupta Empire?

Around A.D. 320, Chandra Gupta I came to power in the north. He was not related to the first emperor. He took the title of king and began to conquer other areas.

His son followed the same policy. For 40 years, he fought to win new lands for the **Gupta Empire.** His son, Chandra Gupta II, brought the empire to its largest size. He managed to take parts of western India, including some important ports on the Indian Ocean. With these, the Guptas were able to take part in the rich trade that connected India, Southwest Asia, and the world of the Mediterranean Sea. The Gupta empire stretched all across northern India.

Most Indians lived in villages and were farmers. Part of each crop that they grew had to be paid to the king each year. Farmers also had to set aside part of each month to work on community resources, such as wells or dams. Craft workers and those who worked in trade lived in special sections of each village, town, or city.

Most families in northern India were **patriarchal.** They were headed by the oldest male. But in southern India, some Tamil families were **matriarchal.** This meant the mother was head of the family. Property, and sometimes the throne, were passed through the female side of the family.

The Gupta kings were *patrons* of the arts. Artists *flourished* during the Gupta rule. The people were happy, according to a Chinese traveler who spent many years in India. However, this period of calm ended not long after the death of Chandra Gupta II. Another wave of invaders moved into India. Soon the great Gupta Empire had broken up into several smaller kingdoms.

3. How did the Gupta Empire end?

_____

_____

_____

Name _____ Date _____

CHAPTER 7 Section 2 (pages 177–180)

Trade Spreads Indian Religions and Culture

BEFORE YOU READ

In the last section, you read about the Mauryan and Gupta Empires.

In this section, you will learn how trade caused changes in religion and culture.

AS YOU READ

Use the chart below to show changes in India.

TERMS AND NAMES
Mahayana Sect of Buddhism that offers salvation to all and allows popular worship
Theravada Sect of Buddhism focusing on strict spiritual discipline
Brahma Creator of the world, in Hinduism
Vishnu Preserver of the world, in Hinduism
Shiva Destroyer of the world, in Hinduism
Kalidasa One of India's greatest poets and playwrights
Silk Roads Caravan routes that crisscrossed central Asia

```
                    Changes
                    in India
          ┌───────────┼───────────┬───────────┐
          ▼           ▼           ▼           ▼
      Buddhism    Hinduism    Art and      Spread of
   Divides into                Science       Trade
   two sects;
   becomes a
   popular
   religion
```

Changes in Religious Thought
(pages 177–178)

How did Buddhism and Hinduism change?

Over time, the religions of Hinduism and Buddhism became more and more distant from the common people. A special class of priests controlled Hinduism. Followers of the Buddha found it difficult to find the promised goal of release from this world. As new peoples moved into India, they brought new ideas. These ideas had an impact on these religions.

The Buddha had taught that a tough spiritual life was the way to escape from the suffering of the world. But *self-denial* was difficult for most people. Many people came to worship the Buddha himself as a god, even though he had forbidden it. Some came to believe that other people could become Buddhas themselves. They could do this through good works and sacrifice.

These ideas created a new kind of Buddhism, the **Mahayana** sect. Those who held on to the stricter beliefs belonged to the **Theravada** sect. The new Mahayana approach helped Buddhism become a popular religion. All believers had the

CHAPTER 7 INDIA AND CHINA ESTABLISH EMPIRES **69**

chance to be saved. This change caused an increase in art. Buddhists with money built temples and shrines and then paid artists to decorate them with sculptures and paintings.

Hinduism changed, too. By the time of the Mauryan empire, only priests were involved in many rituals of the faith. For centuries, Hinduism had been a religion of many gods. Now other religions based on only one god were becoming more important. Many Hindus began to emphasize three gods in particular. One was **Brahma,** creator of the world. Another was **Vishnu,** preserver of the world. The third was **Shiva,** destroyer of the world. By devoting themselves to one of these gods, people began to feel the religion more directly in their lives.

1. What changes did the split in Buddhism bring?

_____

_____

Flowering of Indian Culture
(pages 178–179)

What advances occurred in the arts and sciences?

The amount and quality of Indian art increased. Poets and playwrights, such as **Kalidasa,** wrote beautiful works of literature. Other artists laid the foundations for the classical form of dance in India.

The scientists of India proved that Earth was indeed round 1,000 years before Columbus. They made great advances in mathematics, too. They invented the idea of zero and of decimal numbers. The doctors of India became highly skilled. They knew more than 1,000 diseases and used hundreds of medicines from plants to help their patients.

2. What advances did scientists and mathematicians make?

_____

_____

_____

The Spread of Indian Trade
(pages 179–180)

How did India's trade increase?

Soon Indians learned about the **Silk Roads.** These were *caravan* routes that crisscrossed central Asia. Indian traders joined in the trade along these routes. Indians traded cotton cloth and animals to China for silk. Traders brought spices from Southeast Asia to India and then sold them to Rome and other western peoples.

This trade was so busy that large numbers of Roman coins have been found in India. The Indians also traded their own cotton cloth in Africa for ivory and gold. They sent rice and wheat to Arabia for dates and horses. They carried out this trade by land and sea.

Indians culture spread beyond India. The art and architecture of many lands in Southeast Asia show the influence of Indian art. Some people adopted Hinduism, and many began to follow Buddhism.

3. In addition to goods, what did India send to different parts of the world?

_____

_____

_____

Name _____ Date _____

CHAPTER 7 Section 3 (pages 181–187)

Han Emperors in China

BEFORE YOU READ

In the last section, you read about the spread of Indian religions and culture.

In this section, you will read about the Han Dynasty in China.

AS YOU READ

Use the web below to take notes on the Han Dynasty.

TERMS AND NAMES

Han Dynasty Chinese dynasty that ruled for most of the period from 202 B.C. to A.D. 220

centralized government Government that concentrates power in a central authority

civil service Administrative departments of a government; also, word describing government jobs and employees

monopoly One group's complete control over the production and distribution of certain goods

assimilation Policy of encouraging conquered peoples to adopt the institutions and customs of the conquering nation

```
        Government
     centralized government;
     highly organized; civil
         service jobs
Fall                          Technology

            Han
          Dynasty

Rebellion                     Business

          Culture
```

The Han Restore Unity to China
(pages 181–183)

What changes did Han leaders make?

A strong empire also arose in China. The Chinese had been united briefly under the Qin empire. But it fell apart in a period of civil war. In 202 B.C., Liu Bang named himself the first emperor of the **Han Dynasty.** The Han would rule parts of China for the next 400 years. They set many patterns for Chinese culture for centuries to come.

Liu Bang created a **centralized government.** Local officials reported to the emperor. The rule of the previous emperor had been very harsh. Liu Bang took a different approach. He lowered taxes. He gave lighter penalties for crimes. Life became easier for the Chinese people.

From 141 to 87 B.C., the emperor Wudi ruled Han China. He made his empire almost the size of modern China. He defeated nomads in the north. He moved troops and settlers to the west. He sent soldiers to the north into modern Korea and to the south to modern Vietnam.

1. What changes did Liu Bang make?

_____

_____

CHAPTER 7 INDIA AND CHINA ESTABLISH EMPIRES **71**

A Highly Structured Government; Han Technology, Commerce, and Culture (pages 183–186)

What advances took place?

Wudi changed the government in important ways. He had a large number of officials, who reached down to the smallest village. They filled **civil service** jobs. Those who wanted these jobs had to pass an exam. The exam tested them on their knowledge of the writings of the Chinese philosopher Confucius. Wudi also built schools around the country that taught this knowledge.

To support this large government, Wudi collected taxes. Farmers paid part of the crops they gathered. Merchants paid taxes on the goods they traded. Peasants also gave one month's worth of labor each year to the government. They worked on public building projects, such as dams and roads.

Under Han rule, the Chinese created many new inventions. One was paper. Paper made books more available and increased learning.

The Chinese also improved farming by inventing a new two-bladed plow. This change was important because the number of Chinese people had grown greatly. As Han emperors told their people, farming was the most important work.

At the same time, several industries became important. The government had a **monopoly** on, or took complete control of, the mining of salt and making of iron, coins, and alcohol. For a while, the government also made silk. This expensive cloth was in great demand in other lands.

China now included many different peoples. The Han rulers encouraged **assimilation**—making sure that these people learned Chinese ways. They urged the Chinese to marry them.

One group that did not do well in Han China was women. According to the teachings of Confucius, women were supposed to meet the needs of their husband and children and not become involved in other areas of life.

2. Why were changes in farming so important?

_____

Rebellion and Restoration
(pages 186–187)

Why was there a rebellion?

The Han empire began to have problems. Rich people got richer, while the poor were forced to pay heavy taxes. Members of the court were caught up in plots to gain power. Eventually, the peasants rebelled against their high taxes and poor lives.

A government official named Wang Mang took the throne. He tried to help the poor by taking land from the large landholders. But in the middle of these changes, a terrible flood struck China. The peasants rebelled again, and Wang Mang was killed. The Han Dynasty was *restored* when a member of the Han family was put on the throne. This was called the Later Han Dynasty.

For the next few decades, China enjoyed peace and wealth. But the same problems arose. The gap between rich and poor was too great. By A.D. 220, the Han Dynasty had fallen for good.

3. What caused the fall of the Han Dynasty?

_____

Two Great Empires: Han China and Rome	
Han Dynasty—202 B.C. to A.D. 220	**Roman Empire—27 B.C. to A.D. 476**
• Empire replaced rival kingdoms	• Empire replaced republic
• Centralized, bureaucratic government	• Centralized, bureaucratic government
• Built roads and defensive walls	• Built roads and defensive walls
• Conquered many diverse peoples in regions bordering China	• Conquered many diverse peoples in regions of three continents
• At its height—area of 1,500,000 square miles and 60,000,000 people	• At its height—area of 3,400,000 square miles and 55,000,000 people
• Chinese became common written language throughout empire	• Latin did not replace other written languages in empire
• Ongoing conflict with nomads	• Ongoing conflict with nomads

Skillbuilder

1. Which empire at its height covered more land?

2. What did the two empires have in common?

Name _____ Date _____

Glossary — CHAPTER 7 India and China Establish Empires, 300 B.C.–A.D. 550

caravan Word describing a route on which many traders traveled in groups
commerce Business
dominated Controlled
flourished Did extremely well
patrons Financial supporters
provinces Political divisions like states
restored Brought back
sect Branch that breaks off from a larger group, usually due to disagreements
self-denial Not taking part in life's pleasures

AFTER YOU READ

Terms and Names

A. Write the name or term in each blank that best completes the meaning of the paragraph.

Vishnu
Theravada
Mahayana
Brahma
Shiva

Both Hinduism and Buddhism underwent changes. Because the Buddha's teachings were so difficult to follow in real life, a new sect, **1** _____ Buddhism, arose. It offered salvation to more people. Those who held on to the stricter teachings of the Buddha belonged to the **2** _____ sect. Changes also occurred in Hinduism. Gradually, Hindus shifted from the worship of hundreds of gods to concentration on three main gods. These were **3** _____, creator of the world; **4** _____, preserver of the world; and **5** _____, destroyer of the world.

B. Write the letter of the name or term next to the description that explains it best.

a. monopoly
b. assimilation
c. patriarchal
d. matriarchal
e. civil service

____ **1.** Administrative parts of a government; also describes government jobs and employees

____ **2.** Relating to a social system in which the father is the head of the family

____ **3.** Relating to a social system in which the mother is the head of the family

____ **4.** One group's complete control over the making and selling of a certain good

____ **5.** Policy to get conquered peoples to adopt the culture of the conquering nation

CHAPTER 7 INDIA AND CHINA ESTABLISH EMPIRES 73

Name _____ Date _____

AFTER YOU READ (continued) **CHAP 7** INDIA AND CHINA ESTABLISH EMPIRES

Main Ideas

1. Describe the rule of Chandragupta Maurya.
   _____
   _____
   _____

2. What happened in the 500 years between the Mauryan and Gupta Empires?
   _____
   _____
   _____

3. Explain the role of the Silk Roads in changing and spreading Indian culture.
   _____
   _____
   _____

4. Explain how Wudi changed his empire.
   _____
   _____
   _____

5. What were two cultural facts of life in Han China?
   _____
   _____
   _____

Thinking Critically
Answer the following questions on a separate sheet of paper.

1. Compare and contrast the rule of Chandragupta Maurya and Asoka.

2. What basic problem was there in Han China that led to its fall?

74 CHAPTER 7 REVIEW

Name _____ Date _____

CHAPTER 8 Section 1 (pages 193–198)

Diverse Societies in Africa

BEFORE YOU READ

In the last section, you read about empires in China.

In this section, you will learn how African people developed diverse societies.

AS YOU READ

Use the web below to show some of the features of Africa's geography.

TERMS AND NAMES
Sahara Large desert in Africa
savanna Grassy plain
Sahel Land at the southern edge of the Sahara
desertification Steady process of drying of the soil
extended family Parents and children, plus grandparents, aunts, uncles, and cousins
clan Group that shares common ancestors
animism Religion in which spirits play a role in daily life
griot West African storyteller
Djenné-Djeno Oldest known city in Africa south of the Sahara
Nok African people who lived in what is now Nigeria from 500 B.C. to A.D. 200

(web diagram with center "Africa's geography" and one filled bubble: "large coastline; few harbors")

A Land of Geographic Contrasts
(pages 193–195)

What are some of the geographic contrasts in Africa?

Africa is the second largest continent in the world. It stretches 4,600 miles from east to west and 5,000 miles from north to south. It has about one-fifth of the earth's land. Much of the land is a high plateau, with lower land near the coasts. The rivers that flow along this high land often form waterfalls or rapids. As a result, boats cannot use these rivers to travel either to or from the coast. Also, the coast has few harbors for so large a landmass.

Africa has many different environments, even though much of the continent lies in the tropics. There are hot, dry deserts; steamy, wet rain forests; and high, cool mountains.

CHAPTER 8 AFRICAN CIVILIZATONS **75**

About a third of Africa's land is desert. Few people live there. Deserts form a barrier to people who want to move from one area to another. The **Sahara** Desert in the north of Africa is about one-third the size of the United States. Dense rain forests cover much of the central part of Africa. This area receives heavy rainfall.

The northern and southern regions of Africa have large numbers of people. They have good soil for farming and plenty of grass for animals to eat. They have pleasant climates. Most Africans live on the **savannas,** grasslands that cover almost half of the continent. They grow grains, including rice and wheat, and tend cattle.

The land at the southern edge of the Sahara Desert is the **Sahel.** Each year, the Sahara Desert takes over a little more of this Sahel. This steady process of drying of the soil is called **desertification.**

1. Name three contrasting features of African geography.

_____

Early Humans Adapt to Their Environments (pages 195–197)

When and where did people begin to farm?

The first humans in Africa got food by hunting animals and gathering plants. Even today, some African peoples still use this method to get food.

Over time, these people learned to tame animals and raise them for food. Like the hunters and gatherers, these herders were *nomadic* people. As they moved, they looked for grass and for water for their animals. When food or water was used up in one area, they moved to another.

About 10,000 B.C., some people in Africa began to farm. People used to farm in the area of the Sahara before it became a desert. They also farmed in the Nile Valley and West Africa or on the grasslands. Some moved to the rain forest.

The *diverse* environments of Africa created much variety in the way different African peoples lived. The people who lived south of the Sahara, though, had these features in common:

- The family was the most important unit of society. The family was an **extended family** that included grandparents, aunts, uncles, and cousins. In some groups, family included all the people who came from common *ancestors*. This is called a **clan.**
- They believed that one god created the world. Their beliefs included **animism.** They felt that plants, animals, and other natural forces all have spirits that play an important role in life.
- They relied on oral storytelling, rather than writing, to pass on the traditions of their people. In West Africa, for example, storytellers, or **griots,** kept history alive.

2. What features did people living south of the Sahara have in common?

_____

Early Societies in West Africa
(pages 197–198)

What early societies existed?

An ancient city in West Africa, named **Djenné-Djeno,** rested on the banks of the Niger River. About 50,000 people lived there at its height. At first, they lived in round huts made of *reeds* and covered with mud. Later they lived in houses of mud bricks. They grew rice, raised cattle, and made iron. They traded these goods for gold and copper.

Djenné-Djeno is the oldest known African city south of the Sahara. It dates from about 250 B.C. But a culture has been found from an even earlier time. The West African **Nok** culture existed from about 500 B.C. to A.D. 200. The Nok people made pottery figures and were the first people in Africa who knew how to make iron. Some styles of Nok pottery are still found in Africa today.

3. What is Djenné-Djeno?

_____

Name _____ Date _____

CHAPTER 8 Section 2 (pages 199–202)

The Kingdom of Aksum and East African Trade

TERMS AND NAMES
Aksum African kingdom that reached the height of its power in the fourth century A.D.
Adulis Chief seaport of Aksum
Ezana King of Aksum who conquered Kush

BEFORE YOU READ

In the last section, you read about different ways of life in Africa.

In this section, you will learn about the kingdom of Aksum and its role in trade.

AS YOU READ

Use the time line below to show the rise and fall of Aksum.

| 1000 B.C. Aksum begins as Arabians and Kushites mix | 350 | 710 |

| early A.D. 300s | 600s |

The Rise of the Kingdom of Aksum (pages 199–200)

How did Aksum arise?

The peoples in East Africa had a great deal of contact with people from other areas. The Kushite kingdom of Nubia had close relations with Egypt. Its kings even ruled Egypt for a while. That kingdom continued for many centuries as a trading power. It was then replaced by the kingdom of **Aksum** in what is now modern Ethiopia. The dynasty that ruled Aksum and later Ethiopia included the 20th-century ruler Haile Selassie.

Aksum may have begun as early as 1000 B.C. when Arabian traders mixed with the people of Kush. It became an important part of world trade.

Salt, emeralds, brass, copper, gold, cloth, olive oil, and wine all moved through Aksum. Its trade routes helped link Rome to India. Traders crowded into its chief seaport, **Adulis.**

In the early A.D. 300s, Aksum had a strong new king named **Ezana.** He brought the kingdom to its height during his rule. Ezana captured more land on the Arabian peninsula, and then conquered Kush in 350.

1. Why was Aksum an important trading center?

_____
_____
_____
_____

CHAPTER 8 AFRICAN CIVILIZATONS **77**

A Cosmopolitan Culture Develops (pages 200–201)

What was unique about Aksum's culture?

Aksum was a *cosmopolitan* trading center. It was home to peoples from many different cultures. There were people from Aksum's widespread trading partners, including Egypt, Arabia, Greece, Rome, Persia, India, and even Byzantium. At the time of King Ezana, these different peoples all spoke to one another in Greek.

The Aksumites, like other ancient Africans, traditionally believed in one god. They also worshiped the spirits of nature and honored their dead ancestors. During his rule, King Ezana decided to become a Christian. The religion slowly spread throughout the land.

The people of Aksum also developed a special way of building. They made structures out of stone, not mud baked into bricks by the hot sun. Their kings built tall *pillars* of stone that reached as high as 60 feet. They were among the tallest structures in the ancient world.

Aksum made other advances as well. Aside from Egypt and the city of *Meroë*, it was the only culture of ancient Africa to have a written language. The language of Aksum had been brought to the land by Arab traders many hundreds of years before. Aksum was also the first state south of the Sahara to *mint* its own coins.

The people of Aksum also developed a new way of farming. They cut steps into the steep mountainsides in their country. The steps helped the land hold water instead of letting it run down the mountain in a heavy rain. This was called terrace farming. The people of Aksum also used dams and stone tanks to store water and used ditches to channel it to their fields.

2. What achievements and advances were made in Aksum?

_____
_____
_____
_____

The Fall of Aksum (pages 201–202)

Why did Aksum fall?

Aksum remained an important power in East Africa for 800 years. It was first challenged in the 600s, after the new religion of Islam came to Arabia. The followers of Islam captured the lands that Aksum held in the Arabian peninsula. Within a few decades, they had taken much of North Africa.

At first, these conquerors left Aksum alone. Aksum remained an island of Christianity in a sea of Islam. In 710, however, the conquerors destroyed Adulis. The Aksum kings moved their capital over the mountains to a hard-to-reach area, in present-day northern Ethiopia. Aksum was now cut off from other Christian lands. It was also isolated from the sea trade. Aksum began to *decline* as a world power.

3. Why did the rulers of Aksum move their capital?

_____
_____
_____
_____

Name _____ Date _____

CHAPTER 8 Section 3 (pages 203–205)

Patterns of Change: Migration

TERMS AND NAMES
Bantu-speaking peoples People who speak one of a group of languages related to Bantu

BEFORE YOU READ
In the last section, you read about the kingdom of Aksum.

In this section, you will read about the causes and effects of migration among Bantu-speaking peoples.

AS YOU READ
Use the chart below to record reasons for the movement of Bantu-speaking peoples.

- Farming methods used up the soil
- [ ]
- [ ]

→ **Movement of Bantu-Speaking People**

Migrations Through History
(page 203)

What are the main reasons for migrations?

Throughout human history, many peoples have felt the urge to move from their homes to a new land. There are many reasons that people make such a move. But they can be grouped into four main causes. They are environmental change, economic pressure, political and religious *persecution,* and technological development.

People have moved for these reasons since the beginning of human life. The large-scale movement of people in modern times can be traced in written records. In studying times before written history, though, researchers need to look for other clues to these migrations. One clue they use is language.

People take their language with them when they move to a new place. When historians find two languages from two distant areas that have words that are somewhat similar, they can conclude that those two languages may have both come from the same language. They say that the original speakers of the language simply moved to the two different areas long before. Then, the two languages changed independently of one another. This kind of clue has given historians a way of understanding the early history of Africa.

CHAPTER 8 AFRICAN CIVILIZATONS **79**

1. Name four key reasons for migration.

_____

_____

Massive Migrations (pages 204–205)
Who were the Bantu-speaking peoples?

Many languages spoken in Africa today developed from the same parent language called *Proto-Bantu*. The speakers of all these different languages are called the **Bantu-speaking peoples.** The people who spoke Bantu first lived in a part of modern Nigeria. In the first few centuries A.D., they began to move south and east. Over time, they spread throughout Africa south of the Sahara Desert, reaching the southern tip around 500 years ago. They brought their language and their culture with them.

One reason that these people moved had to do with how they farmed. Their method was to clear forest land by burning down trees. This left a plot of rich soil that was suitable for growing food—for a few years. After that, however, the soil no longer could produce good crops. The people then needed to move to a new area to clear new ground.

Another reason they moved was that their farming was so successful. Farming helped them produce more food than they could by hunting and gathering. With more to eat, groups became larger—and the land more crowded. They could not move north, where the Sahara Desert made a barrier. So they had to move farther and farther south.

As they reached new areas, the Bantu peoples met other peoples. Sometimes these meetings were violent. The Bantus, who knew how to make iron, had better weapons than those they met, who only had stone tools. Some of the peoples that they met are still found in Africa. But they live in small areas with very harsh environments. The Bantus took the better land.

2. Why did the Bantu peoples keep moving to new areas?

_____

_____

PATTERNS OF CHANGE: Migration

Cause	Example	Effect
Environmental change	Shift in climate, depletion of natural resources, drought, earthquake	Redistribution of world's population, blending of cultures
Economic pressure	Increasing population, famine, unemployment	Shifts in population
Political and religious persecution	Slave trade, war, ethnic cleansing, repression	Dislocation and oppression of peoples, spread of ideas and religions
Technological development	Tools, agriculture, iron smelting, communications and transportation networks	Development of civilizations and empires

Skillbuilder

1. Which causes of migration are still important today?

_____

_____

2. What effect does economic pressure have?

_____

_____

Name _____ Date _____

Glossary   CHAPTER 8 African Civilizations

ancestors Relatives who came before or long ago
cosmopolitan Worldly, sophisticated
decline Weaken, lose power
diverse Varied; different
Meroë City on the Nile River in ancient Africa
mint Produce money by stamping metal
nomadic Wandering
pillars Thin columns
Proto-Bantu Parent language from which the Bantu languages came
reeds Plants with long, hollow stems

AFTER YOU READ

Terms and Names

A. Write the name or term in each blank that best completes the meaning of the paragraph.

Nok
animism
clan
extended family
Djenné-Djeno

Societies that developed south of the Sahara shared certain characteristics. The basic social unit was the **1** _____. Besides parents and children, this group often included grandparents, aunts, uncles, and cousins. These ties often included an entire **2** _____, a group sharing common ancestors. These African people tended to believe in one creator and shared beliefs in **3** _____, a religion in which spirits played an important role in daily life. Early cultures have been found south of the Sahara in West Africa. These include the city of **4** _____ on the Niger River. Scientists have also unearthed remains of Africa's earliest known culture, the **5** _____ culture.

B. Write the letter of the name or term next to the description that explains it best.

a. savanna
b. griot
c. Adulis
d. Sahel
e. Ezana

____ **1.** West African storyteller
____ **2.** Land at the southern edge of the Sahara
____ **3.** Grassland
____ **4.** King of Aksum who conquered Kush
____ **5.** Chief seaport of Aksum

Name _____ Date _____

AFTER YOU READ (continued)   CHAPTER 8   African Civilizations

Main Ideas

1. Explain where the Sahel is and what is happening there.

_____
_____
_____
_____

2. What was the Nok culture?

_____
_____
_____
_____

3. Who was Ezana, and what did he accomplish?

_____
_____
_____
_____

4. Name three features of the culture that developed in Aksum.

_____
_____
_____
_____

5. How has language provided clues to the early history of Africa?

_____
_____
_____
_____

Thinking Critically

Answer the following questions on a separate sheet of paper.

1. What impact did geography have on the way human societies developed in Africa?

2. Why was Aksum important?

Name _____ Date _____

CHAPTER 9   Section 1 (pages 211–215)

Hunters and Farmers in the Americas

> **TERMS AND NAMES**
> **Ice Age** Time when sheets of ice covered large portions of North America
> **Beringia** Land bridge between Asia and the Americas
> **maize** Corn; the most important crop of the Americas

BEFORE YOU READ
In the last chapter, you read about African civilizations.
In this section, you will read about the Americas' first inhabitants.

AS YOU READ
Use the chart below to take notes on changes related to or brought about by the end of the Ice Age.

Ice Age Ends
- Glaciers melt
-
-

The Earliest Americans (pages 211–213)

How did the earliest people come to the Americas?

North and South America form a single stretch of land. It stretches from the Arctic Circle in the north to the waters around Antarctica in the south. The Atlantic and Pacific Oceans separate the Americas from Africa, Asia, and Europe.

But that was not always the case. From around 1.6 million years ago until about 10,000 years ago, the earth went through an **Ice Age.** During this time, huge sheets of ice called *glaciers* spread south from the Arctic Circle. The level of the world's oceans went down. The lowered oceans *exposed* land that is today again covered by water.

One strip of land, called **Beringia**, connected Asia and North America. Wild animals crossed this rocky *land bridge* and entered North America for the first time. Some of the Asian people who hunted these animals followed them. The people became the first Americans.

No one knows for sure when these first people arrived. Some scholars say the people came to the Americas as long ago as 40,000 B.C. Others say as late as 12,000 B.C. A discovery in Chile suggests that people were well-settled in that part of the Americas by 10,500 B.C. Since Chile lies far south of the land bridge, some experts say that people needed many thousands of years to travel that far. For this reason, they think that the first people must have crossed the land bridge in about 20,000 B.C.

These first Americans lived as hunters. One of their favorite hunting targets was the huge *mastodon.* Over time, all the mastodons died. People were forced to look for other food. They began to hunt smaller animals and to fish. They also began to gather plants and fruits to eat. They

CHAPTER 9   THE AMERICAS: A SEPARATE WORLD   **83**

no longer had to roam over large areas to search for the mastodon, so they settled for part of the year in one spot.

Between 12,000 and 10,000 B.C.., the climate changed. The Ice Age ended, and the world warmed up again. The huge sheets of ice melted, and the oceans rose again to cover the land bridge that connected Asia to the Americas. By this time, though, people lived from north to south in the Americas. They lived in many different environments and found ways of life suited to the place where they lived.

1. Where did the first Americans come from?

_____

_____

Agriculture Prompts a New Way of Life (pages 213–215)

How did agriculture change ways of life?

About 7000 B.C., the people living in central Mexico started a quiet revolution—farming. It was the same kind of *radical* change that had happened in several spots in Asia and Africa. By 3400 B.C., they had several foods that they grew, including squashes, beans, chilies, and the most important one—**maize,** or corn. Corn grew so well that a family of three could, in four months, grow enough corn to feed it for two years.

Over many centuries, farming spread throughout the Americas. In what is now the eastern United States and in the region of the Andes, people may have discovered the idea of farming on their own. In central Mexico, farmers became so skilled at growing corn that they could enjoy three harvests each year.

Farming had the same results in the Americas that it did in Asia and Africa. Growing food gave people a larger and more reliable food supply. As more people could be fed, they were healthier and lived longer. As a result, the population grew.

Because farmers produced so much food, some people could concentrate on other ways of making a living. They began to work in different arts and crafts and learned new skills. Some people became rich. They owned more than others and enjoyed a higher position in society. Some people became rulers. Others became their subjects.

2. Why was maize so important?

_____

_____

The Effects of Agriculture

Before Agriculture
- People hunted or gathered what they ate.
- Families continually moved in search of big game.
- Groups remained small due to the scarcity of reliable sources of food.
- Humans devoted much of their time to obtaining food.

After Agriculture
- People enjoyed a more reliable and steady source of food.
- Families settled down and formed larger communities.
- Humans concentrated on new skills: arts and crafts, architecture, social organization.
- Complex societies eventually arose.

Skillbuilder

1. How did the development of agriculture lead to population growth?

_____

_____

2. How did the development of agriculture change daily life?

_____

_____

Name _____ Date _____

CHAPTER 9 Section 2 (pages 216–220)

Early Mesoamerican Civilizations

TERMS AND NAMES
Mesoamerica Area that stretches south from central Mexico to the northern part of modern-day Honduras
Olmec People who flourished along the Mesoamerican coast of the Gulf of Mexico from 1200 B.C. to 400 B.C.
Zapotec Early Mesoamerican civilization that was centered in the Oaxaca Valley of what is now Mexico
Monte Albán First urban center in the Americas, built by the Zapotec

BEFORE YOU READ

In the last section, you read about the first inhabitants of the Americas.

In this section, you will read about the first civilizations in America.

AS YOU READ

Use the time line below to take notes on the rise and fall of early Mesoamerican civilizations.

| 1200 B.C. Olmec begin to flourish | 500 B.C. | A.D. 700 |

| 1000 B.C. | 400 B.C. |

Mesoamerica's Mother Culture
(pages 216–218)

Who were the Olmec?

The story of American civilizations begins in **Mesoamerica.** This area stretches south from central Mexico to the northern part of present-day Honduras.

The earliest known American civilizations arose in southern Mexico, an area of hot rain forests. The people are called the **Olmec.** They *flourished* from about 1200 to 400 B.C. Their culture had a great influence on their neighbors and on peoples who lived long after them.

The Olmec lived along the coast of the Gulf of Mexico in a land of *dense* forests and heavy rains.

The land gave them many benefits. It had good clay that could be used for pottery. Wood and rubber could be taken from the forest. The mountains to the north had stone for building. The rivers could be used to move people and goods. The soil was excellent for growing food.

Archaeologists have found earthen *mounds*, courtyards, and pyramids built of stones. On top of the mounds were many monuments made of stone. Some of these stone structures are very large. They weigh as much as 44 tons.

Researchers are not sure whether the Olmec sites were monuments to rulers or areas important for religious reasons. They do think that the Olmec had many gods who stood for important forces of nature. The most important god, it seems, was the

CHAPTER 9 THE AMERICAS: A SEPARATE WORLD **85**

jaguar spirit. Many stone monuments show figures that are half-human and half-jaguar.

The Olmec traded with other people in the region. In return for the products they made, they received iron ore and different kinds of stone. Along with their trade goods, they spread their culture to other people. For some reason, the Olmec disappeared around 400 B.C. Historians still do not understand why. But their influence lived on.

1. What evidence of Olmec civilization has been found?

Zapotec Civilization Arises
(pages 218–219)

Who were the Zapotec?

Another important early culture of Mexico was that of the **Zapotec** people. Their home was to the southwest of the Olmec in a valley that had excellent soil for farming and plenty of rainfall. By about 1000 B.C., the Zapotec built stone platforms and temples. A few hundred years later, they developed a kind of writing and a calendar.

Around 500 B.C., the Zapotec built the first city in the Americas. The city was called **Monte Albán.** As many as 25,000 people lived there. The city lasted as late as A.D. 700. Monte Albán had tall pyramids, temples, and palaces made out of stone. It had an *observatory* that could be used to look at the stars. But the Zapotec culture collapsed. As with the Olmec, historians do not know why.

2. What evidence of Zapotec civilization has been found?

The Early Mesoamericans' Legacy (pages 219–220)

How did the early Mesoamericans influence later peoples?

Both of these cultures left their mark on later cultures. The jaguar figure of the Olmec continued to appear in the sculpture and pottery of people who came later. Also, the look of Olmec towns—with pyramids, open space, and huge stone sculptures—was repeated in later times. The *ritual* ball games of the Olmec continued to be played.

The Zapotec also shaped the lives of later peoples. Their way of writing and their calendar were used by other groups. The city of Monte Albán also influenced later peoples, who built their own cities in similar ways. These cities combined religious purposes with the needs of the common people who lived in them.

3. How did the Zapotec influence later peoples?

Name _____ Date _____

CHAPTER 9 Section 3 (pages 221–223)

Early Civilizations of the Andes

TERMS AND NAMES
Chavín First influential culture in South America, which flourished from around 900 B.C. to 200 B.C.
Nazca Culture that flourished along the southern coast of Peru from around 200 B.C. to A.D. 600
Moche Culture that flourished along the northern coast of Peru from around A.D. 100 to A.D. 700

BEFORE YOU READ
In the last section, you read about the first Mesoamerican civilizations.

In this section, you will read about the civilizations of the Andes.

AS YOU READ
Use the time line below to take notes on the early civilizations of the Andes.

```
┌─────────────────────────┐    ┌─────────────────────────┐    ┌─────────────────────────┐
│ 900 B.C.                │    │ A.D. 100                │    │ A.D. 700                │
│ The Chavín culture      │    │                         │    │                         │
│ begins to flourish      │    │                         │    │                         │
│ in South America        │    │                         │    │                         │
└─────────────────────────┘    └─────────────────────────┘    └─────────────────────────┘

         ┌─────────────────────────┐    ┌─────────────────────────┐
         │ 200 B.C.                │    │ A.D. 600                │
         │                         │    │                         │
         └─────────────────────────┘    └─────────────────────────┘
```

Societies Grow in the Andes Regions (pages 221–222)

What *geographic factors made it unlikely for a civilization to arise?*

Other interesting civilizations arose in the Americas far to the south of the Olmec and Zapotec peoples. These civilizations grew in a very harsh environment—the *Andes* in South America. This mountain range has many peaks that are more than 20,000 feet high.

Toward the northern part of South America, along these mountains, lies the modern country of Peru. In this area, the mountains are steep and very rocky. Ice and snow cover the tops of the mountains during the entire year. Travel is hard. The climate changes quickly from being hot during the day to bitter cold at night. The soil is poor.

It was in the mountains of this difficult land that a new civilization arose. That culture is called **Chavín**. It takes its name from a major ruin, Chavín de Huántar, in the Andes. At this site, researchers have found pyramids, open spaces, and large mounds made of earth. The Chavín culture was at its height from 900 B.C. to 200 B.C. It is considered the first influential civilization in South America.

Scientists have found objects that suggest that the Chavín culture helped shape other cultures to the north and south of this site. At these other sites are the art styles and symbols of religion found at Chavín. Scientists think that the main site was not

CHAPTER 9 THE AMERICAS: A SEPARATE WORLD **87**

the center of a political empire but was the chief site of a spiritual or religious movement. People from other areas may have made trips to the main site to pay their respects. The Chavín culture, like the Olmec in Mexico, may have been a "mother culture," one that gave the first form to the ideas and styles of the area.

1. What theories do scientists have about the Chavín culture?

_____

_____

_____

_____

Other Andean Civilizations Flourish (pages 222–223)

What other Andean civilizations developed?

Two other important cultures arose in Peru. The **Nazca** culture developed along the coast of the Pacific Ocean in the south of Peru. It lasted from 200 B.C. to A.D. 600. The Nazca people built large and complex systems to bring water to their farmlands. They made beautiful cloth and pottery.

The Nazca are most famous for the *Nazca Lines.* They are huge pictures scraped on the surface of a rocky plain. The drawings include a monkey, a spider, some birds, and other creatures. The pictures are so large that they can be seen and appreciated only from high in the air. Some experts think that the Nazca drew these pictures for their gods to see.

The other culture of early Peru arose along the Pacific Coast but far to the north. This was the **Moche** culture. It lasted from A.D. 100 to A.D. 700. The Moche tapped into rivers that flowed down from the mountains. They built ditches to bring water to their fields. They raised corn, beans, potatoes, squash, and peanuts. They also fished, caught wild ducks and pigs, and hunted deer.

Archaeologists have found some tombs of the Moche people. They show that the culture had great wealth. They have found objects made of gold, silver, and jewels. The Moche people made beautiful pottery that showed scenes of everyday life. So, even though they never had a written language, it is possible to learn much about how they lived.

Eventually, the Moche culture also fell. As with the other peoples of the Americas, the reason for this fall is not known. For the next hundred years, other cultures would rise and fall in the Americas. But most of them remained separate from one another.

2. Name three characteristics of the Moche people.

_____

_____

_____

_____

_____

Name _____ Date _____

Glossary   **CHAPTER 9**   The Americas: A Separate World

Andes Mountain range in South America
archaeologists Scientists who learn about past human life and activities
dense Thick
exposed Uncovered
flourished Did well
glaciers Huge sheets of ice

land bridge Strip of land linking two larger land masses
mastodon Large prehistoric animal like an elephant
mounds Raised masses of earth created by humans for burial, ceremonial, or other purposes

Nazca Lines Huge drawings made by the Nazca people by scraping the surface of a rocky plain and which can only be properly observed from the air
observatory Place to observe heavenly bodies
radical Extreme
ritual An event or ceremony with order, form, and significance

AFTER YOU READ

Terms and Names

A. Write the name or term in each blank that best completes the meaning of the paragraph.

Zapotec
Nazca
Olmec
Chavín
Moche

Early civilizations in the Americas developed in the Andes of South America as well as in Mesoamerica. In the Andes, the **1** _____ culture was the first to develop. This culture was followed by two other significant Andean civilizations. Both the **2** _____ and the **3** _____ developed in what is now Peru. In Mesoamerica, the **4** _____ culture, which has come to regarded as a "mother culture," developed a little ahead of the **5** _____ culture.

B. Write the letter of the name or term next to the description that explains it best.

a. Monte Albán
b. Mesoamerica
c. maize
d. Ice Age
e. Beringia

____ **1.** Corn

____ **2.** Area stretching from present-day central Mexico to northern Honduras

____ **3.** Land bridge between Asia and the Americas

____ **4.** Period when sheets of ice covered large portions of North America

____ **5.** First urban center in the Americas

CHAPTER 9 THE AMERICAS: A SEPARATE WORLD **89**

Name _____ Date _____

AFTER YOU READ (continued)   CHAPTER 9   The Americas: A Separate World

Main Ideas

1. Explain how scholars know when the first people arrived in the Americas.
_____
_____
_____

2. What changes did the rise of farming cause in the Americas?
_____
_____
_____

3. What geographic advantages did the Olmec enjoy?
_____
_____
_____

4. What is the significance of Monte Albán?
_____
_____
_____

5. What made the Andes an unlikely place for civilizations to arise?
_____
_____
_____

Thinking Critically

Answer the following questions on a separate sheet of paper.

1. What did the first Americans hunt, and what happened when that supply of food disappeared?

2. What do the Olmec and Chavín cultures have in common?

Name _____ Date _____

CHAPTER 10 Section 1 (pages 233–237)

The Rise of Islam

BEFORE YOU READ

In the last section, you read about early civilizations in South America.

In this section, you will read about the rise of Islam.

AS YOU READ

Use the chart below to take notes on the rise of Islam.

TERMS AND NAMES
Muhammad Arab prophet who founded Islam
Allah One god of Islam
Islam Religion based on the belief in Allah
Muslim Follower of the religion Islam
Hijrah Muhammad's move from Mecca to Yathrib (Medina) in 622
mosque Islamic house of worship
hajj Pilgrimage to Mecca
Qur'an Holy book of Islam
Sunna Islamic model for living based on the life and teachings of Muhammad
shariah Body of Islamic law

BATTLE/POLITICAL ISSUE	EFFECT
geography of the Arabian peninsula	desert nomadic way of life near trade routes
Muhammad	
Islamic beliefs	

Deserts, Towns, and Travelers
(pages 233–234)

How did the desert help shape Arab life?

The harsh environment of the Arabian peninsula left its mark on the Arab peoples. The land is almost completely covered by desert. The desert people were nomads. They herded animals, leading them from one *fertile* spot, or *oasis*, to another. Over time, many of these people, called *Bedouins*, began to live in towns and cities. They also began to trade goods.

By the early 600s, trade became an important activity in the Arabian peninsula. Merchants from the north brought goods to Arabia. They traded for spices and other goods. They also brought new ideas.

At this time, some Arab people believed in many gods. Religious pilgrims came to Mecca to worship at an ancient shrine called the *Ka'aba*.

1. When and how did trade become important?

_____
_____

CHAPTER 10 THE MUSLIM WORLD 91

The Prophet Muhammad
(pages 234–235)

Who was Muhammad?

Around the year 570, **Muhammad** was born into this Arab society. At around age 40, he took religion as his life's mission and became a *prophet*. According to Muslim belief, the angel Gabriel visited Muhammad and told him to speak the word of God to his people.

Muhammad began to teach that there was only one god—**Allah.** The religion based on his teachings is called **Islam.** Its followers are called **Muslims.**

At first many people in Mecca opposed Muhammad's views. They feared Meccans would neglect traditional Arab gods. Muhammad and his followers were forced to leave Mecca for Yathrib (later called Medina) in 622. This became known as the **Hijrah.** The Hijrah was a turning point for Muhammad.

Gradually, Muhammad and his followers gained power. Finally, in 630, Muhammad went to the Ka'aba in Mecca and destroyed the *idols*. Many of the people of Mecca adopted Islam. They began to worship Allah as the only God. Muhammad died soon after, in 632. Much of the Arabian peninsula was already united under Islam.

2. What was the Hijrah?

_____

_____

_____

Beliefs and Practices of Islam
(pages 236–237)

What do Muslims believe and practice?

Muslims have five duties to perform. These duties include faith, prayer, *alms, fasting,* and pilgrimage. The duties show a person's acceptance of the will of Allah:

- A Muslim must state the belief that, "There is no God but Allah, and Muhammad is the Messenger of Allah."
- A Muslim must pray to Allah, facing Mecca, five times every day. This may be done at a **mosque,** an Islamic house of worship.
- A Muslim must give alms, or money for the poor, through a tax.
- A Muslim must fast during the holy month of Ramadan. Muslims eat only one meal a day, after sunset, every day during this month.
- A Muslim should perform the **hajj**—a trip to the holy city of Mecca—at least once in his or her life.

The central ideas of Islam are found in the **Qur'an.** Muslims believe this book states the will of Allah as revealed to Muhammad. Muslims are also guided by the example of Muhammad's life, called the **Sunna,** and by a set of laws and rules, the **shariah.**

Muslims believe that Allah is the same God that Jews and Christians worship. To Muslims, the Qur'an perfects the earlier teachings of God found in the Jewish Torah and the Christian Bible. Because their holy books were related to the Qur'an, Jews and Christians enjoyed special status in Muslim societies.

3. What are the five duties of Muslims?

_____

_____

_____

_____

_____

Name _____ Date _____

CHAPTER 10 Section 2 (pages 238–241)

The Spread of Islam

BEFORE YOU READ

In the last section, you read about the rise of Islam.
In this section, you will read about the spread of Islam.

AS YOU READ

Use the chart below to take notes on how Islam spread.

TERMS AND NAMES

caliph Highest political and religious leader in a Muslim government
Umayyads Dynasty that ruled the Muslim Empire from A.D. 661 to 750
Shi'a Branch of Islam whose members believe the first four caliphs are the rightful successors of Muhammad
Sunni Branch of Islam whose members believe Ali and his descendants are the rightful successors of Muhammad
Sufi Muslim who tries to achieve direct contact with God
Abbasids Dynasty that ruled much of the Muslim Empire from A.D. 750 to 1258
al-Andalus Muslim-ruled area in what is now Spain
Fatimid Member of a Muslim dynasty that traced its ancestry to Muhammad's daughter Fatima

```
                The Spread
                 of Islam
          ┌──────────┼──────────┐
          ▼          ▼          ▼
   ┌─────────────┐ ┌──────────┐ ┌──────────────┐
   │Abbasid Dynasty│ │al-Andalus state│ │Fatimid Dynasty│
   │Iraq, Iran,    │ │          │ │              │
   │ central Asia  │ │          │ │              │
   └─────────────┘ └──────────┘ └──────────────┘
```

Muhammad's Successors Spread Islam (pages 238–239)

How did other leaders spread Islam?

When Muhammad died, his followers elected a new leader, Abu-Bakr. He had been loyal to Muhammad. He was given the title **caliph.** This means *"successor"* or *"deputy."* A successor is a person who comes after and takes the place of someone else. A deputy is an assistant who acts on behalf of a leader who is absent.

Abu-Bakr reacted quickly when a group of Arabs abandoned Islam. He defeated them in battle over a two-year period. Abu-Bakr died soon after. But his army began to conquer new lands. By 750, the Muslim Empire stretched from the Indus River in India west to the Atlantic Ocean.

Many of the people conquered by the Muslims accepted Islam. Some found the message of Islam appealing. Others liked the fact that by becoming Muslims they avoided paying a tax put only on non-Muslims. But the Qur'an prevented Muslims from

CHAPTER 10 THE MUSLIM WORLD 93

forcing others to accept the religion. Muslim rulers allowed people to follow whatever beliefs they chose.

1. How did Abu-Bakr spread Islam?

_____

_____

_____

Internal Conflict Creates a Crisis
(pages 239–240)

What disagreements arose?

After the murder of a ruling caliph in 656, different Muslim groups began to struggle for control of the empire. Ali, a cousin and son-in-law of Muhammad, was chosen caliph. After a few years, he was also killed. The system of electing caliphs died with him.

A family known as the **Umayyads** took control of the empire. They did not follow the simple life of earlier caliphs. Instead, they surrounded themselves with wealth. This created a split in the Muslim community.

Most Muslims accepted Umayyad rule. But a different view of the office of caliph also developed. The **Shi'a** group—the "party" of the deceased Ali—felt that caliphs needed to be relatives of Muhammad. Those who did not openly resist Umayyad rule became known as the **Sunni**. Among them were many Muslims who felt that the Umayyads had lost touch with their religion. Another group, the **Sufi**, reacted to the Umayyads' life of luxury. The Sufis emphasized a more spiritual way of life. They helped keep Muslims focused on the Qur'an and tradition.

2. How did the Shi'a and Sunni groups arise?

_____

_____

_____

Muslims Control Areas of Three Continents (pages 240–241)

What Muslim states arose?

After 750, there were Muslim *dynasties* on three continents. The **Abbasids** (750–1258) took power and murdered members of the Umayyad family.

The Abassids controlled the lands of modern Iraq, Iran, and central Asia. They built the city of Baghdad in southern Iraq as their capital. They used their location to control the rich trade between China and Europe.

One Umayyad prince escaped the murders and went to Spain. Muslims known as Berbers already lived there. The prince set up a Muslim state called **al-Andalus**. The Umayyads of al-Andalus (756–976) controlled parts of Spain and North Africa. Another Muslim state—the **Fatimid Dynasty** (909–1171)—sprang up in North Africa. This dynasty spread to western Arabia and Syria. Although the Muslims were divided politically, all of the different communities were linked by religion, language, culture, and trade.

3. Who were the Abbasids?

_____

_____

_____

_____

94 CHAPTER 10 SECTION 2

Name _____   Date _____

CHAPTER 10 Section 3 (pages 242–247)

Muslim Achievement

TERMS AND NAMES
House of Wisdom Center of learning established in Baghdad in the 800s
calligraphy Art of beautiful handwriting

BEFORE YOU READ

In the last section, you read about the spread of Islam.
In this section, you will read about the achievements of Muslim society.

AS YOU READ

Use the web below to take notes on the achievements and advances made by Muslims.

- **Scholarship**: Collected, translated, and saved ancient works
- **Art**
- **Science**
- **Muslim Achievement**
- **Literature**
- **Math**

Muslim Society (pages 242–243)

Where and how did Muslims live?

The Muslim Empire included people of many different lands and cultures. Major cities arose in the Muslim world. They included Córdoba and Cairo, centers of Muslim rule in Spain and North Africa, and Baghdad, the Abbasid capital.

Muslim society was divided into four groups. At the top were people who were Muslims from birth. Next came those who converted to Islam. The third group included Jews, Christians, and Zoroastrians—protected because Muslims shared some of their beliefs. The fourth group was slaves, none of whom were Muslims.

According to Muslim law, women should obey men. But Muslim women still enjoyed more rights than did those living in European society at the time. The Qur'an allowed them to divorce and protected their right to inherit property. In early Muslim society, women could also have an education and take part in public life. Later they lost those rights.

1. Name the four groups of Muslim society.

_____

_____

CHAPTER 10 THE MUSLIM WORLD 95

Muslim Scholarship Extends Knowledge (pages 243–244)

How did Muslim scholars keep learning alive?

Muslims placed a high value on learning and *scholarship*. Muslim scholars added much to human knowledge. Europe was in chaos and much of the knowledge of Europeans was in danger of being lost. During this time, Muslim scholars collected ancient Greek, Indian, and Persian works of science and philosophy. The scholars translated these works into Arabic. One center of this study was the **House of Wisdom** in Baghdad. Later, this ancient learning returned to Europe when the works of Muslim scholars were translated.

2. **Explain how Muslim scholars helped save the learning of the West.**

_____

_____

Arts and Sciences Flourish in the Muslim World (pages 244–247)

What were some achievements of Muslim society?

Muslim scholars made great advances in medicine and mathematics. The physician al-Razi wrote an encyclopedia that collected all that was known about medicine from Greece to India. A mathematician named al-Khwarizmi wrote a textbook that introduced algebra.

In science, Muslims studied the work of ancient Greek scientists but took a new approach. The Greeks had tried to learn about nature by using logic to reach conclusions. In contrast, Muslims used experiments to test ideas. One Muslim scientist made new discoveries about how people see. His findings helped lead to the invention of the telescope and microscope.

In philosophy, the Muslim scholar Ibn Rushd tried to join together the thinking of ancient Greeks with Muslim ideas.

Literature was a strong tradition before Islam. Later, the Qur'an became the standard for all Arabic poetry. One branch of poetry came from the Sufis, who wrote about their efforts to reach spiritual growth. The collection *The Thousand and One Nights* included many entertaining stories, fairy tales, and legends.

Muslims had their own special practices in art. For instance, artists could not draw pictures of people. Only Allah, the religion said, could create life. Unable to draw these images, Muslims developed a new art form. They practiced **calligraphy,** or the art of beautiful handwriting.

3. **Name four achievements of Muslim scientists and mathematicians.**

_____

_____

Urban Centers, A.D. 900

(Bar graph showing population: Baghdad ~900,000; Constantinople ~300,000; Córdoba ~200,000; Rome ~50,000)

Source: Tertius Chandler and Gerald Fox, *3,000 Years of Urban Growth.*

Skillbuilder

1. **Approximately how many times larger was Baghdad than Constantinople?**

_____

_____

2. **How does the population of Córdoba shown in this graph compare with the population of your own city or town?**

_____

_____

Name _____ Date _____

> **Glossary** **CHAPTER 10** The Muslim World
>
> **alms** Money for the poor
> **Bedouins** Nomadic people of Arabia, North Africa, or Syria
> **deputy** An assistant or representative who can take over when the leader is absent
> **dynasties** Series of rulers from a single family
> **fertile** Word that describes soil that is good for growing crops
> **fasting** Restricting what one eats
> **flourish** Do well
> **idols** Images or objects that people worship
> **Ka'aba** Muslim shrine
> **oasis** Place in a desert with enough water to support plant life
> **prophet** Person said to speak the word of God
> **scholarship** Learning
> **successor** Person who comes after and takes the place of someone else

AFTER YOU READ

Terms and Names

A. Write the name or term in each blank that best completes the meaning of the paragraph.

shariah

hajj

Allah

Islam

Muslim

Muhammad is the prophet of the religion called **1** _____. The word that names a follower of this religion is **2** _____. One of the central beliefs of this religion is that there is only one god, **3** _____. Among the required practices of followers is the giving of alms, or aid, for the poor. Followers must also make a **4** _____, or pilgrimage, to Mecca at least once in a lifetime. Believers also follow a body of law known as **5** _____. It gives guidance on practical matters of daily life.

B. Write the letter of the name or term next to the description that explains it best.

a. Umayyad

b. Fatimid

c. Abbasid

d. Hijrah

e. Sufi

____ **1.** Muhammad's move from Mecca to Yathrib (Medina)

____ **2.** Member of a Muslim dynasty that traced its ancestry to Muhammad's daughter

____ **3.** Dynasty that ruled much of the Muslim Empire from A.D. 750 to 1258

____ **4.** Dynasty that ruled the Muslim Empire from A.D. 661 to 750

____ **5.** Muslim who tries to achieve direct contact with God

Name _____ Date _____

AFTER YOU READ (continued) — CHAPTER 10 The Muslim World

Main Ideas

1. Who was Muhammad, and what did he teach?

_____
_____
_____
_____

2. Explain the importance of the Qur'an and Sunna in Muslim life.

_____
_____
_____
_____

3. Why did many conquered peoples accept Islam? What happened to those who did not?

_____
_____
_____
_____

4. What factors linked the three separate dynasties—the Abbasids, the Umayyads of al-Andalus, and the Fatimids?

_____
_____
_____
_____

5. What rights did women have in early Muslim society?

_____
_____
_____
_____

Thinking Critically

Answer the following questions on a separate sheet of paper.

1. Explain the importance of Mecca and Yathrib (Medina) in the life of Muhammad.

2. Explain the relationship between these terms: Umayyads, caliph, Sunni, and Shi'a.

Name _____   Date _____

CHAPTER 11 Section 1 (pages 269–273)

Byzantium Becomes the New Rome

BEFORE YOU READ

In the last chapter, you read about the Muslim world.
In this section, you will learn about the Byzantine Empire.

AS YOU READ

Use the chart below to take notes on people, places, and developments in the Byzantine Empire.

TERMS AND NAMES

Justinian Code Body of Roman law collected and organized by the Byzantine emperor Justinian around A.D. 534

Hagia Sophia Church destroyed by mobs of rioters in 532 and rebuilt by Justinian

patriarch Leader of the Eastern church

icon Religious image used in practices by eastern Christians

iconoclast Icon breaker

excommunication Formal declaration that someone is no longer a member of the Church

schism Split

Cyrillic alphabet Alphabet invented by Saints Cyril and Methodius, in which most Slavic languages, including Russian, are written

| THE BYZANTINE EMPIRE ||
Action	Result
Justinian moves the capital	
Justinian creates the law	
The empire is weakened	
The church divides	

A New Rome in a New Setting
(page 269)

How did the Roman Empire change?

In the A.D. 300s, the emperor Constantine moved the capital of the Roman Empire to the east. He was worried about the growing power of German tribes. He thought that he could better meet that threat in the east. He built a great new capital city, Constantinople. It was on the site of the old port city of Byzantium. Constantinople became the center of the empire. Power moved eastward.

The Roman Empire was officially divided in 395. The western area was overrun by German tribes. It did not exist after 476. However, the Byzantine, or eastern, part remained strong. It lasted for hundreds of years

In 527, Justinian became the Byzantine emperor. He sent an army to try to regain control of Italy. He hoped to restore the Roman Empire once again. By about 550, Justinian ruled over almost all of the territory of the old Roman Empire.

CHAPTER 11 BYZANTINES, RUSSIANS, AND TURKS INTERACT **99**

1. Who was Justinian?

Building the New Rome; Byzantium Preserves Learning
(pages 270–271)

What changes did Justinian bring?

Justinian directed legal experts to create a complete code of laws based on the laws of ancient Rome. This body of civil law—the **Justinian Code**—served the empire for 900 years.

Justinian also worked at making Constantinople a strong but also a beautiful capital. He built high, sturdy walls to protect the city from attack. He constructed a huge palace, public baths, courts, schools, hospitals, and many churches. The main street of the city was lined with shops and open-air markets. People bought and sold goods from Asia, Africa, and Europe there.

In 532, riots broke out against the emperor. Justinian's troops maintained control of the city, killing thousands of rioters. A church called **Hagia Sophia** ("Holy Wisdom," in Greek) had been destroyed by the mobs. Justinian rebuilt it to become the most beautiful church in the Christian world.

2. How did Justinian make Constantinople a strong and beautiful capital?

The Empire Confronts Its Enemies (page 272)

What weakened the empire?

The Byzantine Empire faced many dangers. A terrible disease broke out in 542. It was probably caused by rats. The illness killed thousands of people and returned every 8 to 12 years until about 700. This weakened the empire.

Also, the empire was forced to *confront* many enemies over the centuries. German tribes, the Sassanid Persians, and Muslim armies all tried to gain control of Byzantine land. Constantinople remained safe during this time despite many attacks. Eventually, though, the empire shrank. By 1350, the empire included only the capital city and lands in the *Balkans*—part of southeastern Europe.

3. What were the two biggest problems the empire faced?

The Church Divides (pages 272–273)

Why did the church divide?

Although it was based on the Roman Empire, the Byzantine Empire had developed a culture of its own. People in the Byzantine Empire spoke Greek, not Latin. They belonged to the Eastern Orthodox Church, not the Catholic Church. The Eastern Church was led by the **patriarch,** the leading bishop. However, even the patriarch had to obey the emperor.

The feeling of separateness from Rome grew worse when one emperor *banned* the use of **icons.** Icons are religious images used by eastern Christians to aid their *devotions.* The emperor thought this was like *idol* worship. **Iconoclasts,** or "icon breakers" went into churches destroying images. This caused the people to riot and the *clergy* to rebel. The pope became involved. He supported the use of icons. One pope even ordered the **excommunication** of a Byzantine emperor. That means that the pope said the emperor could no longer be a member of the Church.

Slowly the Eastern and Roman churches grew further apart. In 1054, the split, or **schism,** became permanent.

Some *missionaries* traveled from the Byzantine Empire to the north. Two missionaries, Saint Methodius and Saint Cyril, met the Slavic peoples who lived in Russia. They developed an alphabet for the Slavic languages. Many Slavic languages, including Russian, are now written in what is called the **Cyrillic alphabet.**

4. What are two differences between the Eastern and Roman churches?

Name _____ Date _____

CHAPTER 11 Section 2 (pages 274–278)

Russians Adapt Byzantine Culture

TERMS AND NAMES
Slavs People from the forests north of the Black Sea
boyars Landowning nobles of Russia
Olga Russian princess who converted to Christianity in 957
Vladimir Grandson of Olga who ordered all his subjects to adopt Christianity
Yaroslav the Wise Russian ruler who helped Kiev gain power and wealth
Alexander Nevsky Russian noble who gained power in Moscow
czar Russian emperor

BEFORE YOU READ

In the last section, you read about the establishment and decline of the Byzantine Empire.

In this section, you will learn about the spread of Byzantine culture to Russia.

AS YOU READ

Use the time line below to show key events in the early development of Russia.

800s Vikings enter the lands of the Slavs	1019	1453
957	1200s	1480

Both Slavic and Greek (pages 274–275)

Who were the Slavs?

The **Slavs** lived in what is today eastern Russia. The area was bounded by the Ural Mountains and the Black Sea on the south and the Baltic Sea on the north.

The Slavs lived in the forest areas. They worked as farmers and traders. In the 800s, some Vikings called the Rus came from the north. They built forts along the rivers and blended with the *Slavic* people. They founded the cities of Novgorod and Kiev and became the rulers of the land. They began to trade in Constantinople. With them, they brought furs, timber, and the Slavs who were their subjects. They sold these people as slaves. In fact, the word slave comes from Slav.

Over time, the Vikings adopted the culture of the Slavs. Divisions between Vikings and Slavs disappeared. But the society was sharply split between the great mass of peasants and the few nobles, or **boyars.**

In 957 Princess **Olga** of Kiev *converted* to Christianity. Her grandson, **Vladimir,** also converted to Byzantine Christianity. He was the ruler of Russia. He ordered all of his subjects to adopt this religion. Now more than trade linked Russia to the Byzantine Empire. Russia also looked to Constantinople for religious leadership. Teachers from the empire gave the Russian people instructions in the new religion. The king liked the idea that the ruler of the empire was also the head of the church.

CHAPTER 11 BYZANTINES, RUSSIANS, AND TURKS INTERACT **101**

1. How did Olga and Vladimir influence the Slavic people?

Kiev's Power and Decline
(pages 275–276)

What caused Kiev's rise?

Under the influence of Byzantine culture, Kiev grew to be a large, wealthy, and cultured city. It continued to grow as Vladimir took land to the west and to the north. His son, **Yaroslav the Wise,** came to power in 1019. He proved to be an able ruler as well. Under him, Kiev grew even more wealthy through trade and *alliances* made with western nations.

Then the state centered in Kiev began to have problems. After Yaroslav's death in 1054, his sons fought one another for control of the land. Trade *declined,* cutting the wealth of Kiev.

2. What caused Kiev's decline?

Mongol Invasions Favor the Rise of Moscow (pages 276–278)

How did the Mongol invasions change Russia?

In the middle 1200s, the *Mongols* reached Kiev. They quickly overran the Russian state, killing many people. The Mongols held control of the area for more than 200 years.

The Mongols had been fierce conquerors, but they were not harsh rulers. As long as the Russian people did not rebel, the Mongols let them keep their customs, including their Eastern Christian religion.

The Mongols made the Russians pay tribute, a sum of money that was owed every year. They used Russian nobles to collect the *tribute.* One of those nobles, **Alexander Nevsky,** gained power. His *heirs* became princes of Moscow. They later used this city as their base of power.

Control by the Mongols had important effects on Russia. It isolated the Russians from western Europe. Russian society developed in its own way. Rule by the Mongols united many different areas of Russia under one central authority. Before then, what is now Russia had been ruled by a number of princes. Mongol rule also led to the rise of Moscow, which had a good location near three major rivers—the Dnieper, the Don, and the Volga.

Ivan I increased the influence of Moscow. Over time, Ivan and his successors added to the land that Moscow controlled. In the late 1400s, under Ivan III, Russia grew to be a mighty empire. In 1453, the Byzantine Empire had fallen, defeated by the Turks. In 1472, Ivan married the niece of the last Byzantine emperor. From that time, he called himself **czar**—the Russian version of *Caesar.* In 1480, Ivan finally broke with the Mongols.

3. Name three effects of Mongol rule on Russia.

Skillbuilder
Use the illustration to answer these questions.

1. What kinds of items are the Vikings carrying in their boat?

2. What conclusions can you draw about the Vikings from this woodcut?

Name _____ Date _____

CHAPTER 11 Section 3 (pages 279–281)

Turkish Empires Rise in Anatolia

TERMS AND NAMES
mamelukes Turkish military slaves
Seljuks Turkish group that migrated into the Abbasid Empire in the 10th century and later established their own empire
vizier Prime minister in a Muslim kingdom or empire
Malik Shah Famous Seljuk sultan

BEFORE YOU READ

In the last section, you read about the blending of cultures in Russia.

In this section, you will learn about the Turks in Anatolia.

AS YOU READ

Use the time line below to record important events in the rise and fall of the Seljuk Turks.

```
┌─────────────────────────┐      ┌─────────────────────────┐
│ 945                     │      │ 1095                    │
│ Persians take control   │      │                         │
│ of the abbasid Empire   │      │                         │
└─────────────────────────┘      └─────────────────────────┘
        │                                │
┌─────────────────────────┐      ┌─────────────────────────┐
│ 1055                    │      │ 1258                    │
│                         │      │                         │
│                         │      │                         │
└─────────────────────────┘      └─────────────────────────┘
```

The Turks March from Central Asia (pages 279–280)

Who were the Seljuk Turks?

The Turks were nomads from central Asia. They lived by herding sheep and goats. They traded with the settled peoples of the Abbasid Empire. Beginning in the 900s, they moved into the lands of that empire and began converting to Islam.

The Turks were fierce and highly skilled fighters. The rulers of the empire began to buy them as children to train them for their armies. These Turkish military slaves were known as **mamelukes.** The Turks became an important political factor in the empire. Turkish soldiers many times removed caliphs from the throne in Baghdad and put new rulers in their place.

While the Turkish influence was growing, the empire itself was shrinking. Local leaders in several areas split off to establish their own states. In 945, a Persian army seized control of the empire. Members of the Abbasid family continued to hold the position of caliph and act as religious leaders. The new rulers of the government were from outside the dynasty. They were called *sultans.*

Large numbers of Turks settled in the empire as these changes took place. They were called **Seljuks** after the name of the family that led them. In 1055, the Seljuks captured Baghdad and took control of the government. In the next few decades, the Seljuks used their force to take land from another empire—the Byzantine Empire. They won almost all of Anatolia. Anatolia was the name for the peninsula where modern Turkey is

CHAPTER 11 BYZANTINES, RUSSIANS, AND TURKS INTERACT **103**

located. In this position, the Seljuks stood almost at the gates of Constantinople.

The Seljuks relied on the government experience of Persians in ruling their empire. They chose the Persian city of Isfahan as the capital of their kingdom. They gave Persians important positions in the government. For example, Nizam al-Mulk was a Persian who served as **vizier,** or prime minister. In return, Persians became loyal supporters of Turkish rule.

The Turks also adopted Persian culture. The nomadic Seljuk Turks had arrived in Southwest Asia as basically *illiterate*. They were not familiar with the traditions of Islam, which they had just adopted. They looked to Persian scholars to teach them the proper way to follow Islam. They began to use the Persian language for art and education. Turkish rulers even took the Persian word for "king"—*shah*—as their title.

One of the greatest Seljuk rulers, **Malik Shah,** became a *patron* of the arts. He made the capital city more beautiful by building many mosques, or Muslim houses of worship. Persian became so important that Arabic—the language of the Qur'an—almost died out in Seljuk lands.

1. What influence did Persians and Persian culture have on the Seljuks?

_____

_____

_____

Seljuks Confront Crusaders and Mongols (page 281)

Why did the Seljuk Empire collapse?

After Malik Shah died unexpectedly in 1092, the Seljuk Empire collapsed quickly. Weak rulers could not maintain it. Collapse was also due to the *Crusades*. Rulers in western Europe sent armies to capture the lands of ancient Palestine. These were places sacred to Christians.

The First Crusade began in 1095, and the Christian armies captured Jerusalem. They established a Latin Kingdom that lasted about a century. Eventually, the Turks gathered enough strength to fight back. They retook the city in 1187.

Just when the Crusades became less of a threat to the Muslim world, the Mongols moved in from the east. They were led by a brutal leader, Genghis Khan. They killed tens of thousands of people and overran huge stretches of territory. Baghdad was captured in 1258. The Mongols killed the last caliph and took control of the government from the Seljuk Turks.

2. What brought the Seljuk Empire to an end?

_____

_____

_____

Name _____ Date _____

Glossary **CHAPTER 11** Byzantines, Russians, and Turks Interact

alliances Agreements, usually for the sake of trade or protection
Balkans Region of southeastern Europe now occupied by Greece, Bulgaria, Albania, Romania, the European part of Turkey, and the former republics of Yugoslavia
banned Forbade completely; outlawed the use or practice of
civil law Law dealing with the rights of private citizens
clergy Officials of the church
confronts Faces; meets

converted Officially changed from one religion to another
Crusades Series of attempts made by Western rulers to capture the Holy Land
decline Weakening; lessening power
devotions Prayers and other acts of worship
heirs People, usually relatives, who inherit the power or holdings of those who died before them
idol Image or object used in worship

illiterate Unable to read or write
missionaries People who bring Christianity to others
patron Supporter
shah Persian word for "king;" title of some Persian and Turkish rulers
Slavic Relating to the Slavs
sultans Rulers of a Moslem country, especially what is now Turkey
tribute Payment made by a conquered people to its rulers

AFTER YOU READ

Terms and Names

A. Write the name or term in each blank that best completes the meaning of the paragraph.

patriarch
excommunication
iconoclasts
schism
icons

There were many reasons for the **1** _____ that occurred between the Eastern Orthodox Church and the Roman Catholic Church. One reason was leader of the Eastern Church, the **2** _____, had to be subject to the emperor. The authority of the emperor was tested when one emperor banned the use of **3** _____. These were important in the religious practices of eastern Christians. They were outraged when **4** _____ went into churches breaking these images. Another outrage occurred when a Roman pope ordered the **5** _____ of a Byzantine emperor.

B. Write the letter of the name next to the description that explains it best.

a. Hagia Sophia
b. Alexander Nevsky
c. Malik Shah
d. Vladimir
e. Yaroslav the Wise

____ **1.** Seljuk sultan
____ **2.** Grandson of Olga who ordered all his subjects to adopt Christianity
____ **3.** Church rebuilt by Justinian
____ **4.** Russian ruler who helped Kiev gain power
____ **5.** Russian noble who gained power in Moscow

Name _____ Date _____

AFTER YOU READ (cont.) *CHAP 11* Byzantines, Russians, and Turks Interact

Main Ideas

1. What was the importance of Constantinople?
_____
_____
_____

2. Describe the accomplishments of the emperor Justinian.
_____
_____
_____

3. What relationship did the Slavs have to the Vikings?
_____
_____
_____

4. Explain the changes that occurred in Russia during the rules of Ivan I and Ivan III.
_____
_____
_____

5. Explain the role the mamelukes played in the Abbasid Empire.
_____
_____
_____

Thinking Critically

Answer the following questions on a separate sheet of paper.

1. What influences combined to produce Russian culture?

2. Explain how the Turks eventually displaced both the Abbasids and the Byzantine Empire.

Name _____ Date _____

CHAPTER 12 Section 1 (pages 287–291)

Two Great Dynasties in China

TERMS AND NAMES
Tang Taizong Great emperor of the Tang Dynasty
Wu Zhao Tang ruler and only woman in China ever to assume the title of emperor
movable type Wood or metal blocks, each with a single character, that can be arranged to make up a page for printing
gentry Powerful upper class

BEFORE YOU READ

In the last section, you read about the Turkish empires.
In this section, you will read about changes in China during the Tang and Song Dynasties.

AS YOU READ

Use the web below to show developments during the Song Dynasty.

- agriculture
- science and technology
  movable type
  gunpowder
- trade
- **The Song Dynasty**
- art
- society

The Tang Dynasty Expands China (pages 287–288)

What *changes occurred during the Tang Dynasty?*

Starting in A.D. 220, China went through a long period of troubles. There were no strong rulers. China was not united. Then in 589, Sui Wendi brought order. He united the northern and southern regions. He also named himself the first emperor of the *Sui Dynasty*.

This dynasty lasted only about 30 years. Just two rulers reigned. Both were important. They built the *Grand Canal*. This waterway connected China's two major rivers. The canal was a trade route between northern and southern China. Cities were in the north. Areas that grew rice were in the south.

The *Tang Dynasty* followed. It lasted for 300 years. **Tang Taizong** was a mighty emperor. He and other Tang rulers made the empire larger. They gained back lands lost since the fall of the Han Dynasty. **Wu Zhao** was another great Tang leader. She was the only woman ever to rule China as emperor. During her reign, parts of Korea were added to the dynasty.

Early Tang rulers made the government stronger. They won support from the peasants.

CHAPTER 12 EMPIRES IN EAST ASIA **107**

Schools were set up to train people for political jobs. They had to pass tough tests. Only then could people work for the government.

By the mid-700s, the Tang Dynasty grew weaker. Rulers charged heavy taxes. The Chinese people faced more hardship. Invaders attacked the empire's lands. Chinese rebels became violent. In 907, they killed last Tang ruler.

1. How did Tang rulers change China?

_____

_____

_____

The Song Dynasty Restores China (pages 288–289)

What happened during the Song Dynasty?

The *Song Dynasty* replaced the Tang Dynasty. The Song Dynasty also lasted about 300 years. Its empire was smaller than the Tang. But China was still strong under Song rule.

This dynasty did have military troubles, though. Invaders forced the Song to move south. The dynasty of the Southern Song arose in 1127.

2. How was the Song Dynasty related to the Tang Dynasty?

_____

_____

_____

An Era of Prosperity and Innovation (pages 289–290)

What advances occurred during the Tang and Song periods?

During the Tang and Song rule, the Chinese made many advances. They invented useful things. **Movable type** made printing faster. Gunpowder was another important invention. It led to the design of exploding weapons. The Chinese made progress in farming, too. They improved ways of growing rice.

Trade increased under the Tang and Song emperors. Goods were carried over land routes. Later, ocean trade became important. Ideas were also exchanged. Buddhism spread. This religion traveled from China to Japan, Korea, and Vietnam.

The Tang and Song dynasties were creative periods. Great poets wrote about life. Artists made beautiful paintings.

3. Name three advances in technology.

_____

_____

_____

Changes in Chinese Society (page 291)

How did China change under the Tang and Song?

Chinese society changed during the Tang and Song periods. The old noble families lost power. Key officials in government gained power. They formed a new upper class. This wealthy group is called the **gentry.**

Next came the middle class. They lived in the cities. People such as store owners and traders belonged to this group. Below them were workers, soldiers, and servants. In country areas, peasants made up the largest class. The position of women became worse.

4. What social changes occurred in China during the Tang and Song periods?

_____

_____

_____

Name _____ Date _____

CHAPTER 12 Section 2 (pages 294–298)

The Mongol Conquests

TERMS AND NAMES
pastoralist Person who herds tamed animals
clan Large group of people related to a common ancestor
Genghis Khan Leader who brought together the Mongol clans

BEFORE YOU READ

In the last section, you read about the Tang and Song Dynasties.

In this section, you will read about rise and conquests of the Mongols.

AS YOU READ

Use the chart below to record facts about the Mongols and their empire.

Life as Nomads	Herded animals Lived on dry grassland
The Rise of the Mongols	
The Mongol Empire	

Nomads of the Asian Steppe
(pages 294–295)

How did the nomads of the Asian steppe live?

Much of Central Asia is covered by dry grassland. Such a region is called the *steppe*. Very little rain falls on the steppe. Only short hardy grasses grow in this dry region. It gets very cold in winter and very hot in the summer.

Herders lived in this area. They were **pastoralists.** They herded *domesticated* animals. The herders were *nomads.* They moved from place to place. They searched for grass to feed the sheep and goats.

Herders often rode on horseback. They traveled together in large groups. These groups formed **clans.** The clans made up of people related to a common ancestor.

The nomads often rode out from the steppes and made contact with the settled peoples who lived in towns and villages. Often they traded peacefully with one another. But sometimes the nomads attacked the villages and took what they wanted by force. A nomadic group, called the Mongols, became very powerful.

1. Name three characteristics of the nomads of the steppes.

_____

_____

_____

CHAPTER 12 EMPIRES IN EAST ASIA **109**

The Rise of the Mongols
(pages 295–296)

Who united the Mongols?

Around 1200, a leader tried to bring the Mongol clans together. His name was Temujin. In 1206, he took the title **Genghis Khan.** This means "universal ruler." Over the next 21 years, he ruled the Mongols. They conquered much of Central Asia, including China.

Genghis Kahn was a huge military success for these reasons. First, he organized his soldiers well. He followed the Chinese model of creating armies of 10,000 men. The armies were broken into brigades of 1,000 men, companies of 100 men, and platoons of 10 men.

Second, Genghis Khan was able to trick his enemies. He set traps for his opponents. He also used dummies to make his army look bigger than it was. And he used spies well.

Third, he used new weapons made by his enemies, such as the catapult. Finally, he used cruelty. His terror made many of enemies surrender.

2. Name four reasons for the success of the Mongols as conquerors.

_____

_____

_____

The Mongol Empire (pages 297–298)

How did the Mongol Empire spread and divide?

Genghis Khan died in 1227. His son, Ogadai, took control of the entire Mongol Empire. Ogadai became the Great Khan. His armies conquered China. They took parts of Korea. They invaded the city of Kiev in Russia. Mongol forces threatened Venice and Vienna in eastern Europe. Then Ogadai died in 1241. The conquests ended.

By 1260, the Mongol empire was divided into four areas. These were called *khanates*. Each was ruled by a descendant of Genghis Khan.

The Mongols destroyed many things in their invasions. Some towns were completely wiped out. They destroyed irrigation systems in the Tigris and Euphrates valleys. People could no longer live in some of those areas.

Over time, Mongol rulers borrowed from the cultures in the areas they ruled. Rulers in the west became Muslims. Those in China used Chinese inventions. Differences in culture split up the Empire.

The Mongols were able rulers. They brought about a long period of peace in Central Asia. Trade thrived. The exchange of ideas between Asia and Europe increased. However, the Mongols may have also brought the *bubonic plague* to Europe. In the 1300s, this deadly disease killed many people in Europe.

3. What were two effects of the Mongol empire on central Asia?

_____

_____

_____

Name _____   Date _____

CHAPTER 12 Section 3 (pages 299–302)

Empire of the Great Khan

> **TERMS AND NAMES**
> **Kublai Khan** Mongol leader and Chinese emperor
> **Marco Polo** Traveler from Venice who served Kublai Khan for 17 years

BEFORE YOU READ

In the last section, you read about the rise of the Mongols and their conquests.

In this section, you will read about the Mongol leader who became emperor of China.

AS YOU READ

Use this diagram to show the effects of Kublai Khan's rise to power and rule.

Effects of Kublai Khan's Rule

political	social	international
China united		

Kublai Khan Conquers China
(pages 299–300)

How did Kublai Khan rule China?

Genghis Khan began the conquest of China in 1215. His grandson, **Kublai Khan,** conquered all of China in 1279. He was the first foreigner to rule the whole country.

Kublai Khan became China's new emperor. He began the *Yuan Dynasty.* It ruled China for almost 100 years. This era was important. Kublai Khan united China for the first time in 300 years. He opened China to more foreign trade. The Mongols did not *disrupt* Chinese government or culture. Kublai Khan built a new capital. It was located in the modern city of Beijing.

The Mongols tried to conquer other lands. Kublai Khan attacked Japan in 1274 and 1281. The Mongols forced the Koreans to build and supply ships for the planned invasions. It was very expensive and almost ruined Korea. Both attacks failed because storms destroyed the Mongol fleets.

1. Why was the Yuan Dynasty important in Chinese history?

_____

_____

_____

CHAPTER 12 EMPIRES IN EAST ASIA **111**

Mongol Rule in China (pages 300–301)

What changes occurred under Mongol rule?

Mongol rulers were very different from the Chinese. The Mongols kept the top government jobs for themselves. They also hired many people from other lands for these posts. Mongol rulers did not trust the Chinese.

Kublai Khan was a great leader. He rebuilt the Great Canal. He helped foreign trade increase. Chinese goods—such as silk and porcelain—were in demand. West Asia and Europe wanted Chinese inventions. These included gunpowder and paper money.

Kublai Khan welcomed merchants from other countries to China. **Marco Polo** was a trader from Venice, Italy. He came to Kublai Khan's court around 1275. Polo learned several Asian languages and served under Kublai Kahn for 17 years. Polo traveled to different Chinese cities in his work for Kublai Khan.

Polo returned to Italy in 1292. He told amazing stories about his journeys. He described China's cities, riches, and customs. He also recorded the way the Khan's government worked. Later, Polo's tales were collected in a book. The book was popular in Europe.

2. How did Kublai Khan help China?

_____

_____

_____

_____

The End of Mongol Rule (pages 301–302)

How did Mongol rule end?

In the last years of his rule, Kublai Khan ran into trouble. Attacks on Southeast Asia failed. Many lives and much equipment were lost.

To pay for these wars, as well as public works and the luxuries enjoyed by the Yuan court, the Khan raised taxes. The Chinese resented the heavy burden these taxes placed on them.

Kublai Khan died in 1294. Afterward, Mongol leaders struggled for power. They fought over control of the empire. These fights weakened Mongol rule.

Rebellions broke out in many parts of China in the 1300s. In 1368, Chinese rebels took over the government. Mongol rule ended. The rebels set up a new dynasty. It was called the Ming.

By this time, the whole Mongol Empire was falling apart. Mongols lost control of Persia and Central Asia. The Mongols held on to Russia, though, until 1480.

3. Name two reasons why Mongol rule came to an end.

_____

_____

_____

_____

_____

Name _____ Date _____

CHAPTER 12 Section 4 (pages 303–307)

Feudal Powers in Japan

TERMS AND NAMES
Shinto Japan's earliest religion, based on respect for nature and ancestors
samurai Japanese warrior who served a lord
Bushido Code that samurai lived by—"the way of the warrior"
shogun Highest military commander in feudal Japan, ruling in the name of the emperor

BEFORE YOU READ

In the last section, you read about Mongol rule in China.

In this section, you will learn about the early Japanese and their system of government.

AS YOU READ

Use the chart below to take notes on the development of Japan.

Geography	Made up of islands
Early Religion	
Early Emperors	
Feudalism	

The Growth of Japanese Civilization (pages 303–304)

How did geography help shape Japan?

Japan benefited from its location. It was near China. Thus Chinese culture influenced Japan. However, there was enough distance between these two countries to prevent Chinese attacks.

Japan is made up of about 4,000 islands. They vary in size. Most people live on the four largest islands. The country has many mountains. There is not much good farmland. The islands have few natural resources, such as coal and oil.

Early Japan was broken up into many small areas. Each was controlled by a clan. These clans believed in their own gods. Later, all these beliefs became combined. They formed Japan's earliest religion, called **Shinto**. The main ideas of Shinto are respect for nature and ancestors.

In the 400s, the *Yamato clan* became the most powerful. The Yamato claimed that they were related to a sun goddess. By the 600s, Yamato leaders began to call themselves emperors. The emperor remained an important figure in Japan.

1. Who were the Yamato?

_____

_____

CHAPTER 12 EMPIRES IN EAST ASIA 113

The Japanese Adopt Chinese Ideas; Life in the Heian Period
(page 304–305)

How *did Chinese culture influence Japanese culture?*

By 500, contact between China and Japan grew. Japan became more aware of Chinese ways. Buddhism from China reached Japan. It became an important religion in Japan.

Japan's emperor sent people to China. They learned about the culture. The Japanese adopted the Chinese system of writing. Japanese artists imitated Chinese paintings. For a while, Japan even used China's government as a model. Yet Japan still held on to its own traditions.

From 794 to 1185, Japan's noble families ruled. This era is called the *Heian Period*. Heian was the new capital of the royal court. Japanese culture thrived there.

The gentleman and ladies of the court lived in splendor. Art and good manners formed the center of their lives. The best accounts of Heian society come from the writings of women of the court.

2. Name two parts of Chinese culture that Japan adopted?

_____
_____

Feudalism Erodes Imperial Authority (pages 305–307)

How *did feudalism arise in Japan?*

Over time, the power of ruling family members decreased. The central government grew weaker. Wealthy land owners lived away from the capital. They set up their own armies. These soldiers began to *terrorize* farmers.

In exchange for protection, farmers gave up some of their land to the lords. This is how the feudal system began in Japan. It was similar to the feudal system in Europe during the Middle Ages.

Each lord used a group of trained soldiers. They were called **samurai.** They protected their lord from attacks by other lords. Samurai followed a strict code of behavior. It was called **Bushido.** This word means "way of the warrior."

After a period of war, one of these lords arose as the most powerful. The emperor named him the **shogun.** This means "superior general of the emperor's army." The emperor remained in power in name. But the new shogun ran the country. This pattern continued in Japan from 1192 to 1868. Shoguns defended Japan against Mongol invaders from China.

3. Who were the samurai?

_____
_____

Japanese Samurai	European Knights
• Live by code of honor called Bushido, which values bravery and loyalty to their lord above all else. Will commit ritual suicide rather than face defeat or dishonor.	• Live by code of honor called chivalry, which values bravery and loyalty to heavenly God, earthly lord, and chosen lady. Code also demands that knights show humility.
• Fight for lord in exchange for an allowance.	• Fight for lord in exchange for land.
• Expect women to live up to same values of honor and courage.	• Regard women as weak creatures to be idolized and defended.
• Enter into battle with iron and leather armor, swords, and bows and arrows.	• Enter into battle with chain mail or plate armor, broadsword, and lance.

Skillbuilder
Use the chart to answer the questions.

1. Name two ways in which samurai and knights were alike.

_____

2. Name two ways in which samurai and knights were different.

_____

Name _____ Date _____

CHAPTER 12 Section 5 (pages 308–311)

Kingdoms of Southeast Asia and Korea

TERMS AND NAMES
Khmer Empire Empire that ruled what is now Cambodia
Angkor Wat Temple complex of the Khmer Empire
Koryu Dynasty Dynasty that ruled Korea from 935 to 1392

BEFORE YOU READ

In the last section, you read about early Japan and the rise of feudalism.

In this section, you will learn about smaller kingdoms in East and Southeast Asia.

AS YOU READ

Make a web like the one below. Use it to take notes on Southeast Asia and Korea.

- Srivijaya Empire
- Khmer Empire — *Main power on mainland Southeast Asia (800 to 1200)*
- Vietnam
- Korea under the Han
- Koryu Dynasty

(Center: **Southeast Asian Kingdoms**)

Kingdoms of Southeast Asia
(pages 308–310)

What was the Khmer Empire?

Southeast Asia lies between the Indian and Pacific oceans. It stretches from China to Australia. Southeast Asia includes mainland areas and many islands.

The region has never been united culturally or politically. Rivers and valleys cut through the mainland from north to south. Between the valleys are hills and mountains that make travel difficult in the region.

Political power in the area has often come from control of trade routes. Powerful lords charged high fees for the use of ports or safe passage on waterways. This worked well for local lords because Southeast Asia lies on the most direct sea route between the Indian Ocean and the South China Sea.

India and China had a great influence on Southeast Asia. Hindu and Buddhist missionaries spread their faiths. Kingdoms in the area followed these religions as well as Indian political ideas. Many Southeast Asian writers wrote in the Indian language of Sanskrit.

Chinese ideas spread to the area through trade and migration. Sometimes the Chinese exerted

CHAPTER 12 EMPIRES IN EAST ASIA **115**

political influence over the region.

From about 800 to 1200, the **Khmer Empire** was the main power. It was located on the mainland of Southeast Asia in what is now Cambodia. Growing rice was its chief source of wealth. The Khmer used large irrigation works to bring water to their fields. Rulers built huge temples and palaces. One of these is called **Angkor Wat.** It is among the world's greatest achievements in architecture.

At the same time, a dynasty called *Srivijaya* arose on Java. Java is an island. This dynasty reached its height from the 600s the 1200s. Nearby islands fell under its rule. The capital, Palembang, was located on Sumatra. Pelembang was a center for the study of Buddhism.

Vietnam fell under the influence of China. China controlled the area from about 100 B.C. to A.D. 900. Vietnam became independent in 939. The Vietnamese resisted three Mongol invasions. These failed conquests took place in the late 1200s.

The Vietnamese borrowed from Chinese culture. For example, Buddhism became important. The Vietnamese, though, kept their own culture. Women in Vietnam, for instance, had more rights than women in China.

1. What kingdoms arose in Southeast Asia?

_____
_____
_____

Korean Dynasties (pages 310–311)

How did China influence Korea?

Korea, like Japan and Vietnam, was influenced by China. Korea also preserved its own traditions. In 108 B.C., the Han Dynasty of China conquered Korea. Leaders set up a military government. From China, the Koreans learned about two religions—Buddhism and Confucianism. Koreans also learned about China's central government and system of writing.

Korean tribes began to gather into groups. One group, the Silla chased out the Chinese in the 600s and took control of the Korean peninsula.

The **Koryu Dynasty** ruled Korea from 935 to 1392. It had a government similar to China's. Korea used examinations to fill government jobs. But this did not keep wealthy landowners from controlling society. The dynasty, though, produced great works of art—including celadon pottery, fine poetry, and wood blocks to print the entire Buddhist canon.

Korea fell to the Mongols. They were under the Mongols until the 1350s. The Mongols demanded heavy taxes. The Koreans rebelled. The Mongols lost power. Then a new dynasty, the Choson, took over of Korea. It ruled for 518 years.

2. What was the Koryu Dynasty?

_____
_____
_____

116 CHAPTER 12 SECTION 5

Name _____ Date _____

Glossary CHAPTER 12 Empires in East Asia 600–1350

bubonic plague Deadly disease that struck Europe in the 1300s
disrupt Break up
domesticated Tamed for human use
Grand Canal Long waterway connecting China's major rivers and linking the north and south
Heian Period Time in Japanese history of great cultural achievement from 794 to 1195

khanates Four areas into which the Mongol empire was divided
nomads Groups who move from place to place
Song Dynasty Important and long-lasting Chinese dynasty that followed the Tang
Srivijaya Powerful island dynasty in Southeast Asia
steppe Large, dry area of grassland

Sui Dynasty Short-lived Chinese Dynasty that gave way to the Tang Dynasty
Tang Dynasty Important Chinese dynasty that followed the Sui Dynasty
terrorize Use of force or threats to frighten people
Yamato clan Powerful early Japanese clan
Yuan Dynasty Chinese dynasty founded by Kublai Khan

AFTER YOU READ

Names and Terms

A. Write the name or term in each blank that best completes the meaning of the paragraph.

Genghis Khan

Kublai Khan

Marco Polo

clans

pastoralists

The Mongol Empire arose on the grasslands of Asia. There, nomads lived as **1** _____. They moved from place to place in large family units called **2** _____. A ruler who adopted the name **3** _____ brought these groups together into one empire. He conquered China and central Asia. Later, his grandson, **4** _____, ruled China and founded the Yuan Dynasty. One important visitor to China at this time was the European traveler **5** _____ .

B. Write the letter of the name or term next to the description that explains it best.

a. Koryu Dynasty

b. Tang Taizong

c. Khmer Empire

d. Bushido

e. Wu Zhao

____ **1.** Early and brilliant emperor of the Tang Dynasty

____ **2.** Samurai code of honor

____ **3.** Korean dynasty

____ **4.** Tang emperor; only female emperor of China

____ **5.** Southeast Asian empire that ruled in the area now known as Cambodia

Name _____ Date _____

AFTER YOU READ (continued)   CHAPTER 12   Empires in East Asia

Main Ideas

1. Name three social changes that occurred in China during the Song Dynasty.

_____
_____
_____

2. How did Genghis Khan change the Mongols?

_____
_____
_____
_____

3. Why did the Mongol Empire fall?

_____
_____
_____

4. Expain Shinto and its main ideas.

_____
_____
_____
_____

5. What happened in Korea before the Koryu Dynasty?

_____
_____
_____

Thinking Critically

Answer the following questions on a separate sheet of paper.

1. Compare and contrast the Tang and Song Dynasties.

2. What was the relationship between a Japanese shogun and the emperor?

Name _____ Date _____

CHAPTER 13 Section 1 (pages 317–321)

Germanic Kingdoms Unite Under Charlemagne

TERMS AND NAMES
Middle Ages Period of European history from 500 to 1500
Franks Germanic people who held power in the Roman province called Gaul
monastery Religious community of people devoting their lives to worship and prayer
secular Concerned with worldly things
Carolingian Dynasty Dynasty of Frankish rulers, lasting from 751 to 987
Charlemagne Powerful Frankish ruler who built a huge empire

BEFORE YOU READ

In the last section, you read about Southeast Asian kingdoms and Korean dynasties.

In this section, you will read about the rise and fall of Charlemagne's empire.

AS YOU READ

Take notes on the time line below. Fill it in with key events related to the rise of Germanic kingdoms and Charlemagne's empire.

```
┌──────────────────┐        ┌──────────────────┐
│       496        │        │       771        │
│ Clovis and his   │        │                  │
│ warriors become  │        │                  │
│   Christian      │        │                  │
└──────────────────┘        └──────────────────┘
         │                           │
┌──────────────────┐        ┌──────────────────┐
│       590        │        │       800        │
│                  │        │                  │
└──────────────────┘        └──────────────────┘
```

Invasions Trigger Changes in Western Europe (page 317)

How did invasions by Germanic groups change Europe?

The slow decline of the Roman Empire marked the beginning of a new era in European history. This period is called the **Middle Ages**. It lasted from around 500 to 1500.

By the end of the fifth century, various Germanic groups invaded the Roman Empire in the west. These invasions led to a series of changes. Trade was halted. Moving goods from place to place became unsafe. Cities were no longer centers of trade and government. Many people then fled to the countryside. They returned to *rural* ways of life. People also became less educated.

As Germanic groups settled in different areas, they began to blend Latin with phrases of their own language. Many kinds of *dialects* developed. Europe no longer had a single language understood by all.

1. Name three effects of the Germanic invasions.

_____

_____

CHAPTER 13 EUROPEAN MIDDLE AGES **119**

Germanic Kingdoms Emerge
(page 318)

How did Europe change?

As Rome's power faded, a new kind of government appeared. Warring Germanic groups carved out kingdoms. The borders of these kingdoms changed often because of warfare. There was no central rule. Family ties and loyalty to a local leader bound Germanic peoples together. Europe was in *chaos*. The Church provided a sense of order, though.

The **Franks,** a Germanic people, established a large kingdom. It was located in the Roman province of Gaul. In 496, Clovis, the king of the Franks, and his warriors became Christian. From then on, the pope in Rome supported Clovis.

2. What new kind of government arose during Rome's decline?

_____

_____

Germanic Peoples Adopt Christianity (pages 318–319)

How did Christianity spread?

Other Frankish rulers helped spread Christianity. The Church also tried to convert people. It set up religious communities called **monasteries.** There Christian men called *monks* devoted their lives to God. *Nuns* were women who led this religious way of life. Monasteries became centers of learning. Their libraries preserved some writings of ancient Rome.

The Church grew in importance when Gregory I became pope in 590. He made the pope the *guardian* of the spiritual lives of all Christians. He also made the pope a worldly, or **secular,** power in governing part of Italy. Gregory used Church wealth to raise armies and fix roads. He took part in making peace treaties with invaders. His influence in politics grew.

3. What role did monasteries play during this period?

_____

_____

A European Empire Evolves
(pages 319–320)

How did the Carolingian Dynasty arise?

The kingdom of the Franks covered much of modern France. By the 700s, the most powerful official was the mayor of the palace. He made laws and controlled the army.

In 719, Charles Martel became mayor of the palace. He expanded the lands controlled by the Franks. He also won a battle in 732. He defeated a Muslim force moving north from Spain. This victory ended the Muslim threat to Europe and made Charles Martel a Christian hero.

His son, Pepin, was crowned king. Pepin began the reign of the Frankish rulers called the **Carolingian Dynasty.** One of Pepin's sons, **Charlemagne,** became king of the whole Frankish kingdom in 771.

4. Who were Charles Martel and Pepin?

_____

_____

Charlemagne Takes Center Stage (pages 320–321)

What did Charlemagne achieve?

Charlemagne had great military skill. He made his kingdom larger than any other known since ancient Rome. By 800, he held most of modern Italy, all of modern France, and parts of modern Spain and Germany. Pope Leo III crowned him emperor. This event marked the joining of Germanic power, the Church, and the *heritage* of the Roman Empire.

Charlemagne cut the power of the nobles in his empire and increased his own. He traveled throughout his lands, visiting the people and judging cases. He brought well-read men to his court and *revived* learning. However, Charlemagne's empire fell apart soon after his death.

5. What was important about Charlemagne's being crowned as emperor?

_____

_____

Name _____ Date _____

CHAPTER 13 Section 2 (pages 322–326)

Feudalism in Europe

BEFORE YOU READ

In the last section, you read about Charlemagne and his empire.

In this section, you will read about feudalism.

AS YOU READ

Use the chart below to take notes on feudalism

TERMS AND NAMES
lord Landowner
fief Land granted by a lord to a vassal
vassal Person receiving a fief from a lord
knight Warrior on horseback who promised to defend his lord's land in exchange for a fief
serf Peasant who could not lawfully leave the place where he or she was born
manor Lord's estate
tithe Church tax; usually one-tenth of a peasant family's income

BATTLE / POLITICAL ISSUE	EFFECT
Feudal relationships	• Lord promised land and protection to his vassal • Vassal helped his lord in battle
Social classes	
Manor system	

New Invasions Trouble Western Europe (pages 322–323)

Who invaded Western Europe?

Between 800 and 1000, new invasions threatened Europe. From the north came the most feared fighters of all. They were the Vikings, or Norsemen.

The Vikings raided villages and monasteries. By around the year 1000, though, the Vikings had settled down in many parts of Europe. They adopted Christianity and stopped raiding to become traders and farmers.

The Magyars were Turkish nomads. They attacked from the east and reached as far as Italy and western France. They sold local people as slaves. The Muslims struck from the south. They attacked areas along the Atlantic and Mediterranean coast.

The attacks by Vikings, Muslims, and Magyars made life in western Europe difficult. People suffered and feared for their futures. With no strong central government, they went to local leaders for protection.

1. Why did the people need to turn to local leaders for help?

Feudalism Structures Society
(pages 323–324)

How did feudalism affect society?

Europe's feudal system arose around the ninth and tenth centuries. Feudalism was based on an agreement between a **lord,** or landowner, and a **vassal,**

CHAPTER 13 EUROPEAN MIDDLE AGES **121**

a person who received land from a lord. In exchange for land, or a **fief,** a vassal promised to help his lord in battle.

Under feudalism, society in western Europe was divided into three groups. Those who fought were the nobles and **knights.** Those who prayed were the officials of the Church. Those who worked were the peasants. Peasants were by far the largest group. Most peasants were **serfs,** who were not free to move about as they wished. They were tied to the land of their lord.

2. What were the three main groups of feudal society?

_____

_____

Manors: The Economic Side of Feudalism (pages 325–326)

What was life like on a manor?

The lord's land was called the **manor.** Manors became the centers of economic life. The lord gave peasants some land, a home, and protection from raiders. The lord controlled much of their lives. The peasants worked the land to grow food, giving part of each year's crop to the lord. They paid taxes on their grain. Peasants also paid a tax, called a **tithe,** to the Church.

Peasants lived in small villages of 15 to 30 families. They produced almost everything they needed. Peasants rarely traveled far from their homes.

Life on the manor was often harsh. Peasants' cottages had just one or two rooms with only straw mats for sleeping. They had poor diets. Peasants *endured* these conditions. They believed that God had set their place in society.

3. What was the job of peasants on the manor?

_____

_____

_____

Skillbuilder

Use the diagram to answer the questions.

1. How are rank and position organized on this pyramid?

_____

_____

2. What members of feudal society are not represented on this chart?

_____

_____

Name _____   Date _____

CHAPTER 13 Section 3 (pages 327–331)

The Age of Chivalry

TERMS AND NAMES
chivalry Code of behavior for knights, stressing ideals such as courage, loyalty, and devotion
tournaments Staged battles for entertaining audiences and training knights
troubadours Poet-musicians at the castles and courts of Europe

BEFORE YOU READ

In the last section, you read how feudalism shaped society. In this section, you will read about the code of chivalry for knights and its influence.

AS YOU READ

Use the web below to take notes on knighthood during the Middle Ages.

- **Duties** — Fight battles
- **Equipment**
- **Knighthood**
- **Training**
- **Code of conduct**

Warriors on Horseback (page 327)
What was the role of knights?

Nobles were constantly at war with one another. They raised private armies. The armies included knights, soldiers who fought on horseback. These knights became the most important warriors during the Middle Ages.

By about the year 1000, nobles used their armies of *mounted* knights to fight over control of land. When nobles won battles, they gave some of the new land to their knights. The knights could use the wealth from this land to pay for weapons, armor, and horses. Knights devoted much of their time to improving their skill at fighting.

1. What was the main duty of knights?

_____

_____

Knighthood and Chivalry (page 328)
What was required of a knight?

By the 1100s, a new code of *conduct* for knights arose. This code of **chivalry** required that knights fight bravely for three masters: their lord, God, and their chosen lady. Knights were also required to protect the weak and poor. While the code set high standards, few knights met them. Most knights were harsh and cruel to peasants.

CHAPTER 13 EUROPEAN MIDDLE AGES **123**

The son of a noble began training to become a knight at an early age. At around age 7, his parents sent him off to the castle of another lord. There he would learn good manners. The boy would also practice fighting skills. At around age 14, he would become the servant of a knight. Then at age 21, he would finally become a knight himself.

Knights gained experience by fighting in staged combats called **tournaments.** These fights were fierce, but real battles, especially those fought at castles, were far more violent. To protect their lands and homes, nobles built stone castles.

2. **Give two examples of training for knighthood.**

The Literature of Chivalry (page 330)

What was the literature of chivalry about?

The literature about knights did not reflect real life. Many stories glorified castle life. Others centered on the code of chivalry. Songs and poems were often about a knight's loyalty to the woman he loved. Some long poems, called epics, told the story of legendary kings, such as King Arthur and Charlemagne.

Troubadours were poet-musicians at the castles and courts of Europe. They wrote and sang about the joys and sorrows of romantic love. Many troubadours traveled to the court of Eleanor of Aquitaine. She was the rich, powerful ruler of a land in southern France.

3. **Who were the troubadour's songs about?**

The Shifting Role of Women
(page 331)

How did the roles of women change?

The knights' ideals of love and devotion to a noble lady seemed to give women a high position in the society of the Middle Ages. In fact, the position of women actually worsened in this period. They were limited to working in the home or living in *convents.* Noble women could sometimes rule the land when their husbands were away from home. But they could not inherit land. It usually passed from father to son.

Most women during the Middle Ages, however, were poor. They held no power. They worked in the fields and took care of their families. Poor women struggled to survive—just as they had always done.

4. **What new limits did women of the upper class face?**

Name _____ Date _____

CHAPTER 13 Section 4 (pages 332–335)

The Church Wields Power

TERMS AND NAMES
clergy Religious officials
sacrament Important religious ceremony
canon law Law of the church
Holy Roman Empire Kingdom originally made up of what is now Germany and Italy
lay investiture Appointment of religious officials by kings or nobles

BEFORE YOU READ

In the last section, you read about knighthood and the literature of chivalry.

In this section, you will learn about power struggles between church leaders and political leaders.

AS YOU READ

Use the chart below to take notes on the authority of the Church.

CHURCH STRUCTURE	CHURCH JUSTICE
Different ranks of clergy—priests, bishops, pope	

The Scope of Church Authority
(pages 332–333)

How did the Church control most aspects of life?

With the central governments of Europe weak, the Church became the most important force in *unifying* European society. An early pope believed that God had made two areas of influence in the world—religious and political. The pope was in charge of spiritual matters. The emperor and other rulers were in charge of political affairs. Over the years, though, the difference was not so clear. Popes often tried to influence the actions of rulers, who *clashed* with them in struggles for power.

The Church established its own organization. It consisted of different ranks of **clergy,** or church officials. At the bottom were the priests who led services at local churches. Above them were bishops, who oversaw all the priests in a large area. At the top was the pope. He was the head of the Church.

The Middle Ages was an Age of Faith. People were bound together by their belief in God and the teachings of the Church. Though their lives were hard, Christians during this time hoped for *salvation*—eternal life in heaven. One path for achieving this goal was through the **sacraments.** These

CHAPTER 13 EUROPEAN MIDDLE AGES **125**

were important religious ceremonies.

The law of the Church, called **canon law,** was a set of standards that applied to all Christians during the Middle Ages. These standards guided such matters as marriage and religious practices. The Church also set up courts. People who broke canon law were put on trial.

Two punishments were especially harsh. If the Church *excommunicated* a person, he or she was out of the Church forever. The person was denied the chance for eternal life in heaven. Popes often used this power to threaten rulers. The other punishment was interdiction. When a ruler disobeyed the pope, the Church leader could place the land under *interdiction.* That meant that no sacred actions of the Church could officially take place there. The people of the area deeply feared this. They might then be doomed to eternal suffering in hell.

1. What powerful punishments could the Church hand down?

The Church and the Holy Roman Empire; Holy Roman Emperor Clashes with the Pope (pages 333–334)

What was the conflict between Pope Gregory VII and Henry IV?

The **Holy Roman Empire** was the strongest kingdom that arose from Charlemagne's fallen empire. The kingdom was mainly made up of what is now Germany and Italy. Henry IV was an emperor who ruled over this area. He and Pope Gregory VII became caught in a conflict.

For a long time, rulers had the power to name the bishops who led the Church in their lands. This power was known as **lay investiture.** In 1075, Pope Gregory VII *banned* this practice. Henry IV was angry. He persuaded his bishops to say that this pope had no real authority.

Gregory then excommunicated Henry. Henry's nobles supported Gregory. So Henry begged the pope for forgiveness. The pope forgave him.

The larger issue of excommunication was left open until 1122. Then an agreement stated that only the pope could name bishops. However, the emperor had the right to turn down any appointment he did not like.

2. Why did Henry IV beg Pope Gregory VII for forgiveness?

Renewed Church Conflicts Under Frederick I; German States Remain Separate (page 335)

Who was Frederick I?

In the late 1100s, a strong German king came to power. His name was Frederick I. He repeatedly invaded the cities of Italy but lost an important battle.

When Frederick died in 1190, his empire fell apart. It was broken up into feudal states. These German states did not unify during the Middle Ages.

3. What happened to the Holy Roman Empire after Frederick I's death?

Name _____ Date _____

Glossary — CHAPTER 13 European Middle Ages, 500–1200

chaos Complete disorder
conduct Behavior
convert Change to another religion
dialects Varieties of a language
endured Lived through; managed against odds
excommunicated Banished from the Church
guardian One who watches over the welfare of another
heritage Traditions passed down or received from the past
interdiction Church ruling prohibiting sacred actions of the Church from taking place in a certain area
banned Officially forbidden
monks Christian men devoted to a religious life
mounted On horseback
nuns Christian women devoted to a religious life
province Part of a country with its own government
revived Brought back
rural Having to do with the country
salvation Eternal life in heaven after death
unifying Bringing together

AFTER YOU READ

Names and Terms

A. Write the name or term in each blank that best completes the meaning of the paragraph.

vassal
serf
fief
knight
lord

The feudal system was based on an exchange. The **1** _____, or landowner, granted land to a person called a **2** _____. The land granted to him was his **3** _____. In return, that person gave the landowner military protection. This meant he might go into battle, performing the duties of a **4** _____. People who worked the land were mostly peasants. Among the peasants were many people who were not free to leave the land. The term used to describe one of these peasants is **5** _____.

B. Write the letter of the name or term next to the description that explains it best.

a. Franks
b. Holy Roman Empire
c. Carolingian Dynasty
d. Middle Ages
e. Charlemagne

____ **1.** Period of European history from 500 to 1500

____ **2.** A Frankish ruler who built a huge empire and unified Europe for the first time since the Roman Empire

____ **3.** Dynasty of Frankish rulers, lasting from 751 to 987

____ **4.** Germanic people who held power in the Roman province called Gaul

____ **5.** Empire established in the 10th century mainly consisting of what is now Germany and Italy

Name _____ Date _____

AFTER YOU READ (continued) CHAPTER 13 European Middle Ages

Main Ideas

1. Who was Clovis?
_____
_____
_____

2. Give three examples describing how Charlemagne ruled his empire.
_____
_____
_____
_____

3. Why was life on the manor often harsh for peasants?
_____
_____
_____
_____

4. What did the code of chivalry require?
_____
_____
_____
_____

5. How did Pope Gregory show his power in political affairs?
_____
_____
_____
_____

Thinking Critically
Answer the following questions on a separate sheet of paper.

1. How did invasions contribute to the beginning of the feudal system?

2. Why was the Church so important during in the Middle Ages?

Name _____ Date _____

CHAPTER 14 Section 1 (pages 341–346)

Church Reform and the Crusades

BEFORE YOU READ

In the last section, you read about the authority and role of the Church during the Middle Ages.

In this section, you will read about changes in the Church and the launching of the Crusades.

AS YOU READ

Use the diagram below to take notes on impact of the Age of Faith—a new age of religious feeling.

TERMS AND NAMES

simony Practice of selling positions in the church
St. Francis of Assisi Spiritual leader who gave up his own wealth and founded the Franciscan friars
Gothic Style of architecture of the cathedrals during the Middle Ages
Urban II Pope who called for the first Crusade
Crusade Campaign to regain the Holy Land
Saladin Famous Muslim leader of the 1100s
Richard the Lion-Hearted English king who fought Saladin in the Third Crusade
Reconquista Effort by Christian leaders to drive the Muslims out of Spain
Inquisition Church court that tried people suspected of having opposing religious beliefs

```
                 Effects of
               the Age of Faith
              /       |        \
    Changes in    Cathedrals    Crusades
    the Church
  • growth of monasteries
  • enforcement of
    Church laws
```

Monastic Revival and Church Reform (pages 341–342)

What changes did the Church undergo?

Starting in the 1000s, a new age of spiritual feeling arose in Europe. This era was called The Age of Faith. It led to many changes. The reform movement began with the founding of a *monastery*. It was located at Cluny in France. About 300 related monasteries were set up in Europe.

Many problems troubled the Church. Popes made reforms. They enforced Church laws. They tried to end certain practices. One was the marriage of priests. Another was **simony**, or the selling of positions in the Church.

In the early 1200s, a new Church group arose. They were called *friars*. They moved from place to place spreading the ideas of the Church. Friars owned nothing. They begged for food. **St. Francis of Assisi** was a very famous friar. He treated all creatures as his spiritual brothers and sisters. Women also played a role during the Age of Faith. Many entered convents to devote themselves to God.

1. What three developments in the Church showed the new spiritual feeling of the times?

_____

_____

CHAPTER 14 THE FORMATION OF WESTERN EUROPE **129**

Cathedrals—Cities of God (page 342)

How did the new cathedrals reflect the new Age of Faith?

The Age of Faith was shown in the building of great *cathedrals*. In the early 1100s, these huge churches were built in a new style of architecture. This style was called **Gothic.** The cathedrals were towering. They seemed to reach toward heaven. Light streamed in through colorful stained-glass windows.

2. What was the new style of church architecture?

_____

_____

The Crusades (pages 343–345)

Why were the Crusades fought?

Renewed faith also led to war. In 1093, the Byzantine emperor asked for help against Muslim Turks. They were threatening to conquer Constantinople. This city was his capital. Pope **Urban II** urged the leaders of Western Europe to begin a holy war—a **Crusade.** He wanted Christians to gain control of Jerusalem and the entire Holy Land. Rulers and the Church favored the Crusades. Both knights and common people joined the Crusades. Their motive was deep religious feeling.

The First Crusade began in 1096. It was badly organized. Yet the Crusaders still captured some of the Holy Land, including Jerusalem. Muslims won back some of this land. Then other Crusades followed. During the Second Crusade, the Muslim leader **Saladin** recaptured Jerusalem.

Three powerful European rulers led the Third Crusade. One was the English king. His name was **Richard the Lion-Hearted.** He fought Saladin. The two reached a *truce*. But the Crusades were not over.

The Fourth Crusade ended in disaster. In 1204, knights *looted* Constantinople. This helped make a lasting split between western and eastern Christian churches.

3. Why did people support the Crusades?

_____

_____

The Crusading Spirit Dwindles
(pages 345–346)

What happened to Muslims and Jews in Spain?

A later Crusade took place in Spain. Christian rulers tried to drive the Muslims out of Spain. This long fight was called the **Reconquista.** It lasted from the 1100s until 1492.

Thousands of Jews lived in Spain. During the late 1400s, many Spanish Jews and Muslims became Christians. Jewish and Muslim converts were suspected of *heresy*. They were believed to hold beliefs that differed from the teachings of the Church. Queen Isabella and King Ferdinand of Spain conducted the **Inquisition.** Suspects might be questioned for weeks and even tortured. Those who confessed were often burned at the stake.

The Crusades had many effects on Europe. The failure of later Crusades cut the pope's power. The deaths of many knights reduced the nobles' power. Contact with the East revived trade. The Christians' harsh treatment of Muslims in the Holy Land led to bitterness that has lasted to the present.

4. What was the Reconquista?

_____

_____

Name _____ Date _____

CHAPTER 14 Section 2 (pages 348–351)

Trade, Towns, and Financial Revolution

TERMS AND NAMES
three-field system Farmland divided into three equal-sized fields, in which crops were rotated
guild Group of people working at the same job
burgher Person who lived in a town
vernacular Everyday language
Dante Alighieri Italian author of *The Divine Comedy*
Geoffrey Chaucer English author of *The Canterbury Tales*
Thomas Aquinas Scholar who argued that the most basic religious truths could be proved by sound reasoning
scholastics Scholars who gathered and taught at universities

BEFORE YOU READ

In the last section, you read about the Crusades.
In this section, you will read about the rise of towns and trade.

AS YOU READ

Use the diagram below to take notes on changes occurring in towns and cities during the Middle Ages.

```
  [Agriculture]         [Trade]          [Finance]
  use of horses
           \              |              /
            \             |             /
             → [Towns and Cities Grow] ←
```

A Growing Food Supply (page 348)

Why did the food supply increase?

The climate in Europe became warmer between the years 800 and 1200. This helped farming. Farmers also developed better ways to produce crops. Horses pulled plows. Horses could do twice the work of oxens. A new harness made the use of horses possible.

Farmers also used a new method of rotating the crops planted in an area. They planted two-thirds of their fields, leaving one-third unplanted. This **three-field system** help farmers grow greater amounts of food.

1. Give three reasons why the food supply increased.

_____
_____
_____

Trade and Finance Expand (page 349)

Why did trade and finance increase?

Along with the growth in the food supply, trade and finance increased. Craft workers began to make goods. These goods were traded all over Europe. Towns held fairs each year. There merchants sold

CHAPTER 14 THE FORMATION OF WESTERN EUROPE **131**

cloth, food, leather, and other wares.

Supporting the fairs were new organizations—the **guilds.** They were made up of groups of workers who did the same job. As towns grew, craft guilds formed. These included bakers, tailors, and glass makers. Members set standards and prices for their products. They also made rules for young people learning the craft.

With more trade, merchants needed more cash. They had to borrow money to buy goods to sell. Christians didn't lend money. The Church had rules against charging a fee for loaning money. Jews, who were outside the Church, became the chief sources of loans. Later, the Church relaxed its rules. Then Christians began to form banks.

2. What were the guilds?

_____
_____
_____

Urban Splendor Reborn (pages 349–350)
Why did towns grow larger?

In the early 1100s, the population of western Europe grew quickly. Trade was booming. Towns grew larger and more important. Towns were dirty places, with narrow streets. Wooden houses in the towns were fire hazards.

Many peasants fled to the towns. After living there a year and a day, they became free. Other town *dwellers*, known as **burghers,** organized themselves. They demanded more rights.

3. Why did peasants move to the towns?

_____
_____
_____

The Revival of Learning (pages 350–351)
Why did learning spread?

Growing trade and wealth helped lead to a growing interest in education. New centers of learning arose in Europe. They were called universities.

At this time, most writers were still using Latin. However, some began to use the **vernacular.** This was their native, everyday language. **Dante Alighieri** wrote *The Divine Comedy* in Italian. **Geoffrey Chaucer** wrote *The Canterbury Tales* in English. These writers brought literature to many people.

During the Crusades, contact with Muslims helped increase learning. Muslim scholars had preserved books from ancient Rome and Greece. These works then became available in Europe.

Ancient writings influenced Christian thinkers, such as **Thomas Aquinas.** He reasoned that the most basic religious truths could be proved by logic. Aquinas and his fellow scholars met at the great universities. They were known as schoolmen, or **scholastics.**

4. How did the use of the vernacular help spread learning?

_____
_____
_____

132 CHAPTER 14 SECTION 2

Name _____ Date _____

CHAPTER 14 Section 3 (pages 352–355)

England and France Develop

BEFORE YOU READ

In the last section, you read about the growth of towns and trade.

In this section, you will read about the development of France and England.

AS YOU READ

Use the time line below to take notes on the development of France and England.

TERMS AND NAMES
William the Conqueror Duke of Normandy who invaded England in 1066 and claimed the English crown
Henry II English king who added to English holdings by marrying Eleanor of Aquitaine
Eleanor of Aquitaine Former Queen of France who became Queen of England through marriage to Henry II
Magna Carta Great Charter, which guaranteed certain basic political rights
parliament Body of representatives that makes laws for a nation
Philip II One of the most powerful Capetian kings
Louis IX Grandson of Philip II, who included commoners in a meeting to gain support of his policies

```
[987 Capetain dynasty of French kings begins.] — [1215] — [1302]
                    |                              |
                 [1066]                         [1295]
```

England Absorbs Waves of Invaders (pages 352–353)

Who invaded England?

England was formed by the blending of cultures. Danish Vikings invaded the island in the 800s. Some Germanic groups arrived there much earlier. Over time, the Vikings and Anglo-Saxons were united under one rule and kingdom.

In 1066, King Edward died. A power struggle followed. This led to one last invasion. The invader was **William the Conqueror.** He was the duke of Normandy, a land in northern France. He won control of England declared it his personal realm.

1. Who invaded England before the William the Conquerer?

_____

_____

_____

England's Evolving Government
(pages 353–354)

What were some of England's earliest steps toward democracy?

Later English kings, *descendants* of William, tried to hold and add to the land they still had in France.

CHAPTER 14 THE FORMATION OF WESTERN EUROPE **133**

They also wanted to increase their control over the government and the Church in England.

Henry II ruled from 1154 to 1189. He was one of the strongest of William's descendants. He married **Eleanor of Aquitaine,** who had been married to King Louis VII of France. From this marriage, Henry gained more territory in France. In England, he began the practice of trial by jury.

One of Henry's sons, King John, had serious problems. He was a poor military leader. His harsh rule caused nobles to rebel against him. In 1215, they forced John to sign an important paper called the **Magna Carta.** It put limits on the power of the king. The document protected the power of nobles only. Common people, though, said that parts of the Magna Carta also applied to them.

Another step toward limiting the king came in the 1200s. Edward I needed to raise taxes for a war against the French. He called a meeting of representatives from all parts of England. It was called a **parliament.** The purpose of this meeting was approve his tax plan. His *Model Parliament* met in 1295. Bishops, nobles, and common people attended.

2. Why was the Magna Carta important?

_____

_____

_____

Capetian Dynasty Rules France
(pages 354–355)

What was the Capetian Dynasty?

In France, a new dynasty of kings came to power. They were called the Capetians. They were named for the first of these rulers, Hugh Capet, who had been a duke from the middle of France. This dynasty ruled from 987 to 1328.

France was split into 30 separate small territories. Each was ruled by a different lord. The kings held only a small area centered in Paris. They tried to gain control of all the land. Gradually, the growth of royal power would unite France.

One of the most successful kings was **Philip II.** He ruled from 1180 to 1223. He tripled the lands under his control. He also made a stronger central government. This gave the king more control over his subjects.

His grandson, **Louis IX,** ruled from 1226 to 1270. He carried on Philip's work. Louis set up royal courts. There, people could appeal their lords' decisions. These courts increased the king's power. In 1302, Philip IV called for a meeting of representatives. Like Edward I in England, Philip invited common people. This meeting was called the *Estates General.*

3. How did the kings of France gain more control over their subjects?

_____

_____

_____

_____

134 CHAPTER 14 SECTION 3

Name _____ Date _____

CHAPTER 14 Section 4 (pages 356–361)

A Century of Turmoil

BEFORE YOU READ

In the last section, you read about developments in the governments of France and England.

In this section, you will learn about the plague, religious conflict, and war between England and France.

AS YOU READ

Use the time line to take notes on the events of the 1300s and first half of the 1400s.

TERMS AND NAMES

Avignon City in France where the pope moved temporarily

Great Schism Division in the Church created by having popes in both Avignon and Rome

John Wycliffe English scholar who argued that the Bible was the final authority for Christian life

John Huss Bohemian scholar who taught that the Bible was the final authority for Christian life

bubonic plague Deadly disease that spread across Asia and Europe in the mid-14th century

Hundred Years' War War between England and France waged from 1337 to 1453

Joan of Arc English peasant who led the French army to victory at Orléans

[Timeline: 1300's Pope moves to Avignon — 1305 — 1337 — 1378 — 1429 — 1453]

A Church Divided (pages 356–357)

How was the Church divided?

In 1300, the pope said he had supreme authority over King Philip IV of France. Philip would not obey him. He held the pope prisoner. Philip planned to put him on trial. The pope was rescued but died soon after. The king then forced the election of a French cardinal as pope. In 1305, the new pope moved to **Avignon,** a city in France. There, the new pope was to lead the Church. This action weakened the Church.

In 1378, the French pope at that time died. An Italian was elected the next pope. But the French elected their own pope. Confusion resulted. Church officials had two popes, one in France and the other in Rome. This situation, called the **Great Schism,** lasted 39 years.

At the same time, the pope's authority was challenged. The English scholar **John Wycliffe** and the Bohemian **John Huss** argued that the Bible, not the pope, was the final authority for Christian teaching.

1. What created the Great Schism?

_____

_____

CHAPTER 14 THE FORMATION OF WESTERN EUROPE **135**

The Bubonic Plague Strikes
(pages 357–359)

What happened when the plague struck?

People of the late 1300s experienced an even greater shock than the schism in the Church. A deadly disease—the **bubonic plague**—struck. It swept across Europe. The plague started in 1347. It lasted for decades. Millions of people died. The disease wiped out about one-third of Europe's population.

The plague affected Europe's economy. Trade declined, and prices rose. Towns became smaller. Fewer people meant fewer workers. Peasants demanded wages or their freedom. When nobles resisted these demands, peasants often revolted.

The Church lost *prestige* because it could not stop the plague. Art and literature from the period showed a deep awareness of death. People tended to be *pessimistic* and fearful of the future. The plague helped bring an end to the Middle Ages.

2. Name three effects of the plague.

_____

The Hundred Years' War (pages 359–361)

Why was the Hundred Years' War fought?

A century-long war also helped bring the Middle Ages to an end. The last Capetian king of France died in 1328. He left no *heirs*. Edward III of England claimed the throne. In 1337, he began a war to win control of France. This conflict is known as the **Hundred Years' War.**

English forces won three important battles. At one, their archers used longbows. These weapons launched arrows that killed one-third of the French troops—even armored knights.

By 1429, France was desperate. The French army held the town of Orléans. But England was about to capture it. A teenage peasant girl named **Joan of Arc** arrived on the scene. She led the army of France to victory. Then the French crowned a new king, Charles VII. Later, Joan was captured in battle by *allies* of the English. She was turned over to Church authorities. She was tried as a witch and burned at the stake.

The Hundred Years' War finally ended in 1453. Most of the fighting took place in France. The war brought France much suffering. However, the war produced a strong national feeling in both England and France. It provided the sense that the king was not just a feudal lord. He was also the leader of a nation.

3. What role did Joan of Arc play in the Hundred Years' War?

_____

_____

_____

The Development of England and France

England	France
• William the Conqueror, duke of Normandy, invades England in 1066.	• Hugh Capet establishes Capetian Dynasty in 987, which rules until 1328.
• Henry II (ruled 1154–1189) introduces use of the jury in English courts.	• Philip II (ruled 1180–1223) increases the territory of France.
• Under pressure from his nobles, King John agrees to Magna Carta in 1215.	• Louis IX (ruled 1226–1270) strengthens France's central government.
• Edward I calls Model Parliament in 1295.	• Philip IV (ruled 1285–1314) adds Third Estate to Estates General.

Skillbuilder
Use the chart to answer the questions.

1. Which English King signed one of the most important documents in English history?

_____

_____

2. What is similar about Edward I's and Philip IV's actions?

_____

_____

Name _____ Date _____

Glossary   CHAPTER 14 The Formation of Western Europe

allies Those who joined in a close relationship, often for national protection
cathedrals Large, towering churches
descendants People who come from a common family
dwellers People who live in a certain place
Estates General A meeting of representatives in 1302, called by Philip IV of France
friars Members of a Church religious order who owned nothing and begged for food
heirs People who inherit the power of another
heresy Beliefs differing from the teachings of the Church
looted Robbed
monastery Religious community of monks
Model Parliament A meeting of representatives in 1295, called by Edward I of England
pessimistic Tending to think or believe negative thoughts
prestige High position or status
truce Temporary end of fighting

AFTER YOU READ

Names and Terms

A. Write the name or term in each blank that best completes the meaning of the paragraph.

scholastics

Geoffrey Chaucer

vernacular

Thomas Aquinas

Dante Alighieri

As towns and trade were reborn, learning was revived. One reason for this revival was that some great authors began to write in their own everyday language instead of in Latin. The use of the **1** _____ enabled more people to read their works. For example, **2** _____ wrote *The Divine Comedy* in Italian. **3** _____ wrote *The Canterbury Tales* in English. At this time, ancient thinkers influenced Christian thinkers. The scholar **4** _____ developed an argument about the nature of religious truth. He and his fellow thinkers who met at the great universities of the day were known as the **5** _____.

B. Write the letter of the name or term next to the description that explains it best.

a. John Wycliffe

b. William the Conqueror

c. Henry II

d. Saladin

e. Urban II

____ **1.** Muslim leader who fought in the Crusades

____ **2.** Pope who called for Europe to begin a holy war

____ **3.** Duke of Normandy who conquered England in 1066

____ **4.** Scholar who taught that the Bible was the final authority for Christian life

____ **5.** English king who married Eleanor of Aquitaine

Name _____ Date _____

AFTER YOU READ (cont.) CHAP 14 The Formation of Western Europe

Main Ideas

1. What started the Crusades?
   _____
   _____

2. Why, when, and where did the Inquisition take place?
   _____
   _____

3. Why did Jews become the chief sources of loans?
   _____
   _____

4. Why was the Model Parliament important?
   _____
   _____

5. Why was the Hundred Years' War fought?
   _____
   _____

Thinking Critically

Answer the following questions on a separate sheet of paper.

1. Discuss the effects of the Crusades.

2. What do you think was the most serious problem affecting Europe in the 14th century? Explain your answer.

Name _____ Date _____

CHAPTER 15 Section 1 (pages 367–370)

North and Central African Societies

BEFORE YOU READ

In the last section, you read about disasters in Europe during the 1300s.

In this section, you will read about various societies that arose in North and Central Africa.

AS YOU READ

Use the web below to take notes on the different societies that developed in North and Central Africa.

TERMS AND NAMES
lineage Group of people descended from a common ancestor
stateless societies Societies without central governments
patrilineal Tracing ancestry though the father
matrilineal Tracing ancestry though the mother
Maghrib Part of North Africa that is today the Mediterranean coast of Morocco
Almoravids Islamic group that established an empire in North Africa and southern Spain during the 11th century
Almohads Islamic group that overthrew the Almoravids in the 12th century

Hunting-Gathering
Men hunt animals. Women collect plant foods.

North and Central African Societies

Muslim

Stateless

Hunting-Gathering Societies
(pages 367–368)

What is life like for hunter-gatherers?

People in early African societies depended on hunting and gathering for their food supply. Some societies, such as the Efe, still use these methods today. The Efe live in central Africa. They live in groups of around 50 people. All members of the groups are related to one another. Each family has its own shelter. It is made of grass and brush. The Efe move often in search for food. That is why they keep few belongings.

Women gather plant foods. They look for roots, yams, mushrooms, and wild seeds. These are found in the forest. Men and older boys hunt animals. Sometimes they form groups to hunt. At other times, a hunter goes alone. He uses a poison-tipped arrow as a weapon. Efe men also collect honey.

An older male leads the group. But he does not give orders or act like a chief. Each family makes its

CHAPTER 15 SOCIETIES AND EMPIRES OF AFRICA **139**

own decisions. Families, though, do ask the leader for his advice.

1. How do the Efe get food?

_____

_____

_____

Stateless Societies (pages 368–369)

What are stateless societies?

Family organization is important in African society. In many African societies, families form groups called **lineages.** Members of a lineage believe that they are all descended from a common ancestor. Lineage also includes relatives of the future. These are the children who are not yet born.

Lineage groups sometimes take the place of rulers. They do not have central governments. Such societies are called **stateless societies.** Power in these societies are spread among more than one lineage. This prevents any one family from having too much control and power. Members of a stateless society usually try to get along with one another. They want to share power.

The Igbo people are from southern Nigeria. They first began living in a stateless society in the 800s. Sometimes there were disagreements within an Igbo village. Then the older members from different villages would meet. Together they would solve the problem.

In **patrilineal** societies, lineages are traced through fathers. In **matrilineal** societies, lineages are traced through mothers.

In some societies, children of similar ages belong to groups called age sets. All members of the *age set* take part in ceremonies. These rites mark the movement from one stage of life to the next. Men and women have different life stages.

2. How does lineage help balance the power in some stateless societies?

_____

_____

_____

Muslim States (pages 369–370)

How did Islam spread in north Africa?

Islam was an important influence on African history. Muslims came to northwest Africa in the 600s. By 670, Muslims ruled Egypt. They entered the **Maghrib,** a part of North Africa. This area today is the Mediterranean coast of Morocco, Tunisia, and Algeria.

In their new states, the Muslims set up *theocracies*. In them, the ruler served as both political and religious leader. The Islamic tradition of obeying the law was important. It helped promote order in the government. The common influence of Islamic law also set up ties between the different North African states.

The *Berbers* were a group of North Africans. They *converted* to Islam. In the 11th century, a group of Berbers devoted themselves to spreading Islam. They were called the **Almoravids.** They had many conquests. They conquered modern Morocco, the empire of Ghana, and parts of Spain.

The **Almohads** were another group of Berbers. They overthrew the Almoravids in the 1100s. The Almohads also captured Morocco and then Spain. Their empire reached east to the cities of Tripoli and Tunis. This empire lasted about 100 years. Then it broke up into smaller states.

3. Who were the Berbers?

_____

_____

_____

Name _____ Date _____

CHAPTER 15 Section 2 (pages 371–377)

West African Empires and Civilizations

BEFORE YOU READ

In the last section, you read about societies in North and Central Africa.

In this section, you will read about kingdoms in West Africa.

AS YOU READ

Use the chart below to take notes on the kingdoms and states of West Africa.

TERMS AND NAMES
Ghana West African empire that grew rich from trade
Mali West African empire that grew rich from trade
Sundiata Founder and first emperor of the kingdom of Mali
Mansa Musa Mali ruler who created a large kingdom and adopted Islam
Ibn Battuta 14th century traveler who visited most of the Islamic world
Songhai West African empire that conquered Mali
Hausa West African people who lived in several city states of what is now northern Nigeria
Yoruba West African people who formed several kingdoms in what is now Benin
Benin Kingdom that arose near the Niger River delta and became a major West African state

Ghana	Gained wealth through gold and taxing trade.
Songhai	
Mali	
Benin	
Other States	

Ghana: Land of Gold (pages 371–373)

How did the kingdom of Ghana arise?

Traders crossed the Sahara Desert of North Africa as early as A.D. 200. The desert was harsh. This limited trade. Then the Berbers began using camels. Trade increased.

By the 700s, the rulers of the kingdom of Ghana were growing rich. They taxed the goods that traders carried through their land. The two most important trade goods were gold and salt. Gold was taken from mines and streams in the western and southern parts of West Africa. It was traded for salt from the Sahara region. Arab traders also brought cloth and manufactured goods. These came from cities on the Mediterranean Sea.

The king of Ghana was powerful. Only the king

CHAPTER 15 SOCIETIES AND EMPIRES OF AFRICA **141**

could own *gold nuggets*. He was the religious, military, and political leader. By the year 800, Ghana had become an empire. It controlled the people of nearby lands.

Over time, Muslim merchants and traders brought their religion to Ghana. By the 1000s, the kings converted to Islam. Many common people in the empire, though, kept their traditional beliefs. Later, Ghana fell to the Almoravids of North Africa. Ghana never regained its former power.

1. What goods were traded in Ghana?

_____

_____

Empire of Mali (pages 373–374)
How did Mali rise to power?

By 1235, a new kingdom began—**Mali.** It arose south of Ghana. Mali's wealth and power were also based on the gold trade. **Sundiata** became Mali's first emperor. He was a great military and political leader.

Later Mali rulers adopted Islam. One of them was **Mansa Musa.** He made Mali twice the size of the old empire of Ghana. To rule this large empire, he named governors to head several *provinces*. Mansa Musa was a devoted Muslim. He built *mosques* in two cities. One was Timbuktu. It became a leading center of Muslim learning.

Ibn Battuta was a later traveler to the area. He described how peaceful Mali was. Mali, though, declined in the 1400s. Mali was replaced by another empire that grew wealthy from gold.

2. What did Mansa Musa achieve?

_____

_____

Empire of Songhai (pages 374–375)
How did Songhai arise?

The next trading empire was **Songhai.** It was farther to the east than Mali. Sonhgai arose in the 1400s. It had two great rulers. One was Sunni Ali. He gained control of new areas. His conquests included the city of Timbuktu.

Songhai's other great ruler was Askia Muhammad. He was a devoted Muslim. He ran the government well.

The Songhai Empire fell, however. Its army lacked modern weapons. In 1591, Moroccan troops used gunpowder and cannons to beat Songhai soldiers. They had only swords and spears. This defeat ended the period when empires ruled West Africa.

3. Why did Songhai fall?

_____

_____

Other Peoples of West Africa (pages 375–377)
What other states and kingdoms arose?

In other parts of West Africa, city-states developed. The **Hausea** people lived in the region that is now northern Nigeria. Their city-states first arose between the years 1000 and 1200. The Hausea rulers depended on farmers' crops. They also relied on trade goods. These included salt, grain, and cotton cloth.

The **Yoruba** people also first lived in city-states. These were located in what is now Benin and southwestern Nigeria. Over time, some of the small Yoruba communities joined together. Many Yoruba kingdoms were formed. Yoruba people believed their kings were gods.

The kingdom of **Benin** arose in the 1300s. It was located near the delta of the Niger River. In the 1400s, a ruled named Ewuare led Benin. He made the kingdom more powerful. During his reign, Benin became a major West African state. He strengthened Benin City, his capital. High walls surrounded the city. The huge palace contained many works of art.

In the 1480s, trading ships from Portugal came. They sailed into a major port of Benin. Their arrival was historic. It marked the start of a long period of European involvement in Africa.

4. What was important about Benin?

_____

_____

Name _____ Date _____

CHAPTER 15 Section 3 (pages 378–381)

Eastern City-States and Southern Empires

TERMS AND NAMES
Swahili Language that is a blend of Arabic and Bantu
Great Zimbabwe City that grew into an empire built on the gold trade
Mutapa Southern African empire established by the leader Mutota

BEFORE YOU READ

In the last section, you read about West African kingdoms and states.

In this section, you will read about East African city-states and southern African empires.

AS YOU READ

Use the chart below to take notes on East Africa and southern Africa from 1000 to 1500.

East Coast Trade Cities	Swahili arose.
Great Zimbabwe	
Mutapa Empire	

East Coast Trade Cities
(pages 378–379)

What cultures blended in East Africa?

The east coast of Africa became a region where cultures blended. Africans speaking Bantu languages moved to this area from central Africa. Muslim Arab and Persian traders settled in port cities along the coast. A new blended language formed. It was called **Swahili.**

Arab traders sold *porcelain* bowls from China. They sold jewels and cotton cloth from India. They bought ivory, gold, and other African goods. The traders took these goods back to Asia. By 1300, trade was *thriving* in over 35 cities on the coast. Some cities also manufactured products for trade. These goods included woven cloth and iron tools.

Kilwa was one of the richest trading ports. It was located far to the south. Trade goods from southern lands passed through Kilwa.

In 1497, though, the situation changed. Ships arrived on the east coast of Africa from Portugal. Portuguese sailors were looking for a route to India. They wanted to join in the trade for spices and other goods desired in Europe. Soon the Portuguese attacked Kilwa. They also attacked other trading centers along the East African coast.

CHAPTER 15 SOCIETIES AND EMPIRES OF AFRICA **143**

For the next two centuries, the Portuguese remained a powerful force in the region.

1. Why did Kilwa become an important center of trade?

_____

_____

Islamic Influences
(pages 379–380)

How did Muslim traders influence East Africa?

On the east coast of Africa, contact with Muslim traders grew. This resulted in the spread of Islam. A *sultan*, or governor, ruled each city. Most government officials and wealthy merchants were Muslims. As in West Africa, though, most common people kept their traditional beliefs.

Muslim traders also sold slaves from the East African coast. These slaves were brought to markets in areas such as Arabia and Persia. Some slaves did household tasks. Other were sent to India to be soldiers. This slave trade was still small. Only about 1,000 slaves a year were traded. The later European-run slave trade was much larger.

2. Describe the Muslim slave trade.

_____

_____

Southern Africa and Great Zimbabwe (pages 380–381)

What empires arose in Southern Africa?

In southern Africa, a great city-state arose in the 1000s. The Shona people grew crops in their rich land. The also raised cattle. Their city, **Great Zimbabwe,** linked the gold fields inland with the trading cities on the coast. From the 1200s through the 1400s, the city controlled this trade. The city grew wealthy.

Around 1450, though, the people left the city. No one knows why. One explanation is that overuse had destroyed the grasslands, soil, and timber. About 60 acres of ruins remain. The ruins include stone buildings. A high wall carved with figures of birds also still stands.

The **Mutapa** Empire followed. It began around 1420. A man named Mutota left the area. He moved farther north looking for salt. Mutota and his successors took control of a large area. It was almost all of the land of the modern Zimbabwe. This empire gained wealth from its gold. The rulers forced conquered to mine the gold. The southern region of the empire formed its own kingdom.

In the 1500s, the Portuguese moved in. They failed to conquer the empire. Later, through political schemes, they took over the government.

3. What happened to Great Zimbabwe around 1450?

_____

_____

TRADE GOODS

Raw Materials	Point of Origin	Products Made
• leopard skins	• savanna region	• saddles
• tortoiseshell	• shells of hawksbill sea turtles	• combs
• gold	• mines in southern Africa	• coins, jewelry
• ivory	• tusks from elephants in savanna region	• carved chess pieces and sword hilts

Skillbuilder
Use the chart to answer the questions.

1. Which raw materials came from South African mines?

_____

2. What do most of the raw materials have in common?

_____

Name _____ Date _____

Glossary — CHAPTER 15 Societies and Empires of Africa, 800–1500

age sets Groups of similar ages who take part in the same ceremonies
Berbers North African Muslims
converted Officially changed from one religion to another
dominating Taking control
gold nuggets Small lumps of gold
Kilwa Key East African trading port, especially for trade from India
mosques Islamic houses of worship
porcelain Fine pottery
provinces Divisions of a country
successors Leaders who replace others in charge
sultan Muslim ruler
theocracy Government controlled by a religious leader
thriving Busy and growing

AFTER YOU READ

Names and Terms

A. Write the name or term in each blank that best completes the meaning of the paragraph.

Mali
Songhai
Ibn Battuta
Ghana
Sundiata

Three powerful empires arose in West Africa. The first of these was **1** _____. This empire grew rich from taxing the trade goods that went through its territory. Much later, the empire of **2** _____ arose. The powerful leader **3** _____ became its first emperor. **4** _____, an Islamic traveler, described this great kingdom as peaceful. The last of the great empires to arise was **5** _____. It fell to a Moroccan army.

B. Write the letter of the name or term next to the description that explains it best.

a. Almohads
b. Almoravids
c. Mutapa
d. Maghrib
e. Swahili

____ 1. Part of North Africa that is today the Mediterranean coast of Morocco, Tunisia, and Algeria

____ 2. Arabic-influenced blended language that is used widely in eastern and central Africa

____ 3. Islamic reformers who overthrew the Almoravids to establish an empire in North Africa and southern Spain

____ 4. Southern African empire established by Mutota

____ 5. Islamic brotherhood that spread Islam in North Africa and southern Spain

Name _____ Date _____

AFTER YOU READ (cont.)   CHAPTER 15 Societies and Empires of Africa, 800–1500

Main Ideas

1. What is a stateless society, and how are decisions made in this type of society?
   _____
   _____

2. What role did the Almoravids and Almohads play in North Africa?
   _____
   _____

3. Who were the Hausa and Yoruba?
   _____
   _____

4. Describe the trade that took place in east coast trade cities.
   _____
   _____

5. What was the Mutapa Empire?
   _____
   _____

Thinking Critically

Answer the following questions on a separate sheet of paper.

1. What common feature linked the kingdoms and empires of West Africa?

2. How does Swahili reflkect the blending of cultures in East Africa?

146 CHAPTER 15 REVIEW

Name _____ Date _____

CHAPTER 16 Section 1 (pages 391–394)

Diverse Societies of North America

BEFORE YOU READ

In the last section, you read about diverse societies in Africa.

In this section, you will read about diverse societies in North America.

AS YOU READ

Use the chart below to take notes on Native American societies.

TERMS AND NAMES

potlatch Ceremonial giving practiced by some Native American societies in the Pacific Northwest

Anasazi Early Native American people who lived in the Southwest

pueblos Villages of large apartment-like buildings made of clay and stone by peoples of the American Southwest

Mississippian Related to the mound-builder culture that flourished in North America between A.D. 800 and 1500

Iroquois Native American peoples from the Eastern Great Lakes region of North America who formed an alliance in the late 1500s

totems Animals or other natural objects that serve as symbols of clans or other groups

Pacific Northwest
Resources—sea and forest
Potlatch ceremony

Native American Societies

Complex Societies Build Trade
(pages 391–393)

Where did different Native American societies arise?

Between about 40,000 and 12,000 years ago, hunter-gatherers moved from Asia to North America. (At that time the two continents had a land connection.) These were the first Americans. They spread throughout North and South America. They had many different ways of life, each suited to the place where they lived.

The Pacific Northwest stretches from modern Oregon to Alaska. The peoples who lived there used the rich resources of the region. The sea was the most important of these resources. The people there hunted whales. They also gathered food from the forests on the coast. The people of the Northwest Coast developed societies in which differences in wealth led to the creation of social classes. From time to time, they performed a ceremony called the **potlatch.** In this ceremony, wealthy families could show their rank and prosperity by giving food, drink, and gifts to the community.

CHAPTER 16 PEOPLE AND EMPIRES IN THE AMERICAS **147**

The peoples of the Southwest faced a harsh environment. The *Hohokam* people *irrigated,* or watered, their crops. Their use of pottery and baskets showed that they had contact with the Mesoamerican people to the south.

The **Anasazi** lived where the present-day states of Utah, Arizona, Colorado, and New Mexico meet. They built groups of houses in the shallow caves that broke up the rocky walls of deep canyons. By the 900s, the Anasazi were living in pueblos. **Pueblos** were villages with large, apartment-style groupings. They were made of stone and clay baked in the sun. The Anasazi did not have horses, mules, or the wheel. They relied on human power to make their pueblos. They had small windows to keep out the hot sun. One of the largest pueblos had more than 600 rooms and probably housed about 1,000 people.

Many Anasazi pueblos were abandoned around 1200. Later peoples—including the Hope and Zuni—living in this area continued the traditions of the Anasazi.

In the woods east of the Mississippi River, another culture arose. These people are called the *Mound Builders*. They built large mounds of earth that were filled with copper and stone artwork. When seen from above, some mounds revealed the shapes of animals. The **Mississippians** were a people who lived later in this area. They built thriving villages, such as Cahokia. In the center of Cahokia was a flat-topped pyramid with a temple on top.

The peoples of the eastern woodlands had many different cultures and spoke many different languages. They often fought for control of land. Some groups formed *alliances* to put an end to this fighting. The most successful of these alliances was set up in the late 1500s by the **Iroquois** and was called the Iroquois League. The league linked five tribes in upper New York and lasted about 200 years.

1. **Explain the cultural differences between the Anasazi and the Mississippians.**

   _____
   _____
   _____
   _____

Cultural Connections (pages 393–394)

How were Native American groups similar culturally?

These North American groups had some common features. Trade linked people of all regions of North America. Religious ideas were similar across the continent as well. Nearly all native North Americans thought that the world was full of spirits and that people had to follow certain *rituals* and customs to live in peace. Native Americans also shared great respect for the land, which they did not believe that people could own.

They also shared an emphasis on the family as the most important social unit. Family included parents, children, grandparents, and other relatives. In some tribes, families were linked together with others who shared a common ancestor. These larger groups are called *clans*. Clans were often identified with a **totem.** A totem is a natural object or animal that a person, clan, or family uses to show its identity.

2. **Name three features shared by Native American groups.**

   _____
   _____
   _____
   _____

Name _____ Date _____

CHAPTER 16 Section 2 (pages 395–399)

Mayan Kings and Cities

BEFORE YOU READ

In the last section, you read about societies in North America.

In this section, you will read about the Mayan civilization in Mexico and Central America.

TERMS AND NAMES
Tikal Mayan city in present-day Guatemala
glyph Picture symbol used as part of a writing system
codex Book with pages that can be turned; one of three surviving ancient Mayan books
Popul Vuh Book containing a Mayan story of creation

AS YOU READ

Use the chart below to take notes on Mayan civilization.

```
            Cities
     Religious and trade centers
        Large populations
          Linked by trade
Writing                          Social Classes
            Mayan
          Civilization
Astronomy                        Religion
```

Maya Create Urban Kingdoms
(pages 395–396)

Who were the Maya?

A great civilization arose in what is today southern Mexico and northern Central America. This was the Mayan civilization. It appeared around A.D. 250. Between then and 900, the Maya built large cities such as **Tikal** and Copan. Each city was independent and ruled by a god-king. Each city was a religious center as well as a trade center for the area around it. These cities were large. Tens of thousands of people lived in these cities. The cities were full of palaces, temples, and pyramids. *Archaeologists* have found at least 50 Mayan cities.

Trade linked these cities. Among the trade goods were salt, *flint,* feathers, shells, cotton cloth, and ornaments made of jade. Cacao beans, which are used to make chocolate, were sometimes used as money. Maize, beans, and squash were the main foods.

Mayan society was divided into social classes. The best warriors and priests were at the top. The merchants and craft workers were at the next level. Peasant farmers—the majority of the people—were at the bottom.

1. What is known about Mayan cities?

_____

_____

CHAPTER 16 PEOPLE AND EMPIRES IN THE AMERICAS **149**

Religion Shapes Mayan Life
(pages 396–398)

How did religion shape Mayan life?

The Mayan religion was at the center of their society. There were many gods, including one for each day. The actions of the day's god could be predicted, they thought, by following a calendar. The Maya sometimes cut themselves to offer their blood to the gods in sacrifice. Sometimes they killed enemies and sacrificed them.

The Mayan religion led to the development of mathematics, calendars, and astronomy. Mayan math included the idea of zero. They had two calendars. One calendar was religious, and it had 20 13-day months. The other calendar was based on the sun. It had 18 months consisting of 20 days. The Maya linked the two together to identify days that would bring good fortune.

Mayan astronomy was very accurate. They observed the sun, moon, and stars to make their calendars as accurate as possible. They calculated the time it takes the earth to revolve around the sun almost perfectly.

The Maya also developed the most advanced writing system in the ancient Americas. Mayan writing was made up of about 800 symbols, or **glyphs.** They used their writing system to record important historical events. They carved in stone or recorded events in a bark-paper book known as a **codex.** Three of these ancient books still survive. A famous Mayan book called the ***Popul Vuh*** records a Mayan story of the creation of the world.

2. How does Mayan writing reflect Mayan culture?

_____
_____
_____
_____
_____

Mysterious Mayan Decline
(pages 398–399)

Why did the civilization decline?

In the late 800s, the Maya civilization began to decline. Historians do not know why. One explanation may be that warfare between the different city-states disrupted Mayan societies. The wars interrupted trade and drove many people out of the cities into the jungle. Another may be that the soil became less productive due to intensive farming over a long time. Whatever the cause, the Maya became a less powerful people. They continued to live in the area, but their cities were no longer the busy trade and religious centers they had been.

3. Name two reasons that may explain the civilization's decline.

_____
_____
_____
_____
_____

Name _____ Date _____

CHAPTER 16 Section 3 (pages 400–406)

The Aztecs Control Central Mexico

TERMS AND NAMES
obsidian Hard, glassy rock used by early peoples to make sharp weapons
Quetzalcoatl Toltec god
Triple Alliance Association of city-states that led to the formation of the Aztec Empire
Montezuma II Ruler under whom the Aztec Empire weakened

BEFORE YOU READ

In the last section, you read about Mayan civilization.

In this section, you will read about societies that arose in central Mexico, including the Aztecs.

AS YOU READ

Use the time line below to take notes on the peoples and empires of Central Mexico.

| 500 — Early city-state of Teotihuacan is at its peak | 900 | 1428 |
| 750 | 1200 | 1502 |

The Valley of Mexico (pages 400–401)

What civilizations arose in the Valley of Mexico?

The Valley of Mexico is a mountain valley more than a mile above sea level. It is a good place for people to settle because it has lakes and fertile soil. An early city-state called *Teotihuacan* ("City of the Gods") arose in this area in the first century A.D. The city had as many as 125,000 people at its peak around 500

Many of the city's residents were involved in the trade of **obsidian.** This hard green or black rock was found nearby. Obsidian was used to make sharp weapons. In the city was the huge Pyramid of the Sun, larger at its base than the largest pyramid of Egypt. By 750, Teotihuacan was abandoned. The reasons why are not clear.

The next people to dominate the area were the *Toltecs.* They rose to power around 900 and ruled over central Mexico for about 300 years. The Toltecs were warlike and based their empire on *conquest.* They worshipped a warlike god.

One Toltec king, *Topiltzin,* tried to replace the warlike god with a peaceful one. The peaceful god was called **Quetzalcoatl,** the Feathered *Serpent.* According to legend, Topiltzin and Quetzalcoatl became one and ruled the Toltecs in peace. Followers of the warlike god rebelled and chased Quetzalcoatl away. The Toltecs became warlike again. Someday, it was thought, Quetzalcoatl would return and bring a new *reign* of peace. This legend

CHAPTER 16 PEOPLE AND EMPIRES IN THE AMERICAS **151**

lived on in central Mexico for centuries and has important consequences.

1. What was Teotihuacan?

_____

_____

Aztecs Build an Empire (pages 401–403)

How did the Aztecs build an empire?

Around 1200 the Toltecs were losing control of the region. But another people—the Aztecs—began to gain power. The Aztecs founded a city and, in 1428, they joined with two other city-states to form the Triple Alliance. The **Triple Alliance** became the leading power of the Valley of Mexico. It soon gained control over neighboring regions.

By the early 1500s, the Aztecs controlled a large empire that included somewhere between 5 and 15 million people. This empire was based on military *conquest* and collecting *tribute* from conquered peoples.

Military leaders owned huge amounts of land. Along with government officials and priests, they ruled Aztec society. Below them were commoners—merchants, craft workers, soldiers, and farmers who owned their land. At the bottom of society were the slaves taken as captives in battle. At the top was the emperor. He was treated as a god as well as a ruler.

The capital city—Tenochtitlan—was built on an island in a lake. The Aztecs made long *causeways* to connect the city to the land. The city contained about 200,000 people. It was well-planned and had a large government and religious complex at its center.

2. How was Aztec society organized?

_____

_____

_____

Religion, the Center of Aztec Life (page 403)

What was the role of religion in Aztec life?

Religion played a major role in Aztec society. Temples were built in cities for the many different gods. Priests led religious *rituals*. The most important rituals were for the sun god. Priests made the sacrifice of human blood to make sure that the sun god was happy, and the sun would rise every day. People taken captive in war were sacrificed. The need for a steady supply of victims pushed the Aztecs to fight their neighbors.

3. Why and how did the Aztecs sacrifice to the sun god?

_____

_____

Problems in the Aztec Empire (page 406)

What weakened the Aztec Empire?

Montezuma II became emperor in 1502. The Aztec empire began to have problems during his reign. The Aztecs ordered the other peoples they had conquered to hand over even more people to sacrifice. These other peoples finally rebelled against the Aztecs. In the midst of this conflict, the Spanish arrived and made contact with the Aztecs for the first time. Some saw their arrival as the legendary return of Quetzalcoatl.

4. Why did conquered peoples rebel against the Aztecs?

_____

_____

Name _____ Date _____

CHAPTER 16 Section 4 (pages 407–411)

The Inca Create a Mountain Empire

TERMS AND NAMES
Pachacuti Ruler under whom the Incan Empire grew quickly
ayllu Small community or clan whose members worked together for the common good
mita Requirement for all Incan subjects to work for the state a certain number of days each year
quipu Arrangement of knotted strings on a cord used by the Inca to record numerical information

BEFORE YOU READ
In the last section, you read about the Aztec empire.
In this section, you will learn about the empire of the Inca.

AS YOU READ
Use the chart below to show how the Inca created their empire.

[Chart: Four boxes leading to "The Inca Create Unity". First box filled in: "Organized groups of varying sizes led by chiefs"]

The Inca Come to Power
(pages 407–408)

Who were the Inca?

The Inca civilization arose in the Andes of South America. It was built on the foundations made by several earlier cultures. Inca was the name of the original ruling family.

The Inca united much of the Andes under their rule. They first settled in the Valley of Cuzco, in modern Peru. They built a kingdom there by the 1200s. The Inca believed that their ruler was related to the sun god, who would bring wealth and power to them. Only men from one of 11 noble families could serve as king. When they died, rulers were *mummified* and worshipped by the people. The rulers also kept all the riches that they had won during life. This forced each new ruler to conquer new lands in order to get his own riches.

In 1438, **Pachacuti** became the ruler of the Inca. He made conquest after conquest. By 1500, the Inca ruled an empire that stretched along the Andes from modern Ecuador all the way south to Chile and Argentina. It held about 16 million people. The empire did not grow only through military conquest. Often the Inca offered new peoples the chance to join the empire peacefully as long as they swore loyalty to the emperor. Many peoples became part of the empire in this way. But when force was needed, the Inca were fierce fighters.

1. What beliefs and practices related to Inca rulers?

_____

CHAPTER 16 PEOPLE AND EMPIRES IN THE AMERICAS **153**

Incan Government Creates Unity (pages 408–410)

How did the government unite the empire?

The Inca had a highly organized system to govern their empire. Small groups of people known as **ayllu** worked together for the common good. For example, they built irrigation ditches together. The Inca applied this idea to their empire. Families were placed in groups of 10, 100, 1,000, and so on. Each group was led by a chief.

The Inca usually let local rulers stay in place when they conquered a people—as long as the conquered people met any Inca demands. The most important demand was for all adult workers to spend some days each year working for the state. They might work on state farms or build state roads or buildings. This payment of labor was known as **mita.**

The Inca built a complex network of roads. The roads linked all parts of the empire. The Inca also built all government buildings in the same style. This created a common identity for the government throughout the empire. They made all people speak a common language—the Inca tongue, called *Quechua*.

The Inca controlled the economy. They told people what to grow or make and how it would be distributed. Land was divided into government land, religious land, and community land. People were expected to spend some time farming all three types. The government also took care of people who needed help, such as the very old or ill.

In spite of all these advances, the Inca never developed a system of writing. All records were kept in peoples' memories. They did have a device for counting. It was a set of knotted strings called a **quipu.** The Inca also had day and night calendars for information about their gods.

2. What was mita, and what forms did it take?

_____

_____

Religion Supports the State; Discord in the Empire (pages 410–411)

How were religion and government connected?

The Inca religion played a central role in Inca life. The Inca believed in fewer gods than the peoples of Mexico. The most important of the Inca gods were the creator god and the sun god. Cuzco, the capital, was the most important religious center. It was decorated with gold and other precious objects.

In the early 1500s, the Inca empire was at the height of its power. But King Huayna Capac died while traveling through the empire. Civil war broke out after the king's death and weakened the empire. When the Spanish arrived, they used this weakness to their advantage.

3. Why did the empire fall?

_____

_____

INCA	
Traits of Civilization	**Strength Leading to Power**
Religious beliefs and theocracy	United culture Loyalty to the emperor
Major road systems	Connected entire empire and aided control
Type of welfare state with huge bureaucracy	Care for entire population during good and bad times

Skillbuilder

1. Which trait of Incan civilization is not related to government?

_____

_____

2. How did the road system help the Inca gain power?

_____

Name _____ Date _____

Glossary — CHAPTER 16 People and Empires in the Americas

alliances Agreements between groups or nations to protect common interests
archaeologists People who study past human societies and cultures
causeways Raised roadways that go across water or swampy land
clans Groups made up of people related to a common ancestor
conquest Act of conquering
flint Hard quartz

Hohokam A group of people from Southwest North America
irrigated Watered
Mound Builders Prehistoric Native American people who built mounds, mainly in the valley of the Mississippi River
mummified Condition of a dead body that has been preserved
Quechua Language of the Inca
reign Rule

rituals Ceremonial acts or traditional ways of doing things
serpent Snake
Teotihuacan Early city-state in the Valley of Mexico that reached its peak around 500
Topiltzin Toltec king
Toltecs People who ruled over Central Mexico from approximately 900 to 1200
tribute Payment made to a conqueror

AFTER YOU READ

Terms and Names

A. Write the name or term in each blank that best completes the meaning of the paragraph.

Mississippians

totems

pueblos

Anasazi

Iroquois

Several different Native American societies inhabited North America. One was the **1** _____, who occupied dry, desert lands of the Southwest. They built cliff dwellings and villages made up of apartment-like units called **2** _____. In lands near the Mississippi River, people called **3** _____ built a city called Cahokia that was the center of their culture. Among the Eastern tribes was a woodland group of tribes called the **4** _____. Although each of the Native American societies was distinct, all shared some characteristics. Among these was the use of **5** _____, symbols of a group's or clan's identity.

B. Write the letter of the name or term next to the description that explains it best.

a. obsidian

b. quipu

c. glyph

d. mita

e. codex

____ **1.** Requirement for all Incan subjects to work for the state a certain number of days each year

____ **2.** Arrangement of knotted strings on a cord, used by the Inca to record numerical information

____ **3.** Picture symbol used as part of a writing system

____ **4.** Book with pages that can be turned; one of three surviving ancient Mayan books

____ **5.** Hard, glassy rock used by early peoples to make sharp weapons

Name _____ Date _____

AFTER YOU READ (cont.) CHAP 16 People and Empires in the Americas

Main Ideas

1. Explain who the Anasazi were and what their homes were like.

_____
_____
_____

2. How was Mayan society organized?

_____
_____
_____
_____

3. How did the Aztecs build an empire?

_____
_____
_____
_____

4. How did the Incan Empire grow?

_____
_____
_____
_____

5. What steps did the Inca take to unify the different peoples of their empire?

_____
_____
_____
_____

Thinking Critically

Answer the following questions on a separate sheet of paper.

1. Explain this statement and give examples: Mayan cultural advances were connected to their religious beliefs.

2. Were the Aztecs good engineers? Explain your answer.

156 CHAPTER 16 REVIEW

Name _____ Date _____

CHAPTER 17 Section 1 (pages 417–422)

Italy: Birthplace of the Renaissance

BEFORE YOU READ

In the prologue, you read about the development of democratic ideas.

In this section, you will begin your in-depth reading of modern history starting with the Renaissance.

AS YOU READ

Use this chart to take notes on important changes that occurred during the Renaissance in Italy.

TERMS AND NAMES
Renaissance Period of rebirth of art and learning in Europe lasting from about 1300 to 1600
humanism Focus on human potential and achievements
secular Concerned with worldly rather than spiritual matters
patrons People who financially supported artists
perspective Art technique that recreates three dimensions
vernacular Use of native language instead of classical Latin

CHANGES IN VALUES	CHANGES IN ART	CHANGES IN LITERATURE
Humanism—new focus on human potential and achievements		

Italy's Advantages (pages 417–418)

Why did the Renaissance begin in Italy?

The years 1300 to 1600 saw a rebirth of learning and culture in Europe called the **Renaissance**. This rebirth spread north from Italy. It began there for three reasons. First, Italy had several important cities. Cities were places were places where people exchanged ideas. Second, these cities included a class of *merchants* and bankers who were becoming wealthy and powerful. This class strongly believed in the idea of individual achievement. Third, Italian artists and scholars were inspired by the ruined buildings and other reminders of *classical* Rome.

1. What are three reasons why the Renaissance began in Italy?

_____

_____

CHAPTER 17 EUROPEAN RENAISSANCE AND REFORMATION **157**

Classical and Worldly Values (pages 418–419)

What new values did people hold?

The new interest in the classical past led to an important value in Renaissance culture—**humanism**. This was a deep interest in what people have already achieved as well as what they could achieve in the future. Scholars did not try to connect classical writings to Christian teaching. Instead, they tried to understand them on their own terms.

In the Middle Ages, the emphasis had been mostly on *spiritual* values. Renaissance thinkers stressed **secular** ideas. These ideas centered on the things of the world. One way that powerful or wealthy people showed this interest in worldly things was by paying artists, writers, and musicians to create beautiful works of art. Wealthy people who supported artists were known as **patrons**.

People tried to show that they could master many fields of study or work. Someone who succeeded in many fields was admired greatly. The artist Leonardo da Vinci was an example of this ideal. He was a painter, a scientist, and an inventor. Men were expected to be charming, witty, well educated, well mannered, athletic, and self-controlled. Women were expected too have many accomplishments too. But, women were not to show them in public.

2. What are secular ideas?

_____

_____

Renaissance Revolutionizes Art (pages 419–421)

How did art change during the Renaissance?

Renaissance artists sometimes used new methods. *Sculptors* made figures more *realistic* than those from the Middle Ages. Painters used **perspective** to create the illusion that their paintings were *three-dimensional*. The subject of artwork changed also. Art in the Middle ages was mostly religious. Renaissance artists reproduced other views of life. Michelangelo showed great skill as an architect, a sculptor, and a painter.

3. How did the methods and subjects in art change?

_____

_____

_____

Renaissance Writers Change Literature (pages 421–422)

How did literature change during the Renaissance?

Renaissance writers also achieved greatness. Several wrote in the vernacular. This means they wrote in their native languages. It was a change from the Middle Ages, when most writing was done in Latin. Writers also changed their subject matter. They began to express their own thoughts and feelings. Sometimes they gave a detailed look at an individual. Dante and others wrote poetry, letters, and stories that were more realistic. Niccoló Machiavelli took a new approach to understanding government. He focused on telling rulers how to expand their power. He believed rulers should do what was politically effective, even if it was not morally right.

4. What did Renaissance writers write about?

_____

_____

_____

Name _____ Date _____

CHAPTER 17 Section 2 (pages 423–427)

The Northern Renaissance

TERMS AND NAMES
Utopia An ideal place
printing press Machine for reproducing writing by pressing paper against inked type
Gutenberg Bible First full-size book printed with a movable type printing press

BEFORE YOU READ

In the last section, you read how the Renaissance began in Italy.

In this section, you will learn how Renaissance ideas spread in northern Europe.

AS YOU READ

Use the web below to show what happened during the northern Renaissance.

Ideas came from Italy and spread to northern Europe

THE NORTHERN RENAISSANCE

The Northern Renaissance Begins (page 423)

Why *was the time right for the Northern Renaissance to begin?*

By 1450, the *bubonic plague* had ended in northern Europe. Also, the Hundred Years' War between France and England was ending. This allowed new ideas from Italy to spread to northern Europe. They were quickly adopted. Here too, rulers and merchants used their money to sponsor artists. But the northern Renaissance had a difference. Educated people combined classical learning with interest in religious ideas.

1. How was the northern Renaissance different from the Renaissance in Italy?

_____

_____

CHAPTER 17 EUROPEAN RENAISSANCE AND REFORMATION 159

Artistic Ideas Spread (pages 423–424)

What ideas about art developed in Northern Europe?

The new ideas of Italian art moved to the north, where artists began to use them. Major artists appeared in parts of Germany, France, Belgium, and the Netherlands. Dürer painted religious subjects and realistic *landscapes*. Holbein, Van Eyck, and Bruegel painted lifelike portraits and scenes of *peasant* life. They revealed much about the times. They began to use *oil-based paints*. Oils became very popular, and their use spread to Italy.

2. What did Northern European artists paint?

_____
_____

Northern Writers Try to Reform Society (pages 425–426)

What did northern writers write?

Writers of the northern Renaissance combined humanism with a deep Christian faith. They urged reforms in the Church. They tried to make people more devoted to God. They also wanted society to be more fair. In England, Thomas More wrote a book about **Utopia**, an imaginary ideal society where greed, war, and conflict do not exist.

William Shakespeare is often called the greatest playwright of all time. His plays showed a brilliant command of the English language. They also show a deep understanding of people and how they interact with one another.

3. Who were two of the most famous writers of the northern Renaissance?

_____
_____

Printing Spreads Renaissance Ideas (pages 426–427)

Why was the printing press such an important development?

One reason that learning spread so rapidly during the Renaissance was the invention of *movable type*. The Chinese had invented the process of carving characters onto wooden blocks. They then arranged them in words, inked the blocks, and pressed them against paper to print pages.

In 1440, a German, Johann Gutenberg, used this same practice to invent his **printing press.** He produced his first book—the **Gutenberg Bible**—in 1455 on this press. The technology then spread rapidly. By 1500, presses in Europe had printed nearly 10 million books.

Printing made it easier to make many copies of a book. As a result, written works became available far and wide. Books were printed in English, French, Spanish, Italian, or German. More people began to read. The Bible was a popular book. After reading the Bible, some people formed new ideas about Christianity. These ideas were different from the official teachings of the Church.

4. What effects did the printing press have on northern European life?

_____
_____
_____

Name _____ Date _____

CHAPTER 17 Section 3 (pages 428–432)

Luther Starts the Reformation

BEFORE YOU READ

In the last section, you saw how the Renaissance spread to Northern Europe.

In this section, you will see how Renaissance ideas helped bring about the Reformation.

AS YOU READ

Use the chart below to take notes on the responses to Luther's challenge.

TERMS AND NAMES

indulgence Release from punishments due for a sin
Reformation 16th-century movement for religious reform, leading to the founding of new Christian churches
Lutheran Member of a Protestant church founded on the teachings of Martin Luther
Protestant Member of a Christian church founded on the principles of the Reformation
Peace of Augsburg Agreement in 1555 declaring that the religion of each German state would be decided by its ruler
annul Cancel or put an end to
Anglican Relating to the Church of England

BATTLE/POLITICAL ISSUE	EFFECT
Responses to Luther's Challenge	The Pope threatens Luther with excommunication.

Causes of the Reformation (page 428)

Why was the Church criticized?

By 1500, the influence of the Church on the lives of people had weakened. Some people resented paying taxes to support the Church in Rome. Others sharply criticized the Church for some of its practices. Popes seemed more concerned with luxury and political power than with spiritual matters. The lower *clergy* had faults too. Many local priests lacked education and were not able to teach people. Some lived immoral lives.

Reformers urged the Church to change its ways to become more spiritual and humble. Christian humanists such as Erasmus and Thomas More added their voices to calls for change. In the early 1500s, the calls grew louder.

1. What kinds of changes did Church critics want to make?

_____
_____
_____

CHAPTER 17 EUROPEAN RENAISSANCE AND REFORMATION **161**

Luther Challenges the Church
(page 429)

How did the Reformation begin?

In 1517, a German monk named Martin Luther protested the actions of a Church official. That person was selling **indulgences**. An indulgence was a kind of forgiveness. By paying money to the Church, people thought they could win *salvation*.

Luther challenged this practice and others. He posted a written protest on the door of a castle church. His words were printed and spread throughout Germany. This was the beginning of the **Reformation**, a movement for reform that led to the founding of new Christian churches.

2. What role did Martin Luther play in the Reformation?

_____

_____

The Response to Luther (pages 429–430)

What effects did Luther's protest have?

Pope Leo X punished Luther for his views, but he refused to change them. Holy Roman Emperor Charles V, a strong Catholic, called Luther an outlaw. Luther's books were burned. But it was too late. Many of his ideas were already being practiced. The **Lutheran** Church started around 1522.

In 1524, *peasants* in Germany hoped to use Luther's ideas about Christian freedom to change society. They demanded an end to serfdom—a condition like slavery. When it was not granted, they revolted. Luther disagreed with this *revolt*. German princes killed thousands in putting the revolt down.

Some *nobles* supported Luther's ideas. They saw a chance to weaken the emperor's power over them. Other German princes joined forces against Luther's supporters. They signed an agreement to remain loyal to the pope and the emperor. Supporters of Luther's ideas *protested* this agreement. They were called the Protestants. Eventually, the term **Protestant** meant Christians who belonged to non-Catholic churches.

War broke out between Catholic and Protestant forces in Germany. It finally ended in 1555 with the **Peace of Augsburg**. This treaty granted each prince the right to decide whether his subjects would be Catholic or Protestant.

3. Why did Luther's ideas lead to war?

_____

_____

England Becomes Protestant
(pages 431–432)

How did England become Protestant?

The Catholic Church faced another challenge to its power in England. Henry VIII, the king, was married to a Spanish princess. She gave birth to a daughter. England had never had a female ruler. Henry feared a civil war would start if he had no son. He believed his wife was too old to have another child. He tried to get the pope to **annul**, or put an end to the marriage, so he could remarry. The pope refused.

To remarry, Henry had to get out of the Catholic church. In 1534, Henry had *Parliament* pass laws that created the Church of England. These laws made the king or queen, not the pope, head of the Church of England. Henry no longer had to obey the pope. Henry remarried five times. His only son was from his third wife.

One of Henry's daughters, Elizabeth, became queen in 1558. She finished creating a separate English church. The new church was called **Anglican**. It had some practices that would appeal to both Protestants and Catholics. In this way, Elizabeth hoped to end religious conflict.

Elizabeth's England had to face a threat from Catholic Spain, too. In 1588, King Philip II launched a huge fleet of ships—known as the Spanish Armada—to invade England. This fleet was defeated by a combination of English fighting skill and a terrible storm.

4. What role did Henry VIII play in creating the Church of England?

_____

_____

162 CHAPTER 17 SECTION 3

Name _____ Date _____

CHAPTER 17 Section 4 (pages 433–436)

The Reformation Continues

BEFORE YOU READ

In the last section, you read how the Reformation began.
In this section, you will learn how it developed and spread.

AS YOU READ

Use the chart below to take notes on the reforms that occurred as the Reformation continued.

```
        Continuing
         Reforms
        During the
        Reformation
```

- Calvin begins another Protestant church
- [ ]
- [ ]

TERMS AND NAMES

predestination Doctrine that God has decided all things beforehand, including which people will be saved

Calvinism Religious teachings based on the ideas of the reformer John Calvin

theocracy Government controlled by religious leaders

Presbyterian Member of a Protestant church governed by elders and founded by John Knox

Anabaptist Member of a Protestant group during the Reformation who believed only adults should be baptized. Also believed that church and state should be separate

Catholic Reformation 16th-century Catholic reform movement in response to Protestant Reformation

Jesuits Members of the Society of Jesus, a Roman Catholic religious order founded by Ignatius of Loyola

Council of Trent Meeting of Roman Catholic leaders to rule on doctrines criticized by the Protestant reformers

Calvin Begins Another Protestant Church (pages 433–434)

What did Calvin teach?

Protestantism arose elsewhere in the 1530s. This time under the leadership of John Calvin. Calvin wrote an important book that gave structure to Protestant beliefs. He taught that people are sinful by nature. He also taught **predestination,** the idea that God determines beforehand who will be saved. The religion based on Calvin's teachings is called **Calvinism.**

Calvin created a **theocracy** in Geneva, Switzerland. It was government run by religious leaders. It had strict rules of behavior that required people to live religious lives. Anyone who preached different religious ideas might be burned at the stake.

A preacher named John Knox was impressed by Calvin's high moral ideals. Knox put these ideas into practice in Scotland. This was beginning of the **Presbyterian** Church. Others in Holland, France and Switzerland adopted Calvin's ideas as well. In France, his followers were called Huguenots. Conflict between them and Catholics often turned into violence. In 1572, mobs killed about 12,000 Huguenots.

1. What is Calvinism?

_____

_____

CHAPTER 17 EUROPEAN RENAISSANCE AND REFORMATION **163**

Other Reformers (pages 434–435)

What other reformers were important during the Reformation?

Another new Protestant group was the **Anabaptists.** They preached that people should be baptized into the faith as adults. Anabaptists also taught that the church and state should be separate. In addition, they refused to fight in wars.

Many women played key roles in the Reformation. They included Marguerite of Navarre. She protected John Calvin from being killed for his beliefs. Katherina von Bora was the wife of Martin Luther. She supported an equal role for women in marriage.

2. Who were two women who played important roles in the Reformation?

_____

_____

The Catholic Reformation
(pages 435–436)

What was the Catholic Reformation?

Protestant churches grew all over Europe. To keep Catholic believers loyal, the Catholic Church took steps to change itself. This was called the **Catholic Reformation.**

One Catholic reformer was a Spanish noble named Ignatius. He founded a new group in the Church based on deep devotion to Jesus. Members of this group, called the **Jesuits,** started schools across Europe. They sent missionaries to convert people to Catholicism. In addition, they tried to stop the spread of Protestant faiths in Europe.

Two popes of the 1500s helped bring about changes in the Church. Pope Paul III set up a kind of court called the Inquisition. It was charged with finding, trying, and punishing people who broke the rules of the Church. He also called a meeting of church leaders, the **Council of Trent.** The council, which met in 1545, passed these *doctrines:*
- the Church's interpretation of the Bible was final
- Christians needed good works as well as faith to win salvation
- the Bible and the Church had equal authority in setting out Christian beliefs
- indulgences were valid expressions of faith

The next pope, Paul IV, put these doctrines into practice. These actions helped revive the Church. They also allowed it to survive the challenge of the Protestants.

3. What happened at the Council of Trent?

_____

_____

```
                    Christian
                     Church
                 ┌──────┴──────┐
          Eastern Orthodox   Roman Catholic
                         ┌───────┴───────┐
                         P R O T E S T A N T
   ┌──────┬────────┬────────┬──────────┬──────────┐
 Anglican Calvinist Lutheran Anabaptist Roman Catholic
  │         │          │
  Puritan-  Presbyterian Mennonite
  Congregational
  │         Reformed    Amish
  Methodist Church
  │
  Episcopal
  │
  Baptist
  │
  Quakers
```

Skillbuilder

Use the chart to answer these questions

1. How did the Christian Church split before the Reformation?

_____

_____

2. What were the four major Protestant religions out of which other religions formed?

_____

_____

Name _____ Date _____

Glossary — CHAPTER 17 European Renaissance and Reformation

bubonic plague Deadly disease that spread across Europe and Asia in the mid-14th century, killing millions of people

classical related to ancient Greece and Rome and emphasizing ideas of order, balance, and harmony

clergy Religious officials

doctrines Principles; statements of policy

landscapes Pictures showing scenery or land forms

merchants storekeepers and traders

movable type Printing blocks that did not have to be made one by one but could be moved into new positions and reused

nobles People of high rank

oil-based paints Paints that are made with oil; the oil dries slowly and allows for details, blending, and changes

Parliament Law-making body in England

peasant related to poor or lower class people who worked the land

protested Actively disagreed

realistic Lifelike

revolt Uprising, rebellion

salvation Freedom from the effects of sin

sculptors People who create works of art by carving

spiritual sacred; related to religion

three-dimensional Having length, width, and height; giving a sense of depth

AFTER YOU READ

Terms and Names

A. Fill in the blank with the name or term that best completes the paragraph.

Presbyterian
Anabaptists
Anglican
Lutheran
Reformation
Protestant

In Germany, Martin Luther began a movement for religious change called the **1** _____. He and his followers began a separate religious group called the **2** _____ Church. In England, Elizabeth finished and headed the **3** _____ church. In Scotland, John Knox established yet another branch of the **4** _____ faith. His church was the **5** _____ Church. Other Protestant reformers included the **6** _____, who believed in separation of church and state.

B. Write the letter of the name or term next to the description that best explains it.

a. Jesuits
b. secular
c. Calvinism
d. Peace of Augsburg
e. patrons
f. indulgence
g. Utopia
h. humanism
i. predestination
j. vernacular

_____ 1. Focus on human potential and achievements

_____ 2. An agreement in 1555 declaring that the religion of each German state would be decided by its ruler

_____ 3. Concerned with worldly rather than spiritual matters

_____ 4. Doctrine that God has decided all things beforehand, including which people will be eternally saved

_____ 5. Use of native language instead of classical Latin

_____ 6. Body of religious teachings based on the ideas of the reformer John Calvin

_____ 7. Members of the Society of Jesus, a Roman Catholic religious order founded by Ignatius of Loyola

_____ 8. Imaginary land described in a book by Thomas More; this word now means an ideal place

_____ 9. People who financially supported artists

_____ 10. Release from punishments due for a sin

Name _____ Date _____

AFTER YOU READ (continued)   CHAPTER 17 European Renaissance and Reformation

Main Ideas

1. What changes in the arts occurred during the Italian Rennaisance?
_____
_____

2. What changes in learning and the arts occurred during the Northern Rennaissance?
_____
_____

3. What changes in the Christian Church did Martin Luther bring about?
_____
_____

4. How did the Reformation in Germany change German politcal life?
_____
_____

5. Why and how did the Church change in England?
_____
_____

Thinking Critically

Answer the following questions on a separate sheet of paper.

1. How did the Northern Renaissance differ from the Italian Rennaissance?

2. Which leader—Henry VIII or Luther—do you think had a greater impact? Explain why.

166 CHAPTER 17 REVIEW

Name _____ Date _____

CHAPTER 18 Section 1 (pages 443–447)

The Ottomans Build a Vast Empire

BEFORE YOU READ

In the last chapter, you read about changes in Europe during 1300-1600.

In this section, you will read about the rise of the Ottoman Empire during the same period.

AS YOU READ

Use the time line below to take notes on the major events in the history of the Ottoman Empire.

TERMS AND NAMES
ghazi Warriors for Islam
Osman Successful ghazi who built a small state in Anatolia
Timur the Lame Conqueror of Persia and Russia
Mehmet II Conqueror who made Istanbul his capital
Suleiman the Lawgiver Ruler who brought Ottoman Empire to its height
janissary Soldier slave drawn from conquered Christian territories
devshirme Policy for creating the sultan's army

```
  1300-1326                      1451
  Osman builds a small empire
  in Anatolia


       |                           |
       |_____|
            |              |
          1402          1520-1566
```

Turks Settle in Christian Byzantium (pages 443–444)

How did the Ottoman Empire begin?

In 1300, the world of the eastern Mediterranean was also changing. The Byzantine Empire was fading. The Seljuk Turk state had been destroyed. Anatolia, the area of modern Turkey, was now inhabited by groups of *nomadic* Turks. They saw themselves as *ghazis*, or warriors for *Islam*. They raided the lands where non-Muslims lived.

The most successful ghazi was **Osman**. Western Europeans thought his name was Othman. They called his followers Ottomans. Between 1300 and 1326, Osman built a strong but small kingdom in *Anatolia*. Leaders who came after Osman called themselves *sultans*, or "ones with power." They extended the kingdom by buying land. They also formed *alliances* with other chieftains and conquered everyone they could.

CHAPTER 18 THE MUSLIM WORLD EXPANDS **167**

The Ottomans ruled in a kindly way. Muslims had to serve in the army but paid no taxes. Non-Muslims paid tax but did not serve in the army. Many joined Islam just to avoid the tax. Most people adjusted easily to their new rule.

One warrior did not. He was **Timur the Lame**. He conquered Russia and Persia. In 1402, he defeated the Ottoman forces and captured the sultan.

1. Who were the Ottomans?

_____
_____
_____

Powerful Sultans Spur Dramatic Expansion (pages 444–445)

How did the empire grow?

In Anatolia, the four sons of the last sultan fought for control of the empire. Mehmet I won control. His son and the four sultans who came after him brought the Ottoman Empire to its greatest power. One of them—**Mehmet II**—took power in 1451. He built a force of 100,000 foot soldiers and 125 ships to gain control of Constantinople. In 1453, he took the city and the waterway it controlled. Mehmet made the city his capital. He renamed it Istanbul. The rebuilt city became home to people from all over the Ottoman Empire.

Other emperors used *conquest* to make the empire grow. After 1514, Selim the Grim took Persia, Syria, and Palestine. He then captured Arabia, took the Muslim holy cities of Medina and Mecca, and gained control of Egypt.

2. Who was Mehmet II?

_____
_____
_____

Suleiman the Lawgiver; The Empire Declines Slowly (pages 445-447)

Why was Suleiman the Lawgiver a great leader?

Suleiman I took power in 1520 and ruled for 46 years. His people called him **Suleiman the Lawgiver.** He brought the Ottoman Empire to its greatest size and most impressive achievements. He conquered parts of southeastern Europe. He won control of the entire eastern Mediterranean Sea and took North Africa as far west as Tripoli.

Suleiman ruled his empire with a highly structured government. Thousands of slaves served the royal family. The **janissaries** were a group of soldier slaves. They were Christians taken as children and made slaves. They were trained as soldiers and fought fiercely for the sultan. The policy of making people slaves was called *devshirme.* Other slaves held important government jobs.

The empire allowed people to follow their own religion. Jews and Christians were not mistreated. Suleiman revised the laws of the empire. His empire was also known for great works of art and many fine buildings.

Although the empire lasted long after Suleiman, it spent the next few hundred years in *decline*. That means its power slipped. None of the sultans were as accomplished as Suleiman had been.

3. What were two of Suleiman's accomplishments?

_____
_____
_____

Name _____ Date _____

CHAPTER 18 Section 2 (pages 448–450)

Patterns of Change: Cultural Blending

TERMS AND NAMES
Safavid Member of a Shi'a Muslim group that built an empire in Persia
Isma'il Safavid warrior who seized most of what is now Iran
Shah Abbas Leader during the Safavid golden age
Isfahan Capital city of the Safavid Empire

BEFORE YOU READ

In the last section, you read about the Ottomans.

In this section, you will learn about the development of another empire, the Safavid.

AS YOU READ

Use the chart below to show three of the long-lasting effects of the Safavid Empire.

Effects of the Safavid Empire
- Tension between Shi'a and Sunni Muslims
-
-

Patterns of Cultural Blending
(page 448)

What is cultural blending?

Throughout history, different peoples have lived together. Their cultures have influenced one another. Often these people have blended one culture with another. This can be due to trade, conquest, or movement of people from one area to another. It can also happen when there is a new religion.

Societies that are able to benfit from cultural blending are open to new ways. They are willing to adapt and change.

1. What are the four causes of cultural blending?

_____

_____

The Safavids Build a Shi'i Empire (pages 449–450)

How did the Safavids rise to power?

Cultural blending took place in the Safavid Empire of Persia. The **Safavids** were members of an Islamic group that said it was related to the prophet Muhammad. In the 1400s, they joined with the *Shi'a*, a branch of Islam. The major group of Muslims, the *Sunnis*, *persecuted* the Shi'a for their views. The Safavids feared the Sunni Muslims. They decided to build a strong army to protect themselves.

In 1499, a 14-year-old leader named **Isma'il** led this army to conquer Iran. He took the traditional Persian title of *shah*, or king, and made the new empire a state of Shi'a. He destroyed Baghdad's

CHAPTER 18 THE MUSLIM WORLD EXPANDS **169**

Sunni population. Ottoman Turk rulers—who were Sunni Muslims—in turn killed all the Shi'a that they met. This conflict between the two groups of Muslims continues today.

The Safavids reached their height in the late 1500s under **Shah Abbas.** He created two armies that were loyal to him and him alone. He also gave new weapons to the army to make them better fighters. He got rid of *corrupt* officials in the government. He also brought gifted artists to his empire. They helped make his capital and other cities very beautiful. In taking these steps, Shah Abbas drew on good ideas from other cultures. He used Chinese artists. This helped create gorgeous artwork. The artwork decorated the rebuilt capital of **Isfahan**.

Under Shah Abbas, the Safavids enjoyed good relations with nations of Europe. Through this contact, the demand for Persian rugs increased greatly in Europe. In this period, rug-making, which had been a local craft in Persia, became a major industry for the country.

Like the Ottoman Empire, the Safavid Empire began to decline soon after it had reached its greatest height. Shah Abbas had killed or injured his most talented sons—just as Suleiman had done. Shah Abbas feared that his sons would seize power from him. As a result, a weak and ineffective grandson became shah after him.

While the empire fell, the blended culture that the Safavid Empire had created continued. The main elements of that culture were the joining together of the Persian tradition of learning and sophistication with the strong faith of the Shi'a. These elements are found in Iran even today.

2. What were four reforms made by Shah Abbas?

_____

_____

_____

_____

Skillbuilder

Use the chart to answer the questions.

1. Where are three places where cultural blending has occurred?

_____

2. What are two reasons for interaction?

_____

PATTERNS OF CHANGE: Cultural Blending

Location	Interacting Cultures	Reason for Interaction	Some Results of Interaction
India—1000 B.C.	Aryan and Dravidian Indian	Migration	Vedic culture, forerunner of Hinduism
East Africa—A.D. 700	Arab, African, Indian, Islamic, Christian	Trade, religious converts	New trade language, Swahili
Russia—A.D. 1000	Christian and Slavic	Religious converts	Eastern Christianity, Russian identity
Mexico—A.D. 1500	Spanish and Aztec Indian	Conquest	Mestizo culture, Mexican Catholicism
United States—A.D. 1900	European, Asian, Caribbean	Migration, religious freedom	Cultural diversity

Name _____ Date _____

CHAPTER 18 Section 3 (pages 451–457)

The Mughals Establish an Empire in India

BEFORE YOU READ

In the last section, you learn about how the Safavids established an empire in what is present-day Iran.

In this section, you will learn about the establishment of the Mughal Empire in what is now India.

AS YOU READ

Use the web diagram below to take notes. In each circle, write the name of one important Mughal ruler. Also write two or three words that identify each person or name a major accomplishment or problem of his rule.

> **TERMS AND NAMES**
> **Babur** Founder of the Mughal Empire
> **Mughal** One of the nomads who invaded the Indian subcontinent and established a powerful empire there
> **Akbar** Mughal ruler with a genius for cultural blending, military conquest, and art
> **Jahangir** Weak Mughal ruler; son of Akbar
> **Nur Jahan** Wife of Jahangir; Mughal ruler in all but name
> **Sikh** Nonviolent religious group that became the enemy of the Mughals
> **Shah Jahan** Mughal ruler who built Taj Mahal
> **Taj Mahal** Tomb built by Shah Hahan for his wife
> **Aurangzeb** Last important Mughal ruler

[Web diagram: center circle "Key Mughal Leaders" connected to five outer circles; top-center circle contains "Babur: founder of the empire"; other four circles are blank]

Early History of the Mughal Empire (pages 451–452)

How did the Mughal Empire begin?

Starting in the 600s, India went through a long, unsettled period. Nomads from central Asia invaded the area and created many small kingdoms. In the 700s, Muslims arrived on the scene. This began a long history of fighting with the *Hindus* who had lived in India for centuries.

After about 300 years, a group of Muslim Turks conquered a region around the city of Delhi. They set up a new empire there. They treated the Hindus in their area as conquered peoples. Their rule was brought to an end in 1398.

A little over a hundred years later, a new leader named **Babur** raised an army and began to win large parts of India. He had many talents. He was a lover of poetry and gardens. He was also an excellent general. His empire was called the **Mughal** Empire because he and his families were related to the Mongols.

1. Who was Babur?

_____

_____

CHAPTER 18 THE MUSLIM WORLD EXPANDS **171**

The Golden Age of Akbar (pages 452–453)

Who was Akbar?

Babur's grandson was **Akbar**. His name means "Great One." He ruled with great wisdom and fairness for almost 40 years.

Akbar was a Muslim. He believed strongly that people should be allowed to follow the religion they choose. He hired people in his government based on their ability and not their religion. Both Hindus and Muslims worked in the government.

Akbar ruled fairly. He ended the tax that Hindu pilgrims had to pay. He also ended the tax that all non-Muslims had to pay. To raise money, he taxed people on a percentage of the food they grew. This made it easier for peasants to pay the tax. His land policy was less wise. He gave much land to government officials. However, when they died he took it back. As a result, workers did not see any point in caring for the land.

He had a strong, well-equipped army that helped him win and keep control of more lands. His empire held about 100 million people—more than lived in all of Europe at the time.

During Akbar's reign, many changes in culture took place. His policy of blending different cultures produced two new languages. The languages were blends of several languages. One was *Hindi*, which is widely spoken in India today. The other was *Urdu*. It is now the official language of Pakistan. The empire became famous for its art. The best example of this art was small, highly detailed, colorful pictures called miniatures. Akbar—who could not read—had a huge library of books. He served as a *patron* to many writers. He also sponsored the building of a new capital city.

2. What did Akbar contribute to the Mughal Empire?

_____

_____

Akbar's Successors (pages 453–457)

Who ruled after Akbar?

After Akbar's death in 1605, his son **Jahangir**, took control of the empire. During his reign, the real power was his wife, **Nur Jahan**. She plotted with one son to overthrow another son. She had a bitter political battle with the **Sikhs**, members of a separate, nonviolent religion. That group became the target of attacks by the government.

The next ruler was **Shah Jahan**. He too chose not to follow Akbar's policy of religious toleration. Shah Jahan was a great patron of the arts and built many beautiful buildings. One was the famous **Taj Mahal,** a tomb for his wife. His ambitious building plans required high taxes, though. People suffered under his rule.

His son **Aurangzeb** ruled for almost 50 years. He made the empire grow once again with new conquests. His rule also brought new problems. He was a *devout* Muslim, and he punished Hindus and destroyed their temples. This led to a rebellion that took part of his empire. At the same time, the Sikhs won control of another part of the empire.

3. How did the Mughal Empire change after Akbar?

_____

_____

The Empire's Decline and Decay (page 457)

How did the Mughal Empire lose its power?

Aurangzeb used up the empire's resources. People did not feel loyalty to him. As the power of the state weakened, the power of local lords grew. Soon there was only a patchwork of independent states. There continued to be a Mughal emperor, but he was only a *figurehead*, not a ruler with any real power. As the Mughal empire was rising and falling, Western traders were building power. They arrived in India just before Babur did. Shah Jahan let the English build trading fort in Madras. Aurangzeb handed them the port of Bombay. This gave India's next conquerors a foothold in India.

4. Who established a foothold in India?

_____

_____

172 CHAPTER 18 SECTION 3

Name _____ Date _____

Glossary   CHAPTER 18   The Muslim World Expands

alliances Partnerships
Anatolia Southwest Asian peninsula now occupied by the Asian part of Turkey—also called Asia Minor
conquest Act of conquering, defeating, or taking over
corrupt Having few or no moral values, or having moral values that are unsound
decline Gradual loss of power
devout Devoted to religion or religious duties
figurehead Ruler without real power
Hindi Blend of Persian and local languages still spoken in India
Hindus People who practice the Hindu religion, the main religion of India
Islam Religion that developed in Arabia in the 7th century
nomadic Moving from place to place
patron Sponsor or supporter
persecuted Caused to suffer because of beliefs
shah Persian title meaning king
Shi'a Branch of Islam
sultans Rulers of Muslim states
Sunni Branch of Islam
Urdu Mixture of Arabic, Persian, and Hindi; the official language of Pakistan

AFTER YOU READ

Terms and Names

A. Write the name or term in each blank that best completes the meaning of the paragraph.

Suleiman the Lawgiver
Timur the Lame
Osman
ghazi
Mehmet II

The Ottoman Empire began when a successful **1** _____ built a small state in Anatolia. This warrior's name was **2** _____. The name Ottoman comes from his name. The rise of the Ottoman Empire was interrupted by a warrior named **3** _____. He conquered Persia and Russia. After that time, strong rulers brought power back to the Ottoman Empire. When **4** _____ conquered Constantinople, he opened the city to new citizens of many religions and backgrounds. Although his accomplishments were great, the peak achievement of the Ottoman Empire occurred under **5** _____. He brought a highly structured social organization and many cultural achievements to the Ottomans.

B. Write the letter of the name or term next to the description that explains it best.

a. Babur
b. Isma'il
c. Isfahan
d. Akbar
e. Aurangzeb

_____ **1.** Safavid leader who seized most of what is now Iran

_____ **2.** Capital city of the Safavid Empire under Shah Abbas

_____ **3.** Mughal emperor who drained the empire of its resources while the power of local lords grew

_____ **4.** Founder of the Mughal Empire

_____ **5.** Muslim Mughal leader who defended religious freedom and blended many cultures

Name _____ Date _____

AFTER YOU READ (continued) **CHAPTER 18** The Muslim World Expands

Main Ideas

1. How did the Ottomans come to power?

_____

_____

2. Why was Mehmet II important?

_____

_____

3. How did Suleiman the Lawgiver use slaves in his government?

_____

_____

4. Why did the Safavid Empire decline?

_____

_____

5. What were four of Akbar's great accomplishments?

_____

_____

Thinking Critically

Answer the following questions on a separate sheet of paper.

1. How were cultures blended during the Safavid Empire?

2. How did the leaders who came after Akbar contribute to the end of the Mughal empire?

174 CHAPTER 18 REVIEW

Name _____ Date _____

CHAPTER 19 Section 1 (pages 463-468)

Europeans Explore the East

TERMS AND NAMES
Bartolomeu Dias Portuguese explorer who rounded the tip of Africa
Prince Henry Portuguese supporter of exploration
Vasco da Gama Explorer who gave Portugal a direct sea route to India
Treaty of Tordesillas Treaty between Spain and Portugal dividing newly discovered lands between them
Dutch East India Company Dutch company that established and directed trade throughout Asia

BEFORE YOU READ
In the last chapter, you read about empire building in Asia.
In this section, you will learn why and how Europeans began an age of exploration.

AS YOU READ
Use thie time line below to take notes on important events in European exploration.

```
┌─────────────────────────┐      ┌─────────────────────────┐
│         1419            │      │         1492            │
│   Prince Henry starts   │      │                         │
│  a school of navigation │      │                         │
└─────────────────────────┘      └─────────────────────────┘
            │                                │
┌─────────────────────────┐      ┌─────────────────────────┐
│         1488            │      │         1498            │
│                         │      │                         │
│                         │      │                         │
└─────────────────────────┘      └─────────────────────────┘
```

Many Factors Encourage Exploration (pages 463-464)

Why did Europeans begin to explore new lands?

For many centuries, Europeans did not have much contact with people from other lands. That changed in the 1400s. Europeans hoped to gain new sources of wealth. By exploring the seas, traders hoped to find new, faster routes to Asia— the source of spices and luxury goods. Another reason for exploration was spreading Christianity to new lands.

Bartolomeu Dias, an early Portuguese explorer, explained his motives: "to serve God and His Majesty, to give light to those who were in darkness and to grow rich as all men desire to do."

Advances in technology made these voyages possible. A new kind of ship, the *caravel*, was stronger than earlier ships. It had triangle-shaped sails that allowed it to sail against the wind. Ships

CHAPTER 19 AN AGE OF EXPLORATION AND ISOLATION **175**

could now travel far out into the ocean. The magnetic compass allowed sea captains to stay on course better.

1. What were the two main reasons for European exploration?

_____

_____

Portugal Leads the Way (pages 464-466)

How did Portugal lead the way in exploration?

The first nation to develop and use the caravel and the magnetic compass was Portugal. **Prince Henry** was committed to the idea of exploring. In 1419, he started a school of *navigation*. Sea captains, mapmakers, and navigators met and exchanged ideas there.

Over the next few decades, Portuguese captains sailed farther and farther down the west coast of Africa. In 1488, Bartolomeu Dias reached the southern tip of Africa. Ten years later, **Vasco da Gama** led a ship around Africa, to India, and back. The Portuguese had found a sea route to Asia.

The Spanish, meanwhile, had plans of their own. Christopher Columbus convinced the king and queen that he could reach Asia by sailing west. In 1492, instead of landing in Asia, Columbus touched land in the islands of the Americas. Spain and Portugal argued over which nation had the rights to the land that Columbus had claimed. In 1494, they signed the **Treaty of Tordesillas**. It divided the world into two areas. Portugal won the right to control the eastern parts—including Africa, India, and other parts of Asia. Spain got the western parts—including most of the Americas.

2. How did Spain and Portugal solve their differences over claims to new lands?

_____

_____

Trading Empires in the Indian Ocean (pages 466-468)

Who established trading empires in the Indian Ocean?

Portugal moved quickly to make the new Indian Ocean route pay off. Through military might, Portugal gained power over islands that were rich in desirable spices. They were called the Spice Islands. Spices now cost Europeans one-fifth of what they had cost before, while still making Portugal very wealthy.

Other European nations joined in this trade. In the 1600s, the English and Dutch entered the East Indies. They quickly broke Portuguese power in the area. Then both nations set up an East India Company to control Asian trade. These companies were more than businesses. They were like governments. They had the power to make money, sign treaties, and raise their own armies. The **Dutch East India Company** was richer and more powerful than England's company.

By 1700, the Dutch ruled much of Indonesia. They had trading posts in many other Asian countries and commanded the southern tip of Africa. At the same time, both England and France finally gained footholds in India.

Nevertheless, even though Europeans controlled the trade between Asia and Europe, they had little *impact* on most people living in these areas.

3. How did the Dutch and English become Indian Ocean trading powers?

_____

_____

_____

176 CHAPTER 19 SECTION 1

Name _____   Date _____

CHAPTER 19 Section 2 (pages 469–473)

China Rejects European Outreach

BEFORE YOU READ

In the last section, you read about European exploration in the East.

In this section, you will read about China's reactions to the world around it.

AS YOU READ

Use the chart below to show important developments in the Ming Dynasty and the Qing Dynasty.

TERMS AND NAMES
Hongwu Commander of the rebel army that drove the Mongols out of China in 1368
Ming Dynasty Chinese dynasty that ruled from 1368 to 1644
Yonglo Ming ruler; son of Hongwu
Zheng He Muslim admiral who led seven voyages of exploration during the Ming Dynasty
Manchus People from Manchuria
Qing Dynasty Chinese dynasty that followed the Ming Dynasty and was begun by the Manchus
Kangxi Powerful Manchu emperor of the Qing Dynasty

MING DYNASTY	QING DYNASTY
Hongwu becomes the first emperor.	

The Ming Dynasty (pages 469–470)

What occurred during the Ming Dynasty?

Mongol rule in China ended in 1368 when **Hongwu** led a rebel army that took control of the country. He declared himself the first emperor of the **Ming Dynasty**, which was to last for almost 300 years. Hongwu began his rule by increasing the amount of food produced and improving the government. Later he grew suspicious and untrusting. He caused the deaths of many people whom he suspected of plotting against him.

His son **Yonglo** continued his better policies.

He also launched a major effort at making contact with other Asian peoples. Beginning in 1405, an admiral named **Zheng** led several fleets to Southeast Asia, India, Arabia, and Africa. Wherever he went, he gave away gifts to show Chinese superiority.

Eventually the Chinese changed their position on foreign trade. They began to isolate themselves. China allowed Europeans to trade officially at only three ports, but illegal trade took place all along the coast. Europeans wanted Chinese silk and ceramics, and they paid silver for them. Manufacturing never grew very large in China, however. The *Confucian* ideas that shaped Chinese thinking said

CHAPTER 19 AN AGE OF EXPLORATION AND ISOLATION **177**

that farming was a better way of life, so manufacturing was heavily taxed. *Missionaries* entered China at this time, bringing both Christianity and technology.

1. How was China influenced by foreigners during the Ming Dynasty?

_____

_____

_____

The Qing Dynasty (pages 471-472)
How did China change during the Qing Dynasty?

The Ming Dynasty lost power because the government could not solve several problems. **Manchus**, people who came from a land north of China called Manchuria, took control of the country in 1644. They started the **Qing Dynasty**. Two important emperors were **Kangxi** and his grandson Qian-long. They brought China to its largest size, increased its wealth, and sponsored an increase in artistic production.

The Chinese insisted that Europeans had to follow certain rules in order to continue trading with them. These rules include trading only at special ports and paying fees. The Dutch were willing to do so, and they carried on the largest share of trade with China. The British, though, did not agree to following these rules.

2. Why was trade a problem during the Qing Dynasty?

_____

_____

_____

_____

Daily Life in Ming and Qing China (pages 472-473)
How did changes in agriculture make China different?

In China, the production of rice and the long period of peace gave the people better lives. In the 1600s and 1700s, the number of people in China almost doubled. The huge majority of these people were farmers. Because of the use of fertilizer and better *irrigation*, they could grow more food. The level of nutrition improved. This caused the population to grow.

In Chinese families, sons were valued over daughters. It was felt only sons could carry out family religious duties and tend to the family farm. For that reason, many infant girls were killed, and adult women had few rights.

The invasions by the foreigners from Manchuria and the pressure from European traders bothered the Chinese. They tried to preserve their traditions and their isolation. Artists created books and paintings that showed traditional Chinese values and ideas. At the same time, a feeling of national pride was rising in Korea, which had long been *dominated* by China.

3. Which parts of society improved during this time, and which continued to be the same?

_____

_____

_____

_____

Name _____ Date _____

CHAPTER 19 Section 3 (pages 474-477)

Japan Limits Western Contacts

TERMS AND NAMES
daimyo Warrior-chieftains
Oda Nobunaga Daimyo who hoped to control all of Japan and seized Kyoto
Toyotomi Hideyoshi Daimyo who took control of almost all of Japan
Tokugawa Shogunate Dynasty that ruled Japan from 1603 to 1868
kabuki Type of Japanese theater
haiku Type of Japanese poetry

BEFORE YOU READ

In the last section, you saw how the Chinese reacted to foreigners.

In this section, you will read about civil war in Japan and its effects.

AS YOU READ

Use the chart below to show some ways in which Japan changed after it was unified

```
                    Japan Is Unified
       ┌───────────────┬───────────┬───────────┐
   political        economic     cultural    social
new system of rule—
Tokugawa Shogunate
```

Strong Leaders Take Control
(pages 474-475)

Why were warriors fighting in Japan?

From 1467 to 1568, Japan entered a long, dark period of civil war. Powerful warriors took control of large areas of land. They were called **daimyo**. They became the most important powers in the country. The daimyo fought each other constantly to gain more land for themselves.

In 1568, one of the daimyo, **Oda Nobunaga**, took control of Kyoto. It was the site of the emperor's capital. Another general, **Toyotomi Hideyoshi**, continued the work of bringing all of Japan under one rule. Using military conquest and clever *diplomacy*, he won that goal in 1590. He failed in his effort to capture Korea, however.

The work of *unifying* Japan was completed by Tokugawa Ieyasu. He became the *shogun*, or sole ruler. He moved the capital of Japan to a small fishing village named Edo. Later, it grew to become the city of Tokyo.

While all of Japan was ruled by Tokugawa, the daimyo still held much power in their lands. Tokugawa solved that problem by forcing them to follow his orders. Tokugawa died in 1616. All of the shoguns to follow him were from his family. They maintained a strong central government in Japan. This system of rule, called the **Tokugawa Shogunate**, lasted until 1868.

1. Which three leaders helped bring Japan under one rule?

_____

_____

CHAPTER 19 AN AGE OF EXPLORATION AND ISOLATION **179**

Tokugawa Society and Culture
(pages 475-476)

How was the new society organized?

The new government brought about a long period of peace and *prosperity* for most people. Peasant farmers suffered greatly during this time, however. They worked long and hard on the farms and paid heavy taxes. Many left the countryside to move to the cities. By the mid-1700s, Edo had more than a million people. It was perhaps the largest city in the world. Women found more opportunities for work in this and other cities than they had in the country.

A *traditional* culture thrived. It preferred ceremonial dramas, stories of ancient warriors, and paintings of classical scenes. However, in cities, new styles emerged. Townspeople attended **kabuki,** dramas of urban life. They hung woodblock prints of city scenes in their homes. They also read **haiku**, poetry that presents images instead of expressing ideas.

2. **What kinds of old and new culture were found in the cities?**

_____

Contact Between Europe and Japan (pages 476-477)

Who came to Japan?

In 1543, Europeans began to arrive in Japan. The Portuguese were first. In the beginning, Japanese merchants and the daimyo welcomed them. They even welcomed the Christian missionaries who came after 1549.

Some missionaries scorned traditional Japanese beliefs. They also got involved in local politics. Tokugawa became worried. In 1612, he banned Christianity from the country. Christians were persecuted. Over the next 20 years or so, Japan managed to rid the country of all Christians. This was part of a larger plan to protect the country from European influence. In 1639, leaders sealed Japan's borders except for one port city. It was open to only the Chinese and the Dutch. The Tokugawa shoguns controlled that port city, so they had tight control over all foreign contact. For the next 200 years, Japan remained closed to just about all European contact.

3. **Why did the Japanese seal almost all of their borders?**

_____

JAPANESE SOCIETY

Emperor
Held highest rank in society but had no political power

Daimyo — Large landowners
Shogun — Actual ruler

Samurai Warriors
Loyal to Daimyo and Shogun

Peasants — Four-fifths of the population
Artisans — Craftspeople such as artists and blacksmiths
Merchants — Low status but gradually gained influence

Skillbuilder
Use the illustration to answer these questions.

1. **What three people or groups of people controlled Japanese society?**

_____

2. **What was the relationship of the samurai to the other classes in Japanese society?**

_____

Name _____ Date _____

Glossary   **CHAPTER 19** An Age of Exploration and Isolation

caravel Strong sailing ship designed in the 1400s
Confucian Related to Confucius, who taught principles of social order, harmony, and good
diplomacy Skill in handling affairs between nations
dominated Ruled over or had great power over
irrigation Method of bringing water to crops
missionaries People who bring religious ideas to new places
navigation Finding one's way at sea
rebel Oppose the government by force
shogun Supreme military commander who ruled in the name of the emperor
traditional Based on what has been done in the past
unifying Bringing together under one rule

AFTER YOU READ

Names and Terms

A. Write the name or term in each blank that best completes the meaning of the paragraph.

Kangxi

Yonglo

Hongwu

Zheng He

Manchus

In China, the great Ming Dynasty began when **1** _____ led a rebel army to victory over the Mongols. He made some good changes in China that improved the government and led to the production of more food. His son, **2** _____, continued his better policies. Among other things, he sent the Muslim admiral **3** _____ on journeys of exploration. The power of the Ming Dynasty eventually declined, however. People from Manchuria known as **4** _____ took over. They established the Qing Dynasty. The emperor **5** _____ was one of its most important rulers.

B. Write the letter of the name or therm next to the description that explains it best.

a. haiku

b. Treaty of Tordesillas

c. Vasco da Gama

d. Bartolomeu Dias

e. daimyo

____ **1.** Led voyage around Africa, to India, and back to Portugal

____ **2.** Warrior-chieftains

____ **3.** Led first voyage to reach the southern tip of Africa

____ **4.** Poetry that presents images

____ **5.** Agreement between Portugal and Spain that divided the world into two areas

Name _____ Date _____

AFTER YOU READ (cont.) CHAP 19 An Age of Exploration and Isolation

Main Ideas

1. Who led the way in European exploration, and why?
_____
_____

2. What countries established trading empires in the Indian Ocean?
_____
_____

3. How did the Ming Dynasty come to an end?
_____
_____

4. What was Toyotomi Hideyoshi's greatest accomplishment?
_____
_____

5. How did the Japanese react to the arrival of foreigners?
_____
_____

Thinking Critically

Answer the following questions on a separate sheet of paper.

1. Why did the Europeans begin to explore overseas, and what technological advances made this possible?

2. What factors led to the growth of the Chinese population?

Name _____ Date _____

CHAPTER 20 Section 1 (pages 483-488)

Spanish Conquests in the Americas

BEFORE YOU READ

In the last chapter, you read about European exploration in the East.

In this section, you will study the Spanish and Portuguese exploration of the Americas.

AS YOU READ

Use the web below to show some of the results of Spanish conquest.

TERMS AND NAMES
Christopher Columbus Italian explorer who landed in the Americas
colony Land controlled by another nation
Hernando Cortés Conquistador who defeated the Aztec
conquistadors Spanish explorers in the Americas
Montezuma II Leader of the Aztec at the time of Cortés's arrival
Francisco Pizarro Conquistador who defeated the Inca
mestizo Person with mixed Spanish and Native American blood
encomienda System of mining and farming using natives as slave labor

```
                Effects of Spanish Conquest
                     on the Americas
                              │
          ┌───────────────────┼───────────────────┐
          ▼                   ▼                   ▼
      political             social             economic
     New France
```

Columbus's Voyage Paves the Way (pages 483-485)

How did the voyages of Columbus change the Americas?

In 1492, **Christopher Columbus**, an Italian sailor, led a voyage for Spain. He sailed west hoping to reach Asia. Instead, he landed in the Americas. Columbus thought that he had reached the East Indies in Asia. He misnamed the natives he met there, calling them Indians. He claimed the land for Spain. From then on, Spain began to create **colonies**. Colonies are lands controlled by another nation.

In 1500, a Portuguese explorer claimed Brazil. In 1501, Amerigo Vespucci explored the eastern coast of South America. He said that these lands were a new world. Soon after, a mapmaker showed the lands as a separate continent. He named them America after Vespucci.

Other voyages gave Europeans more knowledge about the world. Balboa reached the Pacific Ocean. Ferdinand Magellan sailed completely around the world.

1. Which voyages gave Europeans new knowledge of the world?

_____

_____

CHAPTER 20 THE ATLANTIC WORLD **183**

Spain Builds an American Empire (pages 485-487)

How did Spain build an empire?

Hernando Cortés was one of the Spanish **conquistadors**, or conquerors. In the 16th century, they began to explore the lands of the Americas. They were seeking great riches. In 1519, Cortés came to Mexico and defeated the powerful *Aztec Empire* led by **Montezuma II**.

About 15 years later, **Francisco Pizarro** led another Spanish force. It conquered the mighty *Inca Empire* of South America. Once again, the Spanish found gold and silver. By the mid-1500s, Spain had formed an American empire that stretched from modern-day Mexico to Peru. After 1540, the Spanish looked north of Mexico and explored the future United States.

One large area of the Americas—Brazil—was the *possession* of Portugal. In the 1830s, colonists began to settle there. Colonists built huge farms called *plantations* to grow sugar, which was in demand in Europe.

The Spanish lived among the people they conquered. Spanish men married native women. Their children and *descendants* were called **mestizo**—people with mixed Spanish and Native American blood. The Spanish also formed large farms and mines that used natives as slave labor. This system was known as *encomienda*.

2. Give two examples of conquistadors and explain what they did.

_____

_____

Spain Expands Its Influence
(pages 487-488)

How did Spain try to gain more power?

Soon Spain began to want even more power in the Americas. It started to look at land that is now part of the United States. Explorers like Coronado led expeditions to the area. Catholic priests went along.

Spanish priests began to make some protests, however. One thing they criticized was the encomienda system. A monk named Bartolomé de Las Casas and others successfully called for the end of the system.

Native Americans also resisted new or continued Spanish rule. One of the most serious *rebellions* occurred in New Mexico. A Pueblo leader named Popé led a well-organized effort. It involved about 17,000 warriors and drove the Spanish back into New Spain for 12 years.

3. What challenges to their power did the Spanish face?

_____

_____

Native Population of Central Mexico
- 1519: 25.3 million
- 1523: 16.8 million
- 1548: 6.3 million
- 1605: 1.0 million

Skillbuilder
Use the graph to answer the questions.

1. Sum up the time frame and the general trend in population shown on this graph.

_____

_____

2. What was the most drastic drop in population?

_____

Name _____ Date _____

CHAPTER 20 Section 2 (pages 490-494)

Competing Claims in North America

BEFORE YOU READ

In the last chapter, you read about Spanish conquests.
In this section, you will see how other nations competed for power in North America.

AS YOU READ

Use the web below to show different claims in North America.

TERMS AND NAMES

New France Area of the Americas explored and claimed by France
Jamestown First permanent settlement in America
Pilgrims Group of English people who founded a colony in Plymouth
Puritans People who did not agree with the practices of the Church of England
New Netherland Dutch colony begun in modern New York City
French and Indian War War between Britain and France over land in North America
Metacom Native American leader who lead an attack on the villages of Massachusetts; also called King Philip

```
      French                             English
    New France
              \                        /
               \                      /
                North America
               /                      \
              /                        \
       Dutch                          Native American
```

European Nations Settle North America (pages 490-492)

What *new colonies were formed in North America?*

In the early 1500s, the French began to explore North America. Jacques Cartier discovered and named the St. Lawrence River. He then followed it to the site of what is now Montreal. In 1608, Samuel de Champlain sailed as far as modern-day Quebec. In the next 100 years, the French explored and claimed the area around the Great Lakes and the Mississippi River all the way to its mouth at the Gulf of Mexico. The area became known as **New France**. The main activity in this colony was trade in beaver fur.

The English also began to colonize North America. The first permanent settlement was at **Jamestown**, in modern Virginia, in 1607. The colony struggled at first. Many settlers died from disease, hunger, or war with the native peoples. Soon, farmers began to grow tobacco to meet the high demand for it in Europe.

In 1620, a group known as **Pilgrims** founded a

CHAPTER 20 THE ATLANTIC WORLD **185**

second English colony in Plymouth, in Massachusetts. These settlers and others who followed were deeply religious people who did not agree with the practices of the Church of England. They were called **Puritans**.

Meanwhile, the Dutch also started a new colony. They settled in the location of modern New York City and called it **New Netherland**. Like the French, they traded fur. The colony became known as a home to people of many different religions and cultures. Europeans also took possession of many islands of the Caribbean. There they built tobacco and sugar plantations that used enslaved Africans as workers.

1. In which two places did English colonists first settle?

___

The Fight for North America
(pages 492-493)

Who fought for control of North America?

The European powers began to fight for control of North America. First, the English forced the Dutch to give up their colony. New Amsterdam was renamed New York. The English also started other colonies along the Atlantic coast, from New Hampshire to Georgia. These English colonists interfered with the French settlers in Canada.

The British and the French clashed over the Ohio Valley in 1754. The fight was called the **French and Indian War**. When it ended in 1763, France was forced to give up all its land in North America to England.

2. How did England gain land from the French?

___

Native American Reaction
(pages 493-494)

How did native people respond to the colonists?

The native peoples responded to the colonists in many different ways. Many worked closely with the French and Dutch, joining in the fur trade and benefiting from it. Those who lived near the English, though, had stormier relations with colonists. More than just trade, the English were interested in settling the land and farming it. This was land that Native Americans would not be able to use for hunting or growing their own food.

Conflicts over land *erupted* into war several times. One of the bloodiest times was known as King Philip's War. The Native American ruler **Metacom** (also known as King Philip) led an attack on 52 colonial villages throughout Massachusetts. However, Metacom's forces were no match for the settlers' guns and cannons.

As in Spanish lands, the native peoples suffered even more from disease than from warfare. Thousands upon thousands of Native Americans died from European illnesses. This made it impossible for them to resist the growth of the colonies.

3. Why did Native Americans lose their way of life?

___

Name _____ Date _____

CHAPTER 20 Section 3 (pages 495-499)

The Atlantic Slave Trade

BEFORE YOU READ

In the last section, you saw how different European nations settled in North America.

In this section, you will read about the slave trade that brought Africans to the Americas.

AS YOU READ

Use the chart below to take notes on the triangular trade system.

TERMS AND NAMES

Atlantic slave trade Buying and selling of Africans for work in the Americas

triangular trade European trade between the Americas, Africa, and Europe involving slaves and other goods

middle passage Voyage that brought captured Africans to the West Indies and the Americas

Who traded?	What was traded?	Where were goods sent?
Spanish, Portuguese, and others		

→ Triangular trade

The Evolution of African Slavery (pages 495-497)

What was the Atlantic slave trade?

Slavery has had a long history in Africa and in the world. For most of that history in Africa, though, large numbers of people had not been enslaved. That changed in the 600s, when Muslim traders started to take many slaves to Southwest Asia.

Most worked as servants, and they did have certain rights. Also, the sons and daughters of slaves were considered to be free. The European slave trade that began in the 1500s was larger. The enslaved Africans also were treated far more harshly.

In the Americas, Europeans first used Native Americans to work farms and mines. When the native peoples began dying from disease, the Europeans brought in Africans. The buying and selling of Africans for work in the Americas became known as the **Atlantic slave trade**. From 1500 to 1870, when the slave trade in the Americas finally ended, about 9.5 million Africans had been *imported* as slaves.

The Spanish first began the practice of bringing Africans to the Americas. However, the Portuguese increased the demand for slaves. They were looking for workers for their sugar plantations in Brazil.

Other European colonies also brought slaves to

CHAPTER 20 THE ATLANTIC WORLD **187**

work on tobacco, sugar, and coffee plantations. About 400,000 slaves were brought to the English colonies in North America. Their population had increased to about 2 million in 1830.

Many African rulers joined in the slave trade. They moved inland to capture people and brought them to the coast to sell to European traders.

1. Why were slaves brought to the Americas?

_____

_____

_____

A Forced Journey (page 497-498)
What kinds of trade included human beings?

Africans taken to the Americas were part of a **triangular trade** between Europe, Africa, and the Americas. European ships brought manufactured goods to Africa, trading them for people. They carried Africans across the Atlantic to the Americas, where they were sold into slavery. The traders then bought sugar, coffee, and tobacco to bring back to Europe.

Another triangle involved ships sailing from the northern English colonies in North America. They carried rum to Africa, people to the West Indies, and sugar and molasses back to the colonies to make more rum.

The part of the voyage that brought people to the Americas was called the **middle passage**. It was harsh and cruel. People were crammed into ships, beaten, and given little food. About 20 percent of the people on these ships died.

2. What was the triangular trade?

_____

_____

_____

_____

Slavery in the Americas; Consequences of the Atlantic Slave Trade (pages 498-499)
What was life like for the slaves?

Life on the plantations was harsh as well. People were sold to the highest bidder. They worked from dawn to dusk in the fields. They lived in small huts and had little food and clothing. Africans kept alive their traditional music and beliefs to try to maintain their spirits. Sometimes they rebelled. From North America to Brazil, from 1522 to the 1800s, there were small-scale slave revolts.

The Atlantic slave trade had a huge impact on both Africa and the Americas. In Africa many cultures lost generations of members. Africans began fighting Africans over the control of the slave trade.

The Africans' labor helped build the Americas. They brought skills and culture too. Many of the nations of the Americas have mixed race populations.

3. How did Africans change the Americas?

_____

_____

_____

_____

188 CHAPTER 20 SECTION 3

Name _____ Date _____

CHAPTER 20 Section 4 (pages 500-503)

The Columbian Exchange and Global Trade

TERMS AND NAMES
Columbian Exchange Global transfer of foods, plants, and animals during the colonization of the Americas
Commercial Revolution New business and trade practices in Europe during the 16th and 17th centuries
capitalism Economic system based on private ownership and the investment of wealth for profit
joint-stock company Company in which people pooled their wealth for a common purpose
mercantilism Economic policy of increasing wealth and power by obtaining large amounts of gold and silver and selling more goods than are bought
favorable balance of trade Condition resulting from selling more goods than are bought

BEFORE YOU READ
In the last section, you read about the slave trade.
In this section, you will learn about other kinds of trade.

AS YOU READ
Use the chart below to take notes on the Columbian Exchange.

| COLUMBIAN EXCHANGE ||
Leaving the Americas	Arriving in the Americas
tomatoes, corn, potatoes	

The Columbian Exchange (page 500)
What was the Columbian Exchange?

There was constant movement of people and products from Europe and Africa to the Americas. The large-scale transfer of foods, plants, and animals was called the **Columbian Exchange**. Important foods such as corn and potatoes were taken from the Americas to Europe, Africa, and Asia.

Some foods moved from the Old World to the New. Bananas, black-eyed peas, and yams were taken from Africa to the Americas. Cattle, pigs, and horses had never been seen in the Americas until the Europeans brought them. Deadly illnesses also moved to the Americas. They killed a large part of the Native American population.

1. What did the Columbian Exchange take from the Americas, and what did it bring?

_____

_____

CHAPTER 20 THE ATLANTIC WORLD **189**

A Commercial Revolution
(pages 500-503)

What was the Commercial Revolution?

The settling of the Americas and the growth of trade started the **Commercial Revolution**. This revolution led to a new set of business practices still followed today. One was the rise of an economic system called **capitalism**. It is based on *private ownership* of property and the right of a business to earn a profit on money it has invested.

Another new business idea was the **joint-stock company**. In this type of company, many investors pool their money to start a business and share in the profits.

During the Commercial Revolution, European governments began to follow an idea called **mercantilism**. According to this theory, a country's power depended on its wealth. Getting more gold and silver increased a country's wealth. So did selling more goods than it bought. Selling more than it bought would result in a **favorable balance of trade**. Colonies played an important role because they provided goods that could be sold in trade.

The American colonies changed European society. Merchants grew wealthy and powerful. Towns and cities grew larger. Still, most people lived in the countryside, farmed for a living, and were poor.

2. Why were colonies important to European mercantilism?

_____

_____

Skillbuilder
Use the chart to answer these questions.

1. Which continents were involved in the Columbian Exchange?

_____

2. What was a harmful effect of the Columbian Exchange?

_____

Name _____ Date _____

Glossary   CHAPTER 20   The Atlantic World

Aztec Empire Great empire in the Valley of Mexico that had strong religious beliefs and a powerful army

descendants People who are offspring or ancestors of one family group

erupted Broke out

imported Brought into one country from another

Inca Empire Largest empire ever in the Americas, located in the Andes

plantations Large farms usually devoted to a single crop

possession Land owned by another country

private ownership Ownership by individuals instead of by groups or governments

rebellions Uprisings against the current government

AFTER YOU READ

Names and Terms

A. Write the name or term in each blank that best completes the meaning of the paragraph.

Puritans
Pilgrims
New France
New Netherland
Jamestown
colony

The first permanent **1** _____ to be established in what is now the United States was at **2** _____. Not long after a group of **3** _____ crossed the ocean and started a colony at Plymouth. They were followed by other **4** _____ who also settled in what is now Massachusetts. Settled by the English, these colonies were a kind of "New England." The empire established by France in American was called **5** _____. The empire established by the Dutch in America was called **6** _____.

B. Write the letter of the name or term that matches the description.

a. mercantilism
b. capitalism
c. middle passage
d. favorable balance of trade
e. Atlantic slave trade

_____ **1.** Buying and selling of Africans for work in the Americas

_____ **2.** Economic condition reached by selling more than is bought

_____ **3.** Economic system that encourages people to make a profit

_____ **4.** Economic policy that said a country's power depended mainly on its wealth

_____ **5.** Voyage of captured Africans to the Americas

Name _____ Date _____

AFTER YOU READ (continued)   *CHAPTER 20*   The Atlantic World

Main Ideas

1. Why did the French and British fight for control of North America, and what happened?
_____
_____
_____

2. How did Native Americans react to the colonists?
_____
_____
_____

3. Describe the middle passage of the triangular trade.
_____
_____
_____

4. What was traded in the Columbian Exchange?
_____
_____
_____

5. Name three new business practices of the Commercial Revolution.
_____
_____
_____

Thinking Critically

Answer the following questions on a separate sheet of paper.

1. How did Spanish conquests forever change the Americas?

2. Discuss the ways the lives of Africans and Native Americans were altered by the European conquest of the Americas.

Name _____ Date _____

CHAPTER 21 Section 1 (pages 513–517)

Spain's Empire and European Absolutism

TERMS AND NAMES
Philip II Spanish king who took control of Portugal but failed in his invasion of England
absolute monarch King or queen with complete control
divine right Idea that a ruler receives the right to rule from God

BEFORE YOU READ

In the last chapter, you read about Europe's new relationship to the Americas.

In this section, you will learn about changes occurring in Europe in the 1500s and 1600s.

AS YOU READ

Use the chart below to record reasons for change in Spain in the 16th century..

CAUSES	EFFECT
Inflation and unfair taxes hurt the poor	Spain's economy declines

Spain's Powerful Empire

(pages 513–514)

How did Spain's power increase and then decrease?

Charles V of Spain ruled the Holy Roman Empire and other European countries. In 1556, he left the throne and split his holdings. His brother Ferdinand received Austria and the Holy Roman Empire. His son, **Philip II**, got Spain and its colonies.

Philip II *expanded* his holdings by taking control of Portugal when the king of Portugal, his uncle, died without an heir. Philip also got its global territories in Africa, India, and the East Indies. When he tried to invade England in 1588, though, he failed. The defeat made Spain weaker. However, Spain still seemed strong because of the wealth—gold and silver—that flowed in from its colonies in the Americas.

1. Who was Philip II?

_____

_____

CHAPTER 21 ABSOLUTE MONARCHS IN EUROPE **193**

Problems Weaken the Spanish Empire (pages 514–515)

What weakened the Spanish Empire?

Spain's new wealth led to some serious problems. The prices of goods constantly rose. Unfair taxes kept the poor from building up any wealth of their own. As prices rose, Spaniards bought more goods from other lands. To finance their wars, Spanish kings had to borrow money from banks in foreign countries. The silver from the colonies began to flow to Spain's enemies.

In the middle of these troubles, Spain lost land. Seven *provinces* of the Spanish Netherlands rose in protest against high taxes and attempts to crush Protestantism in the Netherlands. These seven provinces were Protestant, whereas Spain was strongly Catholic. In 1579, they declared their independence from Spain and became the United Provinces of the Netherlands. The ten southern provinces (present-day Belgium) were Catholic and remained under Spanish.

2. Why did Spain lose its power?

_____

_____

_____

The Independent Dutch Prosper (pages 515–516)

Why did the Dutch prosper?

The United Provinces of the Netherlands was different from other European states of the time. It was a republic, not a kingdom. Each province had a leader elected by the people.

The Dutch also practiced *religious tolerance*, letting people worship as they wished. Dutch merchants established a trading empire. They had the largest fleet of merchant ships in the world. They were also the most important bankers in Europe.

3. Give two reasons for the success of the Dutch in trading.

_____

_____

_____

Absolutism in Europe (pages 516–517)

What is absolutism?

Though he lost his Dutch possessions, Philip continued to hold tight control over Spain. He wanted to control the lives of his people. Philip and others who ruled in the same way were called **absolute monarchs**. They believed in holding all power. They also believed in **divine right**. This is the idea that a ruler receives the right to rule from God.

Absolute rule, or *absolutism,* and its restrictions caused widespread unrest in Europe in the 17th century. Some absolute rulers increased their power by forcing an end to conflicts within their countries. That is what happened in France.

4. What did absolute monarchs believe?

_____

_____

_____

Name _____ Date _____

CHAPTER 21 Section 2 (pages 518–523)

France's Ultimate Monarch

BEFORE YOU READ

In the last section, you were introduced to the idea of absolutism.

In this section, you will read about absolute power in France.

AS YOU READ

Use the time line below to show important events in France.

TERMS AND NAMES
Edict of Nantes Order that gave Huguenots the right to live in peace in Catholic France
Cardinal Richelieu Chief minister of France who reduced the power of the nobles
skepticism Belief that nothing could be known for certain
Louis XIV French king who was an absolute ruler
intendant Official of the French government
Jean Baptiste Colbert Chief Minister of Finance under Louis XIV
War of the Spanish Succession War fought by other European nations against France and Spain when those two states tried to unite their thrones

```
┌─────────────────────┐         ┌─────────────────────┐
│     1562-1598       │         │        1643         │
│ Religious wars between│        │                     │
│ Catholics and Protestants│     │                     │
└──────────┬──────────┘         └──────────┬──────────┘
           │                               │
┌──────────┴──────────┐         ┌──────────┴──────────┐
│        1598         │         │      1700-1713      │
│                     │         │                     │
└─────────────────────┘         └─────────────────────┘
```

Religious Wars Create a Crisis
(pages 518–519)

What changes were occurring in France?

France was torn by eight religious wars between Catholics and Protestants from 1562 to 1598.

In 1589, a Protestant prince, Henry of Navarre, became King Henry IV. In 1593, he changed religions. He became a Catholic to please the majority of his people. In 1598, he issued an order called the **Edict of Nantes**. It gave Huguenots—French Protestants—the right to live in peace and have their own churches in some cities.

Henry rebuilt the French economy and brought peace to the land. He was followed by his son, Louis XIII, a weak king. However, Louis had a very capable chief minister, **Cardinal Richelieu**. Richelieu ruled the land for Louis and increased the power of the crown.

The cardinal ordered the Huguenots not to build walls around their cities. He also said nobles had to destroy their castles. As a result, Protestants and nobles could not hide within walls to *defy* the king's power. Richelieu used people from the middle class—not nobles—to work in his government. That also reduced the power of the nobles.

French thinkers had reacted to the religious wars with horror. They developed a new philosophy called **skepticism**. Nothing could be known

CHAPTER 21 ABSOLUTE MONARCHS IN EUROPE 195

for certain, they argued. Doubting old ideas was the first step to learning the truth, they said.

1. How did the monarchy get stronger in France?

___

Louis XIV Rules Absolutely
(pages 519–520)

How did Louis XIV rule?

In 1643, **Louis XIV** became king at the age of five. Cardinal Mazarin, who succeeded Richelieu as minister, ruled for Louis until he was 23. Louis became a powerful ruler, who had total control of France. He was determined to never let nobles challenge him.

He kept the nobles out of his government. He gave more power to government officials called **intendants** and made sure that they answered only to him. He also worked hard to increase the wealth of France. His chief minister of finance, **Jean Baptiste Colbert**, tried to build French industry. Colbert wanted to persuade French people to buy French-made goods and not those from other countries. He urged people to settle in the new French colony of Canada in North America. The fur trade there brought wealth to France.

2. How did Louis make sure he kept his power?

___

Louis's Grand Style; Louis Fights Disastrous Wars (pages 520–523)

What changes did Louis make?

Louis enjoyed a life of luxury at his court. He built a huge and beautiful palace at Versailles near Paris. He also made sure that nobles had to depend on his favor to advance in society.

Louis made France the most powerful nation in Europe. France had a larger population and a bigger army than any other country. However, Louis made some mistakes that later proved costly. After winning some wars against neighboring countries, he became bolder and tried to seize more land. Other nations allied to stop France in the late 1680s. The high cost of these wars combined with poor harvests to produce problems at home in France.

The final war fought in Louis's time was fought over *succession* to the throne of Spain and lasted from 1700 to 1713. In this **War of the Spanish Succession,** France and Spain attempted to set up united thrones. The rest of Europe felt threatened and joined in war against them. Both France and Spain were forced to give up some of their American and European colonies to England. England was the new rising power.

3. How did Louis XIV bring disaster to France?

___

[Graph: French debt in livres (in millions), years 1643, 1648, 1661, 1683, 1699, 1708, 1715. Scale 0–2,000.]
A livre is equal to approximately $10.50 in 1992 U.S. dollars.
Source: *Early Modern France 1560-1715*

Skillbuilder
Use the graph to answer these questions.

1. What is the general trend shown in this graph?

___

2. What was the difference in the debt, in millions of livres, between 1683 and 1715?

___

Name _____ Date _____

CHAPTER 21 Section 3 (pages 526-530)

Central European Monarchs Clash

BEFORE YOU READ

In the last section, you read how absolute power grew in France.

In this section, you will learn about absolutism in Austria and Prussia.

AS YOU READ

Use the time line below to take notes on key events in Central Europe.

TERMS AND NAMES

Thirty Years' War Conflict over religion, territory, and power among European ruling families

Maria Theresa Empress of Austria whose main enemy was Prussia

Frederick the Great Leader of Prussia who sought to increase its territory

Seven Years' War Conflict from 1756 to 1763 in which the forces of Britain and Prussia battled those of Austria, France, Russia, and other countries.

```
┌─────────────────────────┐      ┌─────────────────────────┐
│      1618-1648          │      │       1756-1763         │
│ Thirty Years' War fought│      │                         │
└─────────────────────────┘      └─────────────────────────┘
              │                              │
              └──────────────┬───────────────┘
                   ┌─────────────────────────┐
                   │         1740            │
                   │                         │
                   └─────────────────────────┘
```

The Thirty Years' War (pages 526–528)

What caused the Thirty Years' War?

Germany had suffered from religious wars that ended in 1555. Rulers of each German state agreed that they would decide whether their lands would be Catholic or Protestant. Relations between sides became tense over the next decades. Then in 1618, a new war broke out and lasted for 30 terrible years. It was called the **Thirty Years' War**.

During the first half of the war, Catholic forces led by Ferdinand, the Holy Roman Emperor, won. However, Germany suffered because he allowed his large army to *loot* towns. Then the Protestant king of Sweden, Gustavus Adolphus, won several battles against him.

In the last years of the war, France helped the Protestants. Although France was a Catholic nation, Richelieu feared the growing power of the Hapsburg family, which was headed by Frederick.

The Thirty Years' War ended in 1648 with the Peace of Westphalia. It had been a disaster for Germany. About 4 million people had died, and the economy was in ruins. It took Germany two centuries to recover.

The peace treaty weakened the power of Austria and Spain. But it made France stronger. The French gained German territory. The treaty also made German princes independent of the Holy Roman emperor. It ended religious wars in Europe. Lastly, the treaty introduced a new way of negotiating peace—a method still used today. All states involved in the fighting meet to settle the problems of a war and decide the terms of peace.

CHAPTER 21 ABSOLUTE MONARCHS IN EUROPE **197**

1. What were three results of the Thirty Years' War?

_____
_____
_____

Central Europe Differs from the West (pages 528–529)

Who ruled Austria?

The formation of strong states took place slowly in central Europe. The economies there were less developed than in western Europe. Most people were still peasants. This region had not built an economy based in towns. Nobles enjoyed great influence. This helped them hold down the serfs and to prevent the rise of strong rulers. Still, two important states arose.

The Hapsburg family ruled Austria, Hungary, and Bohemia. Their empire linked many different peoples—Czechs, Hugarians, Italians, Croatians, and Germans. **Maria Theresa**, the daughter of Charles VI, was empress of Austria in the mid–1700s. She managed to increase her power and reduce that of the nobles. She was opposed by the kings of Prussia, a new powerful state in northern Germany.

2. Who were the Hapsburgs?

_____
_____
_____

Prussia and Austria Clash (pages 529–530)

What was Prussia?

Like Austria, Prussia rose to power in the late 1600s. Like the Hapsburgs of Austria, Prussia's ruling family, the Hohenzollerns, also had ambitions.

Prussia was a strong state that gave much power to its large, well-trained army. In 1740, **Frederick the Great** of Prussia invaded one of Maria Theresa's lands. Austria fought hard to keep the territory, but lost. Still, in fighting the War of the Austrian Succession, Maria Theresa managed to keep the rest of her empire *intact*.

The two sides fought again, beginning in 1756. In the **Seven Years' War**, Austria abandoned Britain, its old *ally*, for France and Russia. Prussia joined with Britain. The Prussians and British won. In that victory, Britain gained complete control of the overseas colonies of France.

3. What effect did fighting between Austria and Prussia have on Britain?

_____
_____
_____
_____

198 CHAPTER 21 SECTION 3

Name _____ Date _____

CHAPTER 21 Section 4 (pages 531–535)

Russian Czars Increase Power

TERMS AND NAMES
Ivan the Terrible Ruler who added lands to Russia, gave it a code of laws, and also used his secret police to execute "traitors"
boyars Russian nobles who owned land
Peter the Great Important leader of Russia who started westernization
westernization Use of western Europe as a model of change

BEFORE YOU READ

In the last section, you read how Austria and Prussia became strong states.

In this section, you will learn how Russia developed into a powerful state.

AS YOU READ

Use the chart below to take notes on the changes made in Russia by Peter the Great.

Peter the Great's Changes

political	social	cultural	economic
Increased power of the czar			

From Ivan to the Romanovs
(pages 531–532)

Who was Ivan the Terrible?

Ivan III had made Moscow the center of a new Russian state with a central government. His son, Vasily, continued the work of adding territory to the growing Russian state. Ivan's grandson, Ivan IV, was called **Ivan the Terrible**. He came to the throne in 1533, when he was three years old.

At first, landowning nobles, known as **boyars**, tried to control Ivan. Eventually, he ruled successfully on his own. He added lands to Russia and gave the country a code of laws. After his wife, Anastasia, died, however, his rule turned harsh. He used secret police to hunt down enemies and kill them. Ivan even murdered his oldest son.

A few years after he died, Russian nobles met to name a new ruler. They chose Michael Romanov, the great nephew of Ivan the Terrible's wife. He began the Romanov dynasty that ruled Russia for about 300 years.

1. What good and bad did Ivan the Terrible do?

_____

_____

Peter the Great Takes the Throne (pages 532–533)

Who was Peter the Great?

The Romanovs restored order to Russia. In the late 1600s, Peter I came to power. He was called **Peter the Great** because he was one of Russia's greatest

CHAPTER 21 ABSOLUTE MONARCHS IN EUROPE **199**

reformers. He began an intense program of trying to modernize Russia. He also continued the trend of increasing the czar's power.

When Peter came to power, Russia was still a land of boyars and serfs. Serfdom lasted much longer in Russia than it did in western Europe. It continued into the mid–1800s.

When a Russian landowner sold a piece of land, he sold the serfs with it. Landowners could give serfs away as presents or to pay debts. It was also against the law for serfs to run away from their owners.

Most boyars knew little of western Europe. But Peter admired the nations of western Europe. He traveled in Europe to learn about new technology and ways of working. It was the first time a czar traveled in the West. He returned to Russia determined to make his country more advanced.

2. Why did Peter the Great visit Europe?

_____

_____

_____

Peter Rules Absolutely (page 535)

What changes did Peter the Great make?

Peter the Great wanted Russia to be the equal of the countries of western Europe. He wanted Russia to be strong both in its military and in its trade.

To meet these goals, Peter changed Russia. His first steps were to increase the powers of the czar, or ruler, so he could force people to make the changes he wanted. He put the Russian Orthodox Church under his control. He reduced the power of nobles. He built up the army and made it better trained.

Peter also changed Russia through **westernization**. He took several steps to make Russia more western. He brought in potatoes as a new food, began Russia's first newspaper, gave more social status to women, and told the nobles to adopt western clothes. He promoted education.

Peter also knew Russia needed a seaport that would make it easier to travel to the west. He fought a long war with Sweden to gain land along the shores of the Baltic Sea. There he built a grand new capital city, St. Petersburg. By the time of Peter's death in 1725, Russia was an important power in Europe.

3. How did Peter the Great increase his power?

_____

_____

_____

_____

200 CHAPTER 21 SECTION 4

Name _____ Date _____

CHAPTER 21 Section 5 (pages 536–539)

Parliament Limits the English Monarchy

BEFORE YOU READ

In the last section, you saw how power was becoming more absolute in Russia.

In this section, you will see how the power of the monarch was challenged and weakened in England.

AS YOU READ

Use the time line below to take notes on key changes in the government of England.

TERMS AND NAMES

Charles I King of England who was executed

English Civil War War fought from 1642 to 1649 between the Royalists, or Cavaliers, and the Puritan supporters of Parliament

Oliver Cromwell Leader of the Puritans

Restoration Period after the monarchy was restored in England

habeas corpus Law giving prisoners the right to obtain a document saying that the prisoner cannot go to jail without being brought before a judge

Glorious Revolution Bloodless overthrow of King James II

constitutional monarchy Government in which laws limit the monarch's power

cabinet A group of government ministers that was a link between the monarch and Parliament

```
  1642                          1660                          1689
  English Civil War begins

           1649                          1688
```

Monarchs Clash with Parliament (pages 536–537)

Why was there tension between the monarchy and Parliament?

When Queen Elizabeth I died, her cousin James, king of Scotland, became king of England. The reign of James I began a long series of struggles between king and Parliament. They fought over control of the English government. James thought that the king had the god-given right to rule and did not have to answer to any authority. Parliament disagreed. His religious policies also angered the Puritans in Parliament. They wanted to reform the Church of England to remove any Catholic practices. James was not willing to make these changes.

During the reign of his son, **Charles I**, there was continued conflict between king and Parliament. Parliament forced Charles to sign the Petition of Right in 1628. By signing, Charles agreed that the king had to answer to Parliament. But he then *dissolved* Parliament and tried to raise money without it. This went directly against the Petition of Right.

Other actions of Charles had caused Scotland to threaten to invade England. Charles needed

CHAPTER 21 ABSOLUTE MONARCHS IN EUROPE **201**

money to fight. When Charles called a new Parliament to get money, it quickly passed laws to limit his power. Charles responded by trying to arrest its leaders.

1. How did Charles I make Parliament angry?

___

English Civil War (pages 537–538)

Who fought the English Civil War?

Soon England was fighting a civil war. Charles and his Royalists were opposed by the supporters of Parliament. Many of Parliament's supporters were Puritans.

The **English Civil War** lasted from 1642 to 1649. Under the leadership of **Oliver Cromwell**, the forces of the Puritans won. They tried and executed Charles for *treason*. This was the first time a king had faced a public trial and execution. Cromwell became a military dictator, ruling until 1658. He crushed a rebellion in Ireland and tried to reform society at home.

2. What happened as a result of the English Civil War?

___

Restoration and Revolution
(pages 538–539)

What was the Restoration?

Soon after Cromwell's death, the government collapsed. A new Parliament asked Charles's older son to restore the monarchy. Charles II began to rule in 1660. The period of his rule is called the **Restoration.**

Charles II's reign was calm. Parliament passed an important guarantee of freedom called **habeas corpus.** It gave every prisoner the right to get an order to be brought before a judge. The judge would then decide whether the prisoner should be tried or set free. This kept monarchs from putting people in jail just for opposing them. It also meant that people would not stay in jail forever without a trial.

After Charles II's death in 1685, his brother became King James II. His pro-Catholic policies angered and worried the English. They feared that he would restore Catholicism. Finally, in 1688, seven members of Parliament contacted James's older daughter, Mary, and her husband, William of Orange, prince of the Netherlands. Both were Protestants. The members of Parliament wanted William and Mary to replace James II on the throne. When that took place, it was called the **Glorious Revolution.** James was forced to flee to France in this bloodless revolution.

3. Why did the Glorious Revolution take place?

___

Political Changes (page 539)

How was the power of the monarchy decreased in England?

William and Mary agreed to rule according to the laws made by Parliament. That is, Parliament became their partner in governing. England was now a **constitutional monarchy,** where laws limited the ruler's power.

William and Mary also agreed to accept the Bill of Rights. It guaranteed the English people and Parliament certain rights.

By the 1700's, it was clear that the government of England would come to a standstill if the monarch disagreed with Parliament or vice versa. This led to the development of the **cabinet.** This group of government ministers became the first link between the monarch and the majority in Parliament.

4. What three changes gave Parliament more power in England?

___

Name _____   Date _____

Glossary — CHAPTER 21 Absolute Monarchs in Europe

absolutism Condition that occurs when a ruler has absolute, or total, power
ally State associated with another state because it has signed a treaty or formed an alliance
defy Go against
dissolved Broken up
expanded Made bigger
intact Whole
loot Rob places that have been conquered or have experienced other disasters
provinces Political divisions, like states
religious tolerance Acceptance of more than one set of religious beliefs
succession Order in which people follow one another to the throne
treason Action to betray or overthrow government

AFTER YOU READ

Names and Terms

A. Write the name or term in each blank that best completes the meaning of the paragraph.

Glorious Revolution
English Civil War
Oliver Cromwell
Charles I
Restoration

The **1** _____ was fought from 1642 to 1649. The Puritans who supported Parliament were led by **2** _____ . They fought against the Royalists who supported **3** _____ . Although the Puritans won the war, their power did not last long. When Charles II came to the throne, the **4** _____ began. Nevertheless, the very next king to take power was overthrown. The bloodless overthrow of James II is known as the **5** _____ .

B. Write the letter of the name or term next to the description that explains it best.

a. Maria Theresa
b. Jean Baptiste Colbert
c. Frederick the Great
d. Peter the Great
e. Cardinal Richelieu

____ **1.** Louis XIV's minister of finance
____ **2.** Minister of France with enormous power
____ **3.** Leader who westernized Russia
____ **4.** Leader of Austria
____ **5.** Leader of Prussia

CHAPTER 21 ABSOLUTE MONARCHS IN EUROPE 203

Name _____ Date _____

AFTER YOU READ (cont.)   **CHAPTER 21**   Absolute Monarchs in Europe

Main Ideas

1. How did Spain lose some of its power?
_____
_____
_____

2. What kind of ruler was Louis XIV?
_____
_____
_____

3. How did the Thirty Years' War affect Germany?
_____
_____
_____

4. What did Peter the Great do to change Russia?
_____
_____
_____

5. How is a constitutional monarchy different from an absolute monarchy?
_____
_____
_____

Thinking Critically

Answer the following questions on a separate sheet of paper.

1. How did Richelieu and Louis XIV increase the power of the French king?

2. What are some of the events that led to the development of a constitutional monarchy in England?

Name _____ Date _____

CHAPTER 22 Section 1 (pages 545–550)

The Scientific Revolution

BEFORE YOU READ
In the last chapter, you learned about wars and political changes in Europe.

In this section, you will read how the Enlightenment transformed Europe and helped lead to the American Revolution.

AS YOU READ
Use the web diagram below to record important events that occurred during the Scientific Revolution.

TERMS AND NAMES
Scientific Revolution New way of thinking about the natural world based on careful observation and a willingness to question
Nicolaus Copernicus Astronomer who said the earth revolved around the sun
heliocentric theory Theory that the sun is at the center of the universe
Johannes Kepler Mathematician who proved the accuracy of Copernicus's theory
Galileo Galilei Scientist who was forced by the Catholic Church to take back scientific ideas that disagreed with the church's view
scientific method Logical procedure for gathering and testing ideas
Francis Bacon Writer who helped advance the scientific method
René Descartes Mathematician who helped promote the scientific method
Isaac Newton Scientist who discovered laws of motion and gravity

[Web diagram with center circle labeled "Discoveries and Developments" connected to six outer circles. One outer circle is filled in: "Copernicus—heliocentric theory"]

The Roots of Modern Science
(pages 545–546)

How did modern science begin?

During the Middle Ages, few scholars questioned beliefs that had been long held. Europeans based their ideas on what ancient Greeks and Romans believed or on the Bible. People still thought that the earth was the center of the universe. They believed that the sun, moon, other planets, and stars moved around it.

In the mid-1500s, attitudes began to change. Scholars started what is called the **Scientific Revolution**. It was a new way of thinking about the natural world. It was based on careful observation and the willingness to question old beliefs. European voyages of exploration helped to bring about the Scientific Revolution. When Europeans explored new lands, they saw plants and animals that ancient writers had never seen. These discoveries led to new courses of study in the universities of Europe.

1. What was the Scientific Revolution?

_____

_____

CHAPTER 22 ENLIGHTENMENT AND REVOLUTION **205**

A Revolutionary Model of the Universe (pages 546–547)

How did new ideas change accepted thinking in astronomy?

The first challenge to accepted thinking in science came in *astronomy*. In the early 1500s, **Nicolaus Copernicus**, a Polish astronomer, studied the stars and planets. He developed a **heliocentric theory**. Heliocentric meant sun-centered. It said that earth, like all the other planets, revolved around the sun. And the moon revolved around the earth. Copernicus did not publish his findings until just before his death. He had been afraid that his ideas would be attacked. They went against the accepted belief that the earth was at the center of the universe. In the early 1600s, **Johannes Kepler** used mathematics to prove that Copernicus's basic idea was correct.

An Italian scientist—**Galileo Galilei**—made several discoveries that also undercut ancient ideas. He made one of the first telescopes and used it to study the planets. He found that Jupiter had moons, the sun had spots, and Earth's moon was rough. Some of his ideas about the earth, the sun, and the planets went against the teaching of the Catholic Church. Church authorities forced Galileo to take back his statements. Still, his ideas spread.

2. What old belief about the universe did the new discoveries destroy?

_____

_____

The Scientific Method (pages 547-548)

Why was the scientific method an important development?

Interest in science led to a new approach, the **scientific method**. With this method, scientists ask a question based on something they have seen in the physical world. They form a *hypothesis*, or an attempt to answer the question. Then they test the hypothesis by making experiments or checking other facts. Finally, they change the hypothesis if needed.

The English writer **Francis Bacon** helped create this new approach to knowledge. He said scientists should base their thinking on what they can observe and test. The French mathematician **René Descartes** also influenced the use of the scientific method. His thinking was based on logic and mathematics.

3. What thinkers helped advance the use of the scientific method?

_____

_____

Newton Explains the Law of Gravity; The Scientific Revolution Spreads (pages 548–550)

What scientific discoveries were made?

In the mid-1600s, the English scientist **Isaac Newton** described the *law of gravity*. Using mathematics, Newton showed that the same force ruled both the motion of planets and the action of bodies on the earth.

Other scientists made new tools to study the world around them. One invented a microscope. Others invented tools for understanding weather.

Doctors also made advances. One made drawings that showed the different parts of the human body. Another learned how the heart pumped blood through the body. In the late 1700s, Edward Jenner first used the process called *vaccination* to prevent disease. By giving a person the germs from a cattle disease called cowpox, he helped that person avoid getting the more serious human disease of smallpox.

Scientists made progress in chemistry as well. One questioned the old idea that things were made of only four elements—earth, air, fire, and water. He and other scientists were able to separate oxygen from air.

4. How did the science of medicine change?

_____

_____

Name _____ Date _____

CHAPTER 22 Section 2 (pages 551–556)

The Enlightenment in Europe

TERMS AND NAMES
Enlightenment Age of Reason
social contract According to Thomas Hobbes, an agreement people make with government
John Locke Philosopher who wrote about government
natural rights Rights that John Locke said people were born with: life, liberty, and property
philosophe Social critics in France
Voltaire Writer who fought for tolerance, reason, freedom of religious belief, and freedom of speech
Montesquieu French writer concerned with government and political liberty
separation of powers Montesquieu's idea that power should be divided between different branches of government
Jean Jacques Rousseau Enlightenment thinker who championed freedom
Mary Wollstonecraft Author who wrote about women's rights

BEFORE YOU READ

In the last section, you read how the Scientific Revolution began in Europe.

In this section, you will learn how the Enlightenment began in Europe.

AS YOU READ

Use the chart below to take notes on important Enlightenment ideas.

THINKER	IDEA
Hobbes	social contract between people and government

Two Views on Government
(pages 551–552)

What were the views of Hobbes and Locke?

The **Enlightenment** was an *intellectual* movement. Enlightenment thinkers tried to apply reason and the scientific method to laws that shaped human actions. They hoped to build a society founded on ideas of the Scientific Revolution. Two English writers—Thomas Hobbes and John Locke—were important to this movement. They came to very different conclusions about government and human nature.

Hobbes wrote that there would be a war of "every man against every man" if there were no government. To avoid this war, Hobbes said, people formed a **social contract**. It was an agreement between people and their government. People gave up their rights to the government so they

CHAPTER 22 ENLIGHTENMENT AND REVOLUTION **207**

could live in a safe and orderly way. The best government, he said, is that of a strong king who can force all people to obey.

John Locke believed that people have three **natural rights**. They are life, liberty, and property. The purpose of government is to protect these rights. When it fails to do so, he said, people have a right to overthrow the government.

1. How were Hobbes's and Locke's views different?

_____

The Philosophes Advocate Reason (pages 552–555)

Who were the philosophes?

French thinkers called **philosophes** had five main beliefs: (1) thinkers can find the truth by using reason; (2) what is natural is good and reasonable, and human actions are shaped by natural laws; (3) acting according to nature can bring happiness; (4) by taking a scientific view, people and society can make progress and advance to a better life; and (5) by using reason, people can gain freedom.

The most brilliant of the philosophes was the writer **Voltaire**. He fought for tolerance, reason, freedom of religious belief, and freedom of speech. Baron de **Montesquieu** wrote about **separation of powers**—dividing power among the separate branches of government. The third great philosophe was **Jean Jacques Rousseau**. He wrote in favor of human freedom. He wanted a society in which all people were equal. Cesare Beccaria was an Italian philosphe. He spoke out against *abuses* of justice.

2. Name the types of freedoms that Enlightenment thinkers championed.

_____

Women and the Enlightenment; Impact of the Enlightenment (pages 555–556)

What were Enlightenment views about individuals?

Many Enlightenment thinkers held traditional views about women's place in society. They wanted equal rights for all men but paid no attention to the fact that women did not have such rights. Some women protested this unfair situation. "If all men are born free," stated British writer **Mary Wollstonecraft**, "how is it that all women are born slaves?"

Enlightenment ideas strongly influenced the American and French Revolutions. Enlightenment thinkers also helped spread the idea of progress. By using reason, they said, it is possible to make society better. Enlightenment thinkers helped make the world less religious and more worldly. They also stressed the importance of the individual.

3. Explain the influence of Enlightenment ideas.

_____

Major Ideas of the Enlightenment

Idea	Thinker	Impact
Natural rights—life, liberty, property	Locke	Fundamental to U.S. Declaration of Independence
Separation of powers	Montesquieu	France, United States, Latin American nations use separation of powers in new constitutions
Freedom of thought and expression	Voltaire	Guaranteed in U.S. Bill of Rights and French Declaration of the Rights of Man and Citizen; European monarchs reduce or eliminate censorship
Abolishment of torture	Beccaria	Guaranteed in U.S. Bill of Rights; torture outlawed or reduced in nations of Europe and the Americas
Religious freedom	Voltaire	Guaranteed in U.S. Bill of Rights and French Declaration of the Rights of Man and Citizen; European monarchs reduce persecution
Women's equality	Wollstonecraft	Women's rights groups form in Europe and North America

Skillbuilder

Use the chart to answer these questions.

1. Which Enlightenment thinkers inflenced the United States government?

_____

2. Which Enlightenment ideas are in the United States Bill of Rights?

_____

Name _____ Date _____

CHAPTER 22 Section 3 (pages 558–562)

The Spread of Enlightenment Ideas

BEFORE YOU READ

In the last section, you read how Enlightenment ideas began.

In this section, you will learn about the spread of these ideas.

AS YOU READ

Use the chart below to take notes on how Enlightenment ideas were spread.

TERMS AND NAMES

salon Social gathering for discussing ideas or enjoying art
baroque Grand, ornate style
neoclassical Simple style that borrowed ideas from classical Greek and Rome
enlightened despot Ruler who supported Enlightenment ideas but did not give up power
Catherine the Great Russian ruler who took steps to reform and modernize Russia

Enlightenment Ideas Spread

general knowledge	art and architecture	literature	music
The Encyclopedia gathers all known knowledge.			

A World of Ideas (pages 558–559)

How did ideas spread from individual to individual?

In the 1700s, Paris was the cultural center of Europe. People came there from other countries to hear the new ideas of the Enlightenment. Writers and artists held social gatherings called **salons**. A woman named Marie-Thérèse Geoffrin became famous for hosting these discussions.

Geoffrin also supplied the money for one of the major projects of the Enlightenment. With her funds, Denis Diderot and other thinkers wrote and published a huge set of books called the *Encyclopedia*. Their aim was to gather all that was known about the world. The French government and officials in the Catholic Church did not like many of the ideas that were published in the *Encyclopedia*. They banned the books at first. Later, however, they changed their minds.

The ideas of the Enlightenment were spread throughout Europe by works like the *Encyclopedia* and through meetings in homes. The ideas also spread to the growing middle class. This group was becoming wealthy but had less social status than

CHAPTER 22 ENLIGHTENMENT AND REVOLUTION **209**

nobles. They also had very little political power. Ideas about equality sounded good to them.

1. **Why were salons important?**

_____

_____

_____

Art and Literature in the Age of Reason (pages 559–561)

How did art and literature change?

The arts—painting, architechture, music, and literature—moved in new directions in the late 1700s. They used Enlightenment ideas of order and reason.

Earlier European painting had been very grand and highly decorated. It was a style known as **baroque**. Now styles began to change. A new simpler, yet elegant, style of painting and architecture developed. This style borrowed ideas and themes from Classical Greece and Rome. That is the reason it was called **neoclassical**.

In music, the style of the period is called classical. Three important composers of the time were Franz Joseph Haydn, Wolfgang Amadeus Mozart, and Ludwig von Beethoven. They composed music that was elegant and original. New musical forms were developed, including the sonata and the symphony.

In literature, the novel became popular. This new form presented long stories with twisting plots. It explored the thoughts and feelings of characters. A number of European authors, including women, began writing novels. These books were popular with the middle-class. They liked entertaining stories in everyday language.

2. **What new styles and forms appeared in art, music, and literature?**

_____

_____

_____

Enlightenment and Monarchy (pages 561–562)

Who were the enlightened despots?

Some Enlightenment thinkers believed that the best form of government was a monarchy. In it, a ruler respected people's rights. These thinkers tried to influence rulers to rule fairly. Rulers who followed Enlightenment ideas in part but were unwilling to give up much power were called **enlightened despots**.

Frederick the Great of Prussia was an enlightened despot. He gave his people religious freedom and improved schooling. He also *reformed* the justice system. However, he did nothing to end *serfdom*, which made peasants slaves to the wealthy landowners. Joseph II of Austria did end serfdom. Once he died, though, the nobles who owned the lands were able to undo this reform.

Catherine the Great of Russia was another of the rulers influenced by Enlightenment ideas. She tried to reform Russia's laws but met resistance. She had hoped to end serfdom. But a bloody peasants' revolt persuaded her to change her mind. Instead, she gave the nobles even more power over serfs. Catherine did manage to gain new land for Russia. Russia, Prussia, and Austria agreed to divide Poland among themselves. As a result, Poland disappeared as a separate nation for almost 150 years.

3. **In what way was Frederick the Great typical of an enlightened despot?**

_____

_____

_____

Name _____ Date _____

CHAPTER 22 Section 4 (pages 563–567)

American Revolution: The Birth of a Republic

BEFORE YOU READ

In the last section, you read about the spread of Enlightenment ideas in Europe.

In this section, you will learn how Enlightenment ideas influenced the American Revolution.

AS YOU READ

Use the web below to take notes on the influence of the Enlightenment on the early Untied States.

TERMS AND NAMES

Declaration of Independence Document declaring American independence from Britain

Thomas Jefferson Author of the Declaration of Independence

checks and balances System in which each branch of government checks, or limits, the power of the other two branches

federal system System of government in which power is divided between the national and state governments

Bill of Rights First ten amendments to the U.S. Constitution; protections of basic rights for individuals

(web diagram: center oval labeled "Documents/Ideas Based on Enlightenment Thinking" connected to five ovals; one is filled in with "Declaration of Independence")

Britain and Its American Colonies (page 563)

How were the colonies governed?

The British colonies in North America grew in population and wealth during the 1700s. Population went from about 250,000 in 1700 to 2,150,000 in 1770. Economically, they prospered on trade with the nations of Europe. The 13 colonies also had a kind of self-government. People in the colonies began to see themselves less and less as British subjects. Still, Parliament passed laws that governed the colonies. One set of laws banned trade with any nation other than Britain.

1. How did the colonists' image of themselves clash with their status as colonists?

_____

_____

CHAPTER 22 ENLIGHTENMENT AND REVOLUTION **211**

Americans Win Independence
(pages 563–565)

What caused Britian and America to grow apart?

The high cost of the French and Indian War led Parliament to pass laws that put taxes on the colonists. The colonists became very angry. They had never before paid taxes directly to the British government. They said that the taxes *violated* their rights. Since Parliament had no members from the colonies, they said, Parliament had no right to tax them.

The colonists met the first tax, passed in 1765, with a *boycott* of British goods. Their refusal to buy British products was very effective. It forced Parliament to *repeal* the law.

Over the next decade, the colonists and Britain grew further apart. Some colonists wanted to push the colonies to independence. They took actions that caused Britain to act harshly. Eventually, the conflict led to war. Representatives of the colonies met in a congress and formed an army. In July 1776, they announced that they were independent of Britain. They issued the **Declaration of Independence**. It was based on Enlightenment ideas. **Thomas Jefferson** wrote it.

From 1775 to 1781, the colonies and the British fought a war in North America. The colonists had a poorly equipped army, and Britain was one of the most powerful nations in the world. However, in the end, the colonies won their independence.

The British people grew tired of the cost of the war and pushed Parliament to agree to a peace. The Americans were also helped greatly by aid from France. In 1783, the two sides signed a treaty. In it, Britain recognized the independent United States of America.

2. Name some of the steps that led to the American Revolution.

_____
_____
_____

Americans Create a Republic
(pages 565–567)

What are some fundamental ideas in the U.S. Constitution?

The 13 states formed a new government under the Article of Confederation. This government was very weak. States held all the power and the central government had little. This proved unworkable. In 1787, American leaders met again. They wrote a new framework of government.

The Constitution of the United States drew on many Enlightenment ideas. It used Montesquieu's idea of separation of powers into three branches of government. Through a system of **checks and balances**, each branch was able to prevent other branches from abusing their power. The Constitution also set up a **federal system**. Under this system, power was divided between national and state governments.

The Constitution also used Locke's idea of putting power in the hands of the people. It used Voltaire's ideas to protect the right to free speech and freedom of religion. It used Beccaria's ideas about a fair system of justice.

Many of these rights were ensured in a set of additions to the Constitution called the **Bill of Rights.** The inclusion of a bill of rights helped win approval for the Constitution.

3. Explain how the Constitution divides power.

_____
_____
_____

Name _____ Date _____

Glossary **CHAPTER 22** Enlightenment and Revolution

abuses Improper uses, misuses
astronomy Study of the universe beyond the earth
boycott Organized refusal to buy a certain good or participate in a certain action
hypothesis Attempt to answer a question that needs to be proven or disproven

intellectual Related to thinking or to the mind
law of gravity Idea linking motion in the heavens with motion on the Earth and based on the principle that every object attracts every other object
reformed Changed for the better
repeal Take back a law

serfdom State or condition of using workers as slaves
vaccination Introduction of weakened or killed viruses or bacteria into the body to protect against a specific disease
violated Went against

AFTER YOU READ

Terms and Names

A. Write the term or name in each blank that best completes the meaning of the paragraph.

Isaac Newton

Johannes Kepler

Nicolaus Copernicus

René Descartes

Francis Bacon

Many thinkers contributed to the Scientific Revolution. In astronomy, **1** _____ first developed the idea that the earth revolved around the sun. **2** _____ later used mathematics to prove that theory. Interest in science led to new approaches to thinking. Two thinkers who helped put forth the ideas that led to the scientific method were writer **3** _____ and mathematician **4** _____. Another great pioneer in science at this time was **5** _____. He described the law of gravity.

B. Write the letter of the name or term next to the description that explains it best.

a. Mary Wollstonecraft

b. John Locke

c. Montesquieu

d. Thomas Jefferson

e. Voltaire

____ **1.** Philosopher who said people have natural rights

____ **2.** Thinker known for ideas about separation of powers

____ **3.** Writer who championed freedom of speech and freedom of religion

____ **4.** Writer who championed women's rights

____ **5.** Author of the Declaration of Independence

Name _____ Date _____

AFTER YOU READ (cont.) CHAPTER 22 Enlightenment and Revolution

Main Ideas

1. How did European exploration help lead the way to the Scientific Revolution?
_____
_____
_____

2. Who were the philosophes, and what did they believe in?
_____
_____
_____
_____

3. What was one of Montesquieu's key ideas about government?
_____
_____
_____
_____

4. How did the arts change as a result of the Enlightenment?
_____
_____
_____
_____

5. How did the government of the United States reflect Enlightenment ideas?
_____
_____
_____
_____

Thinking Critically

Answer the following questions on a separate sheet of paper.

1. How was the Scientific Revolution related to the Enlightenment?

2. How did monarchs react to Enlightenment ideas?

Name _____ Date _____

CHAPTER 23 Section 1 (pages 573–576)

Revolution Threatens the French King

BEFORE YOU READ

In the last chapter, you read about the Enlightenment and the American Revolution.

In this section, you will learn about the beginning of the French Revolution.

AS YOU READ

Use this chart to take notes on important changes that occurred during the Renaissance in Italy.

TERMS AND NAMES
Old Regime System of feudalism
estate Social class of people
Louis XVI Weak king who came to French throne in 1774
Marie Antoinette Unpopular queen; wife of Louis XVI
Estates-General Assembly of representatives from all three estates
National Assembly French congress established by representatives of the Third Estate
Tennis Court Oath Promise made by Third Estate representatives to draw up a new constitution
Great Fear Wave of panic

causes | effects

Old regime—society unequal

Causes of Revolution

The Old Regime (page 573)

How was French society unequal?

In the 1700s, France was the leading country of Europe. It was the center of the new ideas of the Enlightenment. However, beneath the surface there were major problems. Soon the nation would be torn by a violent revolution.

One problem was that people were not treated equally in French society. A system of feudalism called the **Old Regime** remained in place. The French were divided into three classes, or **estates**. The *First Estate* consisted of the Roman Catholic clergy. The *Second Estate* was made up of nobles. Only about two percent of the people belonged to these two estates. Yet they owned 30 percent of the land. They had easy lives.

Everybody else belonged to the *Third Estate*. This huge group included three types of people:
- the *bourgeoisie*—mostly well-off merchants and skilled workers who lacked the status of nobles
- city workers—cooks, servants, and others who were poorly paid and often out of work
- peasants—farm workers, making up about 80 percent of the French people

CHAPTER 23 FRENCH REVOLUTION AND NAPOLEON **215**

Members of the Third Estate were angry. They had few rights. They paid up to half of their income in taxes, while the rich paid almost none.

1. What were the three classes of French society?

_____

_____

_____

The Forces of Change (pages 574–575)

Why were the French ready for the revolution?

Three factors led to revolution. First, the Enlightenment spread the idea that everyone should be equal. The powerless people in the Third Estate liked that. Second, the French economy was failing. High taxes kept profits low, and food supplies were short. The government owed money. Third, **King Louis XVI** was a weak, unconcerned leader. His wife, **Marie Antoinette**, was unpopular. She was from Austria, France's long-time enemy, and was noted for her extravagant spending.

In the 1780s, France was deep in debt. Louis tried to tax the nobles. Instead, they forced the king to call a meeting of the **Estates-General**, an assembly of *delegates* of the three estates.

2. What three factors led to revolution?

_____

_____

_____

Revolution Dawns (pages 575–576)

How did the Revolution begin?

The meeting of the Estates-General began in May 1789 with arguments over how to count votes. In the past, each estate had cast one vote. The Third Estate now wanted each delegate to have a vote. The king and the other estates did not agree to the plan because the Third Estate was larger and would have more votes.

The Third Estate then broke with the others and met separately. In June 1789, its delegates voted to rename themselves the **National Assembly.** They claimed to represent all the people. This was the beginning of *representative government* for France.

At one point, the members of the Third Estate found themselves locked out of their meeting. They broke down a door leading to a tennis court. Then they promised to stay there until they made a new constitution. This promise was called the **Tennis Court Oath.**

Louis tried to make peace. He ordered the clergy and nobles to join the National Assembly. However, trouble erupted. Rumors flew that Swiss soldiers paid by Louis were going to attack French citizens. On July 14, an angry crowd captured the *Bastille*, a Paris prison. The *mob* wanted to get gunpowder for their weapons in order to defend the city.

3. Why did the National Assembly form?

_____

_____

_____

A Great Fear Sweeps France (page 576)

What was the Great Fear?

A wave of violence called the **Great Fear** swept the country. Peasants broke into and burned nobles' houses. They tore up documents that had forced them to pay fees to the nobles. Late in 1789, a mob of women marched 12 miles from Paris to the king's palace at *Versailles*. They were angry about high bread prices and demanded that the king come to Paris. They hoped he would end hunger in the city. The king and queen left Versailles, never to return.

4. What happened during the Great Fear?

_____

_____

_____

Name _____ Date _____

CHAPTER 23 Section 2 (pages 577–583)

Revolution Brings Reform and Terror

BEFORE YOU READ

In the last section, you read how the French Revolution began.

In this section, you will learn what course it took and where it led.

AS YOU READ

Use the time line below to take notes on major events.

TERMS AND NAMES
Declaration of the Rights of Man Revolutionary statement guaranteeing rights such as liberty and property
Legislative Assembly Assembly that replaced the National Assembly in 1791
émigrés Nobles and others who left France during the peasant uprisings and who hoped to come back to restore the old system
sans-culottes Radical group of Parisian wage-earners
guillotine Machine for beheading people
Maximilien Robespierre Revolutionary leader who tried to wipe out every trace of France's past monarchy and nobility
Committee of Public Safety Committee led by Robespierre that tried so-called "enemies of the republic" and had them executed
Reign of Terror Period of Robespierre's rule

```
┌─────────────────────────┐      ┌─────────────────────────┐
│ 1789                    │      │ 1792                    │
│ National Assembly issues│      │                         │
│ Declaration of Rights of│      │                         │
│ Man                     │      │                         │
└─────────────────────────┘      └─────────────────────────┘
           │                                │
┌─────────────────────────┐      ┌─────────────────────────┐
│ 1791                    │      │ 1793-1794               │
│                         │      │                         │
└─────────────────────────┘      └─────────────────────────┘
```

The Assembly Reforms France
(pages 577–578)

What reforms resulted from the revolution?

In August 1789, the National Assembly took steps to change France. It made a revolutionary statement called the **Declaration of the Rights of Man.** One new law ended all the special rights that members of the First and Second Estates had enjoyed. Another law gave all French men equal rights. Though women did not get these rights, it was a bold step. Other laws gave the state power over the Catholic Church.

The new laws about the church divided people who had supported the Revolution. Catholic peasants remained loyal to the church. They were angry that the church would be part of the state. Thereafter, many of them opposed the Revolution's reforms.

For months, the assembly worked on plans for a new government. During this time, Louis was fearful for his safety. One night, he and his family tried to escape the country. They were caught, brought back to Paris, and placed under guard. This escape attempt made the king and queen more unpopular. It also increased the power of his enemies.

1. What new laws came into being?

_____

_____

CHAPTER 23 FRENCH REVOLUTION AND NAPOLEON **217**

Conflicting Goals Cause Divisions (pages 578–579)

What groups called for different kinds of changes?

In the fall of 1791, the assembly drew up a new constitution. It took away most of the king's power. The assembly then turned over its power to a new assembly, the **Legislative Assembly.**

This new assembly soon divided into groups. Some wanted an end to revolutionary changes. These were the **émigrés,** nobles and others who had fled France during the uprisings. Another group of assembly members wanted even more *radical* changes. They included the **sans-culottes.** These wage-earners and small shopkeepers wanted a greater voice in government.

2. In what ways did the émigrés and sans-culottes have opposite goals?

___

___

War and Extreme Measures (pages 579–580)

What caused the French people to take extreme measures?

At the same time, France faced serious trouble on its borders. Kings in other countries feared that revolution would spread to their lands. They wanted to use force to restore control of France to Louis XVI. Soon foreign soldiers were marching toward Paris. Many people thought that the king and queen were ready to help the enemy. Angry French citizens imprisoned them. Many nobles were killed in other mob actions.

The government took strong steps to meet the danger from foreign troops. It took away all the king's powers. In 1792, the National Convention—another new government—was formed. It declared Louis a common citizen. He was then tried for treason and convicted. Like many others, the king was beheaded by a machine called the **guillotine.** The National Convention also ordered thousands of French people into the army.

3. What happened to the king?

___

___

Terror Grips France; End of Terror (pages 582–583)

What was the Reign of Terror?

Maximilien Robespierre became leader of France. He headed the **Committee of Public Safety.** It tried and put to death "enemies of the republic." Thousands were killed. Robespierre's rule, which began in 1793, was called the **Reign of Terror.** It ended in July 1794, when Robespierre himself was put to death.

The French people were tired of the killing and the unrest. They wanted a return to order. Moderate leaders drafted a new, less revolutionary plan of government.

4. Where did the Reign of Terror lead?

___

___

Beheading by Class

More than 2,100 people were executed during the last 132 days of the Reign of Terror. The pie graph below displays the breakdown of beheadings by class.

☐ First Estate
■ Second Estate
■ Third Estate

Skillbuilder

1. Which estate had the greatest number of members sent to the guillotine during the Reign of Terror?

___

___

2. Why do you think the most beheadings were in this estate?

___

___

Name _____ Date _____

CHAPTER 23 Section 3 (pages 584–588)

Napoleon Forges an Empire

BEFORE YOU READ

In the last section, you read about the Revolution's extremes, including the Reign of Terror.

In this section, you will learn how Napoleon grabbed power and brought order to France.

AS YOU READ

Use the time line below to take notes on Napoleon's changing power.

TERMS AND NAMES

Napoleon Bonaparte Military leader who seized power in France
coup d'état A sudden takeover of a country
plebiscite Vote by the people
lycée Government-run public school
concordat Agreement
Napoleonic Code Complete set of laws set up by Napoleon that eliminated many injustices
Battle of Trafalgar British defeat of Napoleon's forces at sea

```
┌─────────────────────────────┐   ┌─────────────────────────────┐
│           1795              │   │           1804              │
│ Napoleon leads soldiers     │   │                             │
│ against French royalists.   │   │                             │
└─────────────────────────────┘   └─────────────────────────────┘
             │                                   │
             └───────────────┬───────────────────┘
                             │
      ┌──────────────────────┴──────────────────┐
      │                                          │
┌─────────────┐                          ┌─────────────┐
│    1799     │                          │    1805     │
└─────────────┘                          └─────────────┘
```

Napoleon Grasps the Power
(pages 584–585)

How did Napoleon rise to power?

Napoleon Bonaparte was born in 1769 on the Mediterranean island of Corsica. When he was nine years old, his parents sent him to military school in northern France. In 1785, he finished school and became an artillery officer. When the revolution broke out, Napoleon joined the army of the new government.

In 1795, Napoleon led soldiers against French *royalists* who were attacking the National Convention. For this, he was thought of as the savior of the French republic.

By 1799, the unsettled French government had lost the people's support. In a bold move, Napoleon used troops to seize control of the government. This was a **coup d'état,** or a sudden takeover of power. Napoleon then assumed dictatorial powers.

1. How did Napoleon get control of the government?

_____

_____

_____

CHAPTER 23 FRENCH REVOLUTION AND NAPOLEON **219**

Napoleon Rules France (pages 585–586)

How did Napoleon use the Revolution's ideas in his government?

Napoleon pretended to be the rightfully elected leader of France. In 1800, a **plebiscite,** or vote of the people, was held to approve a new constitution. The people voted for it overwhelmingly, and Napoleon took power as first consul.

Napoleon made several changes that were meant to build on the Revolution's good ideas:

1. He made tax collection more fair and orderly. As a result, the government could count on a steady supply of money.
2. He removed dishonest government workers.
3. He started **lycées**—new public schools for ordinary citizens.
4. He gave the church back some of its power. He signed a **concordat** (agreement) with the pope. This gave him the support of the organized church.
5. He wrote a new set of laws, called the **Napoleonic Code,** which gave all French citizens the same rights. However, the new laws took away many individual rights won during the Revolution. For example, they limited free speech and restored slavery in French colonies.

2. What changes did Napoleon make?

_____
_____
_____
_____

Napoleon Creates an Empire
(pages 586–588)

What goals did Napoleon have beyond France's borders?

Napoleon had hoped to make his empire larger in both Europe and the New World. In 1801, he had sent soldiers to retake the island of present-day Haiti. Slaves in that colony had seized power during a civil war. But his troops failed. Napoleon then gave up on his New World plans. In 1803, he sold the largest part of France's North American land—the huge Louisiana Territory—to the United States.

Napoleon had been stopped in the Americas. So he then moved to add to his power in Europe. In 1804, he made himself *emperor* of France. He took control of the Austrian Netherlands, parts of Italy, and Switzerland. Napoleon's only loss during this time was to the British navy in the **Battle of Trafalgar.** This loss kept him from conquering Britain.

3. Where did Napoleon succeed in adding lands, and where did he fail?

_____
_____
_____
_____
_____

Name _____ Date _____

CHAPTER 23 Section 4 (pages 589–592)

Napoleon's Empire Collapses

BEFORE YOU READ

In the last section, you read how Napoleon built his power. In this section, you learn why he lost it.

AS YOU READ

Use the chart below to take notes on mistakes Napoleon made.

TERMS AND NAMES
blockade Forced closing of ports
Continental System Napoleon's policy of preventing trade and communication between Great Britain and other European nations
guerrilla Spanish peasant fighter
Peninsular War War that Napoleon fought in Spain
scorched-earth policy Policy of burning fields and slaughtering livestock so that enemy troops would find nothing to eat
Waterloo Battle in Belgium that was Napoleon's final defeat
Hundred Days Napoleon's last bid for power, which ended at Waterloo

[Chart: Four boxes feeding into "Napoleon's Empire Collapses". First box: "Blockade of Britain fails."]

Napoleon's Three Costly Mistakes (pages 589–590)

What mistakes did Napoleon make abroad?

Napoleon's own personality posed a threat to his empire. His love of power pushed him to expand his empire. His efforts to extend French rule led to his empire's collapse.

Napoleon made three costly mistakes. His first mistake was caused by his desire to crush Britain. He wanted to hurt the British economy. So in 1806 he ordered a **blockade**. This was an effort to stop all trade between Britain and the other European nations. Napoleon called this policy the **Continental System**. It was supposed to make continental Europe more self sufficient.

The effort failed because some Europeans secretly brought in British goods. At the same time, the British put their own blockade around Europe. Because the British navy was so strong, it worked well. Soon the French economy, along with others on the European continent, weakened.

Napoleon's second mistake was to make his brother king of Spain in 1808. The Spanish people were loyal to their own king. With help from

CHAPTER 23 FRENCH REVOLUTION AND NAPOLEON **221**

Britain, bands of peasant fighters called **guerrillas** fought Napoleon for five years. Napoleon lost 300,000 troops during this **Peninsular War.** (The war gets its name from the Iberian Peninsula on which Spain is located.)

Napoleon's third mistake was perhaps his worst. In 1812, he tried to conquer Russia, far to the east. He entered Russia with more than 400,000 soldiers. As the Russians retreated, however, they followed a **scorched-earth policy.** They burned their fields and killed their livestock so Napoleon's armies could not eat what they left behind.

Although the French got as far as Moscow, winter was coming. Napoleon was forced to order his soldiers to head back. On the way home, bitter cold, hunger, and Russian attacks killed thousands. Thousands more *deserted*. By the time Napoleon's army left Russian territory, only 10,000 of his soldiers were able to fight.

1. What happened to Napoleon in Russia?

_____

_____

_____

_____

Napoleon's Downfall (pages 591–592)

What other defeats did Napoleon suffer?

Other leaders saw that Napoleon was now weaker. Britain, Russia, Prussia, Sweden, and Austria formed an alliance and attacked France. Napoleon was defeated at the battle of Leipzig, in Germany, in 1813. In 1814, Napoleon gave up his throne and was exiled, or sent away, to the tiny island of Elba off the Italian coast.

Louis XVIII took the throne in Paris. But he quickly became unpopular. The peasants feared the new king would undo the land reforms of the revolution.

News of Louis XVIII's trouble was all Napoleon needed to try to regain his empire. In March 1815, he escaped from Elba and boldly returned to France. He took power and raised another army.

The rest of the European powers raised armies to fight against Napoleon. Led by the Duke of Wellington, they defeated Napoleon in his final battle near a Belgian town called **Waterloo.** This defeat ended Napoleon's last attempt at power, which was called the **Hundred Days.** He was then sent to the far-off island of St. Helena in the southern Atlantic Ocean. He died there in 1821.

2. What was Napoleon's last attempt at power, and where did it end?

_____

_____

_____

_____

Name _____ Date _____

CHAPTER 23 Section 5 (pages 593–596)

The Congress of Vienna Convenes

BEFORE YOU READ

In the last section, you saw how Napoleon's empire collapsed.

In this section, you will learn how the rest of Europe reacted to both the French Revolution and Napoleon's rise and fall.

AS YOU READ

Use the chart below to take notes on the ways that leaders and people of other nations were affected by the ideas and results of the French Revolution.

TERMS AND NAMES

Congress of Vienna Meetings in Vienna for the purpose of restoring order to Europe

Klemens von Metternich Key leader at the Congress of Vienna

balance of power Condition in which no one country becomes a threat to the other

legitimacy Bringing back to power the kings that Napoleon had driven out

Holy Alliance League formed by Russia, Austria, and Prussia

Concert of Europe Series of alliances to help prevent revolution

```
         Effects of the French Reveolution
         and Napoleon's Rule on Europe
              /         |         \
    Congress of
    Vienna held
```

Metternich Restores Stability
(pages 593–594)

What was the Congress of Vienna?

After Napoleon's first defeat, in 1814, leaders of many nations met to draw up a peace plan for Europe. This series of meetings was called the **Congress of Vienna.** The most important person at the Congress of Vienna was the foreign minister of Austria, **Klemens von Metternich.** He shaped the peace conditions that were finally accepted.

Metternich had three goals at the congress. First, he wanted to make sure that the French would not attack another country again. Second, he wanted a **balance of power** in which no one nation was strong enough to threaten other nations. Third, he wanted **legitimacy.** This meant restoring kings to the thrones they had before Napoleon's conquests. The leaders agreed with Metternich's ideas.

Metternich achieved his first goal when the

CHAPTER 23 FRENCH REVOLUTION AND NAPOLEON **223**

congress strengthened the small nations that surrounded France. Meanwhile, France was not punished too severely. It remained independent and kept some overseas possessions. This helped achieve Metternich's second goal to create a balance of power.

The congress also worked to fulfill Metternich's third goal. Many Bourbon and Hapsbury rulers were returned to power in states throughout Europe, including France.

The Congress of Vienna created very successful peace agreements. None of the great powers fought against one another until 1853. Some did not fight in a war for the rest of the century.

1. What three goals did Metternich have?

_____

_____

_____

_____

Political Changes Beyond Vienna (pages 595–596)

How *did European leaders respond to the effects of the French Revolution?*

Many European rulers were nervous about the effects of the French Revolution. In 1815, Czar Alexander, Emperor Francis I of Austria, and King Frederick William III of Prussia formed the **Holy Alliance.** Other alliances created by Metternich were called the **Concert of Europe.** The idea of these alliances was for nations to help one another if revolution came.

Across Europe, *conservatives* held control of European governments. Conservatives were people who opposed the ideals of the French Revolution. They also usually supported the rights and powers of royalty. They did not encourage individual liberties. They did not want any calls for equal rights.

But many other people still believed in the ideals of the French Revolution. They thought that all people should be equal and share in power. Later they would again fight for these rights.

People in the Americas also felt the desire for freedom. Spanish colonies in the Americas revolted against the restored Spanish king. Many colonies won independence from Spain. National feeling grew in Europe, too. Soon people in areas such as Italy, Germany, and Greece would rebel and form new nations. The French Revolution had changed the politics of Europe and beyond.

2. What happened to ideas about freedom and independence?

_____

_____

_____

_____

_____

Name _____ Date _____

Glossary — CHAPTER 23 THE FRENCH REVOLUTION AND NAPOLEON

Bastille Paris prison
bourgeoisie Well-off merchants and skilled workers
conservatives Those favoring established or traditional ways of thinking and acting
delegates Representatives
deserted Left without permission; ran away
emperor Absolute ruler
First Estate Class made up of Roman Catholic clergy
mob Unpredictable crowd that acts as a single body
radical Revolutionary; extreme
representative government Government in which lawmakers represent the will of the people
royalists Supporters of the monarchy
Second Estate Class made up of nobles
stability Order; safety and security
Third Estate All merchants, skilled workers, city workers, and peasants
Versailles Site of the extremely luxurious palace of the kings of France

AFTER YOU READ

Terms and Names

A. Write the name or term in each blank that best completes the meaning of the paragraph.

National Assembly

Legislative Assembly

Declaration of the Rights of Man

Old Regime

estates

Before the revolution in France, a system known as the **1** _____ was in place. In this system, the French were divided into three **2** _____. These groups were unequal. In June 1789, the lowest of these groups renamed itself the **3** _____. By 1791, this group would hand its power over to a new assembly called the **4** _____. Before doing so, however, it drafted the **5** _____.

B. Write the letter of the name or term next to the description that explains it best.

a. Committee of Public Safety
b. Continental System
c. Congress of Vienna
d. Concert of Europe
e. Hundred Days

____ **1.** Napoleon's policy of cutting Britain off from the rest of Europe
____ **2.** Napoleon's last attempt at power
____ **3.** Group led by Robespierre that tried and killed many people
____ **4.** Series of alliances to protect European nations against revolutions
____ **5.** Meeting of European nations to decide the fate of Europe after Napoleon

Name _____ Date _____

AFTER YOU READ (cont.) **CHAPTER 23** FRENCH REVOLUTION AND NAPOLEON

Main Ideas

1. What problems led to the French Revolution?
_____
_____
_____

2. What happened during Robespierre's reign in France?
_____
_____
_____
_____

3. What did Napoleon do to bring back order in France?
_____
_____
_____
_____

4. What costly mistakes did Napoleon make in Spain and Russia?
_____
_____
_____

5. What important ideas did Metternich bring to the Congress of Vienna?
_____
_____
_____
_____

Thinking Critically

Answer the following questions on a separate piece of paper.

1. In what ways did the revolution in France create divisions instead of uniting people in a common goal?

2. Why did Napoleon's Empire collapse?

Name _____ Date _____

CHAPTER 24 Section 1 (pages 603–608)

Latin American Peoples Win Independence

TERMS AND NAMES
peninsulares Latin Americans born in Spain
creoles Spaniards born in Latin America
mulattos Africans or people of mixed European and African ancestry
Simón Bolívar Leader of Venezuelan independence movement
José de San Martín Leader who helped win independence for Chile and Argentina
Miguel Hidalgo Priest who began the revolt against Spanish rule in Mexico
José Morelos Leader of the Mexican revolt after Hidalgo was defeated

BEFORE YOU READ
In the last section, you read about revolution and the Congress of Vienna.

In this section, you will learn how Latin American countries got their independence.

AS YOU READ
Use the time line below to take notes on when each country got its independence.

1804	1818	1822
Haiti declares its independence		

1816	1821

Revolution in Haiti (page 603)

Where *in Latin America was independence first declared?*

In the early 1800s, colonial peoples in Latin America fought for independence. The French colony of Saint Domingue was the first Latin American colony to fight for independence.

Almost all of the people who lived in the French colony were slaves of African origin. In 1791, about 100,000 of them rose in revolt. Toussaint L'Ouverture, a former slave, became their leader. In 1802 Napoleon sent troops to the island to end the rebellion. They failed. In 1804, the colony declared its independence as Haiti.

1. How did Haiti become independent?

_____

Latin America Sweeps to Freedom (pages 604–605)

What *classes existed in Latin American society?*

In Latin America, society was divided into six classes of people. **Peninsulares**—those born in Spain—were at the top. Next were **creoles,** or Spaniards who had been born in Latin America. Below them were *mestizos*. Mestizos had mixed European and Indian ancestry. Next were **mulattos,** with mixed European and African ancestry, and then Africans. At the bottom were Indians.

CHAPTER 24 NATIONALIST REVOLUTIONS SWEEP THE WEST **227**

Creoles felt that they were not treated fairly. This bad feeling boiled over when Napoleon overthrew the king of Spain and named his own brother as king. Creoles in Latin America had no loyalty to the new king. They revolted. Even after the old king was restored, they did not give up their fight for freedom.

2. Which class revolted, and why?

The *Libertadores* End Spanish Rule (page 605)

Who were the libertadores?

Two leaders pushed much of South America to independence. **Simón Bolívar** was a writer, fighter, and political thinker. He survived defeats and *exile* to help win independence for Venezuela in 1821. **José de San Martín** helped win independence for Argentina in 1816 and Chile in 1818. Bolívar led their combined armies to a great victory in 1824. This victory gained independence for all the Spanish colonies.

3. Which two great leaders led the fights for independence in Venezuela, Chile, and Argentina?

Mexico Ends Spanish Rule; Brazil's Loyal Liberator (pages 607–608)

How did Mexico and Brazil achieve independence?

In Mexico, mestizos and Indians led the fight for independence. In 1810, **Miguel Hidalgo,** a village priest, called for a revolt against Spanish rule. Creoles united with the Spanish government to put down this revolt by the lower classes.

Hidalgo lost, but Padre **José María Morelos** took over leadership of the rebels. Fighting continued until 1815, when the creoles won.

After a revolution in Spain put a new government to power, the creoles joined with the other groups fighting for independence. In 1821, Mexico's won its independence. In 1823, the region of Central America separated itself from Mexico.

In Brazil, 8,000 creoles signed a paper asking the son of Portugal's king to rule an independent Brazil. He agreed. Brazil became free that year through a bloodless revolt.

4. How were the drives for independence in Mexico and Brazil different?

Independence Brings Disunity
(page 608)

How did the fight for independence affect Latin America?

The rebellions hurt the societies and economies of Latin America. *Turmoil* continued in the region. The new countries were split up into smaller units. In 1830, the territory of Gran Colombia divided into Colombia, Ecuador, and Venezuela. In 1841, the United Provinces of Central America split into five republics.

5. How did territories and countries change as a result of the fight for independence?

The Divisions in Spanish Colonial Society in 1789

- Mestizos (7.3%) — 1,030,000
- Mulattos (7.6%) — 1,070,000
- EUROPEANS
  - Peninsulares (0.1%) — 15,000
  - Creoles (22.8%) — 3,070,000
- Indians (55.8%) — 7,860,000
- Africans (6.4%) — 900,000

Skillbuilder
Use the chart above to answer these questions.

1. What were the largest and smallest groups in society?

2. What was the total number of Europeans?

Name _____ Date _____

CHAPTER 24 Section 2 (pages 609–612)

Revolutions Disrupt Europe

BEFORE YOU READ
In the last section, you read about Latin American independence movements.
In this section, you will learn about revolutions in Europe.

AS YOU READ
Use the web below to show changes that occurred in Europe at this time.

TERMS AND NAMES
conservatives People who supported the monarchy
liberals People who wanted to give more power to elected legislatures
radicals People who wanted to end the rule by kings and give full voting rights to all people
nationalism Belief that a person's loyalty belongs to the nation itself instead of to the nation's ruler
nation-state Country with its own independent government
the Balkans Region including all or part of present-day Greece, Albania, Bulgaria, Romania, Turkey, and former Yugoslavia
Louis-Napoleon Winner of the presidential election in France in 1848; later emperor
Alexander II Ruler of Russia who freed the serfs

[Web diagram: "Changes in Europe" in center, connected to "Greece — Wins self-rule from the Ottomans," "France," and "Russia"]

Nationalism Changes Europe
(pages 609–610)

What forces and peoples struggled for power?

There was a power struggle in Europe in the first half of the 1800s. Three forces were involved. **Conservatives** wanted to continue to support the kings who had ruled these lands for many centuries. These were nobles and other people who owned large amounts of property. **Liberals** wanted to give more power to elected *legislatures*. They were typically middle-class merchants and business people. They wanted to limit voting rights to people who were educated and owned property. **Radicals** wanted the end of rule by kings and full voting rights for all people.

At the same time, another movement arose in Europe—**nationalism.** This was the belief that a person's loyalty should go not to the country's ruler but to the nation itself. When the nation also had its own independent government, it became a **nation-state.** Nationalists thought that people with a common language and culture were a nation. And they had the right to their own government. These ideas grew out of the French Revolution.

The first people to win self-rule during this period were the Greeks. Greece had been part of the Ottoman Empire for centuries. The Ottomans controlled most of **the Balkans.** That region includes most of modern Greece, Albania, Bulgaria, Romania, Turkey, and the former Yugoslavia. In 1821, the Greeks revolted against Turkish rule. The Greeks won their independence by 1830.

CHAPTER 24 NATIONALIST REVOLUTIONS SWEEP THE WEST **229**

1. What different goals did conservatives, liberals, and radicals have?

_____

_____

_____

The Tide of Reform in Western Europe (pages 610–612)

What changes were occurring in Western Europe?

Other revolts broke out in other parts of Europe. In 1830, the Belgians declared their independence from rule by the Dutch. Nationalists began a long struggle to *unify* all of Italy. The Poles revolted against Russian rule. Conservatives managed to put down these rebellions. However, new ones broke out again in 1848 among Hungarians and Czechs. Once again, they were put down forcibly.

Events differed in France. Riots in 1830 forced the king to *flee,* and a new king was put in his place. Another revolt broke out in 1848. The king was overthrown and a republic established. However, the radicals who had won this victory began arguing. They differed over how much France should be changed. Some wanted only political changes. Others wanted social and economic changes that would help the poor.

When these forces began to fight in the streets, the French gave up on the radical program. They introduced a new government. It had a legislature and a strong president. The new president was **Louis-Napoleon,** Napoleon Bonaparte's nephew. He later named himself emperor of France. He built railroads and helped industry. The economy got better and more people had jobs.

In the early 1800s, Russia still did not have an industrial economy. The biggest problem was that serfdom still existed there. Peasants were bound to the nobles whose land they worked. Russia's rulers were reluctant to free the serfs, though. They feared they would lose the support of the nobles.

A new ruler of Russia, **Alexander II,** decided to free the serfs. Though it seemed bold, Alexander's move went only part way. Nobles kept half their land and were paid for the other half that went to the peasants. The former serfs were not given the land. They had to pay for it. This debt kept them still tied to the land. The *czar's* efforts to make changes ended when he was assassinated in 1881. Alexander III, the new czar, brought back tight control over the country. He also moved to make the economy more industrial.

2. What major reform was made in Russia at this time?

_____

_____

_____

_____

Name _____   Date _____

CHAPTER 24 Section 3 (pages 613–618)

Patterns of Change: Nationalism

TERMS AND NAMES
Camillo di Cavour Prime minister who unified northern Italy
Giuseppe Garibaldi Leader of the Red Shirts who won control over parts of southern Italy
Red Shirts Name for a group of Italian nationalists led by Garibaldi
Otto von Bismarck Leader who worked to expand Prussia
realpolitik Tough, practical politics
kaiser Emperor

BEFORE YOU READ
In the last section, you read about revolutions and reform in western Europe.
In this section, you will learn about nationalism.

AS YOU READ
Use a chart like the one below to take notes on the effects of nationalism.

Divided Empires
- Austrian Empire
- [ ]
- [ ]

Effects of Nationalism

Unified Nations
- [ ]
- [ ]
- [ ]

The Ideal of Nationalism (page 613)
What is nationalism?

Nationalists thought that many factors linked people to one another. First was nationality, or a common *ethnic* ancestry. Shared language, culture, history, and religion were also seen as ties that connected people. People sharing these traits were thought to have the right to a land they could call their own. Groups with their own government were called nation-states.

Leaders began to see that this feeling could be a powerful force for uniting a people. The French Revolution was a prime example of this.

1. What shared characteristics can unite people and create a strong national feeling?

_____
_____

Nationalism Shakes Aging Empires (page 614)
Why did nationalism divide empires?

Feelings of nationalism threatened to break apart three aging empires. The Austrian Empire was forced to split in two parts—Austria and Hungary.

CHAPTER 24 NATIONALIST REVOLUTIONS SWEEP THE WEST **231**

However, nationalist feeling continued to plague Austria and Hungary for 40 years. Later these kingdoms broke up into several smaller states. In Russia, harsh rule and a policy of forcing other peoples to adopt Russian ways helped produce a revolution in 1917. This revolution overthrew the czar. Like the other two, the Ottoman Empire broke apart around the time of World War I.

2. What three empires were torn apart by nationalism?

_____

_____

_____

Cavour Unites Italy (pages 615–616)
How did nationalism unite Italy?

Italians used national feeling to build a nation, not destroy an empire. Large parts of Italy were ruled by the kings of Austria and Spain. Nationalists tried to unite the nation in 1848. But the revolt was beaten down. Hopes rested with the Italian king of the state of Piedmont-Sardinia. His chief minister was Count **Camillo di Cavour.** Cavour worked to expand the king's control over other areas of the north.

Meanwhile, **Giuseppe Garibaldi** led an army of patriots that won control of southern areas. He and his army became known as the **Red Shirts** because they wore red shirts in battle. Garibaldi put the areas he conquered under control of the king. In 1866, the area around Venice was added to the king's control. Four years later, the king completed the uniting of Italy.

However, Italy faced an uncertain future. Political parties were in conflict. The government was disorganized. And the country had severe economic problems.

3. Who helped unify Italy?

_____

_____

_____

The Rise of Prussia; The Balance of Power Shifts (pages 616–618)
How was Germany united?

Germany had also been divided into many different states for many centuries. Since 1815, 39 states had joined in a league called the German Confederation. Prussia and Austria-Hungary controlled this group. Over time, Prussia rose to become more powerful. Leading this move was prime minister **Otto von Bismarck.** He was a master of **realpolitik**—tough power politics.

Bismarck joined with Austria to gain control of new lands. He then turned against Austria to gain even more territory. Other German states formed a new *confederation*. It was controlled by Prussia alone. Bismarck's next step was to win the loyalty of the remaining German areas in the south. He purposefully angered a weak France so that it would declare war on Prussia. When Prussia won the Franco-Prussian War in 1871, Bismarck reached his goal. The war with France gave the southern German states a nationalistic feeling. They joined the other states in naming the king of Prussia as emperor, or **kaiser,** of a strong united Germany.

These events changed the balance of power in Europe. Germany and Britain were the strongest powers, followed by France. Austria, Russia, and Italy were all even weaker.

4. What was the result of the defeat of France and the uniting of Germany?

_____

_____

_____

Name _____ Date _____

CHAPTER 24 Section 4 (pages 619–623)

Revolutions in the Arts

TERMS AND NAMES
romanticism Movement in art and ideas that focused on nature and the thoughts and feelings of individuals
realism Movement in art that tried to show life as it really was
impressionism Style of art using light and light-filled colors to produce an "impression"

BEFORE YOU READ

In the last section, you read how political borders changed in Europe.

In this section, you will learn about changes in the arts in Europe.

AS YOU READ

Use the chart below to show new movements in the arts.

MOVEMENT	DEFINITION	AUTHORS/COMPOSERS
romanticism	Focus on nature; focus on thoughts and feelings	William Wordsworth, Beethoven

The Romantic Movement
(pages 619–621)

What is romanticism?

In the early 1800s, the Enlightenment gradually gave way to another movement, called **romanticism**. This movement in art and ideas focused on nature and on the thoughts and feelings of individuals. Gone was the idea that reason and order were good things. Romantic thinkers valued feeling, not reason, and nature, not society. Romantic thinkers held idealized views of the past as simpler, better times. They valued the common people. As a result, they enjoyed folk stories, songs, and traditions. They also supported calls for democracy. However, not all romantic artists and thinkers supported all of these ideas.

Romantic writers had different themes. The Brothers Grimm wrote on history and the national pride that it fostered. During the first half of the 19th century, they collected German folk tales. They also created a German dictionary and worked on German grammar. These works celebrated being German long before there was a united German nation. Other writers wrote about strong individuals. Some wrote about beauty and nature.

Painters also used these themes. For example, the English painter Joseph Turner captured the raging of the sea. Another English painter, John Constable, celebrated the peaceful English countryside.

Germany produced one of the greatest early Romantic writers. Johann Wolfgang von Goethe wrote *The Sorrows of Young Werther*. It was a story about a young man who kills himself after he falls in love with a married woman.

French author Victor Hugo—who wrote *The Hunchback of Notre Dame*—told stories of the poor individual who fights against an unfair society. British Romantic poets William Wordsworth and Samuel Taylor Coleridge honored nature as the source of truth and beauty. Novels such as Mary Shelley's *Frankenstein* were horror tales about good and evil.

Romanticism was important in music as well. Composers wrote music to appeal to the hearts and souls of listeners. Ludwig van Beethoven, a German, was the foremost of these composers. Romanticism made music a popular art form.

1. What did Romantic thinkers and artists value?

_____

_____

_____

The Shift to Realism (pages 621–623)
What is realism?

In the middle 1800s, the *grim* realities of industrial life made the dreams of romanticism seem silly. A new movement arose—**realism**. Artists and writers tried to show life as it really was. They used their art to protest unfair social conditions. French writer Emile Zola's books revealed harsh working conditions for the poor. They led to new laws aimed at helping those people. In England, Charles Dickens wrote many novels that showed how poor people suffered in the new industrial economy.

A new device, the camera, was developed in this period. Photographers used cameras to capture realistic images on film.

In the 1860s, Parisian painters reacted against the realistic style. This new art style—**impressionism**—used light and light-filled colors to produce an impression of a subject or moment in time. Impressionist artists like Claude Monet and Pierre-Auguste Renoir glorified the delights of the life of the rising middle class in their paintings.

2. For what purposes did writers use realism?

_____

_____

_____

_____

Name _____ Date _____

Glossary — CHAPTER 24 Nationalist Revolutions Sweep the West

confederation Group that joins together for a common purpose
czar Emperor of Russia
ethnic Related to a religious, racial, national, or cultural group
exile State of being sent away from one's own country
flee Run away
grim Harsh; hard to bear
legislatures Law-making bodies
mestizos People with mixed European and Indian ancestry
turmoil Disorder or confusion
unify Unite; create one country out of separate states or other political divisions

AFTER YOU READ

Terms and Names

A. Write the name or term in each blank that best completes the meaning of the paragraph.

Camillo di Cavour
Giuseppe Garibaldi
the Balkans
nationalism
nation-state

In Europe, feelings of **1** _____ were developing. People no longer felt loyal to a king, queen, or other ruler. Instead, they felt loyal to their own particular country, group, or **2** _____. These feelings led to fights for self-rule by the Greeks. They had been part of a large region controlled by the Ottomans called **3** _____. Feelings of national pride and a desire for unity also helped **4** _____ bring together the northern part of Italy. These same feelings helped **5** _____ unite the southern part of Italy.

B. Write the letter of the name or term next to the description that explains it best.

a. Otto von Bismarck
b. Miguel Hidalgo
c. José de San Martín
d. Louis-Napoleon
e. Simón Bolívar

____ **1.** Emperor of France
____ **2.** Liberator of Chile and Cuba
____ **3.** Liberator of Venezuela
____ **4.** Prussian leader
____ **5.** Priest who began the Mexican revolution

Name _____ Date _____

AFTER YOU READ (continued) — CHAPTER 24 Nationalist Revolutions Sweep the West

Main Ideas

1. How did Mexico end Spanish rule?

_____
_____
_____

2. How did the wars for independence affect Latin America?

_____
_____
_____

3. Why was nationalism a force for change in Europe?

_____
_____
_____
_____

4. How did Otto von Bismarck unite Germany?

_____
_____
_____
_____

5. What new artistic movements began in Europe at this time?

_____
_____
_____

Thinking Critically

Answer the following questions on a separate sheet of paper.

1. Explain how the result of German unification was different than that of Italian unification.

2. Why do you think realism replaced romanticism?

236 CHAPTER 24 REVIEW

Name _____ Date _____

CHAPTER 25 Section 1 (pages 633–637)

The Beginnings of Industrialization

BEFORE YOU READ

In the last section, you read about romanticism and realism in the arts.

In this section, you will read about the beginning of the Industrial Revolution.

AS YOU READ

Use this chart to take notes on important developments and conditions that led to industrialization.

TERMS AND NAMES

Industrial Revolution Great increase in machine production that began in England in the 18th century

enclosure Large closed-in field for farming

crop rotation Planting a different crop in a different field each year

industrialization Process of developing machine production of goods

factors of production Conditions needed to produce goods and services

factory Building where goods are made

entrepreneur Person who organizes, manages, and takes on the financial risk of a business enterprise

```
┌──────────────┐   ┌──────────────┐   ┌──────────────┐
│ Agricultual  │   │  Factors of  │   │  Inventions  │
│  Revolution  │   │  Production  │   │              │
│ Increased    │   │              │   │              │
│ population   │   │              │   │              │
└──────┬───────┘   └──────┬───────┘   └──────┬───────┘
       └──────────────────┼──────────────────┘
                   ┌──────▼───────┐
                   │Industrialization│
                   └──────────────┘
```

The Industrial Revolution Begins (pages 633–634)

How *did the Industrial Revolution begin?*

The **Industrial Revolution** was the great increase in production that began in England during the 18th century. Before the Industrial Revolution, people made most goods by hand. By the middle of the 1700s, more and more goods were made by machines.

The Industrial Revolution began with an *agricultural revolution*. In the early 1700s, large landowners in Britain bought much of the land that had been owned by poorer farmers. The landowners collected these lands into large fields closed-in by fences or hedges. These fields were called **enclosures.** Many of the poor farmers who lost their lands became *tenant farmers*. Others gave up farming and moved to the cities.

New farm methods made farmers more productive. For example, Jethro Tull invented a seed drill that made planting more efficient. Farmers also practiced **crop rotation.** Crop rotation is the practice of planting a different crop in a different field each year.

The increase in farm *output* made more food available. People enjoyed better diets. The population of Britain grew. Fewer farmers were needed to grow food. More people began to make goods

CHAPTER 25 THE INDUSTRIAL REVOLUTION 237

other than food. The growth in the number of people in cities to work in factories helped create the Industrial Revolution.

For several reasons, Britain was the first country to industrialize. **Industrialization** is the process of developing machine production of goods.

Great Britain had all the resources needed for industrialization. These resources included coal, water, iron ore, rivers, harbors, and banks. Britain also had all the **factors of production** that the Industrial Revolution required. These factors of production included land, labor (workers), and capital (wealth).

1. Why was Britain the first country to industrialize?

_____

_____

_____

Inventions Spur Technological Advances (pages 635–637)

What inventions helped change business?

The Industrial Revolution began in the *textile* industry. Several new inventions helped businesses make cloth and clothing more quickly. Richard Arkwright invented the water frame in 1769. It used water power to run spinning machines that made yarn. In 1779, Samuel Compton invented the spinning mule that made better thread. In 1787, Edmund Cartwright developed the power loom. The power loom was a machine that sped up the cloth-making process.

These new inventions were large and expensive machines. Business owners built large, water-powered **factories** to house and run these machines. These factories were built near rivers because these machines needed water-power to run them.

The invention of the steam engine in 1705 brought in a new source of power. The steam engine used fire to heat water and produce steam. The power of the steram drove the engine. Eventually steam-driven engines were used to run factories.

At the same time, improvements were being made in transportation. Robert Fulton, an American, invented the first steam-driven boat. This invention allowed people to send goods more quickly over rivers and canals.

Starting in the 1820s, steam brought a new burst of industrial growth. George Stephenson, a British engineer, set up the world's first railroad line. It used a steam-driven locomotive. Soon, railroads were being built all over Britain.

The railroad *boom* helped business owners move their goods to market more quickly. It created thousands of new jobs in several different industries. The railroad had a deep effect on British society. For instance, people could now travel throughout the country more quickly.

2. What effects did the invention of the steam engine have?

_____

_____

_____

_____

Name _____ Date _____

CHAPTER 25 Section 2 (pages 638–642)

Patterns of Change: Industrialization

TERMS AND NAMES
urbanization City building and the movement of people to cities
middle class A social class of skilled workers, professionals, business people, and wealthy farmers

BEFORE YOU READ

In the last section, you saw how the Industrial Revolution began.

In this section, you will read about some of its effects.

AS YOU READ

Use the chart below to record the effects of industrialization.

Negative effects
- Crowded Cities
- [ ]
- [ ]

Industrialization

Positive effects
- [ ]
- [ ]
- [ ]

Industrialization Changes Ways of Life (pages 638–640)

How did industrialization change people's ways of life?

Industrialization brought many changes to the British people. More people could use coal to heat their homes, eat better food, and wear better clothing.

Another change was **urbanization**—city building and the movement of people to cities. For centuries, most people in Europe had lived in the country. By the 1800s more and more people lived in cities.

Living conditions were bad in crowded cities. Many people could not find good housing, schools, or police protection. Filth, garbage, and sickness were part of life in the *slums*. A person in a city could expect to live 17 years. In the countryside, a person could expect to live 38 years.

Working conditions were also bad. The average worker spent 14 hours a day on the job, 6 days a week. Many workers were killed or seriously injured in accidents.

Some people's lives were improved in the new economy. The Industrial Revolution created new wealth for the **middle class,** which included skilled workers, professionals, business people, and wealthy farmers. People in the middle class enjoyed comfortable lives in pleasant homes. This class began to grow in size. Some people grew

CHAPTER 25 THE INDUSTRIAL REVOLUTION **239**

wealthier than the nobles who had been in control for many centuries.

The Industrial Revolution had many good effects. It created wealth. It created jobs for workers and over time helped many of them live better lives. It produced better diets, better housing, and better clothing at lower prices.

1. What were three positive and three negative effects of industrialization?

_____
_____
_____
_____

The Mills of Manchester (pages 641–642)

What changes occurred in Manchester?

The English city of Manchester is a good example of how industrialization changed society. Rapid growth made the city crowded and filthy. The factory owners risked their money and worked long hours to make their businesses grow. In return, they enjoyed huge profits and built huge houses. The workers also worked long hours, but had few benefits. Many of these workers were children, some only six years old. The British government did not limit the use of children as workers until 1819.

The large amount of industry in Manchester caused environmental problems. Coal smoke and cloth dyes from the factories polluted the air and water.

2. Why is Manchester a good example of how industrialization changed cities?

_____
_____
_____
_____
_____

Manchester's Growth

Year	Population
1801	93,400
1831	232,800
1871	476,000

Skillbuilder

Use the chart to answer these questions.

1. How many years does this data cover?

_____
_____
_____
_____

2. What was the rate of growth in Manchester between 1801 and 1871?

_____
_____
_____
_____

Name _____ Date _____

CHAPTER 25 Section 3 (pages 643–646)

Industrialization Spreads

TERMS AND NAMES
corporation Business owned by stockholders who share in its profits but are not responsible for its debts

BEFORE YOU READ
In the last section, you read about some of the effects of industrialization.

In this section, you will see how industrialization spread to other nations.

AS YOU READ
Use the chart below to take notes on how, where, and why industrialization began in other countries.

```
                    Spread of
                 Industrialization
         ┌──────────┬──────────┬──────────┐
   United States   Belgium   Germany    France
  Begins in Northeast
  in textile industry
```

Industrial Development in the United States (pages 643–645)

How did industrialization begin in the United States?

Other countries began to industrialize after Great Britain. The United States was one of the first. Like Britain, the United States had a great deal of coal and water to create power. There was also plenty of iron. In addition, the immigrants that came to the United States created a large supply of workers.

The United States also benefited from conflict with Britain. During the War of 1812, Britain stopped shipping goods to the United States. As a result, American industries began to make many of the goods that Americans wanted.

In the United States, industrialization began in the textile industry. In 1789, Samuel Slater, a British worker, brought the secret of Britain's textile machines to North America. Slater built a machine to spin thread.

In 1813, a group of Massachusetts investors built textile factories in Waltham, Massachusetts. Just a few years later they built even more factories

CHAPTER 25   THE INDUSTRIAL REVOLUTION   **241**

in the Massachusetts town of Lowell. Thousands of workers, mostly young girls, came to these towns to work in the factories.

American industry first grew in the Northeast. In the last decades of the 1800s, industrial growth spread to other areas of the nation. This boom was fueled by large supplies of coal, oil, and iron. New inventions, including the electric light, also helped. As in Britain, a railroad building was also a big part of American industrial growth.

Businesses needed huge sums of money to do big projects. To raise money, companies sold *stock*. Stocks are shares of ownership in a company. All those who held stock were part owners of the company. This form of business organization is called a **corporation**.

1. How did industrialization begin in the United States?

_____
_____
_____

Industrialization Reaches Continental Europe (pages 645–646)

Where *did industrialization begin in Continental Europe?*

Industrial growth also spread from England to the European continent. Belgium was the first to industrialize. It was rich in iron and coal and had good waterways.

Germany was divided politically until the late 1800s. As a result, it did not develop much industry at first. However, the Ruhr Valley in Western Germany was rich in coal. The Ruhr Valley eventually became a leading industrial region.

Across Europe, small areas began to change to the new industries. Industrial growth did not occur in France until after 1850. The government then began to build a large network of railroads. Some countries, such as Austria-Hungary and Spain, faced transportation problems that stopped them from industrializing.

2. Which nations industrialized first, and why?

_____
_____
_____
_____

Worldwide Impact of Industrialization (page 646)

How *did industrialization change the world?*

The Industrial Revolution changed the world. Countries that industrialized gained more wealth and power than those that did not. The countries of Europe soon began to take advantage of lands in Africa and Asia.

The Europeans wanted to use these lands as sources of *raw materials* for their factories. European merchants saw the people on other continents as little more than markets for European goods. The European nations took control of the lands in many areas of the world outside of Europe. This practice is called *imperialism*.

3. How did industrialization lead to imperialism?

_____
_____
_____
_____

Name _____ Date _____

CHAPTER 25 Section 4 (pages 647–652)

An Age of Reforms

BEFORE YOU READ

In the last section, you saw how industrialization spread to different nations.

In this section, you will learn about new ideas and reforms.

AS YOU READ

Fill in the web below with the major ideas and changes you read about.

TERMS AND NAMES
laissez faire Economic theory that argues that governments should not interfere with business affairs
Adam Smith Philosopher who defended laissez faire economics
capitalism Economic system in which people invest money to make a profit
utilitarianism Belief that an idea is only as good as it is useful
socialism Belief that businesses should be owned by society as a whole
Karl Marx Economic thinker who wrote about a radical form of socialism
communism Form of socialism in which all production is owned by the people
union Organized groups of workers that bargain with business owners to get better pay and working conditions
collective bargaining Talks and agreements between organized workers and business owners
strike Organized refusal to work

(web diagram with center "New Ideas and Reforms" and one filled bubble "Laissez faire economics")

The Philosophers of Industrialization (pages 647–648)

What is capitalism?

Industrialization led to new ways of thinking about society. Some economists thought that the government should leave business owners alone. Their view is called **laissez faire.**

Adam Smith argued that governments should not put limits on business. He believed this freedom would help a nation's economy grow. He and other writers supported a system called **capitalism.** In a capitalist economy, people invest their money in businesses to make a profit. Smith and others believed that society would benefit over time from this system. Supporters of laissez faire opposed laws to protect workers.

Other writers challenged these ideas. One group was called the utilitarians. According to **utilitarianism,** an idea or practice is good only if it is useful.

The utilitarians thought it was unfair that workers should work so hard for such little pay and live in such poor conditions. They thought the govern-

CHAPTER 25 THE INDUSTRIAL REVOLUTION **243**

ment should work to end great differences in wealth among people.

1. How does capitalism work?

_____

_____

Rise of Socialism (pages 648–650)
What is socialism?

Some thinkers wanted society as a whole to own businesses. This way a few people would not grow wealthy at the expense of everyone else. Instead, all people would enjoy the benefits of increased production. This view—called **socialism**—grew out of a belief in progress and a concern for justice and fairness.

A German thinker named **Karl Marx** proposed a form of socialism that became known as *Marxism*. He said that factory owners and workers would struggle for power. Over time, he said, the capitalist system would destroy itself. The great mass of workers would rebel against the wealthy few.

Marx wrote *The Communist Manifesto*. It described **communism,** a form of socialism in which production is controlled by the people. In the early 1900s, these ideas would bring revolution.

2. How are capitalism and socialism different?

_____

_____

Unionization and Legislative Reform (pages 650–651)
How did workers take action to improve their lives?

While thinkers discussed these different ideas, workers fought to improve their lives. Many workers joined **unions.** A union is a group of workers that tries to bargain with employers for better pay and better working conditions.

When employers *resisted* these efforts, the workers went on **strike,** or refused to work. British and American workers struggled for a long time to win the right to form unions. By the late 1800s, workers in both countries had made some progress.

The British Parliament and reformers in the United States also tried to fix other social problems. Britain passed laws to limit how much work women and children could do. Groups in the United States pushed for similar laws.

3. How did both the government and workers themselves try to improve workers' lives?

_____

_____

_____

Other Reform Movements
(pages 651–652)
What other reforms were taking place at this time?

Another major reform movement of the 1800s was the effort to *abolish* slavery. The British Parliament ended the slave trade in 1807. It then abolished slavery throughout British territories in 1833.

Slavery was finally abolished in the United States in 1865, after the Civil War. Spain ended slavery in Puerto Rico in 1873 and in Cuba in 1886. In 1888 Brazil became the last country to *ban* slavery.

Women were active in many reform movements. As they fought for the end of slavery, many women began to fight for equal rights for women. The movement for equality began in the United States in 1848. In 1888, women from around the world formed a group dedicated to this cause.

Reformers took on other projects as well. Some pushed for—and won—improved education. Others hoped to improve conditions in prisons.

4. Name two major reform movements of the 1800s.

_____

_____

_____

Name _____ Date _____

Glossary CHAPTER 25 The Industrial Revolution

abolish To end
agricultural revolution Changes that led to great increases in the amount of food farmers produced
ban To forbid
boom A time of increased activity, wealth, and prosperity
economists People who study the ways that goods are made, sold, and bought
imperialism Actions or policies by which one country controls another
Marxism Form of socialism proposed by Karl Marx
output Amount of something produced or manufactured
raw materials Materials used in factories to create goods
resisted Worked against
slums Areas of poverty and poor housing
stock Shares of ownership in a company
tenant farmers Farmers who work land rented from someone else
textile Related to cloth or clothing

AFTER YOU READ

Terms and Names

A. Write the term or name in each blank that best completes the meaning of the paragraph.

Karl Marx
Adam Smith
socialism
capitalism
laissez faire

A great economic thinker who believed in free markets was **1** _____. He also supported a policy of leaving businesses alone to run the economy. This philosophy is called **2** _____. Ideas like this are part of a larger economic system called **3** _____. Another great economic and social thinker was **4** _____. He described an economic and government system called communism. This system is a form of **5** _____.

B. Write the letter of the name or term next to the description that explains it best.

a. industrialization
b. urbanization
c. corporation
d. utilitarianism
e. factors of production

____ **1.** Process of developing machine production of goods
____ **2.** Belief that an idea or thing is only as good as it is useful
____ **3.** Resources needed to produce goods and services
____ **4.** Business owned by stockholders
____ **5.** City building and movement of people to cities

Name _____ Date _____

AFTER YOU READ (continued)   CHAPTER 25   The Industrial Revolution

Main Ideas

1. What was the agricultural revolution, and what caused it?

_____
_____
_____

2. What inventions played a key role in the early development of the Industrial Revolution?

_____
_____
_____

3. How did the Industrial Revolution change cities?

_____
_____
_____

4. Name two countries in which industrialization got an early start. Explain why.

_____
_____
_____

5. What were three of the most important social reforms that followed the Industrial Revolution?

_____
_____
_____

Thinking Critically
Answer the following questions on a separate sheet of paper.

1. Discuss the major negative effects of industrialization on society.

2. How did the Industrial Revolution affect economic thought?

Name _____ Date _____

CHAPTER 26 Section 1 (pages 659–663)

Democratic Reform and Activism

BEFORE YOU READ

In the last section, you read about the Industrialization Revolution.

In this section, you will read about democratic reforms in Great Britain and France.

AS YOU READ

Use the time line below to take notes on key events in Britain and France.

TERMS AND NAMES
suffrage Right to vote
Chartist movement Movement in England to give the right to vote to more people and to obtain other rights
Queen Victoria Leader of Britain when democratic changes were occurring
Third Republic Government formed in France after Napoleon III was exiled
Dreyfus affair Events surrounding the framing of a Jewish officer in the French army
anti-Semitism Prejudice against Jews
Zionism Movement to establish a separate homeland in Palestine for the Jews

```
1832                        1890
Britain: Reform Bill of 1832 gives
more people the right to vote.


          1875                        1903
```

Britain Adopts Democratic Reforms (pages 659–660)

How did Britain become more democratic?

Since the 1600s, Britain's government had been a constitutional monarchy. A king or queen ruled the country, but the elected legislature—Parliament—held the real power.

Still, very few people could vote for members of Parliament. Only men who owned property—about six percent of the population—had the right to vote. That situation changed in the 1800s. The Reform Bill of 1832 was the first step. Middle-class people across England protested the fact that they could not vote. Worried by revolutions sweeping Europe, Parliament passed the Reform Bill. This law gave **suffrage,** the right to vote, to many in the middle class.

Those who still could not vote began the **Chartist Movement.** They wanted the vote and other rights. They presented their demands to Parliament in The People's Charter of 1838. Although they did not get what they wanted at first, over time their demands became law.

The leader of England during all these changes

CHAPTER 26 AN AGE OF DEMOCRACY AND PROGRESS **247**

was **Queen Victoria.** She was queen for 64 years. She performed her duties wisely and capably, but during her reign Parliament gained more power. The era that she was queen is known as the Victorian Age.

1. How did power shift in Britain in the 1800s?

_____

_____

_____

Women Demand the Vote
(pages 660–662)

How did women campaign for the right to vote?

By 1890, a few countries had given the right to vote to all men. But none gave the right to vote to all women. In the 1800s, women in the United States and Britain campaigned peacefully for the vote.

In 1903, a group called the Women's Social and Political Union began a stronger campaign for women's suffrage in Britain. This campaign included rallies, parades, and demonstrations during speeches of government officials. But women in Britain and the United States did not win the right to vote until after World War I.

2. When did women get the right to vote in Britain and the United States?

_____

_____

_____

Democracy in France (pages 662–663)

What was the Dreyfus affair?

The road to democracy in France was rocky. After France lost its war with Prussia in 1870, Napoleon III went to Britain in *exile*. While the National Assembly met to decide on a new government, a group of radicals took control of Paris. Troops put down the movement in bloody fighting.

Finally, in 1875, a new government—the **Third Republic**—was formed. It lasted over 60 years. They were years marked by fighting between many political parties.

In the 1860's, French society was divided over the case of an army officer named Alfred Dreyfus. Dreyfus was accused of being a traitor. The charge was made mainly because Dreyfus was a Jew. Many people believed the charge was true. Dreyfus was found guilty. The issue became known as the **Dreyfus affair.** A few years later, evidence showed that Dreyfus had been *framed*. He was later declared innocent.

The Dreyfus affair revealed **anti-Semitism,** or *prejudice* against Jews, in Europe. In Eastern Europe, anti-Semitism was bad. The Russian government even allowed organized attacks on Jewish villages. From the 1880s on, many Jews fled to the United States. In the 1890s, a movement called **Zionism** began. Its goal was a separate homeland for the Jews in Palestine.

3. Where in Europe was anti-Semitism found?

_____

_____

_____

_____

Name _____ Date _____

CHAPTER 26 Section 2 (pages 664-668)

Self-Rule for British Colonies

BEFORE YOU READ

In the last section, you read about democracy and prejudice in Britain, France, and other parts of Europe.

In this section, you will read about the fight for self-rule in British colonies.

AS YOU READ

Use the web below to show struggles for self-rule and their results.

> **TERMS AND NAMES**
> **dominion** Nation in the British Empire allowed to govern its own domestic affairs
> **Maori** Polynesian people who settled in New Zealand
> **Aborigine** Native people of Australia
> **penal colony** Place where convicts are sent to serve their sentences as an alternative to prison
> **home rule** Local control over domestic affairs

```
   Canada                               New Zealand
 Became a dominion
 after several rebellions
                    The Struggle
                    for Self-Rule
   Australia                            Ireland
```

Canada Struggles for Self-Rule
(pages 664–665)

How was the dominion of Canada formed?

Britain had colonies all over the world. Three of them—Canada, Australia, and New Zealand—were settled by colonists from Europe. Over time, the people in these colonies wanted to control their own governments.

The white settlers of Canada were split into two groups. One group included French-speaking Catholics that lived in the colony. Britain had won Canada from France in 1763. The other group was English-speaking and mostly Protestant. The two groups did not get along. In 1791, Britain split the colony into two *provinces*. Each colony had its own government.

But the French-speaking people were not happy with British rule. After several rebellions, the British Parliament put the two provinces back together under one government. Other smaller colonies were added to create the Dominion of Canada. As a **dominion,** Canada had the right to make all laws concerning its own affairs. But Parliament kept the right to control Canadian relations with other countries. By 1871, Canada stretched all the way from the Atlantic Ocean to the Pacific Ocean.

1. Why does Canada today contain both French-speaking and English-speaking people?

_____

_____

_____

CHAPTER 26 AN AGE OF DEMOCRACY AND PROGRESS **249**

Australia and New Zealand
(pages 665–667)

How were Australia and New Zealand settled?

New Zealand became part of the British Empire in 1769. Britain claimed Australia in 1770. Australia was a **penal colony.** The first settlers there were convicted criminals. The **Aborigines,** as Europeans later called the native people of Australia, were *nomadic*. They fished and hunted. They did not practice warfare among themselves. They offered little resistance to the British settlers.

The settlement of New Zealand went slowly because the British government recognized that the native people—the **Maori**—had rights to the land. By the 1840's, though, the number of British settlers in New Zealand was growing.

During the 1850's, Australia and New Zealand became self-governing. But they stayed in the British Empire. In the early 1900s they became dominions. Australia was the first country to use the *secret ballot* in elections. New Zealand—in 1983—was the first country to give women the right to vote.

2. How were the native people of Australia and New Zealand treated differently?

_____

_____

The Irish Fight for Home Rule
(pages 667–668)

Why did the British hesitate to give Ireland independence?

Irish self-rule took a long time to achieve. The Irish opposed English rule from its start in the 1100s. Religious conflict also divided the Catholic Irish and the small group of English Protestants who lived in the north.

In the 1840s, the Irish suffered a terrible famine. Many died of starvation and disease. Others lost their land. Millions of Irish people emigrated, or left Ireland. Most went to the United States or Britain.

In the late 1800s, some Irish pushed for complete independence. Most argued for **home rule**—the right to govern internal affairs. The British government opposed this move. They were afraid that the Catholic majority would treat harshly the Protestants in the north. In 1914, Parliament finally gave home rule to the southern part of Ireland. When World War I delayed its *enactment*, Irish *nationalists* rebelled.

Finally, Britain split Ireland in two. Northern Ireland remained part of Britain. The southern part became independent. Violence continued in Ireland off and on for decades. In 1998, the people of Ireland and Britain signed an agreement to solve their problems peacefully.

3. Why was Ireland split into two parts?

_____

The Great Famine, 1845–1851

Fate of the Irish during the famine
- 70% remained in Ireland, though millions more Irish emigrated after 1851
- 12% died
- 18% emigrated

Where they emigrated to (1851)
- Australia, 2.5%
- Canada, 11.5%
- Britain, 36%
- United States, 50%

Skillbuilder

1. What percentage of the Irish emigrated at this time?

_____

2. To what two countries did most Irish go?

_____

Name _____ Date _____

CHAPTER 26 Section 3 (pages 669–672)

Expansion and Crisis in the United States

BEFORE YOU READ

In the last section, you read about the struggle for self-rule in British colonies.

In this section, you will read about changes in the United States during the same time period.

AS YOU READ

Use the time line below to take notes on changes that caused the United States to change or to grow in area and numbers.

TERMS AND NAMES
manifest destiny Belief that the United States would rule the land from the Atlantic Ocean to the Pacific Ocean
Abraham Lincoln 16th president of the United States
secede To leave the nation
U.S. Civil War War fought between the North and South from 1861–1865
Emancipation Proclamation 1863 proclamation to free the slaves in the Confederate states
segregation Separation by race

```
  1830s                          1861
  Thousands of Native Americans
  relocated to Oklahoma.
         |                         |
         |_____|
              |              |
            1840s           1941
```

Americans Move Westward
(pages 669–670)

What was manifest destiny?

The United States expanded across North America and fought a bloody civil war. In the early 1800's the nation grew in size. It bought a huge piece of land from France in the Louisiana Purchase. It won a war with Mexico in the 1840's, and gained even more land.

Many believed in **manifest destiny**—the belief that the United States would rule control land from the Atlantic Ocean to the Pacific. As white settlers moved farther west, Native Americans suffered. In the 1830s, thousands of Native Americans were forced to move from their homes in the East to the present state of Oklahoma.

The growth of the nation raised serious questions. The Southern states used slave labor to grow crops such as cotton. People in the South hoped to

CHAPTER 26 AN AGE OF DEMOCRACY AND PROGRESS **251**

extend slavery to the Western lands. But many Northerners believed that slavery was wrong and should be ended.

1. What problems did the movement westward bring?

_____

_____

Civil War Tests Democracy
(pages 670–672)

Why was the Civil War fought?

The struggle over slavery led to the **U.S. Civil War.** The Southern states **seceded,** or pulled out of, the *Union*. The Southerners formed their own nation known as the *Confederate States of America*. War broke out after Confederate forces fired on a Union fort in 1861. The fighting lasted four years.

The North won the war. During the war, President **Abraham Lincoln** issued the **Emancipation Proclamation.** This proclamation declared that the people enslaved in the Confederate states were free. After the war, the Constitution was amended, or changed, to outlaw slavery. Another change to the Constitution made African Americans citizens.

In the first few years after the war, newly freed African Americans enjoyed equal rights. But whites soon regained control of the governments of the Southern states. They passed laws that took away the rights of blacks. The white governments also set up **segregation,** or separation, of blacks and whites. African Americans have continued to fight for equality since then.

2. What changes came about as a result of the Civil War?

_____

_____

Postwar Economic Expansion
(page 672)

What happened after the war?

The economy of the South was destroyed by the Civil War. But the rest of the nation experienced quick industrial growth. A sharp rise in *immigration* from Europe and Asia helped cause this growth. By 1914, more than 20 million people had come to the United States.

Many of these new citizens moved to the West. The government offered free land to people who moved there.

In addition, Congress set aside money to build a railroad across the continent. The railroad linked the different regions of the nation. By 1900, nearly 200,000 miles of track crossed the country. The growth of the railroads helped American industry grow.

3. What helped cause the rise in industrial growth?

_____

_____

252 CHAPTER 26 SECTION 3

Name _____ Date _____

CHAPTER 26 Section 4 (pages 673–679)

Nineteenth-Century Progress

BEFORE YOU READ

In the last section, you read about political change in the United States.

In this section, you will learn about progress in science and other fields.

AS YOU READ

Use the web below to take notes on the changes that occurred during the nineteenth century.

TERMS AND NAMES
assembly line Arrangement by which a product in a factory is moved from worker to worker, with each worker completing a single step in the task
mass culture Art and entertainment appealing to a large audience
Charles Darwin Scientist who developed the theory of evolution
theory of evolution Theory that all life on earth developed from simpler forms of life
radioactivity Form of energy released as atoms decay
psychology Study of the mind

[Web diagram with central oval labeled "Ninteenth-Century Progress" connected to six surrounding ovals. Top oval reads "Discovery of radioactivity"; other five ovals are blank.]

Inventions Change Ways of Life
(pages 673–674)

How did inventions change ways of life?

In the late 1800's, new inventions changed how people lived. Inventors around the world worked to make new machines. Thomas Edison received *patents* on more than 1,000 inventions. Among them were the electric light bulb and phonograph. Alexander Graham Bell invented the telephone. Guglielmo Marconi created the first radio.

There were changes in transportation, too. Henry Ford made the car affordable to ordinary people. He had a factory with an **assembly line.** It allowed him to build cheap cars. These cars were affordable for ordinary people. In 1903, the Wright brothers flew the first motor-powered airplane flight. Soon there was an aircraft industry.

1. What were three important inventions during this period?

_____
_____

CHAPTER 26 AN AGE OF DEMOCRACY AND PROGRESS 253

The Rise of Mass Culture
(pages 674–675)

What is mass culture?

In earlier times, most art, music, and the theater had been of interest to only the wealthy. With the rise of the middle class, a new mass culture developed.

This new **mass culture** appealed to a wide audience. People went to music halls to enjoy singing and dancing. In the early 1900's, they watched the first silent movies. People also enjoyed sporting events, both as participants and as spectators.

2. What new forms of entertainment became popular?

_____
_____
_____

New Ideas in Medicine and Science (pages 675–679)

What new ideas appeared in science and medicine?

Until the mid-1800's, no one knew about germs. French scientist Louis Pasteur discovered that microscopic animals could live in food. Pasteur called these tiny creatures *bacteria*. Scientists soon realized that bacteria could cause disease.

English scientist **Charles Darwin** developed the **theory of evolution.** This theory said that all life on earth had developed from simpler life forms over millions of years. This theory was hotly debated. Many people did not accept this idea. They said it went against the bible.

In the mid-1880's, an Austrian monk named Gregor Mendel showed that parents passed on their personal traits to their offspring. The science of genetics began.

Other scientists made new discoveries in chemistry and physics. They found that all matter is made of tiny particles called atoms. Marie and Pierre Curie discovered **radioactivity.** Radioactivity is the energy that is released when atoms *decay*.

3. Tell what each of the following discovered or developed: Louis Pasteur, Charles Darwin, Gregor Mendel, Marie and Pierre Curie.

_____
_____
_____
_____

The Social Sciences (page 679)

What is psychology?

In the late 1800's, some thinkers began to study the human mind. This new social science was called **psychology.** The Russian scientist Ivan Pavlov conducted a series of experiments. These experiments convinced him that animals and people responded to certain situations because of how they were trained.

Sigmund Freud, an Austrian doctor, argued that a person's actions are shaped by forces in the *subconscious* mind. These views shocked many. They seemed to overturn the idea that people could use their reason to build better lives.

4. What did Freud reveal about the mind?

_____
_____
_____
_____

254 Chapter 26 Section 4

Name _____ Date _____

Glossary — CHAPTER 26 An Age of Democracy and Progress, 1815–1914s

amended Changed
bacteria Microscopic organisms; germs
Confederate States of America Name taken by the states that seceded from the Union leading to the U.S. Civil War
decay Break down
enactment Officially becoming law
exile Absence from one's country
framed Made to appear guilty or assume the guilt for a crime one has not committed
immigration Movement into a country
nationalists People who are loyal to a particular nation or group of people
nomadic Without a fixed home
patents Inventor's rights to make, use, and sell his or her inventions
prejudice Unfair attitudes or beliefs, often aimed at a specific group
provinces Political divisions similar to states
Reform Bill of 1832 Bill that gave some members of the middle class in Britain the right to vote
secret ballots Method of voting in privacy
subconscious Part of the mind below the conscious
Union Name for the United States, often used in reference to the U.S. Civil War

AFTER YOU READ

Terms and Names

A. Write the name or term in the blank that best completes the meaning of the paragraph.

theory of evolution

mass culture

radioactivity

psychology

assembly line

One of the greatest developments in mass production occurred in the nineteenth century. This development was the use of the **1** _____. Another important development in the nineteenth century was the discovery of **2** _____ by Marie and Pierre Curie. Darwin's **3** _____ stated that all life on earth developed from simpler forms of life. Freud made great contributions in the field of **4** _____ . At this time, a new **5** _____ also developed. It produced art and entertainment that appealed to a large audience.

B. Write the letter of the name or term next to the description that explains it best.

a. suffrage

b. anti-Semitism

c. Zionism

d. segregation

e. Third Republic

____ **1.** Separation of races

____ **2.** Government in France established in 1875

____ **3.** Prejudice against Jews

____ **4.** Right to vote

____ **5.** Movement to create a separate homeland for Jews in Palestine

Name _____ Date _____

AFTER YOU READ (cont.) *CHAPTER* **26** An Age of Democracy and Progress

Main Ideas

1. How was the Chartist movement related to suffrage?
_____
_____
_____

2. Why was the Dreyfus affair significant?
_____
_____
_____

3. What problems did Ireland face in its struggle for home rule?
_____
_____
_____

4. How did the lives of African Americans change after the U.S. Civil War? How did they stay the same?
_____
_____
_____

5. How did new inventions change transportation?
_____
_____
_____

Thinking Critically

Answer the following questions on a separate sheet of paper.

1. How were the struggles for self-rule in Canada, Australia, and New Zealand alike?

2. Why were the ideas of Darwin and Freud hard for so many people to accept?

Name _____ Date _____

CHAPTER 27 Section 1 (pages 685–689)

Imperialists Divide Africa

BEFORE YOU READ
In the last section, you read about movements for democracy and self-rule.
In this section, you will learn about imperialism in Africa.

AS YOU READ
Use the chart below to take notes on the reasons why Europeans created overseas empires.

TERMS AND NAMES
imperialism Control by a strong nation over a weaker nation
racism Belief that one race is superior to others
Social Darwinism Use of Charles Darwin's ideas about evolution to explain human societies
Berlin Conference 1884–85 Meeting at which Europeans agreed on rules for colonizing Africa
Shaka Zulu chief who created a large centralized state
Boers Dutch colonists in South Africa
Great Trek Migration of Dutch colonists out of South Africa
Boer War War between the British and the Boers

Economic	Political	Cultural
Sell goods to new markets		

↓ ↓ ↓

Imperialism

Africa Before Imperialism; Nations Compete for Overseas Empires (pages 685–687)

Why did imperialism begin in the 1800s?

In the early 1800s, Europeans controlled a few areas along the coast of Africa. By the mid-1800s, Europeans were to expanding their control to new lands. This policy is called **imperialism.**
There were four basic reasons for imperialism.

The first reason for imperialism had to do with money. Europeans wanted colonies to provide raw materials for their factories. The Europeans also wanted to sell their goods in their new colonies.
Nationalism was a second reason for imperialism. Some nations wanted to gain colonies to show their national strength.
Racism was a third reason for imperialism. Racism is the belief that one race is better than others. Many Europeans believed that whites were better than other races.

CHAPTER 27 THE AGE OF IMPERIALISM 257

Racism is related to Social Darwinism. **Social Darwinism** is the use of Charles Darwin's ideas about evolution to explain human societies. One of Darwin's ideas was "survival of the fittest." This idea was that the fittest, or strongest, species would survive. Weak species would not survive.

People who believed in Social Darwinism argued that fit people and nations survived. They also believed that weak people and nations would not survive.

Christian *missionaries* also supported imperialism. They thought that European rule would end the slave trade. The missionaries also wanted to *convert* the people of other continents to Christianity.

Europeans began to take lands in Africa for these reasons. Technology helped the Europeans succeed. The African peoples were divided. It was hard for them to resist European advances.

1. What are four reasons for imperialism?

_____
_____
_____
_____

African Lands Become European Colonies (pages 687–688)

How did European nations claim African lands?

The *"scramble for Africa"* began in the 1880s. Diamonds were discovered in South Africa in 1867. Gold was discovered there in 1886. Europeans became more interested in the continent.

The European nations did not want to fight over the land. They met at the **Berlin Conference** in **1884–85.** They agreed that any nation could claim any part of Africa by telling the others and by showing that it had control of the area. Europeans quickly grabbed land. By 1914, only Liberia and Ethiopia were free from European control.

2. What was the purpose of the Berlin Conference?

_____
_____
_____
_____
_____

Three Groups Clash over South Africa (page 689)

What groups fought over South Africa?

In South Africa, three groups struggled over the land. In the early 1800s, the Zulu chief **Shaka** fought to win more land. Shaka's successors were not able to keep his kingdom intact. The Zulu land was taken over by the British in 1887.

Meanwhile, the British took control of the Dutch colony on the southern coast. Thousands of Dutch settlers, called **Boers,** moved north to escape the British. This movement is known as the **Great Trek.** The Boers fought the Zulus whose land they were entering.

At the end of the century, Boers fought a vicious war against the British called the **Boer War.** The Boers lost this war. The Boers then joined the British-run Union of South Africa.

3. Who were the Boers, and whom did they fight?

_____
_____
_____
_____
_____

Name _____ Date _____

CHAPTER 27 Section 2 (pages 690-695)

Patterns of Change: Imperialism

TERMS AND NAMES
paternalism Governing in a "fatherly" way by providing for needs but not giving rights
assimilation Absorbing colonized people into the culture of the imperialist nation
Menelik II Leader of Ethiopian resistance

BEFORE YOU READ

In the last section, you learned about the reasons for imperialism.

In this section, you will read about how the colonies were controlled.

AS YOU READ

Use the chart below to contrast direct and indirect rule.

DIRECT RULE	INDIRECT RULE
Colonizers controlled colonial affairs	Local powers controlled daily matters

Colonial Control Takes Many Forms (page 690)

What forms did colonial control take?

Each imperial power had goals for its colonies. Imperialist nations had four forms of control: *colony, protectorate, sphere of influence,* and *economic imperialism.*

A colony is an area ruled by a foreign government. A protectorate runs its own daily affairs, but is controlled by an imperialist nation. A sphere of influence is an area where an imperialist nation has exclusive economic rights. Economic imperialism refers to a situation where an independent nation was controlled by foreign businesses rather than foreign governments.

1. How did a protectorate differ from a colony?

_____

_____

Patterns of Imperialist Management; A British Colony
(pages 691–693)

How did imperialist governments manage their colonies?

The imperialist nations had two basic methods of

CHAPTER 27 THE AGE OF IMPERIALISM **259**

ruling their colonies. Britain used *indirect control*. In this system, local rulers had power over daily matters. There were also councils of native people and government officials. These councils were supposed to help native people learn to govern themselves in the British method. When the United States began to colonize, it also used the indirect method of control.

Britain tried to rule Nigeria through indirect control. The British let local chiefs manage their areas and collect taxes. The system did not always work. Chiefs had not existed before in the east and southwest of Nigeria. The chiefs in these regions did not have the power or status to rule well.

France and other European nations used another method—*direct control*. They felt native peoples could not handle the tough job of running a country. Instead, the imperialist power governed. This policy was called **paternalism.** The French also had a policy of **assimilation.** All colonial institutions were patterned after French institutions. The French hoped that the native peoples would learn French ways.

2. What is meant by direct control and indirect control?

African Resistance (pages 693–694)

How did Africans resist imperialism?

Some Africans resisted imperialism. People in Algeria fought against the French for almost 50 years. In German East Africa, thousands of Africans died when they tried to use magic to fight German machine guns.

Only Ethiopia resisted the Europeans successfully. There, Emperor **Menelik II** played one European country against another. In 1896, he used European weapons to defeat an Italian army.

3. Who resisted imperialism in Africa, and what were the results?

Impact of Colonial Rule (page 695)

How did colonial rule affect Africa?

Africans enjoyed some benefits from *colonial rule*. European governments reduced local conflicts. The Europeans also brought Africa deeper into the world economy. Railroads, dams, and telephone and telegraph lines were built.

But imperialism mostly caused damage. Africans lost control over much of their land. Many African traditions were destroyed. People were forced out of their homes. Many were made to work in bad conditions. The boundaries that Europeans drew had no relation to *ethnic* divisions in Africa. These boundaries caused problems when the colonies became independent nations.

4. What were three benefits and three problems of colonial rule?

Forms of Imperialism	Characteristics
Colony	A country or a region governed internally by a foreign power
Protectorate	A country or territory with its own internal government but under the control of an outside power
Sphere of Influence	An area in which an outside power claims exclusive investment or trading privileges
Economic Imperialism	Independent but less-developed nations controlled by private business interests rather than by other governments

Skillbuilder

1. Under which type of imperialism is the local government most independent?

2. What is the difference between a sphere of influence and economic imperialism?

Name _____ Date _____

CHAPTER 27 Section 3 (pages 697-700)

Muslim Lands Fall to Imperialist Demands

TERMS AND NAMES
geopolitics Interest in or taking of land for its location or products
Crimean War Conflict in which the Ottoman Empire halted Russian expansion near the Black Sea
Suez Canal Man-made waterway connecting the Red and Mediterranean Seas

BEFORE YOU READ
In the last section, you read about imperialism in Africa.
In this section, you will learn about imperialism in Muslim lands.

AS YOU READ
Use the web below to take notes on how other countries took control of Muslim holdings in these lands.

- Egypt
- Europe — *Ottomans lost almost all of their land*
- Muslim Lands
- Persia

Ottoman Empire Loses Power
(page 697)

When *did the Ottoman Empire become weak?*

The Ottoman Empire was based in modern Turkey. But it controlled ands in Eastern Europe, North Africa, and Southwest Asia.

This empire lasted for hundreds of years, but by the 1800s, it was weak. The ruling party broke up into quarreling factions. Corruption and theft caused financial chaos. The Ottomans were once leaders in science and *administration*. But they began to fall behind the Europeans.

Nationalism began to stir among people in the empire. In 1830, Greece won its independence and

CHAPTER 27 THE AGE OF IMPERIALISM **261**

Serbia won the right to govern itself. European nations eyed what remained of the empire hungrily.

1. What happened when the Ottoman Empire weakened?

_____

_____

_____

_____

Europeans Grab Territory
(pages 698–700)

Where did Europeans grab territory?

Geopolitics is the interest in or taking of land for its location or products. It played an important role the fall of the Ottoman Empire. Russia hoped to win control of the Black Sea so it could ship grain into the Mediterranean Sea. Russia fought a war with the Ottomans in the 1850s called the **Crimean War.**

Russia lost the war when Britain and France joined on the side of the Ottomans. Still, the Ottomans later lost almost all of their land in Europe and parts of Africa. Muslim leaders, seeing this decline, decided to modernize their countries.

In Egypt, Muhammad Ali broke away from Ottoman control. He reformed the army and the economy. Ali's grandson continued to modernize the empire. He joined with the French in building the **Suez Canal.** It connected the Mediterranean to the Red Sea.

The canal was extremely expensive to build. Egypt quickly found that it could not afford to repay the money it owed. The British took control of the canal. Later the British took over the rest of the country as well.

In Persia, the Russians and the British competed for control. Russia wanted to use Persia to gain access to the Persian Gulf and Indian Ocean. Twice Russia forced Persia to give territories through military victories.

Britain wanted to use Afghanistan, which was controlled by Persia, as a buffer between India and Russia. In 1857, Britain forced Persia to give up Afghanistan.

In the early 1900s, oil was discovered in Persia. A British company signed an agreement with Persia's ruler to develop these oil fields. Persians rebelled against their ruler, who was corrupt, and the growing influence of Europeans. Then Russia and Britain stepped in and took control of the land.

In Muslim lands, the Europeans gained control by using economic imperialism and creating spheres of influence. Some Muslim countries tried to modernize. But these efforts came too late to prevent Europeans from taking over.

2. What happened in Persia?

_____

_____

_____

_____

_____

Name _____ Date _____

CHAPTER 27 Section 4 (pages 701-705)

British Imperialism in India

TERMS AND NAMES
sepoy Indian soldier under British command
"jewel in the crown" Term referring to India as the most valuable of all British colonies
Sepoy Mutiny Uprising of Indian soldiers against the British
Raj British rule over India from 1757 to 1947.

BEFORE YOU READ
In the last section, you saw how Europeans grabbed Muslim lands.
In this section, you will read about British control of India.

AS YOU READ
Use the chart below to take notes on the causes of the nationalist movement in India.

- Racist attitudes of British
- [ ]
- [ ]
- [ ]

Causes of Nationalist Movement in India

British Expand Control Over India (pages 701–703)

How did British rule affect India?

The Mughal Empire of India fell into decline in the early 1700s. By the mid-1700s, the British East India Company was the most important power in India. The company held huge amounts of land. The company even had its own army. This army was led by British officers. It was staffed by **sepoys,** Indian soldiers.

India was the main supplier of raw materials for Britain. The British called India the **"jewel in the crown"** because it was Britain's most valuable colony.

India enjoyed some benefits from British rule. India's rail system was the third largest in the world. The railroad helped make India's economy more modern. The British made other improvements, too. They built telephone and telegraph lines, dams, bridges, and canals. They also improved *sanitation* and public health and built schools.

But British rule also caused problems. A great

CHAPTER 27 THE AGE OF IMPERIALISM **263**

deal of wealth flowed from India to Britain. Indian industry died out because of British trade laws. Many farmers and villages could no longer feed themselves because they were forced to grow cash crops. India suffered famines in the late 1800s. In addition, most British officials had *racist* attitudes that threatened Indian culture.

1. What problems did British rule bring?

_____
_____
_____
_____

Indians Rebel (pages 703–704)

Why did Indians rebel?

By the mid-1800s, many Indians resented British rule. In 1857, some Indian soldiers heard rumors about British weapons. The rumors offended the Indians' religious feelings. The British handled the situation badly. The Indian soldiers rebelled. This rebellion has been called the **Sepoy Mutiny.** It took the East India Company and British troops a year to put it down.

The Sepoy Mutiny failed because the Indians were divided. Muslims and Hindus did not trust each other. After the revolt, the British government took direct control of British India. The term **Raj** refers to British rule over India from 1757 to 1947.

2. What was the Sepoy Mutiny?

_____
_____
_____
_____

Indian Nationalist Movements Begin (page 705)

What were the goals of the Indian nationalist movement?

Indians also resisted British control in other ways. Leaders such as Ram Mohun Roy urged changes in traditional Indian practices. He wanted to make Indian society more modern and to free India of foreign control.

Nationalist feelings also started to grow in India. Indians resented the British discrimination against them. Indians were barred from the best jobs in the Indian Civil Service. British workers were paid more than Indian workers doing the same job.

Indians formed two groups—the Indian National Congress and the Muslim League. Both groups pushed the British to make changes. In the early 1900s, they called for self-government.

3. What groups called for change?

_____
_____
_____
_____
_____

264 CHAPTER 27 SECTION 4

Name _____ Date _____

CHAPTER 27 Section 5 (pages 706-709)

Western Powers Rule Southeast Asia

TERMS AND NAMES
Pacific Rim Southeast Asian mainland and islands along the rim of the Pacific Ocean
King Mongkut King who helped Siam modernize
Emilio Aguinaldo Leader of Filipino nationalists
annexation Adding of territory
Queen Liliuokalani Last Hawaiian ruler of Hawaii

BEFORE YOU READ

In the last section, you saw how the Indians reacted to imperialism.

In this section, you will read about imperialism in Southeast Asia.

AS YOU READ

Use the web below to show the various lands controlled by each Western nation.

- Dutch (Indonesia)
- British
- Southeast Asia
- Americans
- French

Western Rivalries for Pacific Rim Lands (pages 706–707)

Which *Western powers grabbed land in Southeast Asia?*

European nations also grabbed land in the **Pacific Rim,** Southeast Asia and the islands on the edge of the Pacific Ocean. The lands of Southeast Asia were perfect for plantation agriculture. Sugar, coffee, cocoa, rubber, coconuts, bananas, and pineapples were important products.

The Dutch controlled Indonesia. Many of the Dutch who moved to Indonesia thought of Indonesia as their home. They set up a class system that kept the Dutch at the top. Wealthy and educated Indonesians came next. Plantation workers were at the bottom. The Dutch forced farmers to use one-fifth of their land for export crops.

The British took the port of Singapore plus Malaysia and Burma (modern Myanmar). They used Singapore as a base for trade. It became one of the world's busiest ports. The British encouraged the Chinese to move to Malaysia. The Malaysians have become a minority in their own country. Tension between the Malays and the Chinese remains to this day.

France grabbed Indochina (modern Laos, Cambodia, and Vietnam). The French ruled Indochina directly and tried to push French culture on the Indochinese. The French did not

CHAPTER 27 THE AGE OF IMPERIALISM **265**

encourage industry. Rice became a major crop. Although the Vietnamese grew more rice than before, they ate less of it because so much rice was sent out of the region. This problem set the stage for Vietnamese resistance to French rule.

Colonialism brought some features of modern life to these regions. But economic change benefited Europeans more than the local people. Even so schooling, health, and sanitation were improved. Millions of people migrated to new regions of Southeast Asia. The mix of cultures did not always go so smoothly. Even today, some conflict between groups results from this period.

1. What major problems did colonialism bring?

_____
_____
_____

Siam Maintains Independence
(page 708)

How did imperialism affect Siam?

One land—*Siam* (modern Thailand)—stayed independent. Siam was surrounded by lands taken by the French and British. The French and British did not want the other to control Siam. The Siamese kings played the French and British against one another to remain free of both nations.

King Mongkut and his son modernized Siam. They started schools and reformed the government. They also built railroads and telegraph lines and ended slavery. These changes happened with little social turmoil.

2. How did Siam confront imperialism?

_____
_____
_____
_____

U.S. Acquires Pacific Islands
(pages 708–709)

What lands did the United States acquire?

In the late 1800s, the United States also began to seek colonies. After the Spanish-American War in 1898, the United States took control of Puerto Rico, Guam, and the Philippine Islands.

Filipino nationalists led by **Emilio Aguinaldo** fought against the Americans for their freedom. The United States defeated the rebels but promised to give the Philippines self-rule later. In the meantime, American businesses took advantage of Filipino workers.

American businessmen grew wealthy from sugar plantations in Hawaii. But they wanted to make more money. They also asked for the **annexation,** or addition, of Hawaii to the United States. That way they would get more money when they sold sugar in the United States. The American businessmen had a great deal of power in Hawaii.

In the 1890s, **Queen Liliuokalani** tried to regain control of her country for Hawaiian people. The American businessmen overthrew her. They declared a republic. In 1898, it became a territory of the United States.

3. What happened in the Philippines?

_____
_____
_____
_____

266 CHAPTER 27 SECTION 5

Name _____   Date _____

Glossary — CHAPTER 27 The Age of Imperialism

colonial rule Control of one nation by another
colonialism Imperialism; act of creating colonies
colony Area governed by a foreign power
convert To change religion
direct control System of completely governing a colony
economic imperialism Area controlled by private businesses rather than by a foreign government
ethnic Related to one particular group or race of people
exclusive Only; limited to just one
Filipino Person from the Philippine Islands
indirect control System of running a colony in which local rulers have some power
missionaries People who spread the message of their religion
nationalism Loyalty to a nation or group of people
protectorate Area with its own government under the control of a foreign power
racist Belief that one race is superior to another race
sanitation Cleanliness; measures taken to create a clean or healthy environment
scramble for Africa European grab for African land that began in the 1880s
Siam Old name for what is now modern Thailand
sphere of influence Area claimed as the exclusive investment or trading realm of a foreign power
Zulu Member of a large nation in southeastern Africa

AFTER YOU READ

Terms and Names

A. Write the name or term in each blank that best matches the description.

racism

Social Darwinism

paternalism

imperialism

assimilation

1. _____ Control over a weak nation by a stronger nation
2. _____ Belief that one race is superior to others
3. _____ Use of the theory of evolution to explain human societies
4. _____ Governing in a "fatherly" way by providing for needs but not giving rights
5. _____ Absorbing colonized people into the culture of the imperialist nation

B. Write the letter of the name next to the description that explains it best.

a. Menelik II
b. Shaka
c. Emilio Aguinaldo
d. King Mongkut
e. Queen Liliuokalani

____ 1. Leader who modernized Siam
____ 2. Ruler of Hawaii
____ 3. Leader of Filipino nationalists
____ 4. Zulu chief who created a large state
____ 5. Leader of Ethiopian resistance

Name _____   Date _____

AFTER YOU READ (continued)   **CHAPTER 27** The Age of Imperialism

Main Ideas

1. Explain what happened in the scramble for Africa. Tell which nations remained independent.

_____
_____
_____

2. Explain why indirect control of Nigeria did not work.

_____
_____
_____

3. Why was the Crimean War fought, and what happened?

_____
_____
_____

4. How did Indians rebel against British power?

_____
_____
_____

5. In what way was Siam different from other countries of Southeast Asia?

_____
_____
_____

Thinking Critically

Answer the following questions on a separate sheet of paper.

1. Explain the relationship between these terms: Raj and "jewel in the crown."

2. What was similar and what was different about U.S. imperialism in the Philippines and in Hawaii?

Name _____   Date _____

CHAPTER 28 Section 1 (pages 715–719)

China Responds to Pressure from the West

BEFORE YOU READ

In the last section, you read about imperialism in Asia.

In this section, you will see how China dealt with foreign influence.

AS YOU READ

Use the chart below to take notes on events that occurred in China.

TERMS AND NAMES

Opium War War between Britain and China over the opium trade

extraterritorial rights Rights of foreign residents to follow the laws of their own government rather than those of the host country

Taiping Rebellion Rebellion against the Qing Dynasty

sphere of influence Area in which a foreign nation controls trade and investment

Open Door Policy Policy proposed by the United States giving all nations equal opportunities to trade in China

Boxer Rebellion Rebellion aimed at ending foreign influence in China

CAUSE	EFFECT ON CHINA
British bring opium to China	

China Resists Foreign Influence
(pages 715–716)

Was China able to resist foreign influence?

In the late 1700s, China had a strong farming economy based on growing rice. Other crops, such as peanuts, helped to feed its large population. The Chinese made silk, cotton, and ceramics. Mines produced salt, tin, silver, and iron. China needed nothing from the outside world.

China limited its trade with European powers. All goods shipped to China had to come through one port. Britain bought so much Chinese tea that it was eager to find something that the Chinese would want in large quantities. In the early 1800s, the British began shipping *opium,* a dangerous drug, to China. The opium came mostly from India. The Chinese tried to make the British stop.

As a result of the **Opium War** that followed, the British took possession of Hong Kong. Later, the United States and European nations won **extraterritorial rights** and the right to trade in five ports. The Chinese resented these treaties but could not stop them.

1. What happened as a result of the Opium War?

_____
_____

CHAPTER 28 TRANSFORMATIONS AROUND THE GLOBE **269**

Internal Problems Increase (page 717)
What problems did China face?

China had *internal* problems as well. The population had grown quickly. When rains were too light or too heavy, millions starved. The Chinese government was weak and too corrupt to solve its problems.

A leader arose who hoped to save China. His name was Hong Xiuquan, and he led the **Taiping Rebellion**. More than one million peasants joined his army. The rebels won control of large parts of the south. The government needed 14 years to put down this rebellion. The fighting destroyed much farmland. At least 20 million people died.

2. What was the Taiping Rebellion?

_____

_____

China Wrestles with Reform
(pages 717–718)
What was the official attitude toward reform?

In the late 1800s, a number of young emperors ruled China. But they ruled in name only. It was the Empress Cixi who controlled the country. She supported a few reforms in education, civil service, and the military.

In the late 1800s, each of the European powers and Japan won a **sphere of influence** in China. A sphere of influence is a region in which a foreign nation controls trade and investment.

The United States opposed these spheres of influence. Americans urged an **Open Door Policy**, in which all powers had equal *access* to Chinese markets. The Europeans agreed. This policy did not help China, however. Although it as not a colony or group of colonies, China was *dominated* by foreign powers.

3. How did foreigners begin to gain control over China?

_____

_____

_____

Chinese Nationalism Grows
(pages 718–719)
What actions resulted from growing nationalism?

Humiliated by their loss of power, many Chinese wanted strong reforms. In 1898, the young Emperor Guangxu, Cixi's nephew, tried to put in place broader reforms.

Conservatives didn't like this. The retired EmpressCixi had him arrested and she took back control of the government. China had lost a chance for reform.

Some Chinese peasants and workers formed the Society of Harmonious Fists, known as the Boxers. They wanted to get rid of all Western influence. That included any Chinese who had accepted Western culture or the Christian religion. At the start of the **Boxer Rebellion** in early 1900, Boxers surrounded Beijing's European section. After many weeks, they were driven out by a *multinational* army.

Cixi finally began to allow major reforms. But change came slowly. In 1908, the court said that China would become a *constitutional monarchy* by 1917. However, *unrest* soon returned.

4. What was the Boxer Rebellion?

_____

_____

_____

Name _____ Date _____

CHAPTER 28 Section 2 (pages 720–723)

Japan Modernizes

BEFORE YOU READ

In the last section, you read about foreign influence in China.

In this section, you will learn about the steps taken by Japan to modernize.

AS YOU READ

Use the chart below to take notes on how Japan's power increased at home and abroad.

TERMS AND NAMES
Treaty of Kanagawa Treaty between the United States and Japan opening trade between the two nations
Meiji era Period of rule by Emperor Mutsuhito from 1867 to 1912
Russo–Japanese War War between Russia and Japan fought in 1904
annexation Adding of territory

Growing Japanese Power
- Asks foreigners to give up special rights in Japan
-
-
-

Japan Ends Its Isolation (paged 720–722)

How did isolation end in Japan?

From the early 1600s to the mid-1800s, Japan traded with China and the Dutch and had diplomatic contact with Korea. But beyond that, Japan was largely isolated. British, French, Russian, and American officials tried to convince the Japanese to open up. But the Japanese repeatedly refused.

That situation changed in 1853 when American steamships with cannons entered Japanese waters. The next year, Japan and the United States signed the **Treaty of Kanagawa**. It agreed to open Japan to trade with America. Soon afterwards, Japan made similar deals with European nations.

Many Japanese were upset with the *shogun*, the military dictator, who had agreed to these new treaties. The Emperor Mutsuhito got their support and managed to overthrow the shogun. For the first time in centuries, the emperor ruled Japan directly. He reigned for 45 years, from 1867 to 1912. This period is called the **Meiji era.** The name *Meiji* means "enlightened rule."

The emperor wanted to modernize Japan. He sent government officials to Europe and the United States. From what they saw, they shaped a new Japan. They modeled the government after

CHAPTER 28 TRANSFORMATIONS AROUND THE GLOBE **271**

the strong central government of Germany. They patterned the army after Germany's and the navy after Britain's. They adapted the American system of schooling for all children.

The emperor also supported changes to Japan's economy. The country mined coal and built railroads and factories. In just a few years, Japan's economy was as modern as any in the world.

1. What steps did Mutsuhito take to modernize Japan?

_____

_____

_____

_____

Japanese Imperialism Grows
(pages 722–723)

How did Japan increase its influence in Asia?

By 1890, Japan had the strongest military in Asia. It asked foreigners to give up their special rights in Japan. The European nations agreed. Japan felt equal to the Western nations.

Japan became more imperialistic as its power grew. When China broke an agreement not to send armies into Korea, Japan went to war. It drove China out of Korea and gained Taiwan and some other islands as new colonies. In 1904, Japan and Russia fought the **Russo–Japanese War** over China's Manchurian territory. Japan surprised the world by defeating a larger power that was supposed to be stronger.

The next year, Japan attacked Korea. In 1905, Japan made Korea a protectorate. Japanese officials took more and more power away from the Korean government. The Korean king was unable to get help for his government from other countries. By 1910, Japan achieved **annexation** of Korea.

The Japanese were harsh rulers. They shut down Korean newspapers. They allowed only Japanese history and language to be taught. They took land from Korean farmers and gave it to Japanese settlers. They built factories run by Japanese only. Koreans were not allowed to start new businesses. Koreans resented these actions. They began a nationalist movement and protested against Japanese rule.

2. How did Japan expand its empire to Korea?

_____

_____

_____

_____

_____

Name _____   Date _____

CHAPTER 28 Section 3 (pages 724–727)

U.S. Economic Imperialism in Latin America

BEFORE YOU READ

In the last section, you saw how Japan increased its power and became an imperialist nation.

In this section, you will read about U.S. economic imperialism in Latin America.

AS YOU READ

Use the chart below to take notes on the causes and effects of U.S. imperialism.

TERMS AND NAMES
caudillo Dictator
Monroe Doctrine U.S. statement of opposition to European influence in the Americas
José Martí Cuban writer who fought for Cuban independence
Spanish–American War War fought between the United States and Spain in 1898, in which the Americans supported the Cuban fight for independence
Panama Canal Man-made waterway connecting the Atlantic and Pacific Oceans
Roosevelt Corollary Statement that the United States had the right to exercise "police power" in the Western Hemisphere

causes → U.S. Economic Imperialism → **effects**

(Cause box 1: Poverty and political unrest)

Latin America After Independence (pages 724–725)

What conditions existed among the new nations of Latin America?

In the early 1800s, the new nations of Latin America had serious problems. Most people were poor and unable to read. They worked on farms for large landowners who took advantage of them.

Another problem was political unrest. Local military leaders who wanted power ruled Latin American nations as caudillos, or dictators. Landowners kept the **caudillos** in power. The landowners refused to give power to the mass of poor people. Only people with property could vote.

Sometimes reformers did take office. But they never lasted long. When their reforms threatened the power of the wealthy too much, a dictator would rise and remove them from office.

1. What problems did the people in the new nations of Latin America face?

_____
_____

CHAPTER 28 TRANSFORMATIONS AROUND THE GLOBE **273**

Economies Grow Under Foreign Influence (pages 725–726)

What nations controlled Latin American economies?

Spain's trade laws in Latin America ended when Spain lost control of those lands. The new countries could now trade with any nation. Britain and the United States became the chief trading partners. Businesses in these nations soon dominated Latin American economies.

The Latin American economies depended on exports. Other countries benefited from trade with Latin America more than the Latin Americans did.

Latin America did not develop its own manufacturing industries. It had to *import* manufactured goods. These goods cost more than what was earned from exports.

In addition, Latin American countries often borrowed money from foreign banks. When they could not repay the loans, lenders took control of the businesses. In this way, much of Latin America fell into foreign hands.

2. Why was Latin America's need to import goods a problem?

_____

_____

_____

The United States and Latin America (pages 726–727)

How did the United States gain Latin American territories?

In 1823, President James Monroe issued the **Monroe Doctrine.** It warned European nations against interfering in the American continents. The United States did not really enforce this policy until the end of the century.

In the 1890s, the people of Cuba were fighting for their independence from Spain. The writer **José Martí** was one of them. American businesses had economic interests on the island. Also, Spain had placed many Cuban women and children in concentration camps. This upset many Americans. For these reasons, the United States fought against Spain in the **Spanish–American War.**

The United States won the war and gained several new territories. The United States put a military government in place in Cuba. This step and others made many Cubans angry at the United States.

Into the early part of the 20th century, ships traveling from the east to the west coast had to go around the southern tip of South America. This took many weeks. Americans wanted to find a quicker route. They hoped to build a canal across Panama.

President Roosevelt offered $10 million to Colombia—to which Panama belonged—for the right to build this canal. When Colombia asked for more money, the United States helped the people of Panama revolt for independence. In return, the United States won a ten-mile-wide zone in Panama in which to build the **Panama Canal.** The canal opened in 1914.

In 1904, Roosevelt extended the Monroe Doctrine. He said that the United States had the right to act as "an international police power" in the western hemisphere. This statement is known as the **Roosevelt Corollary.** Over the next few decades, the United States acted on the Roosevelt Corollary many times. When trouble arose in various countries, the United States sent its troops. Sometimes they stayed for many years.

3. How did the United States win a zone in Panama for a canal?

_____

_____

_____

_____

274 CHAPTER 28 SECTION 3

Name _____ Date _____

CHAPTER 28 Section 4 (pages 729–733)

The Mexican Revolution

TERMS AND NAMES
Antonio López de Santa Anna Leader in Mexico's fight for independence
Benito Juárez Leader of *La Reforma*
La Reforma Movement in Mexico aimed at achieving land reform, better education, and other goals
Porfirio Díaz Dictator who came to power after Juárez
Francisco Madero Enemy of Díaz who believed in democracy
Francisco "Pancho" Villa Popular leader of the Mexican revolution
Emiliano Zapata Leader of a powerful revolutionary army

BEFORE YOU READ

In the last section, you read about economic imperialism by the United States in Latin America.

In this section, you will read about revolution and reform in Mexico.

AS YOU READ

Use the time line below to take notes on the reforms and key events of the Mexican Revolution.

```
┌─────────────────────────┐      ┌─────────────────────────┐
│         1858            │      │         1872            │
│ Benito Juárez and his   │      │                         │
│ supporters win control  │      │                         │
│ of the government.      │      │                         │
└─────────────────────────┘      └─────────────────────────┘

┌─────────────────────────┐      ┌─────────────────────────┐
│         1862            │      │         1917            │
│                         │      │                         │
│                         │      │                         │
└─────────────────────────┘      └─────────────────────────┘
```

Santa Anna and the Mexican War (pages 729–730)

Who was Santa Anna?

Antonio López de Santa Anna was a leading figure in the early history of independent Mexico. He fought for Mexican independence from Spain in 1821. He fought against Spain again in 1829 when Spain tried to recapture Mexico. He served as Mexico's president four times.

But in the 1830s, Santa Anna was unable to stop Texas from winning independence from Mexico. In the 1840s, the United States annexed Texas. This angered many Mexicans.

When a border dispute between Mexico and Texas turned into armed conflict, the United States invaded Mexico. Santa Anna led his nation's army and was defeated. Mexico surrendered huge amounts of land to the United States.

1. What losses did Mexicans suffer under Santa Anna?

_____

_____

_____

Juárez and *La Reforma* (pages 730–731)

What was La Reforma?

Another important leader of the middle 1800s was **Benito Juárez.** Juárez wanted to improve conditions

CHAPTER 28 TRANSFORMATIONS AROUND THE GLOBE **275**

for the poor in Mexico. He led a movement called *La Reforma*—the reform. *La Reforma* aimed to break the power of the large landowners and give more schooling to the poor. Juárez and his supporters won control of the government in 1858.

But conservatives who opposed *La Reforma* did not give up. They plotted with France to retake Mexico. In 1862, Napoleon III of France sent an army that captured the country in 18 months. Napoleon III named a European noble as emperor. But Juárez and his followers kept fighting. Five years later, they drove the French from Mexican soil and killed the emperor.

2. How did conservatives oppose *La Reforma*?

_____

_____

Porfirio Díaz and "Order and Progress" (page 732)

Who was Porfirio Díaz?

Juárez again pressed for his reforms. He made some progress but died in office in 1872. Soon after he died, a new leader emerged. **Porfirio Díaz** was a leader in Mexican politics for more than 30 years. Díaz brought order to the country. He ended raids by bandits and brought some economic growth, but he limited political freedom. A leader named **Francisco Madero** called for the overthrow of Díaz.

3. What were the benefits and drawbacks of Díaz's rule?

_____

_____

Revolution and Civil War
(pages 732–733)

Who were Villa and Zapata?

In the early 1900s, calls for reform got louder. **Francisco "Pancho" Villa** and **Emiliano Zapata** called for better lives for the poor. They raised armies and forced Díaz to step down. But political unrest continued. For many years, leaders struggled for power. In 1917, Mexico adopted a new constitution that survived all of the turmoil.

Conflict continued until a new political party gained control of Mexico in 1929. The Institutional Revolutionary Party (PRI) brought peace and political *stability* to a troubled land.

4. What was the main goal of Villa and Zapata?

_____

_____

Reforms of Mexican Constitution of 1917

Land	Religion	Labor	Social Issues
• Breakup of large estates • Restrictions on foreign ownership of land • Government control of resources (oil)	• State takeover of land owned by the Church	• Minimum wage for workers • Right to strike • Institution of labor unions	• Equal pay for equal work • Limited legal rights for women (spending money and bringing lawsuits)

Skillbuilder

1. Which of these reforms were meant to weaken wealthy landowners?

_____

_____

2. Which reforms do you think benefited the poor the most?

_____

_____

Name _____ Date _____

Glossary CHAPTER 28 Transformations Around the Globe

access Means of getting in
Boxers Chinese people who fought against foreign influence in China
concentration camps Places where people are held, usually for being political enemies
conservatives People who do not want change
constitutional monarchy Government in which royal power is limited by the law
dominated Controlled
exports Goods sold to another country
humiliated To have lost pride, dignity, or self-respect
import To buy a good from another country
internal Inside a country
isolated Cut off from other nations
multinational Made up of people from many nations
opium A dangerous drug that the British exported to China from India
plotted Made a secret plan
shogun Japanese military ruler
stability Order; freedom from constant change
unrest Political change and dissatisfaction

AFTER YOU READ

Terms and Names

A. Write the name or term in each blank that best completes the meaning of the paragraph.

Francisco "Pancho" Villa

Emiliano Zapata

Antonio López de Santa Anna

Benito Juárez

Porfirio Díaz

One of the most important leaders in early Mexican history is **1** _____. He helped fight for Mexican independence from Spain. **2** _____ was the leader of *La Reforma*, a Mexican reform movement. Many of the reforms he established were undone by **3** _____, who brought order to the country but also limited freedom. A far more popular leader was **4** _____. Along with **5** _____, he helped the poor fight for better lives.

B. Write the letter of the name or term next to the description that explains it best.

a. Open Door Policy

b. Treaty of Kanagawa

c. Roosevelt Corollary

d. Boxer Rebellion

e. Taiping Rebellion

____ **1.** Policy that gave all nations an opportunity to trade in China

____ **2.** Agreement to open two Japanese ports to American ships

____ **3.** Uprising against foreign influence in China

____ **4.** Revolt against the Qing Dynasty

____ **5.** Addition to the Monroe Doctrine

Name _____ Date _____

AFTER YOU READ (cont.) **CHAP 28** Transformations Around the Globe

Main Ideas

1. Why did the Taiping Rebellion occur?
_____
_____
_____

2. Who was Cixi?
_____
_____
_____

3. What occurred in Japan during the Meiji Era?
_____
_____
_____

4. In what ways did the United States both help and hurt the Cuban people?
_____
_____
_____

5. What are three reforms made by the Mexican constitution of 1917?
_____
_____
_____

Thinking Critically

Answer the following questions on a separate sheet of paper.

1. Describe how Japan acted on its feelings of pride and strength in the late 1800s.

2. What did Juárez, Villa, and Zapata have in common?

Name _____ Date _____

CHAPTER 29 Section 1 (pages 743–746)

The Stage Is Set for War

TERMS AND NAMES
militarism Glorifying war and preparing for it
Triple Alliance Military agreement between Germany, Austria-Hungary, and Italy
Kaiser Wilhelm II Emperor of Germany
Triple Entente Military agreement among Britain, France, and Russia

BEFORE YOU READ
In the last chapter, you read about political changes around the globe.
In this section, you will learn about the First World War.

AS YOU READ
Use this chart to take notes on the causes of World War I.

[Chart with four boxes labeled — first box: "Nationalism"; three blank boxes — all pointing to a box labeled "World War I"]

An Uneasy Peace Grips Europe
(pages 743–744)

Why didn't peace last in Europe?

Many people in Europe had joined groups to work for peace. However, developments would soon lead Europe into war.

One of those developments was *nationalism*—a deep feeling of attachment to one's own nation. This force helped *unify* the people of a country. It also created competition between countries.

By 1900, six nations were *rivals* for power in Europe. These nations, called the *Great Powers*, were Germany, Austria-Hungary, Great Britain, Russia, Italy, and France. They competed economically, and they competed for neighboring land.

Imperialism was another force that helped lead to war. France and Germany were each seeking to control of parts of Africa. They almost came to war twice in the early 1900s. Mistrust was a huge problem.

The third factor leading to war was a growing arms race. Each country in Europe—except Great Britain—built a large army. Glorifying war and preparing for it is called **militarism**.

1. What were three factors leading to war?

_____

_____

_____

CHAPTER 29 THE GREAT WAR **279**

Tangled Alliances (pages 744–745)

What caused countries to fear one another?

Growing *rivalries* led the nations to make military *alliances*. Prussia's chancellor, Otto von Bismarck, feared that France would want revenge for its defeat in the Franco-Prussian War. He set out to *isolate* France. In 1879, he formed a **Triple Alliance** with Austria-Hungary and Italy. He also signed a treaty with Russia.

Kaiser Wilhelm II of Germany did not want to share power with Bismarck. He forced Bismarck to resign and followed his own foreign policy. He let the agreement with Russia end. Russia soon allied itself with France. This alliance meant that Germany would have to fight enemies on its eastern and western borders if there were a war with either country. Wilhelm II then moved to make the German navy larger.

Britain grew alarmed. It began to build more ships. It also entered into the **Triple Entente** alliance with France and Russia. The six Great Powers had now formed two camps—Germany, Austria-Hungary, and Italy against Britain, France, and Russia.

2. What two groups of nations developed?

_____
_____
_____
_____

Crisis in the Balkans (pages 745–746)

What part did the Balkans play in the increasing tensions?

Meanwhile, trouble was brewing in the Balkans, in southeastern Europe. The Ottoman Empire controlled this area. But it was breaking apart. Both Austria-Hungary and Russia wanted some of this land.

The kingdom of Serbia was also in this region. It wanted to bring other Slavic peoples who lived in the Balkans under its control. In 1908, Austria-Hungary seized Bosnia and Herzegovina. These lands had Slavic peoples. This action angered the Serbs. However, their Russian allies were unwilling to support them, and they backed down.

By 1914, the situation was different. Serbia had gained land in other parts of the region and felt strong. Austria worried that Serbia might interfere with its control of Bosnia and Herzegovina.

In June 1914, a Serbian killed Archduke Franz Ferdinand, the *heir* to the throne of Austria-Hungary. Austria-Hungary declared war on Serbia. Russia came to Serbia's defense. Soon most of Europe was at war.

3. How were the Serbians involved in the start of World War I?

_____
_____
_____
_____

Name _____ Date _____

CHAPTER 29 Section 2 (pages 747–751)

War Consumes Europe

BEFORE YOU READ

In the last section, you read how World War I began.

In this section, you will learn the details of this costly and tragic war.

AS YOU READ

Use the chart below to compare and contrast the Western Front and the Eastern Front. Include who fought, where they fought, and how they fought.

TERMS AND NAMES

Schlieffen Plan Germany's plan for winning the war on two fronts

Allies Great Britain, France, Russia, and other nations who fought on their side

Central Powers Germany, Austria-Hungary, and other nations who fought on their side

trench warfare Fighting from trenches dug in the battlefield

Western Front Region of northern France where much fighting took place

Eastern Front Region along German-Russian border where much fighting took place

WESTERN FRONT	EASTERN FRONT
Area in France	

The Alliance System Collapses
(pages 747–748)

How did so many nations become involved?

The system of alliances turned the war between Austria-Hungary and Serbia into a wider war. Russia moved against Austria-Hungary. It figured that Germany would support Austria-Hungary. So it moved troops against Germany as well. Germany declared war on Russia. Soon after, it also declared war on Russia's ally, France.

Germany had a plan for winning the war on two fronts. This was the **Schlieffen Plan**. It called for a rapid push through France, a quick defeat of that nation, and a turn to face Russia in the east. To capture France quickly, Germany moved through Belgium. Belgium was a neutral country. Britain was outraged by Germany's action. It declared war on Germany. France, Britain, and Russia. They were called the **Allies**. They were later joined by Italy, which broke with Germany and Austria-Hungary. Bulgaria and the Ottoman Empire joined Germany and Austria-Hungary. They were called the **Central Powers**.

CHAPTER 29 THE GREAT WAR **281**

1. Who were the Allies and Central Powers?

_____
_____
_____
_____

A Bloody Stalemate Along the Western Front (pages 748–750)

What kind of warfare was used?

After the German army moved almost to Paris, French defenses strengthened and stopped them in September 1914. Both sides became bogged down in a bloody conflict. Soldiers dug deep *trenches* into the ground. **Trench warfare** began.

When soldiers left the trenches to storm enemy lines, they faced powerful weapons. Machine guns, tanks, poison gas, and larger pieces of *artillery* killed hundreds of thousands of soldiers. This was how the war was fought in France, which was called the **Western Front.**

2. What was the war like on the Western Front?

_____
_____
_____
_____

The Battle on the Eastern Front (pages 750–751)

What happened on the Eastern Front?

The war on the **Eastern Front** showed more movement at first—but it was equally *destructive*. Russian armies attacked both Germany and Austria-Hungary. They had some early success but were driven back in both places. One reason was that Russia did not have a fully industrial economy. It could not keep troops supplied.

Still, Russia had a huge population and could send millions to war. The large Russian army provided a constant threat to Germany. This threat prevented Germany from putting its full resources against the Allies in the west.

3. What weaknesses and strengths did Russia have?

_____
_____
_____
_____
_____

Name _____ Date _____

CHAPTER 29 Section 3 (pages 753–757)

War Affects the World

TERMS AND NAMES
unrestricted submarine warfare Using submarines to sink any ship without warning
total war War in which countries use all their resources for the war
rationing Control of the amounts and kinds of goods people can have
propaganda One-sided information designed to persuade
armistice Agreement to stop fighting

BEFORE YOU READ

In the last section, you read how the war was fought in Europe.

In this section, you will learn how the war affected the world.

AS YOU READ

Use the chart below to take notes on the effects of World War I around the world and on the home fronts.

causes

- Allies capture several cities in Southwest Asia.
- [ ]
- [ ]

→ **World War I** →

effects

- [ ]
- [ ]
- [ ]

A Truly Global Conflict (pages 753–755)

What other areas of the world were involved?

The Allies hoped to take a part of the Ottoman Empire called the Dardanelles. The attack failed with great loss of life. A more successful operation was headed by a British officer named T. E. Lawrence. He helped lead an Arab revolt against Ottoman rule. As a result, the Allies were able to capture several important cities in Southwest Asia.

Japan took German colonies in China and the Pacific Ocean. The Allies also captured three of the four German colonies in Africa.

The British had used their strong navy to block all supplies from reaching Germany. The Germans responded by increasing their submarine attacks on ships bringing food and supplies to the Allies. They used **unrestricted submarine warfare**. This meant sinking any ship without warning in the waters around Great Britain.

When American ships were sunk and lives were lost, the American people grew angry. Then the British intercepted a secret message from Germany to Mexico. This message asked Mexico to ally itself with Germany. In return, Germany offered to help Mexico regain land lost to the United States in the 1840s. In April 1917, Congress declared war on Germany.

1. What areas outside of Europe were affected by the war?

_____

CHAPTER 29 THE GREAT WAR **283**

War Affects the Home Front
(page 755–756)

What happened on the home fronts?

By 1917, the war had already killed millions. It had drastically changed the lives of millions more—people at home as well as soldiers. This "Great War," as it was called, was a **total war**. It demanded all the resources of the countries that fought it.

Governments took control of factories. It told them what to produce and how much of it to make. Governments also used **rationing**. This limited how much food and other goods people could buy and hold. That way armies in the field would have the supplies they needed. Governments used **propaganda** to get support for the war. They also took steps to stop *dissent*, or opposition to the war.

With so many men in the military, women played a growing role in the economies of the countries at war. They worked in factories, offices, and shops. They built planes and tanks, grew food, and made clothing. These changes had an impact on people's attitudes toward what kind of work women could do.

2. What were three ways that the war affected people's day-to-day lives?

_____

The Allies Win the War (pages 756–757)

Why did the Allies win?

In 1917, the United States entered the war. And Russia left it. Suffering during the war chipped away at the Russian people's support for the *czar*. In March, he stepped down. The new government hoped to continue fighting the war, but the Russian armies refused. Just months later, a new revolution broke out. Communists seized Russia's government. They quickly made a treaty with Germany and gave up huge amounts of land in return for peace.

In March 1918, Germany tried one final attack. Once again, the German army nearly reached Paris. But the soldiers were tired, and supplies were short. The Allies—now with fresh American troops—drove the Germans back.

Bulgaria and the Ottoman Empire surrendered. In October, a revolution overthrew the emperor of Austria-Hungary. In November, Kaiser Wilhelm II was forced to step down in Germany. The new government signed an **armistice**, an agreement to stop fighting. On November 11, 1918, Europe was finally at peace.

3. What were the final problems that Germany and Austria-Hungary faced?

_____

Unemployment in Germany and Britain

[Line graph showing percentage of work force unemployed from 1914 to 1920 for Germany and Great Britain]

Source: *European Historical Statistics 1750–1975*

Skillbuilder

Use the graph to answer the questions.

1. Which country had a consistently higher unemployment rate?

_____

_____

2. How do political events explain the differences between the rates of unemployment in Germany in 1914 and 1917?

_____

_____

Name _____ Date _____

CHAPTER 29 Section 4 (pages 760–763)

A Flawed Peace

BEFORE YOU READ

In the last section, you read how World War I spread and finally ended.

In this section, you will learn about the harsh peace that followed.

AS YOU READ

Use the web below to take notes on the Treaty of Versailles.

TERMS AND NAMES

Woodrow Wilson President who proposed the Fourteen Points and represented the United States at Versailles

Georges Clemenceau France's premier and delegate at Versailles

David Lloyd George Britain's prime minister and delegate at Versailles

Fourteen Points Plan for a just and lasting peace

self-determination Allowing people to decide for themselves about what kind of government they want

Treaty of Versailles Agreement at the end of World War I between Germany and the Allied Powers

League of Nations International group with the goal of keeping peace among nations

- Ottoman Empire
- League of Nations
- Treaty of Versailles
- Colonial People — *No self-determination*
- German Land in Europe
- Germany's Colonies

The Allies Meet at Versailles
(pages 760–763)

What decisions were made at Versailles?

Many nations sent delegates to the peace talks in Paris. The main leaders were **Woodrow Wilson** of the United States, **Georges Clemenceau** of France, and **David Lloyd George** of Britain. Germany and its allies and Russia were not present.

Wilson pushed for his peace plan called the **Fourteen Points**. He wanted to end secret treaties and alliances and give people **self-determination**, the right to form their own nation. He also hoped to set up a world organization that would police the actions of nations and prevent future wars.

Britain and especially France had different views. They had suffered greatly in the war. They wanted to punish Germany. After long debates, the leaders finally agreed on a peace settlement. It was called the **Treaty of Versailles** and was signed in June 1919.

The treaty called for a **League of Nations**—

CHAPTER 29 THE GREAT WAR **285**

the world organization that Wilson wanted. It would include 32 nations. The United States, Britain, France, Japan, and Italy would make up the leadership. Germany and Russia were left out of the League. The treaty took away German land in Europe and took away its colonies in Africa and the Pacific. Limits were placed on the size of Germany's armed forces. Finally, Germany was given complete blame for the war. That meant it would have to make payments to the Allies for the damage caused.

Germany's former colonies were given to the Allies to govern until they decided which were ready for independence. Poland, Czechoslovakia, and Yugoslavia were all declared independent. Finland, Estonia, Latvia, and Lithuania—once part of Russia—were made independent nations as well. The treaty also broke up the Ottoman Empire. The Ottomans kept control only of Turkey.

The treaty did not make a lasting peace. The United States Senate never approved the treaty or joined the League of Nations. Germans bitterly resented the treaty because placed all the blame for the war on them. Colonial peoples in Africa and Asia were angry because the treaty did not make them independent. Japan and Italy were also upset by getting few *territorial* gains.

1. How did the Treaty of Versailles affect Germany?

_____

_____

_____

_____

The Legacy of the War (page 763)
What was the cost of the war?

The peace was uncertain because the treaty satisfied no one. It was certain, though, that the war had made a major impact on the world. About 8.5 million soldiers had died. Another 21 million had been wounded. Countless civilians had suffered as well. The economies of the warring nations had suffered serious damage, too. Farms were destroyed, and factories ruined. One estimate said the war had caused $338 billion in damage.

The war also had an emotional cost. People felt all the suffering did not seem to have a purpose. The art and literature of the years after the war reflected a new sense of hopelessness.

2. Name one political, economic, and emotional cost of the war.

_____

_____

_____

_____

_____

Name _____ Date _____

Glossary
CHAPTER 29 The Great War

alliances Agreements to help other countries in a military way
artillery Large guns, cannons
czar Ruler of Russia
destructive Causing negative effects, including death and ruin
dissent Disagreement
Great Powers Germany, Austria-Hungary, Great Britain, Russia, Italy, and France

heir Person who inherits; next in line
intercepted Took or received something intended for someone else
isolate Set apart; cut off
legacy Results; lasting effects
nationalism Feeling of attachment to one's own nation
rival One who tries to be better or do better than another

rivalries Competitions
territorial Related to territories; related to colonies or other imperialist holdings
trenches Long, deep holes in the ground dug for protection from enemy fire
unify Bring together as one

AFTER YOU READ

Terms and Names

A. Write the name or term in each blank that best completes the meaning of the paragraph.

Western front
Eastern front
total war
trench warfare
rationing

World War I was a **1** _____. Nations used all their resources to fight it. At home, people were faced with **2** _____. This reserved needed materials for the military. On the battlefield, fighting was brutal. Soldiers used **3** _____ in northern France. This area was known as the **4** _____. On the **5** _____, a bloody war was fought between the Germans, Serbs, and Russians.

B. Write the letter of the name or term next to the description that explains it best.

a. Fourteen Points
b. Allies
c. Central Powers
d. Triple Alliance
e. Triple Entente

____ **1.** Agreement among Germany, Austria-Hungary, and Italy

____ **2.** British alliance with France and Russia

____ **3.** Great Britain, France, Russia, and other nations that fought on their side

____ **4.** Germany, Austria-Hungary, and other nations that fought on their side

____ **5.** Plan for achieving peace

AFTER YOU READ (continued) — CHAPTER 29 The Great War

Main Ideas

1. How did imperialism help lead to World War I?

2. What did the Schlieffen Plan involve?

3. How did America get involved in the war?

4. How did the war help lead to revolution in Russia?

5. What was Wilson's plan for peace, and what did it involve?

Thinking Critically

Answer the following questions on a separate sheet of paper.

1. Explain why this war can be called "a truly global conflict."

2. Discuss the weaknesses of the Treaty of Versailles.

Name _____ Date _____

CHAPTER 30 Section 1 (pages 769–774)

Revolutions in Russia

BEFORE YOU READ

In the last chapter, you read about World War I.

In this section, you will learn about the revolutions in Russia that occurred at the same time.

AS YOU READ

Use the time line below to take notes on key events in Russia's history just before, during, and after the revolutions.

TERMS AND NAMES
pogrom Organized violence against Jews
Trans-Siberian Railway World's longest continuous rail line
Bolsheviks Group of revolutionaries led by Lenin
V. I. Lenin Leader of the Bolsheviks and first ruler of the Soviet Union
Duma Russia's first parliament
Rasputin Eccentric monk assassinated because of his corrupt influence on the Russian royal family
provisional government Temporary government led by Alexander Kerensky
soviet Local governing council

```
1881                          November 1917
Alexander III stops
reforms in Russia

         March 1917              1921
```

Alexander III Upholds the Autocracy (page 769)

How did Alexander III rule?

In 1881 *Czar* Alexander II was killed by *radical* students. The new czar, Alexander III, took back control of the Russian government. Reforms stopped. He cracked down on anyone who seemed to threaten his government. He also mistreated all non-Russian peoples who lived within the Russian empire, especially Jews. A wave of **pogroms**—organized violence against Jews—broke out in many parts of Russia.

1. What negative changes occurred during Alexander III's rule?

_____

_____

Nicholas II Resists Change
(pages 769–770)

What progress occurred during Nicholas II's reign?

In 1894, Nicholas II became czar. He was the son of Alexander III. Nicholas continued his father's firm rule. He started a buildup of Russia's industry. Russia quickly became a leading producer of steel. Russia also built the **Trans-Siberian Railway**—the longest continuous rail line in the world.

Although there was progress, working conditions were poor, wages were low, and children were forced to work. Workers grew angry. Revolutionary groups wanted to overthrow the government. Some followed the teachings of Karl Marx. In 1903, they split into two groups. One group—the **Bolsheviks**—was led by **V. I. Lenin**. He fled

CHAPTER 30 REVOLUTION AND NATIONALISM 289

Russia a few years later to await a better time to put forth his ideas.

2. Who were the Bolsheviks?

_____

_____

Crises at Home and Abroad
(pages 770–771)

What crises did Russia face?

In early 1905, the Russian army killed hundreds of hungry workers who had peacefully gathered to ask for relief. Strikes spread in protest. Nicholas was forced to allow some reforms to take place. He approved the creation of the **Duma,** Russia's first parliament.

The suffering caused by World War I was the final blow against the czar's rule. As the war worsened, the czar lost control of Russia. Soldiers refused to fight, prices shot sky high, and people starved. Meanwhile, his wife fell under the influence of an eccentric monk named **Rasputin**. He spread *corruption* throughout the government.

3. What developments helped lead up to the revolution?

_____

_____

The March Revolution (pages 771–772)

What was the provisional government?

In March 1917, the czar was forced to step down. A year later, he and his family were *executed*. A **provisional government** led by Alexander Kerensky was formed.

Kerensky hoped to keep Russia in the war. The decision cost him the support of soldiers who no longer wanted to fight. He also lost the support of workers and peasants who wanted an end to food shortages. Across the country, these forces formed local councils called **soviets**. In some cities, the soviets had more real power than the government.

In the middle of all this change, Lenin returned to Russia.

4. How did Kerensky lose support?

_____

_____

The Bolshevik Revolution
(pages 772–773)

Who led the Bolshevik Revolution?

Lenin's slogan "Peace, Land, and Bread" was soon taken up by many people. In November 1917, armed workers took control of government offices. Kerensky's power came to an end.

To win the peasants' support, Lenin ordered all farmland be given to them. Workers were given control of the factories. Soon, Lenin agreed to a peace treaty with Germany. It gave away large amounts of Russian land, but it ended the war. Then, forces opposed to Lenin's revolution tried to defeat the Bolshevik army. The civil war lasted three years. The fighting and the famine that followed killed 15 million Russians. In the end, Lenin's Red Army won.

5. Who fought the civil war?

_____

_____

Lenin Restores Order (page 774)

How did Lenin bring back order?

In 1921, Lenin started a new plan to rebuild the Russian economy. It allowed for some private ownership of property. He also changed the government to form a new nation—the Soviet Union. It would be run by the leaders of the Communist Party. By the late 1920s, the Soviet economy had recovered. Farms and factories were producing as much as they had before World War I.

6. What changes did Lenin make?

_____

_____

Name _____ Date _____

CHAPTER 30 Section 2 (pages 775–780)

Patterns of Change: Totalitarianism

BEFORE YOU READ

In the last section, you learned about the factors leading to revolution in Russia.

In this section, you will read about the totalitarian government that resulted.

AS YOU READ

Use the web below to show what Stalin's totalitarian state was like.

TERMS AND NAMES

Joseph Stalin Revolutionary leader who took control of the Communist Party after Lenin
totalitarianism Government that has total control over people's lives
command economy Economy in which the government makes all the economic decisions
collective farm Large, government-owned farm
kulak Member of a group of wealthy peasants brutally mistreated by Stalin's government
Great Purge Arrest, exile, or killing of thousands of suspected enemies of the Communist Party
socialist realism Artistic style that praised Soviet life and communist values

[web diagram: central node "Totalitarianism Under Stalin" connected to five surrounding ovals, one labeled "Great Purge"]

Stalin Becomes Dictator; Stalin Builds a Totalitarian State
(pages 775–776)

Who was Stalin?

Joseph Stalin was a member of Lenin's revolutionary movement. He slowly built his power over time. Lenin died in 1924. Stalin was in control of the Communist Party by 1928. He was not as interested as Lenin was in promoting revolution around the world. Stalin wanted to increase the power of the Soviet Union. To do that, he built a totalitarian state. **Totalitarianism** exists when the government has total control over people's lives.

1. What was Stalin's goal, and what did he create to achieve it?

_____
_____

Stalin Seizes Control of the Economy (pages 776–777)

How did Stalin change the economy?

Stalin built a **command economy**—one in which the government makes all the decisions about economic life. He tried to make the economy fully

CHAPTER 30 REVOLUTION AND NATIONALISM **291**

industrial. All resources went to this effort. As a result, there were shortages of food, housing, and clothing for many years.

Stalin also began a farming revolution. The government took control of people's farms. It put them together into large, government-owned farms called **collective farms.** Wealthy peasants called **kulaks** resisted. Millions were killed, and millions more were exiled to *Siberia*. Stalin got farm output to rise by using these brutal methods.

2. How did Stalin's economic changes result in suffering?

_____

_____

Weapons of Totalitarianism
(pages 777–778)

What were the weapons of totalitarianism?

Stalin kept tight control on the Soviet Union. He did this by creating a powerful secret police. In the mid-1930s, he turned against enemies—both real and imagined—within the Communist Party. Thousands were arrested. Many were sent to exile or killed. This was known as the **Great Purge.**

Stalin also used *propaganda* to keep control.

Official literature praised the government and its success. Any writings that expressed a different point of view were seized. Their authors were punished. Art was used in the same way. **Socialist realism** is an artistic style that praised Soviet life and communist values. Stalin's government also moved against religion. Churches were destroyed. Church leaders were killed or sent into exile.

3. What forms did propaganda take?

_____

_____

Daily Life Under Stalin (page 780)

How did Stalin change Soviet society?

Stalin completely changed Soviet society. Women enjoyed equal rights—though the rights were few. They filled all kinds of jobs on farms and in factories. They studied for careers that before had been closed to them. People in general were more educated. Along with learning new skills, however, they also were given constant propaganda in favor of the government.

4. What benefits did Stalin's rule bring?

_____

The slogan on this poster reads, "Young Communists [are] the Shock Brigade of the Five-Year Plan."

Skillbuilder
Use the poster to answer the questions.

1. What message does this poster send?

_____

_____

2. Why is this an example of propaganda?

_____

_____

Name _____ Date _____

CHAPTER 30 Section 3 (pages 781–784)

Collapse of Chinese Imperial Rule

BEFORE YOU READ

In the last section, you read about totalitarianism in the Soviet Union.

In this section, you will learn about the overthrow of the Qing dynasty and the beginnings of the Communist party in China.

AS YOU READ

Use the time line below to take notes on the changes that occurred in China in the early decades of the 20th century.

TERMS AND NAMES
Sun Yixian One of the first leaders of the Kuomintang; "father of modern China"
Kuomintang Nationalist Party of China that overthrew the Qing Dynasty
May Fourth Movement Chinese nationalist protest against China's fate as decided by the Treaty of Versailles
Mao Zedong Leader of the Communist revolution in China
Long March Escape of Communists to safety after being surrounded by Nationalist forces

```
1912                    1925                    1931
The Kuomintang overthrows
the Qing Dynasty

        1916                    1928
```

Nationalists Overthrow Qing Dynasty (pages 781–782)

Who was Sun Yixian?

The early 20th century was a time of change in China. Many Chinese resented the great control that foreign nations had over their economy. Some wanted to modernize China. They hoped it could regain power.

One of the leaders of this push was **Sun Yixian**. His group was called the **Kuomintang,** or Nationalist Party. In 1912, he led a revolt that overthrew the Qing Dynasty. A republic was established, and he was made the president.

Sun wanted political and economic rights for all Chinese people. He also wanted an end to the foreign control of China. But Sun did not have the support of the military. Six weeks later, he turned over his presidency to Yuan Shikai, a powerful general. Yuan became a military dictator. After he died in 1916, civil war broke out. The people suffered terribly from famine and brutal attacks. Sun could not reorganize the Kuomintang.

China's leaders hoped to win the support of the Allies during World War I. They declared war on Germany. When the war ended, though, they were disappointed. The Treaty of Versailles did not give China freedom from foreign influence. It only changed masters. The parts of China that had been controlled by Germany were handed over to Japan.

Angry Chinese protested during the **May Fourth Movement.** Protesters included **Mao Zedong.** He later became the leader of China's Communist revolution.

CHAPTER 30 REVOLUTION AND NATIONALISM **293**

1. What did China's Nationalists want?

_____

_____

_____

_____

The Communist Party in China
(pages 782–783)

What happened to the Communist Party?

In the 1920s, rebels began to look to Marxism and the Russian Revolution for a solution to China's problems. Meanwhile, Sun Yixian became disappointed in the Western democracies. They refused to support his struggling government. He decided to become allies with the newly formed Communist Party. Sun sought Soviet help, too. He died in 1925. Jiang Jieshi became leader of the Kuomintang.

At first, Jiang Jieshi joined with the Communists to try to defeat the warlords. These warlords ruled as much of the Chinese countryside as their armies could conquer. They terrorized the Chinese peasants. Together the Nationalists and Communists successfully fought the warlords.

Many in the Kuomintang were business people. They now feared Communist ideas about government control of economic life. In 1927, Jiang fought the Communists. The Communists were forced into hiding. In 1928, Jiang became president of China. Soon China was torn by a civil war between the remaining Communists and Jiang's forces.

2. What role did Jiang Jieshi play in creating the civil war?

_____

_____

_____

_____

Civil War Rages in China
(pages 783–784)

Who fought the civil war?

Jiang had promised democracy and political rights to all Chinese. But his government had become less democratic and more corrupt. Nothing was done to improve the life of the rural peasants. Many of them gave their support to the Chinese Communist Party.

Communist leader, Mao Zedong, built an army of peasants. In 1933, Jiang's army surrounded them. But the Communists got away. They began the famous **Long March** of 6,000 miles to the north. Thousands died, but the Communists survived, hiding in caves.

At the same time, China had other problems. In 1931, Japan *invaded* the part of China called Manchuria. Japan took control there and six years later began invading other areas. With this new threat, Jiang and the Communists agreed to unite temporarily to fight the Japanese.

3. What finally united Communist and non-Communist forces?

_____

_____

_____

_____

294 CHAPTER 30 SECTION 3

Name _____ Date _____

CHAPTER 30 Section 4 (pages 785–789)

Nationalism in India and Southwest Asia

TERMS AND NAMES
Mohandas K. Gandhi Leader of the movement for Indian independence from Britain
civil disobedience Disobeying the law for the purpose of achieving some higher goal
Mustafa Kemal Leader of Turkish nationalists who overthrew the last Ottoman sultan

BEFORE YOU READ

In the last section, you read about nationalism and civil war in China.

In this section, you will learn about nationalism in India and Southwest Asia.

AS YOU READ

Use the chart below to take notes on how nationalism brought change.

```
              Nationalism
              Brings Change
    ┌─────────────┼─────────────┬──────────────┐
  India         Turkey         Persia      Saudi Arabia
Gandhi leads
movement for
independence
from Britain
```

Indian Nationalism Grows
(pages 785–786)

Why did feelings of nationalism increase?

Many Indians grew angry at British *domination* of Indian life. Indian nationalism had been growing since the mid-1800's. Some Indians joined the Congress Party or the Muslim League. These were two groups that worked toward independence

More than one million Indians served in the British army in World War I. The British promised to make changes to the government of India. These changes would give the Indian people greater control of their own nation. After the war, though, returning Indian soldiers were once again treated as second-class citizens. Reforms were not made. When Indians protested, the British Parliament passed a law that allowed protesters to be jailed without a trial. Western-educated Indians believed this to be a violation of their rights.

About 10,000 Indians gathered at the city of Amritsar to protest this act in the spring of 1919. The British had also *banned* such public meetings. But the crowd was mostly unaware of that fact. British troops fired on the crowd. Several hundred protesters were killed. The massacre sparked further protests. Almost overnight millions of Indians changed from loyal British subjects to revolutionaries and nationalists.

CHAPTER 30 REVOLUTION AND NATIONALISM 295

1. What were three reasons for the increase of Indian nationalism?

2. How did Indians use nonviolence to achieve their goals?

Gandhi's Principles of Nonviolence; Great Britain Grants India Self-Rule (pages 786–787)

What were Gandhi's ideas about nonviolence?

Mohandas K. Gandhi became the leader of India's protest movement. He had attended law school in England. He had a deeply religious approach to political activity. His teachings contained ideas from all of the major religions of the world, including Hinduism, Islam, and Christianity.

Ghandi organized a campaign of *noncooperation* with the British. It was based on passive resistance, or **civil disobedience,** to unjust laws. He asked Indians to stop buying British goods, attending British schools, paying British taxes, or voting in British-run elections. He also persuaded his followers to take these actions while not using violence. British jails filled with thousands of Indians who broke British laws in order to protest them.

Indians resented a British law that forced them to buy salt only from the government. Gandhi organized a huge march to the sea to make salt by evaporating sea water.

Soon afterward, some demonstrators planned another march. They went to the place where the British government made salt. They wanted to close this site down. The British violently broke up the march. A news story about the event was published everywhere. It helped Ghandi's independence movement gain worldwide support. In 1935, the British finally gave in. They passed a law that allowed local Indian self-government.

Nationalism Spreads to Southwest Asia (pages 788–789)

What countries in Southwest Asia experienced great changes?

Other changes took place in Southwest Asia. **Mustafa Kemal**, a military commander, led nationalists in overthrowing the last Ottoman sultan. Kemel became the leader of a new republic in Turkey. He took many steps to modernize society and the economy in Turkey.

Before World War I, both Britain and Russia had influence in the ancient country of Persia. Britain tried to take control of all of Persia after the war. This led to a nationalist revolt. In 1921, Reza Shah Pahlavi, a Persian army officer, seized power. He later changed his country's name to Iran. In both Turkey and Iran, women gained new rights.

In Arabia, different groups united to form one kingdom called Saudi Arabia.

Starting in the 1920s, Southwest Asia saw a major economic change and development. Western companies discovered large reserves of oil in several countries in this area. Oil brought huge sums of money to these countries. Western nations tried to gain power in the region so they could get some of this wealth.

3. What new countries were formed?

Name _____ Date _____

Glossary — CHAPTER 30 Revolution and Nationalism

banned Made a law or ruling against
corruption Dishonesty; failure to act in the best interests of others
czar Ruler of Russia
domination Control
executed Killed
invaded Entered a country with the goal of taking it over
noncooperation Failure to obey rules and laws
propaganda Information or material used to advance a cause; persuasion for a political purpose
radical Those who favor completely new ways of doing things
Siberia Place of punishment in Russia
slogan Saying

AFTER YOU READ

Terms and Names

A. Write the name or term in each blank that best completes the meaning of the paragraph.

soviets

Duma

V. I. Lenin

Bolsheviks

provisional government

In the early 1900s, a group of revolutionaries called **1** _____ came into being in Russia. Their leader was **2** _____ . A few years later, the czar created a parliamentary body called the **3** _____ . Still, this was not sufficient change for the revolutionaries. In March 1917, the czar stepped down. A **4** _____ was set up. It was led by Alexander Kerensky. Meanwhile, revolutionaries formed groups called **5** _____ . These were local councils that gained a great deal of decision-making power.

B. Write the letter of the name or term next to the description that explains it best.

a. Kuomintang
b. Long March
c. kulaks
d. pogrom
e. command economy

____ **1.** Escape of Communist forces in China
____ **2.** Organized violence against Jews
____ **3.** Class of wealthy peasants
____ **4.** Economic system in which the government makes all decisions
____ **5.** Nationalist party of China

CHAPTER 30 REVOLUTION AND NATIONALISM **297**

Name _____ Date _____

AFTER YOU READ (cont.)   **CHAPTER 30**   Revolution and Nationalism

Main Ideas

1. How did revolution lead to civil war in Russia?
_____
_____
_____

2. What was Stalin's farming revolution?
_____
_____
_____

3. Why did Chinese nationalists overthrow the Qing Dynasty?
_____
_____
_____

4. What is the significance of the Salt March in Indian history?
_____
_____
_____

5. What role did Mustafa Kemal play in Turkish history?
_____
_____
_____

Thinking Critically

Answer the following questions on a separate sheet of paper.

1. How was Stalin's control of the economy typical of totalitarianism?

2. How did the Treaty of Versailles add to China's problems?

Name _____ Date _____

CHAPTER 31 Section 1 (pages 795–800)

An Age of Uncertainty

BEFORE YOU READ

In the last chapter, you read about nationalism and revolution.

In this section, you will learn how new ideas changed old ways of thinking.

AS YOU READ

Use the web diagram below to take notes on changes in the postwar period.

> **TERMS AND NAMES**
> **Albert Einstein** Thinker who developed the theory of relativity
> **theory of relativity** Idea that as moving objects approach the speed of light, space and time become relative
> **Sigmund Freud** Thinker who exposed the workings of the unconscious mind
> **existentialism** Philosophy that says each person must make meaning in a world that has no universal meaning
> **Friedrich Nietzsche** German philosopher who dismissed reason, democracy, and progress as empty ideas
> **surrealism** Art movement in which a dreamlike world, outside of reality, is portrayed or evoked
> **jazz** Lively, loose form of popular music developed in the United States
> **Charles Lindbergh** First person to fly alone across the Atlantic

[Web diagram with "New Ideas" in center, surrounded by bubbles; one labeled "Existentialism"]

Science Challenges Old Ideas
(page 795)

How did Einstein and Freud challenge old ideas?

Two thinkers developed *radical* new ideas that challenged old ways of thinking. **Albert Einstein** completely changed *physics* with his ideas about space, time, matter, and energy. He said that as moving objects neared the speed of light, space and time became relative. That means they change. His idea is the **theory of relativity**.

Sigmund Freud changed the way people thought about the human mind. He said that much of human behavior was *irrational*—due to urges and desires buried in the unconscious mind of each person. At first, people did not want to accept Freud's ideas. Eventually, they gained wide influence.

1. What were Einstein's and Freud's new ideas?

_____

_____

Literature in an Age of Doubt
(page 796)

What caused the "Age of Doubt"?

Many philosophers lost faith in reason and progress after they looked at the destruction caused by World War I. One group developed the ideas

CHAPTER 31 AN AGE OF UNCERTAINTY **299**

known as existentialism. **Existentialism** argues that there is no universal meaning to the world. Each person must give life meaning through his or her own actions.

These thinkers had been influenced by **Friedrich Nietzsche**. Nietzsche was a German philosopher of the late 1800s. He said that reason, democracy, and progress were empty ideas. He urged people to adopt the values of pride and strength.

Some authors, like Franz Kafka, wrote about the horrors of modern life. His novels put people in threatening situations that they could not understand or escape.

2. What is existentialism?

_____

_____

Rebellion in the Arts (page 797)

How was painting of this time different from traditional painting?

Artists rebelled against traditional painting. They did not recreate realistic objects. Paul Klee used bold colors and *distorted* lines. Pablo Picasso founded a style called *Cubism* that broke objects into geometric shapes. *Dadaism* was an art movement that created meaningless, absurd works.

An art movement called **surrealism** showed a dreamlike existence outside reality. Architects created new ways of designing buildings. This new approach emphasized the *function* of the building. The new designs were simple. They had clean lines with little decoration.

Composers created a new style of music. Some, like Igor Stravinsky, used unusual rhythms or harsh, rather than pleasing, sounds. African American musicians in the United States developed a lively, loose form of popular music called **jazz**.

3. What three new styles arose in the visual arts?

_____

_____

Society Becomes More Open
(page 798)

How did society change?

Society changed after World War I as well. Young people rebelled against their parents' teachings. Women set aside earlier forms of dress, wearing new styles that were looser and shorter. Many women also began to work in new careers.

4. In what ways was society more open?

_____

_____

_____

Technology Changes Life
(pages 798–800)

What new technology arose?

Technology brought about changes to society as well. Improvements to the automobile helped make cars more desirable and affordable. More and more people bought cars. They began to move to suburbs.

Another change was the growth in air travel. American pilot **Charles Lindbergh** flew alone across the Atlantic Ocean in 1927. In 1932, Amelia Earhart became the first woman to make the flight alone.

A new invention was radio. In the 1920s, large radio networks were built. Soon millions of people were entertained by radios in their homes. Millions more went to movie theaters to watch motion pictures.

5. What major changes came about in travel and entertainment?

_____

_____

300 CHAPTER 31 SECTION 1

Name _____ Date _____

CHAPTER 31   Section 2 (pages 801–806)

A Global Depression

BEFORE YOU READ

In the last section, you read about new ideas in the postwar world.

In this section, you will learn about economic crisis and worldwide depression.

AS YOU READ

Use the web below to record causes and effects of the Great Depression.

TERMS AND NAMES
coalition government Temporary alliance of several political parties
Weimar Republic Government of Germany after World War I
Great Depression Severe economic downturn that followed the collapse of the U.S. stock market in 1929
Franklin D. Roosevelt President of the United States during the Depression
New Deal Roosevelt's program for creating jobs and improving the American economy

causes

- Boom hid economic problems

→ **The Great Depression** →

effects

Europe After the War (pages 801–803)

What *problems did Europe face after the war?*

After the war, European countries were in bad political and economic shape. Even nations that had democratic governments for many years experienced problems. They had so many political parties that no one party could rule alone. Sometimes a **coalition government** had to be formed. This was an alliance of several political parties. In addition, governments lasted for such a short time that it was hard to develop policies.

The situation was worst in Germany. The people felt little loyalty to the government. Germany's government, the **Weimar Republic**, was very weak. Prices rose sharply, and money lost its value. Later, American bank loans helped the German economy recover.

World nations also took steps to try to make sure there would be lasting peace. France and Germany promised never to attack one another. Most countries of the world signed a treaty in which they *pledged* not to go to war. There was no way to enforce the treaty, however.

CHAPTER 31 AN AGE OF UNCERTAINTY **301**

1. Why was the postwar situation in Germany especially bad?

The Great Depression (pages 803–805)

Where and how did the Great Depression begin?

The economy of the United States enjoyed a *boom* in the 1920s. But this growth hid problems. Consumers were unable to buy all the goods produced. When their purchases slowed, factories slowed production. Farmers faced falling food prices and slow sales. They were unable to repay loans and lost their farms. In 1929, stock prices in the United States plunged. The **Great Depression** had begun.

The depression affected other countries. Nations raised *tariffs*—taxes on goods imported from other countries—to keep import prices high. They hoped to increase sales by local companies. Unfortunately, trade between nations dropped, and unemployment shot up in many countries. The world suffered.

2. What caused the Great Depression?

The World Responds to the Crisis (pages 805–806)

How did various countries meet this crisis?

Each country met the economic crisis in its own way. In Britain, a new multi-party government took over. It took steps that slowly improved the economy and cut unemployment.

In France, the political situation was worse. After several governments lost support, *moderates* and *socialists* combined to form a government. It passed laws to help workers, but companies raised prices to cover their labor costs. Unemployment remained high.

In Sweden, Norway, and Denmark, the governments played active roles in the economy. They taxed people with jobs to have money to pay benefits to people without jobs. The governments also created jobs by hiring out-of-work people to build roads and buildings.

In the United States, **Franklin D. Roosevelt** began a program called the **New Deal**. The government spent large amounts of money on constructing roads, dams, bridges, airports, and buildings. This effort created jobs for millions. Businesses and farmers also got help from the government. The American economy got better, but the *recovery* was slow.

3. How did the United States meet the crisis?

Stock Prices, 1925–1933

Skillbuilder
Use the graph to answer the questions.

1. How did the average price per stock share change between 1925 and 1929?

2. How did the average price per share change between 1925 and 1932?

Name _____ Date _____

CHAPTER 31 Section 3 (pages 807–810)

Fascism Rises in Europe

BEFORE YOU READ

In the last section, you read about the Great Depression.

In this section, you will learn about the rise of fascism in Europe during troubled economic times.

AS YOU READ

Use the web diagram below to show characteristics and examples of fascism.

TERMS AND NAMES
fascism Political movement based on nationalism that gives power to a dictator and takes away individual rights
Benito Mussolini Fascist leader of Italy
Adolf Hitler Fascist leader of Germany
Nazism German brand of fascism
Mein Kampf Book by Hitler outlining his beliefs and goals for Germany
lebensraum Living space

[Web diagram with "Fascism" in the center, connected to six ovals. One oval contains "One party, one leader"; the others are blank.]

Fascist Beliefs and Policies (page 807)
What is fascism?

The economic crisis of the Great Depression led to the loss of democracy in some countries. In these nations, millions of people turned to strong rulers to try to solve their economic problems. Such leaders followed a set of beliefs called **fascism**. Fascist leaders were very nationalistic. They believed in authority and built powerful military forces. Fascist governments were controlled by one party, and that party was ruled by one leader. The leader was the nation's *dictator*. Fascist governments did not let their people have individual rights.

1. Name three characteristics of fascist governments.

_____
_____
_____

Mussolini Comes to Power in Italy (pages 807–808)
Why did fascism arise in Italy?

Fascism arose in Italy. It started there because people were angry that they did not get more territory in the treaty that ended World War I. Also,

CHAPTER 31 AN AGE OF UNCERTAINTY **303**

people with more money feared what had happened in Russia. They did not want unrest in Italy to lead to a Communist government. **Benito Mussolini** came to power by promising to help the economy and build the armed forces. He used armed *thugs* to threaten political opponents. The king of Italy decided Mussolini was the best hope to save his dynasty and let him lead the government.

Mussolini became *Il Duce,* or the leader, of Italy. He abolished democracy and outlawed all political parties except the Fascists. He tried to control the economy. Under Mussolini's leadership, Italy became the model for Fascists in other countries.

2. What did Mussolini promise the Italians?

_____

_____

_____

_____

Hitler Takes Control in Germany
(pages 808–810)

How did Hitler gain control of Germany?

Another Fascist came to power in Germany. **Adolf Hitler** was the leader of the Nazi party. The German brand of fascism was called **Nazism.** He tried to take control of the government of Germany in 1923, but the attempt failed. He was sent to prison. In prison, Hitler wrote a book that summarized his ideas. It was called *Mein Kampf.* Hitler believed that Germans were superior to all other people. He said that the Treaty of Versailles treated Germany unfairly. He also said that a crowded Germany needed more *lebensraum*, or living space. To get that space, he promised to conquer the lands of eastern Europe and Russia.

When the depression hit Germany, the country was in terrible shape. Hitler was named leader of the German government. Soon, he took the powers of a dictator. He became Germany's *führer,* or leader. Those who opposed him were arrested. His economic program gave work to millions but took away their rights to organize into unions or to strike. He took control of all areas of life. He burned books that went against Nazi ideas. He forced children to join Nazi groups.

Hitler also attacked Germany's Jews. Laws took away their rights. In November 1938, mobs attacked Jewish people and destroyed thousands of Jewish-owned buildings. This was the start of a process to eliminate the Jews from German life.

3. What changes did Hitler make?

_____

_____

_____

_____

Other Countries Fall to Dictators (page 810)

What other countries were ruled by dictators?

Fascist dictators took control in other countries as well, including Hungary, Poland, Yugoslavia, Albania, Bulgaria, and Romania. All had dictators or kings who ruled like dictators. Only Czechoslovakia remained as a democracy in eastern Europe.

Elsewhere in Europe, only in nations with strong democratic traditions—Britain, France and the Scandinavian countries—did democracy survive.

4. Why did democracy survive in some countries?

_____

_____

_____

_____

Name _____ Date _____

CHAPTER 31 Section 4 (pages 811–815)

Aggressors on the March

TERMS AND NAMES
appeasement Giving in to keep the peace
Axis Powers Germany, Italy, and Japan
Francisco Franco Spain's fascist dictator
isolationism Belief that political ties with other countries should be avoided
Third Reich German empire
Munich Conference Meeting of world powers in 1938 that allowed Hitler to take part of Czechoslovakia

BEFORE YOU READ

In the last section, you read about the rise of fascism.

In this section, you will learn about military actions that led to a second world war.

AS YOU READ

Use the time line below to show when and where aggression took place.

| 1931 Japan captures Manchuria | 1936 | 1939 |

| 1935 | 1938 |

The World Drifts Toward War
(pages 811–814)

How did the movement toward war begin?

Military leaders took control of Japan during the Great Depression. They wanted to solve the countries' economic problems by foreign expansion.

In 1931, the Japanese army *invaded* Manchuria, a province of China. Manchuria was rich in coal and iron. These were valuable resources for the Japanese economy. Other countries spoke in protest in the League of Nations but did nothing else. Japan ignored the protests. In 1933, it pulled out of the League.

Four years later, Japan invaded China. The powerful Japanese army swept Chinese fighters aside. It killed tens of thousands of civilians and soldiers in the city of Nanjing. In spite of these losses, Chinese forces—both the Nationalists of the government and Communist rebels—continued to fight Japan.

Italy's Mussolini also wanted to expand. He dreamed of an Italian empire in Africa. In 1935 he ordered the invasion of Ethiopia. His troops won an easy victory. Haile Selassie, the emperor of Ethiopia, pleaded with the League of Nations to help. The League did nothing. By giving in to Mussolini in Africa, Britain and France hoped to keep the peace in Europe.

Hitler made moves also. He broke the Versailles Treaty by rebuilding Germany's army. In 1936, he sent troops into an area along the Rhine River between Germany and France that the treaty had forbidden the Germans to enter. The French and British again responded with **appeasement**—

CHAPTER 31 AN AGE OF UNCERTAINTY **305**

giving in to keep the peace.

The German movement into the Rhineland marked a turning point in the march toward war. Also in 1936, Hitler signed an alliance with Mussolini and with Japan. These three nations came to be called the **Axis Powers**.

In 1936, civil war broke out in Spain. The army, led by General **Francisco Franco**, revolted against a government run by liberals and socialists. Hitler and Mussolini sent aid to the army, which was backed by Spanish Fascists. The Soviet Union sent aid to the government. In early 1939, the government's resistance to the army collapsed. Francisco Franco became Spain's Fascist dictator.

1. What places did Germany, Italy, and Japan invade?

_____

_____

_____

Western Democracies Fail to Halt Aggression (pages 814–815)

Why did the world's democracies fail to stop the aggression?

At this time, many Americans resisted accepting the nation's new role as a world leader. They believed that the United States should follow a policy of **isolationism**. Isolationism was the belief that political ties with other countries should be avoided. This, it was thought, would keep the country out of another foreign war.

In March 1938, Hitler moved his troops into Austria. He made it part of the **Third Reich**, or German Empire. This action broke the Versailles Treaty again. France and Britain once more did nothing.

Later that year, Hitler demanded that Czechoslovakia give up a part of its land to Germany. Czechoslovakia refused. The **Munich Conference** was held in September 1938 to solve the problem. At this meeting Germany, France, Britain, and Italy agreed to allow the Germans to take the land. In return, Hitler promised to respect the new borders of Czechoslovakia. A few months later, however, he took the entire country.

In the summer of 1939, Hitler made a similar demand of Poland. That nation also refused to give up land. Britain and France now said that they would protect Poland. But Hitler believed that they would not risk going to war. At the same time, he signed an agreement with Soviet dictator Joseph Stalin. The two countries promised never to attack one another.

The Axix Powers were moving unchecked at the end of the decade. The whole world was waiting to see what would happen next. It seemed that war would break out.

2. What happened at the Munich Conference?

_____

_____

_____

_____

Glossary

CHAPTER 31 An Age of Uncertainty

boom Period of great economic growth
Cubism Art style that portrayed objects in geometric shapes
Dadaism Art style in which meaningless, absurd works were created
dictator Ruler who has absolute authority
distorted Twisted; not in the usual shape

function Purpose
invaded Entered a country for the purpose of taking it over
irrational Not reasonable; not consciously thought out
moderates People who are not liberal (in favor of great change) or conservative (reluctant to change) but in the middle
physics Science of matter and energy

pledged Promised
radical Extreme; carried to the limit
recovery Economic growth following a depression or recession
socialists People who believed in socialist ideas, such as shared ownership of business
tariffs Taxes on goods imported from other countries
thugs People who carry out violent activities on someone else's orders

AFTER YOU READ

Terms and Names

A. Write the name or term in each blank that best completes the meaning of the paragraph.

theory of relativity

existentialism

Sigmund Freud

Friedrich Nietzsche

Albert Einstein

Postwar Europe produced many new thinkers. Among them was the scientist **1** _____. He offered new ideas about space, time, and matter. One of them was his **2** _____. Another important thinker of this time was a doctor who studied the mind. His name was **3** _____. He helped reveal the power of the unconscious mind. An important philosopher whose ideas greatly influenced thinkers of this era was **4** _____. Thinkers of this time developed a new philosophy. This philosophy, **5** _____, says that it is up to individuals to give meaning to a meaningless world.

B. Write the letter of the name or term next to the description that explains it best.

a. Weimar Republic

b. Third Reich

c. coalition government

d. fascism

e. *lebensraum*

____ **1.** German empire

____ **2.** Temporary alliance of several political parties

____ **3.** living space

____ **4.** Government of Germany after the first world war

____ **5.** Political movement emphasizing loyalty to the state

Name _____ Date _____

AFTER YOU READ (continued)   CHAPTER 31   An Age of Uncertainty

Main Ideas

1. How did technology change society after the war?

   _____
   _____
   _____

2. Describe the programs of the New Deal.

   _____
   _____
   _____

3. Name four of Hitler's actions that showed he was an absolute ruler, or dictator.

   _____
   _____
   _____
   _____

4. What beliefs and goals did Hitler express in Mein Kampf?

   _____
   _____
   _____
   _____

5. What were the policies of the United States, France, and Great Britain when the Axis Powers were invading other lands?

   _____
   _____
   _____
   _____

Thinking Critically

Answer the following questions on a separate sheet of paper.

1. What conditions in Europe helped give rise to the rule of dictators?

2. Why did the democracies of Europe fail to stop aggression?

Name _____ Date _____

CHAPTER 32 Section 1 (pages 821–826)

Hitler's Lightning War

TERMS AND NAMES
nonaggression pact Agreement that says countries will not attack or invade one another
blitzkrieg Warfare in which surprise air attacks are followed by massive attacks on land
Charles de Gaulle Leader of the French government-in-exile
Winston Churchill Leader of Britain
Battle of Britain Battle of British and German air forces fought over Britain during 1940–1941
Atlantic Charter Declaration of principles issued by Winston Churchill and Franklin D. Roosevelt in August 1941

BEFORE YOU READ

In the last chapter, you read about actions that led up to World War II.

In this section, you will learn about the first years of the war in Europe.

AS YOU READ

Use the time line below to take notes on key events in the first two years of the war.

| September 1, 1939 — Hitler invades Poland | April 1941 | August 1941 |
| April 1940 | June 1941 | fall of 1941 |

Germany Sparks a New War in Europe (pages 821–822)

What caused Britain and France to declare war?

In 1939, Adolf Hitler decided to move on Poland. He had already conquered Austria and Czechoslovakia. When Hitler signed a **nonaggression pact** with Stalin of the Soviet Union, they agreed not to attack each other. Secretly, they also agreed to split Poland between them. This deal removed the threat of the Soviets attacking Germany from the east.

So, on September 1, the German army invaded Poland in a surprise attack. Using planes, tanks, and troops, it moved suddenly in a technique called **blitzkrieg**, or "lightning war." Britain and France declared war, but Poland fell before they could help.

On September 17, after secret agreement with Hitler, Stalin invaded eastern Poland. Stalin then began annexing the regions covered in a second part of the agreement. Lithuania, Latvia, and Estonia fell without a struggle. However, Finland fought back. In March 1940, Finland was forced to surrender.

For seven months after Poland fell to the Germans, Europe was calm. France and Britain got their armies ready. They waited for Hitler's next move.

1. Why did Poland fall to the Germans so quickly?

_____

_____

_____

CHAPTER 32 WORLD WAR II **309**

The Battle for France and Great Britain (pages 822–824)

What happened when France and Britain were attacked?

Suddenly in April 1940, Hitler's armies invaded Denmark and Norway. Within two months, they also captured Belgium, the Netherlands, Luxembourg, and France. Part of the French army, led by **Charles de Gaulle**, escaped to Britain to remain free and continue the fight. By then, Italy's Benito Mussolini had joined Hitler's side.

Great Britain—now led by **Winston Churchill**—stood alone. The German air force began bombing Britain. It wanted to weaken the country. Germany was getting prepared to invade Britain. But the British air force fought back. It was helped by the newly developed radar. This was an electronic tracking system that warned of coming attacks. Also, the British had broken the German army's secret code. The **Battle of Britain** lasted many months. Unable to break British *defenses*, Hitler called off the attacks in May 1941.

2. Why did Germany lose the Battle of Britain?

_____

_____

_____

The Eastern Front and Mediterranean (pages 824–826)

What countries did Hitler invade?

Hitler then turned his attention to the east and to the Mediterranean. Germany sent troops to North Africa to help Italy fight the British. In April 1941, German armies quickly took control of Yugoslavia and Greece. In June, Hitler began a surprise invasion of the Soviet Union. The Red Army was the largest in the world. But it was not well-equipped or well-trained. The Germans quickly pushed deep into Soviet territory. The Red Army was forced to retreat.

To keep supplies out of German hands, the Red Army destroyed everything left behind. The Germans were stopped from taking Leningrad in the north. They then turned on Moscow, the Soviet capital. A strong Soviet *counterattack*, combined with fierce Russian winter weather, forced the Germans back. Moscow had been saved, and the battle had cost the Germans 500,000 lives.

3. What happened when Germany invaded the Soviet Union?

_____

_____

_____

_____

The United States and its Allies (page 826)

How did the United States take sides?

The United States watched these events. Many Americans did not want to join in the war. President Roosevelt wanted to help the Allies, however. He asked Congress to allow Britain and France to buy American weapons. Soon, American ships were *escorting* British ships carrying guns bought from the United States. By the fall of 1941, U.S. ships had orders to fire on German submarines that threatened the ships. The United States and Germany were fighting an undeclared naval war.

Roosevelt met with Churchill off the coast of Canada in August of 1941. Although the United States was not officially in the war, the two leaders issued a statement called the **Atlantic Charter**. It supported free trade and the right of people to form their own government.

4. Name two ways in which the United States supported the Allies.

_____

_____

_____

Name _____   Date _____

CHAPTER 32   Section 2 (pages 827–830)

Japan Strikes in the Pacific

BEFORE YOU READ

In the last section, you read about the war against Hitler in Europe.

In this section, you will learn about the war against Japan in the Pacific.

AS YOU READ

Use the chart below to record key events in the war in the Pacific.

TERMS AND NAMES
Isoroku Yamamoto Japanese admiral who decided that the U.S. fleet in Hawaii had to be destroyed
Pearl Harbor Navy base in Hawaii attacked by the Japanese
Battle of Midway Sea and air battle in which American forces defeated Japanese forces near Midway Island in the Pacific
Douglas MacArthur U.S. general who commanded Allied forces in the Pacific
Battle of Guadalcanal Six-month battle on the island of Guadalcanal in which American and Australian troops defeated Japanese defenders

	ACTION	RESULT
Pearl Harbor	Japanese bomb American fleet.	
Battle of the Coral Sea		
Battle of Midway		
Battle of Guadalcanal		

Japan Seeks a Pacific Empire
(pages 827–828)

How did the United States fight Japan before declaring war?

The military leaders who ran the Japanese government also had plans to build an empire. Japan was overcrowded and did not have enough raw materials or oil.

The Japanese captured part of China in 1931. In 1937, they invaded the center of China. There they met strong *resistance*. Needing resources for this war, they decided to move into Southeast Asia.

The United States feared that Japanese control of this area would threaten U.S. holdings in the Pacific. Roosevelt gave military aid to China. He also cut off oil shipments to Japan.

Japanese Admiral **Isoroku Yamamoto** decided that the U.S. *fleet* in Hawaii had to be destroyed. On December 7, 1941, the Japanese navy began a surprise attack on the U.S. naval base at **Pearl Harbor** in Hawaii. In just two hours, Japanese planes sank or damaged a major part of the U.S. Pacific fleet—18 ships, including 8 battleships. The next day, Congress declared war on Japan.

The Japanese attack on Pearl Harbor was just

CHAPTER 32 WORLD WAR II **311**

one of many sudden strikes. Japan also captured Guam, Wake, and the Philippine Islands from the United States. It took Indonesia from the Dutch and Hong Kong, Malaya, and Singapore from the British.

Japan then invaded Burma, located between India and China. Japan wanted to stop China from receiving supplies through Burma. Burma fell in May 1942. By that time, Japan had conquered more than 1 million square miles of land with about 150 million people.

Before these conquests, the Japanese had tried to win the support of Asians. They used the anti-colonial slogan "Asia for the Asians." After their victory, the Japanese made it clear that they had come as conquerors.

1. **What countries lost territory to Japan early in the war?**

___

___

___

The Allies Strike Back (pages 829–830)
How did the Allies strike back?

The Japanese seemed unbeatable after a string of victories. But the Allies wanted to strike back in the Pacific. In April 1942, the United States sent planes to drop bombs on Tokyo. The attack raised the *morale* of Americans. In May 1942, the Allies suffered heavy losses at the Battle of the Coral Sea. Still, they were able to stop the Japanese advance and save Australia.

The next month, the U.S. Navy scored an important victory near Midway Island in the central Pacific. In the **Battle of Midway**, Japan lost four aircraft carriers, the most important naval weapon in the war. The victory turned the tide of war against Japan.

The United States now went on the attack. General **Douglas MacArthur** did not want to invade the Japanese-held islands that were most strongly defended. He wanted to attack weaker ones. The first attack came on Guadalcanal, in the Solomon Islands in August. The Japanese were building an air base there. It took six months of fighting for U.S. and Australian troops to drive the Japanese off the island in the **Battle of Guadalcanal**. The Japanese abandoned the island in February 1943.

2. **Name three Allied victories against Japan.**

___

___

___

___

Name _____ Date _____

CHAPTER 32 Section 3 (pages 831–834)

The Holocaust

BEFORE YOU READ

In the last section, you read about the battles in the Pacific.

In this section, you will read about Hitler's "final solution" in Europe.

AS YOU READ

Use the web below to record important information about the Holocaust.

TERMS AND NAMES
Aryans Germanic peoples
Holocaust Mass killing of civilians, especially Jews
Kristallnacht "Night of broken glass," when Nazis attacked Jews throughout Germany
ghettos Neighborhoods in which European Jews were forced to live
"Final Solution" Hitler's plan to kill as many Jews as possible
genocide Systematic killing of an entire people

[Web diagram with "The Holocaust" in the center, connected to six ovals. One oval reads: "Caused by ideas of a 'master race'". The other five are blank.]

The Holocaust Begins (pages 831–832)

What was the Holocaust?

Part of Hitler's new order for Europe included getting rid of "inferior" people. Hitler believed that the **Aryans**, or German peoples, were a "master race." He had a deep-seated hatred of people who were not German. He particularly hated Jews. This led to the **Holocaust**, the killing of millions of Jews and other civilians.

During the 1930s, Hitler passed laws that took away the rights of German Jews. One night in November 1938, Nazi mobs attacked Jews throughout Germany. They destroyed homes and businesses and killed or beat many people. This night became known as ***Kristallnacht,*** or "Night of Broken Glass."

Kristallnacht was a major step-up in the Nazi policy of *persecuting* the Jews. The future for the Jews in Germany looked grim. Thousands of Jews tried to leave Germany. Other countries accepted a large number but were unwilling to take all those who wished to leave.

Hitler ordered all Jews in Germany and his conquered lands to live in certain parts of cities called **ghettos**. The Nazis then sealed off the ghettos with barbed wire and stone walls. They wanted the Jews inside to starve or die of disease. Even under these horrible conditions, the Jews hung on.

CHAPTER 32 WORLD WAR II **313**

1. How did the Holocaust begin?

_____

_____

_____

Hitler's "Final Solution" (pages 833–834)

What was the "Final Solution"?

Hitler soon got tired of waiting for the Jews to starve or die of disease in the ghettos. He decided to take more direct action. He was going to kill as many Jews as possible.

Hitler's plan was the "**Final Solution**" to what the Nazis called the "Jewish problem." It was **genocide**, the *systematic* killing of an entire people. The Nazis also wanted to wipe out many other people to protect the "purity" of the Aryan race. These people included gypsies, Poles, Russians, and those who were mentally or physically disabled. The Germans put the most attention on Jews, however.

Thousands of Jews were shot to death by "killing squads." Millions were gathered and placed in *concentration camps*. These prisons used the *inmates* as slave workers. Many in the camps died of starvation or disease.

Starting in 1942, the Nazis built "death camps." At these camps, thousands of Jews were gassed to death in huge gas chambers. In the end, six million Jews were killed by the Nazis. Fewer than four million European Jews survived.

2. How was the "Final Solution" carried out?

_____

_____

_____

_____

Jews Killed under Nazi Rule*			
	Original Jewish Population	Jews Killed	Percent Surviving
Poland	3,300,000	3,000,000	10%
Soviet Union	2,850,000	1,252,000	56%
Hungary	650,000	450,000	30%
Romania	600,000	300,000	50%
Germany/Austria	240,000	200,000	10%

* Estimates

Skillbuilder

Use the chart to anser these questions.

1. How many Jews were killed under Nazi rule?

_____

_____

2. Which countries lost the greatest percentage of their Jewish populations?

_____

_____

Name _____ Date _____

CHAPTER 32 Section 4 (pages 835–841)

The Allies Are Victorious

BEFORE YOU READ

In the last section, you read about the Holocaust in Europe.

In this section, you will learn how the war was fought and brought to an end around the world.

AS YOU READ

Use the time line below to take notes on key events in the last three years of the war.

TERMS AND NAMES
Erwin Rommel German general who led troops in North Africa
Bernard Montgomery British general who drove the Germans out of Egypt
Dwight D. Eisenhower American general who helped drive the Germans out of Africa
Battle of Stalingrad Battle during which the Red Army forced the Germans out of Stalingrad
D-Day Huge Allied invasion mounted to retake France from the Germans
Battle of the Bulge Final large-scale attack by Germans troops that was forced back by the Allies
kamikaze Japanese suicide pilots

| February 1943 Battle of Stalingrad ends | June 1944 | August 1945 |

| May 1943 | March 1945 |

The Allies Plan for Victory; The Tide Turns on Two Fronts
(pages 835–837)

Where did the tide of war turn in favor of the Allies?

In 1942, Roosevelt, Churchill, and Stalin planned the Allies' strategy. Stalin wanted Britain and the United States to open a second front against Germany to relieve the pressure on his armies. Stalin wanted the attack in France. Roosevelt and Churchill agreed to a second front but chose to attack German General **Erwin Rommel** in North Africa.

In late 1942, the British army led by General **Bernard Montgomery** drove the Germans out of Egypt and back to the west. Meanwhile, American troops under the command of General **Dwight D. Eisenhower** landed behind the Germans and began moving east. The Germans were finally forced out of Africa in May 1943.

At the same time, the Soviets gained a major victory as well. German troops had invaded the Soviet city of Stalingrad in 1942. The Red Army forced the Germans to surrender in February 1943, ending the **Battle of Stalingrad**.

American and British soldiers next invaded Italy and captured Sicily in August 1943. Mussolini was driven from power and the new Italian government surrendered. But Hitler did not want to give up Italy. His army fought there until 1945.

1. What major victories did the Allies win?

___

Life on Allied Home Fronts
(pages 837–838)

What problems did people face at home?

While the Allies continued to fight, people at home suffered. Some British and Soviet citizens died. In the United States, citizens faced shortages. Goods such as food, tires, gasoline, and clothing were in short supply. The government *rationed* these items. It limited how much a person could have so there would be enough for the military.

Some Americans were even imprisoned. Bitter feelings against the Japanese became widespread. As a result, mistrust of Japanese Americans grew. The U.S. government took thousands of Japanese Americans who lived on the west coast and moved them to relocation camps in the western United States. Two-thirds of these people were American citizens.

2. What happened to Japanese Americans?

___

Allied Victory in Europe (pages 838–839)

What were the final battles in Europe?

In early 1944, the Allies built a *massive* force to retake France. In June, an invasion of thousands of ships, planes, and soldiers was launched. It was called **D-Day**. The invasion force suffered heavy losses but gained a foothold in northern France. A month later, Allied forces began to pour through German lines. In August, they marched in triumph into Paris. By September, they had driven the Germans out of France, Belgium, Luxembourg, and much of the Netherlands.

At the same time, the Soviets were pushing the Germans back in eastern Europe. In late 1944, Hitler ordered his army to make one final, large-scale attack in the west. In the **Battle of the Bulge**, it punched through Allied lines until an Allied counterattack forced it back to Germany. By late April 1945, Soviet troops surrounded Berlin, Hitler's headquarters. Five days later, he killed himself. A week later, the Germans surrendered. Roosevelt did not live to see this victory, however. He had died in early April. Harry Truman was now president.

3. Name three events that led directly to Germany's surrender.

___

Victory in the Pacific (pages 839–841)

What led to victory in the Pacific?

In the Pacific, the Allies began to move toward Japan in 1943. They landed troops in the Philippines in the fall of 1944. In the Battle of Leyte Gulf, in October 1944, the Japanese navy was crushed.

As American troops moved closer to Japan, they faced attacks by **kamikaze**. These Japanese suicide pilots sank Allied ships by crashing their bomb-filled planes into them. In March 1945, U.S. Marines captured the island of Iwo Jima, a **strategic** Japanese stronghold. By June, they had won control of Okinawa, an island just 350 miles from Japan.

Japan was the next stop. But the U.S. military feared that an invasion of Japan would cost half a million Allied lives. In August, President Truman ordered that an atomic bomb be dropped on the city of Hiroshima to try to end the war quickly. A second bomb was dropped on Nagasaki three days later. Tens of thousands of Japanese died. Japan surrendered in September.

4. Name two events that led directly to Japan's surrender.

___

Name _____ Date _____

CHAPTER 32 Section 5 (pages 842–845)

The Devastation of Europe and Japan

TERMS AND NAMES
Nuremburg Trials Trials of Nazi leaders charged with crimes against humanity, held in Nuremberg, Germany
demilitarization Breaking down armed forces

BEFORE YOU READ

In the last section, you read about how the war ended.
In this section, you will learn about the war's effects on Europe and Japan.

AS YOU READ

Use the chart below to take notes on the effects of the war on Europe and Japan.

```
              Effects of
              World War II
         ↙        ↓        ↘
   economic   political   social
Hundreds of cities destroyed
```

Europe in Ruins
(pages 842–843)

How did the war change Europe?

The war had left Europe in ruins. Almost 40 million people were dead. Hundreds of cities were reduced to rubble by constant bombing and shelling. The ground war had destroyed much of the countryside. *Displaced persons* from many nations were trying to get back home. Often there was no water, no electricity, and little food. Hunger was constant.

Agriculture had been disrupted. Most able-bodied men had served in the military, and the women had worked in war production. Few had remained to plant the fields. With factories destroyed or damaged, most people had no earnings to buy the food that was available. Also the small harvests did not reach the cities because the transportation system had been destroyed. Suffering continued for many years in Europe.

1. What conditions existed in Europe after World War II?

_____

_____

Postwar Government and Politics (pages 843–844)

Who did the Europeans blame for the war?

Europeans often blamed their leaders for the war and its aftermath. Once Germany was defeated, some prewar governments—like those in Belgium,

CHAPTER 32 WORLD WAR II **317**

Holland, Denmark, and Norway—returned quickly. In Germany, Italy, and France, the old fascist governments had disappeared. At first, the Communist parties grew strong in France and Italy. People who opposed Communism grew alarmed. They voted leaders from other parties into power. Communism lost its appeal when the economies of these lands improved.

During efforts to rebuild Europe, the Allies held the **Nuremberg Trials** in the German city of Nuremberg. There, captured Nazi leaders were charged with crimes against humanity. They were found guilty, and some were executed.

2. What were the Nuremberg Trials?

_____

_____

_____

The Effects of Defeat in Japan; U.S. Occupation Brings Deep Changes (pages 844-845)

What changes were made in Japan?

The defeat suffered by Japan in World War II had *devastated* that country. Two million lives had been lost. The country's major cities were in ruins.

The U.S. Army occupied Japan under the command of General MacArthur. He began a process of **demilitarization**, breaking down the Japanese armed forces. He gave farmers and workers more power in the economy. He led the effort to write a new constitution. It gave all power to the Japanese people, who voted for members of a parliament that would rule the land. All Japanese over age 20—including women—were given the right to vote. In 1951, other nations finally signed a formal peace with Japan. A few months later, U.S. military occupation ended.

3. How did the government of Japan change?

_____

_____

Costs of World War II: Allies and Axis

	Direct War Costs	Military Killed/ Missing	Civilians Killed
United States	$288.0 billion*	292,131	—
Great Britain	$117.0 billion	271,311	60,595
France	$111.3 billion	205,707**	173,260***
USSR	$93.0 billion	13,600,000	7,720,000
Germany	$212.3 billion	3,300,000	2,893,000†
Japan	$41.3 billion	1,140,429	953,000

*In 1994 dollars.
**Before surrender to Nazis.
***Includes 65,000 murdered Jews.
†Includes about 170,000 murdered Jews and 56,000 foreign civilians in Germany.

Skillbuilder

Use the chart to answer the questions.

1. Which nation suffered the greatest human costs?

_____

_____

2. How do the economic costs of the United States and Great Britain compare with those of Germany and Japan?

_____

_____

318 CHAPTER 32 SECTION 5

Name _____ Date _____

Glossary CHAPTER 32 World War II

concentration camps Camp where enemies of the government and other people are held against their will, often under brutal conditions

counterattack Attack made in response to an enemy's attack

defenses Weapons used against, or readiness for, attack

devastated Destroyed

displaced persons People driven from their homeland by war or internal upheaval

escorting Traveling with for the sake of protection

fleet Number of ships operating together under one command

inmates Prisoners

massive Huge

morale Spirit

persecuting Harrassing with ill-treatment, especially because of race, religion, or beliefs

rationed Limited the amount a person could have

resistance Fighting back

strategic Important or essential to a plan of action

systematic Done according to a plan or system

AFTER YOU READ

Terms and Names

A. Write the name or term in each blank that best completes the meaning of the paragraph.

"Final Solution"

Aryans

ghettos

Kristallnacht

Holocaust

During World War II, Hitler began to carry out a plan of mass killing. This was called the **1** _____. Hitler aimed to kill those people who were not **2** _____, or Germanic. Most of the people he killed were Jews. One of his earliest attacks on Jews occurred on November 9, 1938. It has come to be known as **3** _____. Soon, Nazis began placing all the Jews in **4** _____, or separate neighborhoods. Then they began to carry out the plan for getting rid of them forever—the **5** _____.

B. Write the letter of the name next to the description that explains it best.

a. Charles de Gaulle

b. Winston Churchill

c. Erwin Rommel

d. Douglas MacArthur

e. Bernard Montgomery

____ **1.** Leader of the French government-in-exile

____ **2.** Leader of Allied forces in the Pacific

____ **3.** Leader of the British forces in Africa

____ **4.** Leader of Great Britain

____ **5.** Leader of German forces in Africa

Name _____   Date _____

AFTER YOU READ (continued)   CHAPTER 32   World War II

Main Ideas

1. How was Hitler first stopped?
_____
_____
_____

2. What did Japan do in its effort to create a Pacific Empire?
_____
_____
_____
_____

3. What groups were targeted by Hitler for the "Final Solution"?
_____
_____
_____
_____

4. What types of suffering occurred on home fronts during the war?
_____
_____
_____
_____

5. How did the American occupation change Japan?
_____
_____
_____
_____

Thinking Critically

Answer the following questions on a separate sheet of paper.

1. In what ways had the United States begun fighting World War II before it was attacked?

2. Explain and support this statement: Early Allied victories in the Pacific were extremely costly.

Name _____ Date _____

CHAPTER 33 Section 1 (pages 855–860)

Two Superpowers Face Off

BEFORE YOU READ

In the last section, you learned about the end of the Second World War.

In this section, you will learn about the international tensions that followed the war.

AS YOU READ

Use the chart below to take notes on causes and effects of the Cold War.

TERMS AND NAMES
United Nations World organization formed to prevent war
iron curtain Division between Eastern and Western Europe during the Cold War
containment Policy aimed at preventing the spread of communism
Truman Doctrine Policy of giving aid to countries threatened by communism
Marshall Plan Plan to give aid to European countries to help them recover from the war
Cold War State of tension and mistrust between the United States and the Soviet Union after World War II
NATO Military alliance including the United States, Canada, and several countries in Western Europe
Warsaw Pact Military alliance between the Soviet Union and the countries of Eastern Europe
brinkmanship Willingness on the part of the superpower to go to the brink, or edge, of war
U-2 incident Shooting down of a U.S. spy plane and capture of its pilot by the Soviet Union

causes → The Cold War → effects

[First cause box: Different political systems]

Former Allies Diverge (pages 855–856)

What caused the Cold War?

The United States and the Soviet Union were allies during World War II. In February 1945, they agreed to divide Germany into separate zones. Each zone was occupied by the soldiers of one of the Allies. The Allies also helped form the **United Nations** (UN) in 1945. The UN pledged to prevent war.

The United States and the Soviet Union had important differences after the war. The United States suffered few casualties and was the richest nation in the world. The Soviet Union suffered enormous loss of life and damage to its cities.

There were also striking political differences. The United States wanted to create new markets for its goods. It also wanted to encourage democracy. The Soviet Union wanted to set up Communist governments and make sure it did not get attacked again from the west. These differences caused tensions between the two countries.

1. How did U.S. goals and Soviet goals differ after World War II?

_____
_____
_____

CHAPTER 33 RESTRUCTURING THE POSTWAR WORLD **321**

The Soviet Union Corrals Eastern Europe (pages 856–857)

How *did the Soviet Union gain control of Eastern Europe?*

At the end of World War II, Soviet forces occupied lands along its western border. After the war, Stalin made sure Communist governments were in place in these lands: Albania, Bulgaria, Hungary, Czechoslovakia, Romania, Poland, and Yugoslavia. This divided Europe between East and West. Winston Churchill called this division the **"iron curtain."**

2. What countries were separated from the West by the iron curtain?

_____

_____

_____

United States Counters Soviet Expansion (pages 857–859)

How *did the United States respond to communism?*

Truman began a policy of **containment**—blocking the Soviets from spreading communism. Under the **Truman Doctrine,** the United States helped nations that were threatened by communism. The United States also adopted the **Marshall Plan** in 1947. This plan gave food and other aid to European countries to help them recover from the war.

In 1948, the Soviets and Americans *clashed* over Germany. France, Britain, and the United States agreed to pull their troops out of Germany. They let the three zones that they occupied unite. But the Soviets refused to leave their zone. Then they cut off all highway and train traffic into Berlin, which was deep within the Soviet zone. The United States and Britain responded with the *Berlin airlift*. They flew food and supplies into the city for 11 months. Finally, the Soviets lifted the *blockade*.

3. What was the Berlin airlift?

_____

_____

_____

The Cold War and a Divided World (pages 859–860)

Why *did tensions between the superpowers increase?*

The struggle between the United States and the Soviet Union was called the **Cold War.** Many countries supported one superpower or the other.

The United States, Canada, and several countries in Western Europe formed the North Atlantic Treaty Organization (**NATO**). NATO was a military *alliance*. Each nation promised to defend any other member that was attacked. The Soviets and the countries of Eastern Europe made a similar agreement. It was called the **Warsaw Pact.**

In 1949, the Soviet Union announced that it had developed an atomic bomb. Three years later, both superpowers had an even more deadly weapon—the hydrogen bomb. Soon both nations were involved in an arms race. They produced more and more nuclear weapons and developed new ways to deliver them. Both sides were willing to go to the brink, or edge, of war. This became known as **brinkmanship.**

In 1957, the Soviet Union launched *Sputnik*, the world's first human-made satellite. Many people were shocked. Americans felt that the Soviets were far ahead in science and technology. The United States then began spending huge amounts of money to improve math and science education.

The **U-2 incident** brought more tension. The United States sent planes, called U-2 planes, to spy over Soviet territory. One was brought down in 1960. The Soviets held the pilot for 19 months.

4. What are three developments or events that increased tensions during the Cold War?

_____

_____

_____

Name _____ Date _____

CHAPTER 33 Section 2 (pages 862–865)

Communists Triumph in China

TERMS AND NAMES
Mao Zedong Communist leader who defeated the Nationalists and led the People's Republic of China
Jiang Jieshi Nationalist leader who set up a new government in Taiwan
commune Large farm set up in China in which many families work the land and live together
Red Guards Young Chinese students who carried out the Cultural Revolution
Cultural Revolution Uprising in China between 1966 and 1976 that aimed to establish a society of peasants and workers in which all were equal

BEFORE YOU READ

In the last section, you read about tensions between the superpowers.

In this section, you will read about civil war and the rise of communism in China.

AS YOU READ

Use the chart below to take notes on changes in China.

[Diagram: Central oval labeled "Mao Brings Changes" connected to six surrounding ovals. One of the ovals is filled in with "Defeats Nationalists". The other five are blank.]

Civil War in China (pages 862–863)

Who fought the civil war?

Nationalists and Communists fought for control of China in the 1930s. During World War II, they joined forces to fight against the Japanese. The Communists, led by **Mao Zedong,** organized an army of peasants in northwestern China. From there they fought the Japanese in the northeast.

The Nationalists, led by **Jiang Jieshi,** controlled southwestern China. The Nationalists were protected from the Japanese by mountains. The United States sent the Nationalists large amounts of money and supplies, but corrupt officers took much of it. The Nationalists built a large army, but they only fought a few battles against the Japanese.

After the Japanese surrendered, the Communists and Nationalists resumed their civil war. The war lasted from 1946 to 1949. The Communists won because their troops were well-trained in *guerrilla war.* They also enjoyed the backing of the peasants to whom they had

CHAPTER 33 RESTRUCTURING THE POSTWAR WORLD **323**

promised land. In 1949, Jiang Jieshi and other Nationalist leaders fled to the island of Taiwan.

1. What two groups fought the civil war, and who led them?

_____
_____
_____
_____

Two Chinas and the Cold War
(pages 863–864)

How did the two Chinas participate in the Cold War?

The United States helped the Nationalists set up a new government. The Nationalists called their land the Republic of China. Meanwhile, the Soviets helped Mao Zedong and his government, the People's Republic of China.

The Chinese and the Soviets promised to help defend each other if either country were attacked. The United States responded by trying to make its sphere of influence in Asia larger. Communist China also tried to expand its power. They invaded Mongolia, Tibet, and India.

2. How did the superpowers take sides with the two Chinas?

_____
_____
_____
_____
_____

Transformation and Revolution
(pages 864–865)

How did Mao change China?

Mao set out to rebuild China. He seized land and gave it to the peasants. But he also forced the peasants—in groups of 200 to 300 households—to join *collective farms,* or **communes.** On these farms, the land belonged to the group. Mao also took control of China's industries. Under Mao's plan, production of industrial products went up.

With this success, Mao launched the "Great Leap Forward." He wanted to make the communes larger and more productive. The plan failed. People did not like strong government control. The government did not plan effectively. Between 1958 and 1961, famine killed millions.

In 1966, Mao tried to revive the revolution. He encouraged young people to revive the revolution. Students formed groups called **Red Guards.** This was the beginning of the **Cultural Revolution.** The Red Guards struck at teachers, scientists, and artists. They shut down schools and sent intellectuals to the country to work on farms. They killed thousands of people who resisted. China was in chaos. Factories shut down and farm production dropped. In 1976, Mao finally ended the Cultural Revolution.

3. What are three changes Mao made?

_____
_____
_____
_____
_____

Name _____ Date _____

CHAPTER 33   Section 3 (pages 866–870)

War in Korea and Vietnam

BEFORE YOU READ

In the last section, you read about the civil war in China.
In this section, you will read about wars in Korea and Vietnam.

AS YOU READ

Use the time line below to take notes on important events in Korea, Vietnam, and Cambodia.

TERMS AND NAMES

38th parallel Line that separated North Korea and South Korea

Douglas MacArthur Leader of United Nations forces during the Korean War

Ho Chi Minh Vietnamese nationalist who drove the French out of Vietnam and who led North Vietnam

domino theory Theory that nations were like a row of dominoes: if one fell to communism, the others would fall, too

Vietcong Communist rebels in South Vietnam who were supported by North Vietnam

Ngo Dinh Diem Leader of the anticommunist government of South Vietnam

Vietnamization Nixon's plan for gradually withdrawing U.S. troops from Vietnam and replacing them with South Vietnamese troops

Khmer Rouge Communist rebels who set up a brutal government in Cambodia

---

1950 North Korea invades the South	1973	1987
1953	1978	1989

War in Korea (pages 866–867)

How was Korea divided?

When World War II ended, Korea became a divided nation. North of the **38th parallel**, a line that crosses Korea at 38 degrees north *latitude*, the Japanese surrendered to the Soviets. South of that line, the Japanese surrendered to the Allies.

As in Germany, two nations developed. The Soviet Union supported a Communist government in North Korea. The United States supported a non-Communist government in South Korea. On June 25, 1950, North Korea invaded South Korea. President Truman fought this move with help from the UN. The United States and other countries sent troops to assist South Korea. At first, the North Korean army captured almost all of South Korea.

Then the UN army made a bold *counterattack*. The attack was led by General **Douglas MacArthur**. In 1953, the two Koreas agreed to a *cease-fire*. The earlier boundary splitting North

CHAPTER 33 RESTRUCTURING THE POSTWAR WORLD 325

and South Korea remained the same.

North Korea had a Communist government. It had a strong army and tight government control, but it also had many economic problems. For more than 30 years, dictators ruled South Korea. But its economy grew, in part because it received U.S. aid. Free elections were held in South Korea only after a new constitution was accepted in 1987.

1. How did the Korean War change the way Korea was divided?

_____

_____

War in Vietnam (pages 868–870)

How did the United States get involved in Vietnam?

A nationalist named **Ho Chi Minh** drove the French out of Vietnam. This worried the United States. The Americans thought Ho was a Communist. Many Americans thought if one country became Communist, others would too like a row of dominoes. This idea is known as the **domino theory.** A peace conference split Vietnam in two, with Ho taking charge of North Vietnam. The country had a Communist government. Communist rebels—the **Vietcong**—stayed active in the South.

The non-Communist government of the South had been set up by the United States and France. Its leader was **Ngo Dinh Diem.** When his government was threatened by Communists, the United States began to send troops. When they could not win the war on the ground, they tried bombing. Many people in the United States came to oppose the war.

In the late 1960s, President Richard Nixon began a plan called **Vietnamization.** This plan called for a gradual pull out of U.S. troops. At the same time, the South Vietnamese increased their combat role. The last American troops left in 1973. Two years later, North Vietnam overran the South and made Vietnam one country again. Today, Vietnam remains Communist but is looking for other nations to invest in its economy.

Fighting in Vietnam spilled over into Vietnam's neighbor, Cambodia. Rebels there were known as the **Khmer Rouge.** They set up a brutal Communist government. The Khmer Rouge killed 2 million people. In 1978, the Vietnamese invaded the country. They overthrew the Khmer Rouge. Vietnam withdrew in 1989. In 1993, Cambodia held free elections.

2. What happened in Vietnam after the United States withdrew?

_____

_____

Combat Troops Involved

Skillbuilder

1. In which year was the number of U.S. troops in Vietnam the highest?

_____

2. What is the greatest number of troops the South Vietnamese army had at one time?

_____

CHAPTER 33 Section 4 (pages 871–875)

Cold War Around the World

BEFORE YOU READ

In the last section, you read about wars in Korea and Vietnam.

In this section, you will learn about Cold War struggles in other parts of the world.

AS YOU READ

Use the chart below to take notes on Cold War conflicts.

TERMS AND NAMES

Third World Developing nations in Africa, Asia, and Latin America
nonaligned nations Countries that did not take sides with either the United States or the Soviet Union
Fidel Castro Communist leader of Cuba
Anastasio Somoza Nicaraguan dictator
Daniel Ortega Leader of Communist rebels in Nicaragua
Shah Mohammed Reza Pahlavi Pro-West ruler of Iran
Ayatollah Ruholla Khomeini Muslim leader who overthrew the Shah of Iran

COUNTRY	CONFLICT OR CHANGE
Cuba	Castro takes power

Confrontations over Developing Nations (page 871)

How were developing nations affected by the Cold War?

After World War II, the world's nations were grouped into three "worlds." The First World included the United States and its allies. The Second World included the Soviet Union and its allies. The **Third World** consisted of developing nations in Africa, Asia, and Latin America.

Many Third World nations had serious problems. These problems were often the results of imperialism. Some Third World nations faced *political unrest* that threatened the peace. Other problems included poverty and a lack of education and technology. Some of these countries tried to stay *neutral* in the Cold War. They met to form what they called a "third force." It consisted of **nonaligned nations,** or countries that did not take sides between the Soviets and Americans. Others actively sought American or Soviet aid.

CHAPTER 33 RESTRUCTURING THE POSTWAR WORLD **327**

1. What problems did Third World nations face?

Postwar Face-off in Latin America (pages 872–873)

What happened in Latin America?

In Cuba, the United States supported a dictator in the 1950s. In 1959, a young lawyer, **Fidel Castro,** led a successful revolt. Castro received aid from the Soviet Union. In 1962, the Soviets and Americans almost went to war over nuclear missiles that the Soviets placed in Cuba. The Soviets finally pulled the missiles out. Over time, the Cuban economy became more dependent on Soviet aid. When the Soviet Union collapsed in 1991, this aid stopped. It was a serious blow to Cuba's economy.

The United States had also backed a dictator, **Anastasio Somoza,** in Nicaragua. Somoza's government fell to Communist rebels in 1979. The rebels were led by **Daniel Ortega.** When the new government began helping leftist rebels in nearby El Salvador, the United States struck back. It began to support Nicaraguan rebels that wanted to overthrow the Communists. The civil war in Nicaragua lasted more than a decade. Finally, the different sides agreed to hold free elections.

2. Where did Communists gain power in Latin America?

Confrontations in the Middle East (pages 874–875)

What happened in Iran and Afghanistan?

The Middle East often saw conflict between those who wanted a more modern, Western-style society and those who wanted to follow traditional *Islam*. Such a struggle took place in Iran. In the 1950s, a group tried to take control of the government from Iran's ruler, **Shah Mohammed Reza Pahlavi.** The United States helped the Shah defeat them.

Over time, the Shah tried to weaken the influence of Islam in Iran. A Muslim leader, the **Ayatollah Ruholla Khomeini,** led a successful revolt. In 1979, the Shah was forced to leave the country. Khomeini made Islamic law the law of the land. He followed a foreign policy that was strongly against the United States. He also led his country in a long war against its neighbor Iraq.

The Soviets gained influence in Afghanistan after 1950. In the 1970s, Islamic rebels threatened the country's Communist government. The Soviets sent in troops to support the government. The United States felt its Middle East oil supplies were in danger and supported the rebels. In 1989, after a costly occupation, Soviet troops left Afghanistan.

3. How did Khomeini change Iran?

328 CHAPTER 33 SECTION 4

Name _____ Date _____

CHAPTER 33 Section 5 (pages 876–879)

The Cold War Thaws

BEFORE YOU READ

In the last section, you read about Cold War struggles around the world.

In this section, you will read about the major events of the Cold War from the 1950s to the 1980s.

AS YOU READ

Use the time line below to show key events that decreased or increased tensions between the superpowers.

TERMS AND NAMES
Nikita Khrushchev Leader of the Soviet Union after Stalin
destalinization Process of getting rid of Stalin's memory
Leonid Brezhnev Soviet leader after Khrushchev
John F. Kennedy President of the United States from 1961 to 1963
Lyndon Johnson President of the United States from 1963 to 1969
détente Policy to decrease tensions between the superpowers
Richard M. Nixon President of the United States from 1969 to 1974
SALT Talks to limit nuclear arms in the United States and the Soviet Union
Ronald Reagan President of the United States from 1981 to 1989
Star Wars Program to protect America against enemy missiles

1953 Krushchev becomes new Soviet leader	1968	1979
1956	1972	1981

The Soviets Dominate Europe
(pages 876–878)

How did the Soviets keep their control over Eastern Europe?

Nikita Khrushchev became the Soviet leader after Stalin died in 1953. Krushchev began a process of **destalinization.** This meant getting rid of Stalin's memory. Krushchev also believed that the Soviet Union should have "peaceful competition" with the capitalist nations.

In Eastern Europe, many people still resented Soviet rule. Eastern Europeans took part in protest movements against Soviet control. In 1956, protesters and the army overthrew the Communist government of Hungary. Khrushchev sent Soviet tanks to put the Communists back in power. In 1964, **Leonid Brezhnev** replaced Krushchev. When Czechoslovakians began to reform their Communist government in 1968, Brezhnev sent in tanks to stop them.

The Soviets did not have the same control over their larger neighbor, China. Although the Soviet Union and China enjoyed friendly relations at first, they gradually grew apart. The split became so wide that the Soviet Union and China sometimes

CHAPTER 33 RESTRUCTURING THE POSTWAR WORLD **329**

fought along their border. The two nations now have a *fragile* peace.

1. In what two European countries did the Soviets put down revolts against Soviet control?

_____

_____

_____

_____

From Brinkmanship to Détente; Détente Cools (pages 878–879)

Did tensions increase or decrease between the United States and the Soviet Union?

Tensions between the Soviets and the United States had been very high during the presidency of **John F. Kennedy.** Tensions remained high during the presidency of **Lyndon Johnson.** The war in Vietnam helped keep relations tense.

In the early 1970s, the United States began to follow a policy called **détente** under President **Richard M. Nixon.** Détente helped lower the tensions between the superpowers. Nixon became the first U.S. president to visit Communist China and the Soviet Union. In 1972, Nixon and Brezhnev held meetings called the Strategic Arms Limitations Talks (**SALT**). They signed a treaty to limit the number of nuclear missiles each country could have.

The United States retreated from détente when the Soviet Union invaded Afghanistan in 1979. In 1981, **Ronald Reagan,** a fierce anticommunist, became president. He started a program to protect America against nuclear missiles. Some people called this program **Star Wars.** But it was never put into effect.

The Soviets grew angry over American support for the rebels fighting against the Communists in Nicaragua. Tensions between the United States and the Soviet Union increased until 1985 when a new leader came to power in the Soviet Union.

2. Name two actions or events that got in the way of détente.

_____

_____

_____

_____

_____

Glossary

CHAPTER 33 Restructuring the Postwar World

alliance Union of people, groups, or nations to achieve common goals

Berlin airlift Flying of food and supplies into West Berlin by Britain and the United States to break a Soviet blockade

blockade Act of cutting off one place from all others

brink Edge

cease-fire End to fighting

clashed Disagreed strongly

collective farms Large farms worked by many families

counterattack To make a return attack

fragile Delicate; easily broken

guerrilla war Warfare carried out by small, independent groups, often acting secretly in and around their own towns and villages

Islam Religion with a belief in one god that developed in Arabia

latitude A line that measures distance north or south from the earth's equator

neutral Not choosing sides between any particular nations or groups

political unrest State of conflict over the government, its leaders, or its laws

revive To bring back to life; to give new strength

AFTER YOU READ

Terms and Names

A. Write the name in each blank that best completes the meaning of the paragraph.

Leonid Brezhnev

Nikita Khrushchev

Fidel Castro

Shah Mohammed Reza Pahlavi

Ayatollah Ruholla Khomeini

Some leaders have played a greater role in post-World War II politics than others. One of the first Cold War leaders that the United States feared was **1** _____, the leader of Cuba. A leader of Iran who also challenged the United States was **2** _____. He had taken power by overthrowing the pro-American leader, **3** _____. Soviet leaders during the Cold War included **4** _____, the leader of the Soviet Union after Stalin. They also included **5** _____, who sent tanks into Czechoslovakia in 1968.

B. Write the letter of the name or term next to the description that explains it best.

a. Truman Doctrine

b. Marshall Plan

c. containment

d. domino theory

e. Vietnamization

_____ **1.** Idea that the fall of one country to communism would lead other countries to become Communist

_____ **2.** Policy of giving aid to countries threatened by communism

_____ **3.** Gradual replacement of U.S. troops with South Vietnamese troops

_____ **4.** Plan that gave aid to European countries to help them recover from World War II

_____ **5.** Policy aimed at preventing the spread of communism

CHAPTER 33 RESTRUCTURING THE POSTWAR WORLD **331**

Name _____ Date _____

AFTER YOU READ (cont.) *CHAPTER* **33** Restructuring the Postwar World

Main Ideas

1. Why did Truman start his policy of containment?
_____
_____
_____

2. Why did the Nationalists lose the Civil War in China?
_____
_____
_____

3. What changes did the Khmer Rouge bring to Cambodia?
_____
_____
_____

4. Describe what happened in Nicaragua after Anastasio Somoza fell from power.
_____
_____
_____

5. Explain when and how tensions between the superpowers decreased and when and how they increased again.
_____
_____
_____

Thinking Critically

Answer the following questions on a separate sheet of paper.

1. Discuss how disagreements between the United States and the Soviet Union after World War II led to the Cold War.

2. Explain the relationship of Ronald Reagan and Star Wars to détente.

Name _____ Date _____

CHAPTER 34 Section 1 (pages 885–889)

The Indian Subcontinent Gains Independence

TERMS AND NAMES
Congress Party Group consisting mostly of Hindus that led a campaign for India's independence
Muhammed Ali Jinnah Leader of the Muslim League
Muslim League Muslim group that led a campaign for India's independence
Lord Mountbatten Last British viceroy of India
partition Division of India into two nations
Jawaharlal Nehru First prime minister of India
Indira Gandhi Daughter of Nehru who followed him as prime minister
Rajiv Gandhi Son of Indira Gandhi who became prime minister
Benazir Bhutto Former prime minister of Pakistan

BEFORE YOU READ

In the last chapter, you read about the Cold War.
In this section, you will read about changes in India, Pakistan, and Sri Lanka.

AS YOU READ

Use the time line below to take notes on changes in India, Pakistan, and Sri Lanka.

| 1947 India and Ceylon win independence | 1971 | 1983 |

| 1964 | 1972 |

A Movement Toward Independence (page 885)

What led to the movement for independence?

Many Asians served in the armies of the colonial powers during World War II. The fight against the Nazis deepened Asians' desire for independence. Japanese victories over European powers early in the war made Asians believe that the colonial rulers could be defeated. In Europe, people began to doubt that it was right for nations to have colonies.

1. Name two things that increased Asian hopes for independence.

_____
_____

Independence Brings Partition to India (pages 885–887)

What divisions existed between Indian political groups?

In the 1920s, Mohandas Gandhi led a movement for Indian independence. Two groups worked in

CHAPTER 34 THE COLONIES BECOME NEW NATIONS **333**

this effort. The Indian National Congress, also called the **Congress Party,** said that it represented all of India. Most of its members were Hindu. **Muhammad Ali Jinnah** formed the **Muslim League** in 1906. He said that the Congress Party did not care for the rights of Indian Muslims. The British encouraged the division of Hindus and Muslims into two opposing groups. This division helped the British keep control of the country.

After World War II, Britain was ready for India to be independent. But the British did not know which people in India would take power. Riots broke out between the Hindus and Muslims throughout India.

Gandhi tried to end the violence. A Hindu extremist *assassinated* him for protecting Muslims. **Lord Louis Mountbatten,** the last British *viceroy* of India, also tried to stop the violence. He finally accepted the idea that **partition,** or the division of India into two nations, was necessary.

The British Parliament passed a law granting independence in July 1947. It created the separate Hindu and Muslim nations of India and Pakistan. The law gave people only one month to decide which country they wanted to live in and to move there. As millions of people began to move, more violence broke out.

2. What happened when the separate nations of India and Pakistan were created?

_____

_____

_____

Modern India (pages 887–888)

What problems has modern India faced?

Jawaharlal Nehru became the first prime minister of India. He led the country for 17 years.

India and Pakistan went to war over the state of Kashmir. Kashmir bordered both countries. It had a Hindu ruler and a large Muslim population. Conflict over Kashmir continues today.

Nehru tried to reform Indian society. He hoped to improve the status of the lower *castes* and of women. Shortly after he died in 1964, his daughter, **Indira Gandhi,** became prime minister. She took steps to increase food production. In 1984, she ordered an attack on Sikh rebels. A few months later, she was killed by Sikhs. She was followed by her son **Rajiv Gandhi.** He was later assassinated. *Separatist movements* continue to *disrupt* Indian society.

3. Why does conflict continue in Kashmir?

_____

_____

_____

_____

Pakistan and Sri Lanka (page 889)

How have new political divisions led to violence?

Pakistan has faced a great deal of violence, too. When Pakistan was first formed, it had east and west parts that were separated by India. In a bloody fight in 1971, the eastern part won its independence. The new nation took the name Bangladesh. Power struggles have caused problems in the western part since then. Its leaders have included Ali Bhutto and his daughter, **Benazir Bhutto.** She was elected prime minister twice.

Ceylon, an island on the southeastern coast of India, won its independence in 1947 as well. In 1972 it was renamed Sri Lanka. Since 1983, a Hindu minority on the island—the *Tamils*—have led a bloody fight to form a separate nation.

4. Why has violence occurred in Pakistan?

_____

_____

_____

_____

CHAPTER 34 Section 2 (pages 892–895)

Southeast Asian Nations Gain Independence

BEFORE YOU READ

In the last section, you read about independence and conflict in India.

In this section, you will read about independence and the challenges of self-rule in Southeast Asia.

AS YOU READ

Use the web below to show key people and events in each struggle for independence.

TERMS AND NAMES

Ferdinand Marcos Leader of the Philippines who was elected but ruled as a dictator

Corazón Aquino Woman who defeated Marcos in the elections of 1986

Aung San Nationalist leader who helped drive British out of Burma

Aung San Suu Kyi Daughter of Aung San; winner of Nobel Prize for her fight for democracy in Burma

Sukarno Leader of Indonesian independence movement; first president of Indonesia

Suharto Leader who turned Indonesia into a police state

- Philippines: *U.S. presence after independence*
- Burma
- Indonesia
- (center) Challenges of Independence

The United States and the Philippines (pages 892–893)

What happened in the Philippines after it gained independence?

In 1946, the United States gave the Philippines independence. The United States also promised money to help the Filipinos rebuild their economy. To win the aid, however, the Filipinos had to agree to a trade deal. For the next few decades, the United States kept naval and air bases on the islands. Many Filipinos wanted the bases closed. In 1991, the United States left the bases.

From 1966 to 1986, **Ferdinand Marcos** led the country. He was elected president but after a few years ruled as a dictator. He then harshly put down *dissent* and stole millions of dollars from the country. When he lost an election to **Corazón Aquino** in 1986, he refused to leave office. A large public outcry forced him to step down.

1. Who was Ferdinand Marcos?

_____

_____

CHAPTER 34 THE COLONIES BECOME NEW NATIONS **335**

British Colonies Gain Independence (page 894)

Which Southeast Asian British colonies won independence?

Burma was the first British colony in Southeast Asia to become independent. Nationalist leader **Aung San** helped drive the British out of Burma. Burma changed its name to *Myanmar* in 1989. Since 1962, generals have ruled the country. Myanmar has been torn by conflict often. **Aung San Suu Kyi** won the Nobel Peace Prize in 1991 for her opposition to this military rule.

After World War II, the British moved back into the Malay peninsula. They tried to form a country there. But ethnic conflict between Malays and Chinese who lived in the area stopped them. In 1957, independence was given to Malaya, Singapore, and parts of two distant islands.

Singapore later declared independence as a city-state. Singapore is one of the busiest ports in the world. It is also a banking center. Its economy creates a high standard of living.

2. What happened in Burma after it gained independence?

_____

_____

Indonesia Gains Independence from the Dutch (page 895)

What challenges did Indonesia face?

Sukarno led an independence movement in Indonesia while Japan held that country. After World War II, he quickly declared an independent Indonesia. The Dutch at first tried to regain control over their former colony. But in 1949 they recognized Indonesia's independence.

Indonesia is spread out. It has 13,600 islands and includes people from 300 different groups that speak 250 different languages. It has been difficult for leaders to unite the nation. In 1967, a general named **Suharto** took control. He ruled until 1998. Many criticized him for taking over the island of East Timor and for corruption in his government. In the late 1990s Indonesia faced severe economic problems.

3. Why has governing Indonesia proven difficult?

_____

_____

_____

Comparing Economies

Gross Domestic Product is the dollar value of all goods and services produced within a country during one year. In this graph, the GDP is divided by the number of productive workers in each country. This results in the GDP per capita, or per person.

[Bar graph showing GDP per capita for Philippines, Singapore, and United States in 1965, 1985, and 1991]

Sources: *World Statistics in Brief* (1978) and *World Statistics Pocketbook* (1995), published by the United Nations.

Skillbuilder

1. How does the rate of growth in the Philippines compare with that of Singapore?

_____

2. Given the trend on this graph, what might you expect to see in later years?

_____

CHAPTER 34 Section 3 (pages 896–900)

New Nations in Africa

BEFORE YOU READ

In the last section, you read about the struggle for self-rule in Southeast Asian colonies.

In this section, you will read about new nations in Africa.

AS YOU READ

Use the web below to take notes on challenges facing each nation after independence.

TERMS AND NAMES

Negritude movement African movement after World War II to celebrate African culture, heritage, and values

Kwame Nkrumah Leader in the Gold Coast independence movement

Jomo Kenyatta Nationalist who helped lead Kenya to independence

Mau Mau Africans who protested British presence in Kenya

Mobutu Sese Seko Ruler who took control of the Congo in 1965 and renamed it Zaire

FLN (Algerian National Liberation Front) Group that fought for Algeria's independence

Ahmed Ben Bella Leader of the FLN who became the first president and prime minister of Algeria

COUNTRY	CHALLENGES
Ghana	Military rule since 1981
Kenya	
Congo	
Algeria	
Angola	

Background to Independence
(page 896)

Why did independence movements increase after World War II?

During World War II, Africans fought as soldiers along with Europeans. After the war, Africans wanted independence. Many Africans took part in the **Negritude movement.** The purpose of this movement was to celebrate African culture, *heritage,* and values.

1. What was the Negritude movement?

_____

_____

British Colonies Seek Independence (pages 896–898)

What challenges did newly independent nations face?

The British gave Africans a greater part in the colonial government of its Gold Coast colony. **Kwame Nkrumah** led a movement to push Britain to act more quickly. The effort succeeded. In 1957 the Gold Coast colony became independent. The new nation took the name Ghana.

Nkrumah had big plans for building the economy of Ghana. But these plans were very expensive. Opposition grew. Finally, the army seized power in 1966. Ghana has been ruled by a military dictator since 1981.

The strong leadership of nationalist **Jomo Kenyatta** helped Kenya achieve independence in 1963. An uprising of Africans called **Mau Mau** also helped. Mau Mau aimed at frightening the British settlers to leave. Kenyatta became president of the new nation. He tried to unite the many different people in his country. Kenya has faced violence and a weak economy in the 1990s.

2. What problems did the new nations of Ghana and Kenya face?

_____

_____

_____

The Congo Gains Independence
(pages 898–899)

What happened in the Congo after independence?

The Congo won its independence from Belgium in 1960. But the new nation was not well-prepared for self-rule. The Congo quickly fell into civil war.

In 1965, **Mobutu Sese Seko** took control. He renamed the country Zaire and ruled until 1997. Zaire had rich mineral resources. But Mobutu's harsh and corrupt rule made the country poor. He was overthrown in a coup in 1997. The country's name was changed back to the Congo.

3. How did Mobutu rule the Congo?

_____

_____

Algeria Fights for Its Independence (pages 899–900)

How did Algeria achieve independence?

A bloody conflict for independence took place in Algeria. About 1 million French settlers lived there. They were unwilling to give up their property or their control of the colonial government.

Violence broke out in 1945 and continued for many years. In 1954, the Algerian National Liberation Front, or **FLN**, announced its intention to fight for independence. In 1962, the French finally granted independence to Algeria.

Ahmed Ben Bella, a leader of the FLN, was the first prime minister and then the first president of Algeria. From 1965 until 1988, Algerians tried to *modernize* their country. These efforts failed.

An Islamic party won elections in 1991. But the government rejected the vote. Fighting between Islamic *militants* and the government continued through the 1990s.

4. What happened in Algeria after it gained independence?

_____

_____

_____

Angola Gains Its Independence
(page 900)

How did Angola win its independence?

The colonies of Portugal were the last to gain their independence. Portugal did nothing to prepare the people of Angola for self-rule. Three Angolan groups emerged in the 1960s that were determined to control the new government.

In the 1970s, the army of Portugal revolted against its government over the war in Angola. The troops left Angola without putting any group in charge. Angolans fought a long civil war. The war ended in 1989. But no strong government has formed yet.

5. How did Portugal's actions help cause civil war in Angola?

_____

_____

_____

Name _____ Date _____

CHAPTER 34 Section 4 (pages 901–905)

Conflicts in the Middle East

BEFORE YOU READ

In the last section, you read about conflicts in the new nations of Africa.

In this section, you will learn about conflict in the Middle East.

AS YOU READ

Use the time line below to take notes on the conflicts and hopes for peace that followed the creation of the state of Israel.

TERMS AND NAMES

Balfour Declaration British statement of support for a Jewish national homeland in Palestine

Suez Crisis 1956 crisis that occurred when Egypt attacked the Suez Canal before it came under Egypt's control

Six-Day War War fought in 1967 in which Israel defeated Egypt, Iran, Jordan, and Syria

Anwar Sadat Egyptian leader who signed a peace agreement with Israel

Golda Meir Israeli prime minister at the time of the 1973 Arab–Israeli war

Menachem Begin Israeli prime minister who signed a peace agreement with Egypt

Camp David Accords Agreement in which Egypt recognized Israel as a nation and Israel gave the Sinai peninsula back to Egypt

Hosni Mubarak Leader of Egypt after Anwar Sadat

PLO Palestinian Liberation Organization

1948 Jews declare the existence of the nation of Israel

1967

1981

1956

1977

1995

Palestine and Israel
(pages 901–902)

How did Israel come into being?

The movement to settle Jews in *Palestine* began in the late 1800s and early 1900s. These Jews believed that Palestine belonged to them because it was their home 3,000 years ago. But Muslims had lived there for the last 1,300 years.

After World War I, Britain took control of the area. The British found that Jews and Muslims did not live together peacefully. In 1917, Britain said it supported the establishment of a Jewish national homeland in Palestine. This statement is known as the **Balfour Declaration.**

After World War II, the British left the area. The United Nations divided the land into two parts. One part was set aside for the *Palestinians.* The other part was set aside part for Jews.

Islamic countries voted against the plan. The Palestinians opposed it. Many countries backed the idea of a separate Jewish state. They wanted to help make up for the suffering Jews had experienced in World War II. On May 14, 1948, the

CHAPTER 34 THE COLONIES BECOME NEW NATIONS **339**

Jewish people in Palestine declared the existence of the Jewish state of Israel.

1. Why did the creation of Israel cause conflict?

_____

_____

Israel and the Arab States in Conflict (pages 902–903)

How did Arab states respond to the creation of Israel?

On May 15, 1948, six Islamic nations invaded Israel. Israel won the war in a few months with strong support from the United States. This war was the first of many Arab–Israeli wars.

Another war was started by the **Suez Crisis.** The crisis began in 1956 when a group of Egyptian army officers seized control of the government of Egypt from Britain. The British and French had kept control of the Suez Canal. Gamal Abdel Nasser, the new leader of Egypt, attacked the canal. The Israeli army helped the British and French keep control. The peace settlement that followed gave the canal to Egypt anyway.

The **Six-Day War** broke out in 1967 when Egypt and other nations threatened Israel. Israel defeated Egypt, Iran, Jordan, and Syria in just a week. Israel's success brought new areas under its control.

The next war, in 1973, began when Egypt, led by **Anwar Sadat,** and its allies launched a surprise attack. At first, Arab forces won some of the territory lost in 1967. Israel, led by its prime minister, **Golda Meir,** fought back and won control of much of the territory it had lost.

2. What did the Suez Crisis and Six-Day War have in common?

_____

_____

Trading Land for Peace (page 903)

What happened at Camp David?

In 1977, Egyptian leader Sadat signed a peace agreement with Israeli prime minister **Menachem Begin.** In this agreement, Israel gave the Sinai Peninsula back to Egypt. In return, Egypt recognized Israel as a nation. Egypt was the first Islamic country to give this recognition. This agreement became known as the **Camp David Accords.** It was the first signed agreement between Israel and an Arab country. This angered many Arabs. Sadat was assassinated in 1981. His successor, **Hosni Mubarak,** kept peace with Israel.

3. What is significant about the Camp David Accords?

_____

_____

The Palestinians Demand Independence (page 905)

How have the Palestinians responded to living in Israel?

Despite many efforts, Israel and the Palestinians have not made peace. Palestinians living in Israel dislike Israeli rule. They want a nation of their own.

The Palestinian Liberation Organization (**PLO**), led by Yasir Arafat, became a leading group in the struggle for self-rule. During the 1970s and 1980s, the military arm of the PLO made many attacks on Israel. Israel responded by invading Lebanon to attack bases of the PLO. In the late 1980s, many Palestinians in Israel began a revolt called the *intifada*. The intifada continued into the 1990s.

In the early 1990s, the two sides took steps toward peace. Israel agreed to give Palestinians control of an area called the Gaza Strip and of the town of Jericho. The Israeli leader who signed this agreement, Yitzhak Rabin, was assassinated in 1995. He was killed by a Jewish *extremist* who opposed giving in to the Palestinians. The two sides have yet to achieve final peace.

4. What is the state of Israeli–Arab relations today?

_____

_____

Name _____ Date _____

Glossary — CHAPTER 34 The Colonies Become New Nation

assassinated Murdered for political reasons
castes Social groupings
disrupt Disturb; break apart
dissent Disagreement with the government
extremist A person who has extreme views on an issue
heritage Sense of the past of a one's nation, culture, or family
intifada Uprising of the Palestinian people against Israeli rule
militants Aggressive people or parties
modernize To make something modern
Myanmar Name of Burma since 1989
Palestine Region of southwest Asia
Palestinians People from Palestine
separatist movement Movement by ethnic, religious, or other groups within a country to create a separate country
Tamils Hindu group in Sri Lanka that wants to form its own nation
viceroy Kind of governor or top government leader

AFTER YOU READ

Terms and Names

A. Write the name in each blank that best completes the meaning of the paragraph.

Rajiv Gandhi

Indira Gandhi

Muhammad Ali Jinnah

Benazir Bhutto

Jawaharlal Nehru

Important leaders in the history of India and Pakistan during the twentieth century include the leader of the Muslim league, **1** _____. He helped India fight for its independence. The first prime minister of India was **2** _____. India fought a war with Pakistan over Kashmir during his rule. His daughter, **3** _____, followed him in the role of prime minister. She, in turn, was followed to power by her son, **4** _____. One of the important leaders of Pakistan was **5** _____.

B. Write the letter of the name next to the description that explains it best.

a. Aung San
b. Kwame Nkrumah
c. Ahmed Ben Bella
d. Corazón Aquino
e. Mobutu Sese Seko

_____ **1.** Filipino leader who defeated Marcos in national elections

_____ **2.** Nationalist leader who helped drive the British out of Burma

_____ **3.** Leader who helped the Gold Coast gain independence

_____ **4.** Leader who took control of the Congo

_____ **5.** Leader of the Algerian National Liberation Front

Name _____ Date _____

AFTER YOU READ (cont.) CHAPTER 34 The Colonies Become New Nations

Main Ideas

1. What role did the British play in the partition of India and the violence that followed?

2. Describe the leadership of Ferdinand Marcos in the Philippines.

3. What problems has the Congo faced since gaining its independence?

4. Why was the Balfour Declaration so significant?

5. Explain the events and significance of the Suez Crisis.

Thinking Critically

Answer the following questions on a separate sheet of paper.

1. Angola gained its independence in a unique way. How was it different from the way other African nations gained independence?

2. Describe how the Arab–Israeli conflict reaches far back in the past and why it could continue into the future.

Name _____ Date _____

CHAPTER 35 Section 1 (pages 911–915)

Patterns of Change: Democracy

TERMS AND NAMES
Brasília Capital city of Brazil
land reform Breaking up large estates in order to give land to the landless
standard of living Quality of life as judged by the amount of goods people have
recession Decrease in the size of the economy
PRI Institutional Revolutionary Party, which has controlled Mexico for most of the century

BEFORE YOU READ

In the last section, you read about conflicts in the Middle East.

In this section, you will read about the struggles for democracy in Latin America.

AS YOU READ

Use the chart below to take notes on the challenges to democracy in Latin America.

```
                    Mexico

    Brazil                          Argentina
Attempts at land reform give    Challenges
way to military rule.           to Democracy
```

Making Democracy Work
(pages 911–912)

How does democracy work?

For democracy to work, several conditions must exist. There must be free and fair elections. There must also be more than one political party. The people of the country should have a good education. Then they can make informed choices. They should share a common culture. All must accept the idea that everyone has equal rights. Finally, there must be rule by law, not by power. Many nations in Latin America have had difficulty achieving democracy because all these factors are not present.

1. Name at least four factors needed to make democracy work.

_____

_____

From Dictators to Democracy
(pages 912–913)

What challenges has Brazil faced?

After independence in 1822, Brazil started out as a monarchy. After 1930, a dictator ruled. But in 1956, Juscelino Kubitschek was elected president. He tried to improve the economy. He built a new capital city, **Brasília**. He supported **land reform**.

CHAPTER 35 STRUFFLES FOR DEMOCRACY 343

Land reform aimed at breaking up large estates and giving land to the peasants.

Landowners opposed land reform. They backed a group of army leaders who took power in 1964. The military ruled Brazil for 20 years. The country's economy grew. But the people had few rights. Eventually, their **standard of living** also fell. This means the quality of life, judged by the amount of goods people have, went down. By the 1980s a **recession**—a decrease in the size of the economy—hurt Brazil.

2. What changes did land reform bring in Brazil?

_____

_____

_____

_____

One Dominant Party (pages 913–914)

What party has controlled Mexico for most of the century?

Mexico has had a stable government since the 1920s. One political party—now called the Institutional Revolutionary Party (**PRI**)—has been in power during this period. This party has controlled the local, state, and national governments.

At times, the PRI acted harshly to stop any *dissent*. For example, in 1968 the government killed many people who took part in a demonstration for economic reform. In 1994 rebels in the southern Mexican state of Chiapas rebelled. They wanted to improve the lives of the poor people in Chiapas. The government tried find a peaceful settlement with the rebels.

The PRI recently opened up the political system to candidates from other parties. In 1997, two opposition parties won many seats in the national legislature. They ended PRI control of that congress.

3. How has the PRI controlled Mexico?

_____

_____

_____

_____

Argentina Casts off Repression
(page 915)

How has democracy grown in Argentina?

Argentina has also struggled toward democracy. In the 1940s and 1950s, Juan Perón was a popular dictator. He put in place many programs to benefit the masses. But in 1952, the army overthrew him. The army controlled the government for the next 30 years. Army leaders ruled harshly. They killed many people who opposed them.

In 1982, the army suffered a stinging defeat in a war with Britain. The generals agreed to step down. Since 1983, Argentina has been led by freely elected leaders.

4. What happened after Perón was overthrown?

_____

_____

_____

_____

_____

Name _____ Date _____

CHAPTER 35 Section 2 (pages 916–920)

Democratic Challenges in African Nations

TERMS AND NAMES
federal system System in which power is shared between state governments and a central authority
martial law Military rule
dissident Person against government policy
apartheid Strict separation of blacks and whites
Nelson Mandela Leader of the African National Congress who was imprisoned

BEFORE YOU READ
In the last section, you read about challenges to democracy in South America and Mexico.
In this section, you will read about struggles for democracy in Africa.

AS YOU READ
Use the chart below to take notes on the struggles for democracy in Nigeria and South Africa. Record key events and changes in government.

Nigeria
- Nigeria gains independence from Britain.
- Elected government overthrown.

South Africa

(Struggles for Democracy)

Colonial Rule Hampers Democracy (page 916)

What problems did colonial rule create?

African nations have had a hard time setting up democratic governments because of the effects of colonial rule. European powers made borders in Africa that paid no attention to ethnic groupings. They put people who disliked each other in the same area. This practice caused conflict.

Also, the European nations never built up the economies of their colonies. Most of the colonies lacked a middle class or skilled workers. Both are needed for a strong democracy. When Britain and France gave their African colonies independence, they gave them democratic governments. But problems soon arose between rival groups.

CHAPTER 35 STRUGGLES FOR DEMOCRACY **345**

1. Name three things that have slowed democracy in Africa.

_____
_____
_____

Nigeria Erupts in Civil War; Nigeria's Struggle for Democracy (pages 917–918)

What happened after Nigeria gained independence?

In 1960, Nigeria became independent from Britain. It adopted a federal system. In a **federal system,** power is shared between state governments and a central authority. But conflict broke out in just a few years. The people of one ethnic group—the Igbo—tried to break away from Nigeria in 1967. The Igbo lost in a three-year civil war.

A period of **martial law,** or military rule, followed the war. In 1979 Nigeria got an elected government. Some army officers said the government was corrupt. The officers overthrew the government in 1983. Once in power, they treated the people from other ethnic groups harshly. They jailed **dissidents,** opponents of government policy. The military rulers allowed elections in 1993. But they did not accept the results of the elections and continued to rule the land.

2. What happened after Nigeria's civil war?

_____
_____
_____
_____

South Africa Under White Rule
(pages 918–919)

What was apartheid?

In South Africa, the conflict was between races. A white minority ruled a black majority. In 1948, the whites put in place a policy called **apartheid**—the strict separation of blacks and whites. Black South Africans were denied many basic rights. Some joined together in a group called the *African National Congress* (ANC) to fight for their rights. The white government cracked down on the ANC. They put many ANC leaders in prison. **Nelson Mandela,** the leader of the ANC, was one of the people imprisoned.

3. Why was the African National Congress formed?

_____
_____
_____
_____

South Africa Moves Toward Democracy (pages 919–920)

How did apartheid end?

By the late 1980s, several riots had taken place. Blacks angrily struck back against apartheid. People in other nations also opposed apartheid. They *boycotted*, or would not buy, goods produced in South Africa. They hoped the boycott would persuade the South African government to end apartheid.

In 1990, President F. W. de Klerk took that step. He made the ANC legal and released ANC leader Nelson Mandela from prison. The South African parliament passed a law ending apartheid. In April 1994, all South Africans—even blacks—were able to vote in an election for a new leader. The ANC and Mandela won easily. In 1996, the new government approved a new constitution. It gave equal rights to all South Africans.

4. Why did F. W. de Klerk end apartheid?

_____
_____
_____
_____

Name _____ Date _____

CHAPTER 35 Section 3 (pages 921–925)

Gorbachev Moves Toward Democracy

TERMS AND NAMES
Politburo Ruling committee of the Communist party
Mikhail Gorbachev Leader of the Soviet Union from 1985 to 1991
glasnost Gorbachev's policy of openness
perestroika Gorbachev's policy aimed at reforming the Soviet economy
Solidarity Polish workers' movement
Lech Walesa Leader of Solidarity
reunification Uniting of East and West Germany into one nation

BEFORE YOU READ

In the last section, you read about political conflicts in Africa.

In this section, you will read about the democratic changes in Communist nations in Europe.

AS YOU READ

Use the web below to take notes on changes that occurred in Communist countries.

(Web diagram: center oval "Changes in Communist Countries" connected to six surrounding ovals, one labeled "Soviet Union—Gorbachev makes reforms")

Gorbachev's Reforms (pages 921–922)

What changes did Gorbachev make?

During the 1960s and 1970s, the leaders of the Soviet Union kept tight control on society. Leonid Brezhnev and the **Politburo**—the ruling committee of the Communist Party—crushed all political dissent. In 1985, Communist Party leaders named **Mikhail Gorbachev** as the leader of the Soviet Union. He was the youngest Soviet leader since Joseph Stalin. He was expected to make minor reforms. But his reforms led to a revolution.

Gorbachev felt that Soviet society could not improve without the free flow of ideas. He started a policy called **glasnost,** or openness. He opened churches. He let political prisoners out of prison. He allowed books to be published that in the past had been *banned*. Gorbachev also began a policy called **perestroika,** or economic restructuring. It tried to improve the Soviet economy by lifting the tight control on all managers and workers.

In 1987, Gorbachev opened up the political system by allowing the Soviet people to elect representatives to a legislature.

CHAPTER 35 STRUGGLES FOR DEMOCRACY **347**

Finally, Gorbachev changed Soviet foreign policy. He moved to end the war in Afghanistan and the arms race against the United States. Gorbachev also urged Communist leaders in Eastern Europe to change their policies as well. But many of them resisted.

1. Name four changes Gorbachev made.

___

Reforms in Poland and Hungary
(pages 922–923)

How did Poland and Hungary change?

Despite resistance from the old Communist leaders, the people of Eastern Europe wanted reform. Protest movements began to build.

In Poland, years of economic problems troubled the people. Polish workers organized a union called **Solidarity.** Solidarity went on strike to get the government to recognize the union.

The government gave in to Solidarity's demands. But later, the government banned the union and threw **Lech Walesa,** the union's leader, in jail. This caused unrest. Finally, the government was forced to allow elections. The Polish people voted overwhelmingly against the Communists and for Solidarity.

Inspired by the Poles, leaders in Hungary started a reform movement. The reformers took over the Communist party. Then the party voted itself out of existence.

2. What happened when Poland held elections?

___

Communism Falls in East Germany (pages 923–924)

What changes occurred in Germany?

Change soon came to East Germany as well. Its leaders resisted at first. Then thousands of people across the country demanded free elections. Soon, the Berlin Wall, which divided East and West Berlin, was torn down. By the end of 1989, the Communist party was out of power.

The next year **reunification** occurred. The two parts of Germany, East and West, were one nation again. But the new nation had many problems. The biggest problem was the weak economy in the east. And, as the largest nation in central Europe, Germany needed to face its new role in world affairs.

3. What happened after the Berlin Wall fell?

___

Democracy Spreads (page 924–925)

What happened in Czechoslovakia and Romania?

In Czechoslovakia, similar calls for reform took place. When the government cracked down on protesters, thousands of Czechs poured into the streets. One day 500,000 people gathered to protest in the nation's capital. The Communists agreed to give up power.

In Romania, Nicolae Ceausescu, the Communist dictator, ordered the army to shoot at protesters. This caused larger protests. The army then joined the people and fought against the secret police loyal to Ceausescu. He was captured and executed in 1989. General elections quickly followed and the new government reformed the economy.

4. How did the governments of Czechoslovakia and Romania change?

___

Name _____ Date _____

CHAPTER 35 Section 4 (pages 926–930)

Collapse of the Soviet Union

TERMS AND NAMES
Boris Yeltsin Political opponent of Gorbachev who became president of Russia
CIS Commonwealth of Independent States, a loose federation of former Soviet territories
"shock therapy" Yeltsin's plan for changing the Soviet economy
ethnic cleansing Policy of murder and brutality aimed at ridding a country of a particular ethnic group

BEFORE YOU READ

In the last section, you read about changes in the Soviet Union and the fall of communism in several Eastern European nations.

In this section, you will learn about the collapse of the Soviet Union and other changes in Eastern Europe.

AS YOU READ

Use the time line below to take notes on key events leading up to and following the collapse of the Soviet Union.

- **1990** Soviet Union collapses
- **1991**
- **1992**
- **1993**
- **1995**

Unrest in the Soviet Union
(pages 926–928)

What problems did the Soviet Union face?

While revolution was sweeping Eastern Europe, the Soviet Union had serious troubles. People from many different ethnic groups began calling for the right to have their own nation. In 1990, Lithuania declared itself independent. Gorbachev sent troops. They fired on a crowd and kill 14 people. This action and the slow pace of reform cost Gorbachev support among the Soviet people.

Many people began to support **Boris Yeltsin.** Old-time Communists were becoming angry at Gorbachev. They thought his changes made the Soviet Union weaker. In August 1991, they tried to take control of the government. When the army refused to back the *coup* leaders, they gave up.

To strike back, the parliament voted to ban the party from any political activity. Meanwhile, more republics in the Soviet Union declared their independence. By the end of 1991, Gorbachev announced that the Soviet Union would no longer

CHAPTER 35 STRUGGLES FOR DEMOCRACY **349**

exist. Russia and the other 14 republics each became independent states.

Most of the Republics then agreed to form the Commonwealth of Independent States, or **CIS**. It is a loose *federation* of former Soviet territories.

1. Name three events that led up to the collapse of the Soviet Union.

_____

_____

_____

The Yeltsin Era (page 928)
What happened when Gorbachev lost power?

After the coup failed, Gorbachev lost all power. Yeltsin became the most powerful Russian leader. As president of Russia, he faced many problems. He tried to change the economy. His economic plan was known as **"shock therapy."** This move toward capitalism caused suffering.

In addition, rebels in the small republic of Chechnya declared their independence from Russia. Yeltsin refused to allow it. He sent thousands of troops to put down the Chechen rebels. A bloody war raged for two years.

2. What decisions did Yeltsin make about the economy and about Chechnya?

_____

_____

_____

Yugoslavia Falls Apart (pages 928–929)
What happened in Yugoslavia?

Yugoslavia was made up of many different ethnic groups. In the early 1990s they began fighting. When *Serbia* tried to control the government, two other republics—*Slovenia* and *Croatia*—declared independence. Slovenia beat back a Serbian invasion. But Serbia and Croatia fought a bloody war.

In 1992, *Bosnia-Herzegovina* also declared independence. Serbs who lived in that region opposed the move. Using aid from Serbia, they fought a brutal civil war against the Bosnian Muslims, the largest group in Bosnia. The Serbs used murder and other forms of brutality against the Muslims. This **ethnic cleansing** was intended to rid Bosnia of its Muslims. The United Nations helped create a peace agreement, but the situation remains shaky.

3. Who fought in the civil war in Yugoslavia?

_____

_____

_____

Eastern Europe Faces Problems
(page 930)
What problems did Poland and Czechoslovakia face?

The change to democracy and capitalism in Eastern Europe was not smooth. The Polish people were frustrated with how long and painful the process was. In new elections in 1995, they voted Lech Walesa, the former leader of Solidarity, out as president of Poland.

In Czechoslovakia, democracy led to a breakup. In 1993, the country split into two separate nations: the Czech Republic and Slovakia.

4. What caused frustration and change in Poland?

_____

_____

_____

Name _____ Date _____

CHAPTER 35 Section 5 (pages 931–935)

China Follows Its Own Path

BEFORE YOU READ

In the last section, you read about the collapse of the Soviet Union and other changes in Eastern Europe.

In this section, you will learn about the recent history of China.

AS YOU READ

Use the time line below to take notes on the key events in recent Chinese history.

TERMS AND NAMES

Zhou Enlai Chinese leader who worked with President Nixon to improve U.S.–Chinese relations

Deng Xiaoping Chinese leader after Zhou Enlai

Four Modernizations Goals of Deng Xiaoping that called for progress in agriculture, industry, defense, and science and technology

Tiananmen Square Square in the capital of Beijing; scene of a student demonstration and massacre

Hong Kong Island that became part of China again in 1997

```
1966                          1989
Cultural Revolution begins

        1977                          1997
```

Mao's Unexpected Legacy
(page 931)

How did Mao change China?

Mao Zedong had tried to build a China on the ideas of equality, revolutionary spirit, and hard work. But his policies failed to create a strong economy. He reduced incentives for higher production. The Great Leap Forward helped cause an economic disaster.

During Mao's rule, China had little role in world affairs. **Zhou Enlai**, another Chinese leader, worried about this. He worked with U.S. President Richard Nixon to improve U.S.–Chinese relations.

1. How successful were Mao's economic programs?

_____

China and the West (pages 931–932)

How did Deng Xiaoping change China?

After Mao and Zhou died in 1976, *moderates* took control of the government. The most powerful leader was **Deng Xiaoping.** He tried to modernize the economy. Deng had goals known as the **Four Modernizations.** These called for progress

CHAPTER 35 STRUGGLES FOR DEMOCRACY **351**

in agriculture, industry, defense, and science and technology. He ended farming communes and allowed farmers more to sell part of their produce for a profit. Farm production increased greatly.

Deng made similar changes to industry. People's incomes began to rise. They began to purchase appliances and other goods that were once scarce.

2. What were the results of Deng Xiaoping's changes?

_____
_____
_____

Tiananmen Square (pages 932–933)
What caused the protest at Tiananmen Square?

Deng's new plan caused problems. The gap between rich and poor grew wider, which caused unrest. Western political ideas spread throughout the country. In 1989, thousands of Chinese students gathered in **Tiananmen Square** in the capital of Beijing. They called for democracy and freedom. Deng responded by sending army troops and tanks to put down the rally. Thousands were killed or wounded. China has continued to stamp out protests since then.

3. What happened to the protesters at Tiananmen Square?

_____
_____
_____
_____

China in the 1990s (pages 933–935)
What happened to Hong Kong?

Another major issue for China was the status of **Hong Kong.** The island became part of China again in 1997 when the British gave it back after 155 years of colonial rule. China promised to respect Hong Kong's freedom for 50 years. But many worried that China would take away Hong Kong's freedoms.

4. Why do people worry about Hong Kong's new rule?

_____
_____
_____
_____

Mao's Attempts to Change China

Mao's Programs	Program's Results
First Five-Year Plan 1953–1957	• Industry grew 15 percent a year. • Agricultural output grew very slowly.
Great Leap Forward 1958–1962	• China suffered economic disaster—industrial declines and food shortages. • Mao lost influence.
Cultural Revolution 1966–1976	• Mao regained influence by backing radicals. • Purges and conflicts among leaders created economic, social, and political chaos. • Moderates increasingly opposed radicals in Communist Party.

Skillbuilder

1. Why didn't the Great Leap Forward live up to its name?

_____
_____
_____

2. Which of the three programs appears to have been most successful, and why?

_____
_____
_____

Name _____ Date _____

Glossary — CHAPTER 35 Struggles for Democracy

African National Congress (ANC) Group that fought for the rights of black South Africans
banned Forbidden by law
Bosnia-Herzegovina Part of the former Yugoslavia in which Serbs fought a civil war with Muslims and where ethnic cleansing took place
boycotted Refused to buy
coup Sudden overthrow of government
Croatia Part of the former Yugoslavia that fought Serbia
dissent Political disagreement
federation A group with common interests
moderates People who are in the political middle
Serbia Part of the former Yugoslavia that wanted control of the government
Slovenia Part of the former Yugoslavia that fought back an invasion by Serbia

AFTER YOU READ

Terms and Names

A. Write the name or term in each blank that best completes the meaning of the paragraph.

dissidents
martial law
apartheid
reunification
land reform

Reform movements have had many different goals. A key goal in Brazil was **1** _____, which would make land ownership more equal. In South Africa, a key goal was the end of a strict separation of races called **2** _____. The struggle for democracy in East Germany led to the fall of the Berlin Wall. This change also led to the **3** _____ of Germany. The road to democracy can be rocky. Civil war and other power struggles can lead to **4** _____, or temporary military rule, as they did in Nigeria. Under this type of rule, opponents of government policy, **5** _____, are usually silenced.

B. Write the letter of the name or term next to the description that explains it best.

a. PRI
b. CIS
c. Four Modernizations
d. Solidarity
e. Politburo

____ 1. Ruling committee of the Communist party in the Soviet Union
____ 2. Polish labor union that worked for reform and led to the defeat of communism
____ 3. Loose federation of former Soviet territories
____ 4. Deng Xiaoping's goals for progress in China
____ 5. Political party that controlled Mexico for most of the 20th century

Name _____ Date _____

AFTER YOU READ (cont.)   CHAPTER 35 Struggles for Democracy

Main Ideas

1. Name three similarities in the struggles for democracy in Argentina and Brazil.
_____
_____
_____

2. How did apartheid come to an end in South Africa?
_____
_____
_____

3. How did the spirit of reform under Gorbachev in the Soviet Union spill over into Eastern Europe?
_____
_____
_____

4. What caused the civil war in Yugoslavia?
_____
_____
_____

5. How did the events in Tiananmen Square affect the struggle for democracy in China?
_____
_____
_____

Thinking Critically

Answer the following questions on a separate sheet of paper.

1. Give two examples of nations that experienced setbacks in the struggle for democracy. Explain which factors were missing that are needed for democracy to succeed.

2. Compare and contrast Mao Zedong and Deng Xiaoping.

Name _____ Date _____

CHAPTER 36 Section 1 (pages 941–944)

Science and Technology Shape Human Outlook

BEFORE YOU READ

In the last section, you read about struggles for democracy in China.

In this section, you will learn about recent changes in science and technology.

AS YOU READ

Use the chart below to take notes on recent developments and discoveries and their effects.

TERMS AND NAMES
Hubble Space Telescope Powerful telescope put into orbit around Earth in 1990
Internet Worldwide computer network
genetic engineering Use of genes to develop new products and cures
cloning Process of creating identical copies of DNA for research and other purposes
green revolution Attempt to increase food resources worldwide in the 20th century

DEVELOPMENT/DISCOVERY	EFFECT
Satellites	Improved television broadcasts.

Probing the Solar System and Beyond (pages 941–942)

How did competition give way to cooperation in space?

From the 1950s to the 1970s, the United States and Soviet Union took their Cold War rivalry to space. Each nation tried to be the first to reach the moon and beyond.

In the 1970s, the two nations began to cooperate in space exploration. In 1975, United States and Soviet spacecraft *docked*, or joined together, in space. Later, American and Soviet space missions included scientists from other countries. In the mid-1990s, U.S. astronauts began to take the space shuttle to a Russian space station called *Mir*.

Some space missions did not include human crew members. Unmanned flights sent back pictures and information about other planets.

CHAPTER 36 GLOBAL INTERDEPENDENCE **355**

In 1990, the United States and European countries sent the **Hubble Space Telescope** into orbit around the earth. This satellite sent back *unprecedented* images of objects in space.

1. **Give three examples of international cooperation in space.**

___

Expanding Global Communications (pages 942–943)

How has technology changed communications?

Some satellites are owned by private companies. Every day satellites are used to track the weather around the world. They are also used to search for minerals on the planet. Satellites allow television broadcasts to carry events live around the world.

Another advance in technology has been the computer. These machines have become more powerful since they were first invented. At the same time, they have gotten smaller in size. Consumer goods such as microwave ovens, telephones, and cars often include computer chips to keep them running.

Millions of people around the world use personal computers at work or at home. Many of these people are connected through the **Internet,** a worldwide computer network. The Internet allows people to get a great deal of information more quickly and easily than ever before. The Internet also allows people to communicate with one another.

2. **How have computers changed everyday living?**

___

Transforming Human Life
(pages 943–944)

How has new technology changed medicine?

New technology has changed medicine. *Lasers* allow doctors to perform surgery to fix problems in delicate areas, such as in the eye or the brain. New methods for making images of the body help doctors locate problems.

Research into genes has helped unlock the secrets of some diseases. **Genetic engineering** enables scientists to use genes in new ways. For example, scientists can develop plants with special traits. **Cloning** is part of genetic engineering. It is the creation of identical copies of *DNA*. Cloning can be used to produce plants and animals that are identical to the existing plants and animals.

Scientists have also used new understanding of genes to develop better foods. They have made other advances in farming, too. In the **green revolution,** scientists have developed better strains of food crops to help farmers grow more food.

3. **Why is genetic engineering an important development?**

___

356 CHAPTER 36 SECTION 1

Name _____ Date _____

CHAPTER 36 Section 2 (pages 945–950)

Global Economic Development

BEFORE YOU READ

In the last section, you read about changes in science and technology.

In this section, you will read about the new global economy.

AS YOU READ

Use the chart below to show the causes and effects of global economic development.

TERMS AND NAMES
developed nation Industrialized nation
developing nation Nation that is still developing industry
global economy Economy linking the economies of many nations
multinational corporation Corporation that operates in many countries
free trade Absence of barriers that can block trade between countries
Gulf War War fought in 1991 between Iraq and UN forces after Iraq invaded Kuwait
ozone layer Layer of atmosphere that blocks dangerous rays from the sun
sustainable development Economic growth that meets current needs but conserves resources for the future

causes

[New technology]

→ Global Economic Development →

effects

Technology Revolutionizes the World's Economy (pages 945–946)

How have the economies of the developed nations changed?

Technology has changed the world's economies. In the 1950s, scientists found new ways to make plastics, which came to be widely used. In recent years, industries have begun using robots to make products. These changes have required workers to have more skills and different skills than before.

In industrialized nations, or **developed nations,** there are more jobs in service industries. Manufacturing jobs began to grow more quickly in the **developing nations** where wages are lower.

1. What types of jobs are on the increase in developed nations?

_____
_____
_____

CHAPTER 36 GLOBAL INTERDEPENDENCE **357**

The Growth of Japan and the Pacific Rim (pages 946)

Why did growth occur in the Pacific Rim?

Japan's economy grew quickly after World War II. Japan adopted Western technologies and became a manufacturing leader. This success was built in part on Japan's educated and skilled workforce.

South Korea, Taiwan, Hong Kong, and Singapore followed Japan's example. These countries of the Pacific Rim were joined in the 1990s by China and Malaysia as world economic powers.

2. What were the keys to Japan's economic growth?

_____

_____

Growth in World Trade (pages 947–948)

Why is free trade important in a global economy?

A **global economy** continued to develop in the 1980s. Telephone and computer links connect banks and other financial companies around the world. **Multinational corporations** operate in many countries.

After World War II, many leaders believed that world economies would grow best if there were **free trade.** This means there would be no barriers to block goods from one country from entering another country. Many steps have been taken to put free trade in practice. In 1951, some nations in Europe joined together to create free trade. That group, now called the *European Union* (EU), has grown to become a powerful trading block.

The United States, Canada, and Mexico agreed to the North American Free Trade Agreement (NAFTA) in 1994. Another free trade zone was set up in Latin America. Similar groups are being put together in Africa and Asia.

3. Name three steps that have been taken in the direction of free trade.

_____

_____

Challenges Facing Less-Developed Nations; Impacts of Economic Development (pages 948–950)

What challenges do developing nations face?

Some developing nations still face problems in building their economies. Many people in these countries live in poverty. World leaders debate how best to solve this problem.

Economic growth needs many resources. Manufacturing and trade both use huge amounts of energy. Oil has been a major source of this energy. Whenever the flow of oil has been threatened, the world's economies have suffered shocks.

In 1990, Iraq invaded Kuwait. This threatened the flow of Kuwaiti oil. Soon, the countries of the United Nations went to war against Iraq. This was known as the **Gulf War.**

Water has been another source of conflict because of its importance for manufacturing and for farming. Some nations have come in conflict over water supplies.

Economic growth has also caused environmental problems. Burning coal and oil has polluted the air. It has also caused *acid rain* and global warming. The release of some chemicals into the air has weakened Earth's **ozone layer.** This layer of atmosphere blocks dangerous rays from the sun.

One new idea about growth is an idea called sustainable development. **Sustainable development** requires meeting current needs while *conserving* future resources.

4. What environmental problems have resulted from economic growth?

_____

_____

358 CHAPTER 36 SECTION 2

Name _____ Date _____

CHAPTER 36 Section 3 (pages 952–956)

Global Security Issues

BEFORE YOU READ

In the last section, you read about the growth of the global economy.

In this section, you will read about challenges to global security.

AS YOU READ

Use the web below to take notes on threats to global security.

TERMS AND NAMES
Nuclear Non-Proliferation Treaty 1968 treaty in which nations agreed to prevent the spread of nuclear weapons
proliferation Spread
terrorism Use of force or threats to make people or governments change policies
fundamentalism Strict belief in the basic truths and practices of a particular faith
Universal Declaration of Human Rights 1948 United Nations statement of specific rights that all people should have
civil rights movement Effort to fight racial discrimination in the United States

[Web diagram: Threats to Global Security, with one filled bubble labeled "Ethnic and religious conflicts" and three empty bubbles]

Nations Pursue Collective Security (pages 952–953)

How have nations worked together for global security?

After World War II, there were many small, local conflicts. Nations joined together to try to solve these conflicts. The United Nations (UN) was formed at the end of World War II to promote world peace. It now has more than 180 member nations. The UN provides a place for countries—or groups within countries—to share their views.

The UN can also send troops as a *peacekeeping force*. These soldiers—who come from member nations—try to stop violence from breaking out. UN peacekeepers have served in regions such as Central America, Southwest Asia, and Africa.

Another approach to world peace has been to limit weapons of mass destruction. These include *nuclear weapons, chemical weapons,* and *biological weapons*. In 1968, many nations signed a **Nuclear Non-Proliferation Treaty.** The nations that signed the treaty agreed to prevent the **proliferation,** or spread, of nuclear weapons. In the 1990s, the United States and Russia agreed to destroy many of their nuclear weapons. In another treaty, many nations promised not to develop chemical or biological weapons.

CHAPTER 36 GLOBAL INTERDEPENDENCE **359**

Threats to safety remain. **Terrorism** is one of them. Terrorism is the use of force or threats to frighten people or governments into changing their policies.

1. Name two specific approaches toward collective security.

_____

_____

_____

Ethnic and Religious Conflicts Disrupt Peace (pages 953–954)

How do ethnic groups sometimes threaten peace?

Ethnic and religious differences are the sources of many world conflicts. The growth of **fundamentalism** has also helped create conflict. Fundamentalism is a strict belief in the basic truths and practices of a particular faith. Fundamentalists are often unwilling to compromise their beliefs. This brings them into conflict with other people.

2. Why does fundamentalism sometimes create conflict?

_____

_____

_____

Promoting Human Rights Worldwide (page 954–955)

What efforts have been made to ensure human rights?

In 1948, the UN approved the **Universal Declaration of Human Rights**. This declaration gives a list of rights that all people should have. In 1975, many nations signed the Helsinki Accords that also support human rights. Many groups around the world watch to see how well nations do in protecting these rights for their people.

In the 1950s and 1960s, the United States made several reforms to ensure rights for African Americans. The movement to win these reforms has been called the **civil rights movement.** This movement for equality for African Americans inspired other groups—Hispanics, Native Americans, people with disabilities, and women—to insist on equal rights as well.

Women in Western nations work in larger numbers than ever before. Since 1975, the UN has supported efforts to protect women's rights around the world.

3. Name two events that have been important in the worldwide struggle for human rights.

_____

_____

_____

Global Movement of People (page 955–956)

What are some of the causes of the global movement of people?

In recent years, millions of people have moved from one country to another. Some seek better jobs. Others hope to escape harsh treatment at home.

Immigrants can bring many benefits to their new home. While people have a right to leave, every country does not have to accept them. Sometimes these people have to live in crowded *refugee* camps. They suffer hunger and disease. They can also cause political problems for the country where they are held.

4. What problems can result from the global movement of people?

_____

_____

_____

Name _____ Date _____

CHAPTER 36 Section 4 (pages 957–961)

Cultures Blend in a Global Age

TERMS AND NAMES
popular culture Cultural elements—such as sports, music, movies, and clothing—that reflect a group's common background
materialism Placing high value on owning things
accommodation Level of acceptance of ideas from another culture

BEFORE YOU READ
In the last section, you read about global security issues.
In this section, you will learn about the global blending of cultures.

AS YOU READ
Use the chart below to take notes on the blending of cultures around the world.

MAIN IDEA	SUPPORT
sharing of cultures has speeded up	Television and other mass media have sped up cultural sharing

The Sharing of Cultures Accelerates (pages 957–958)

What has speeded up the sharing of cultures?

Changes in technology have made it possible for people to share their cultures with one another. Television is one of the main forces in this trend. It allows people to see things that happen around the world. Movies and radio also have had an impact in bringing the world's people together.

As a result of these *mass media*, the world's popular culture now includes elements from many different cultures. **Popular culture** includes music, sports, clothing styles, food, and hobbies. American television shows have become popular around the world. Broadcasts of some sporting events can reach more than 200 million people in all corners of the globe. Music has also become international.

1. Name three aspects of culture that have become international.

_____
_____

World Culture Blends Many Influences (pages 959–960)

What countries have most influenced cultural blending?

Cultural blending occurs when parts of different cultures are combined. In recent times, the United

CHAPTER 36 GLOBAL INTERDEPENDENCE **361**

States and Europe have been a major force in this blending. One reason is that Western nations dominate the mass media.

The political power of the West has also spread Western culture to other regions. For example, English is now a major world language. About 500 million people speak English as their first or second language. More people speak Mandarin Chinese. But English speakers are more widely spread throughout the world. Western clothes can be seen throughout the world. Western foods—such as hamburgers and cola—are enjoyed everywhere.

Western ideas have also influenced world thought. The Western idea of **materialism**—placing high value on owning things—has also spread. Some ideas have also traveled from East to West. The worlds of art and literature have become more international in recent years.

2. What Western aspects of culture have spread throughout the world?

_____

_____

_____

Future Challenges and Hopes (pages 960–961)

How has the world responded to cultural blending?

Some people think the spread of international culture is a problem. They worry that their own culture will be swallowed up by other cultures. Some countries try to keep foreign words out of their language. Others forbid people to wear certain kinds of clothing.

In some areas, people have returned to old traditions in order to keep them alive. Some nations face issues of accommodation. **Accommodation** is the level of acceptance of ideas from another culture.

The people of the world are becoming more and more dependent on each another. All through human history, people have faced challenges to their survival. In the 21st century, those challenges will be faced by people who are in increasing contact with one another. They have a great stake in living together in harmony.

3. What problems or challenges can cultural blending bring?

_____

_____

_____

_____

Global Interdependence

ECONOMICS
- Service industries grow in developed nations.
- Free trade expands world markets.
- Environmental challenges continue.

CULTURE
- Mass media spreads many cultures.
- Pop culture becomes more international.
- Global interdependence awareness develops.

SCIENCE AND TECHNOLOGY
- Space cooperation stretches horizons.
- Advanced communications allow wider contact.
- Inventions improve life and health.

POLITICS
- Nations take collective security actions.
- Human rights improve worldwide.
- Immigrants change cultures.

Skillbuilder

1. Explain how each year relates to the ones it connects to.

_____

_____

2. What connection might there be between the Science and Technology year and the Culture year?

_____

_____

362 CHAPTER 36 SECTION 4

Name _____   Date _____

Glossary   **CHAPTER 36** Global Interdependence, 1960–Present

acid rain Rain with a high concentration of acids that destroy plant life and life in water
biological weapons Weapons that use disease-spreading microorganisms
chemical weapons Weapons made from chemicals, such as poison gases
conserving Saving
cultural blending Process of combining different cultures
DNA Basic material in chromosomes that transmits the genetic pattern
docked Joined together in space
European Union Powerful European trading block created to promote free trade
lasers Devices that give off light in intense, narrow beams
mass media Communications that reach large numbers of people, including television and radio
nuclear weapons Weapons that use atomic energy
peacekeeping force Soldiers sent by the United Nations to help keep peace
refugee Person who escapes his or her own country
unprecedented Never been done before

AFTER YOU READ

Terms and Names

A. Write the term in each blank that best completes the meaning of the paragraph.

developing nations
developed nations
free trade
global economy
multinational corporations

A new **1** _____ links the economies of many nations. Companies that operate in many nations, known as **2** _____, play an important role in this kind of economy. Often the offices of these companies will be found in countries that have already industrialized, known as **3** _____. The factories, on the other hand, may be found in **4** _____, because wages may be lower there. One thing that many people believe helps world economies to grow is **5** _____. This means that no barriers block goods from one country from entering another country.

B. Write the letter of the name or term next to the description that explains it best.

a. genetic engineering
b. proliferation
c. fundamentalism
d. materialism
e. cloning

____ **1.** Placing high value on owning things

____ **2.** Process of creating identical copies of DNA for research and other purposes

____ **3.** Spread

____ **4.** Strict belief in the basic truths and practices of a particular faith

____ **5.** Use of genes to develop new products and cures

CHAPTER 36 GLOBAL INTERDEPENDENCE **363**

Name _____ Date _____

AFTER YOU READ (continued) — CHAPTER 36 Global Interdependence

Main Idea

1. Explain three major effects of technology on everyday living.
   _____
   _____
   _____

2. How has technology changed world economies?
   _____
   _____
   _____
   _____

3. How has technology helped speed up cultural blending?
   _____
   _____
   _____
   _____

4. What is a UN peacekeeping force, and when and how is it used?
   _____
   _____
   _____
   _____

5. Discuss three responses people make to cultural blending.
   _____
   _____
   _____
   _____

Thinking Critically

Answer the following questions on a separate sheet of paper.

1. How does economic growth strain resources, and what results can this have?

2. Discuss three threats to global security, and explain the possible effects of each one.